"Yes We Can"

PETER LANG

New York • Washington, D.C./Baltimore • Bern
Frankfurt am Main • Berlin • Brussels • Vienna • Oxford

WOLFGANG MIEDER

"Yes We Can"

Barack Obama's Proverbial Rhetoric

PETER LANG
New York • Washington, D.C./Baltimore • Bern
Frankfurt am Main • Berlin • Brussels • Vienna • Oxford

Library of Congress Cataloging-in-Publication Data

Mieder, Wolfgang.
"Yes we can": Barack Obama's proverbial rhetoric / Wolfgang Mieder.
p. cm.
Includes bibliographical references.
1. Obama, Barack—Language. 2. Obama, Barack—Oratory.
3. Proverbs—Political aspects—United States—History—21st century.
4. Rhetoric—Political aspects—United States—History—21st century.
5. Communication in politics—United States—History—21st century.
6. Proverbs—History and criticism. I. Title.
E908.3.M54   973.932092—dc22   2009011568
ISBN 978-1-4331-0668-2 (hardcover)
ISBN 978-1-4331-0667-5 (paperback)

Bibliographic information published by **Die Deutsche Bibliothek**.
Die Deutsche Bibliothek lists this publication in the "Deutsche
Nationalbibliografie"; detailed bibliographic data is available
on the Internet at http://dnb.ddb.de/.

The paper in this book meets the guidelines for permanence and durability
of the Committee on Production Guidelines for Book Longevity
of the Council of Library Resources.

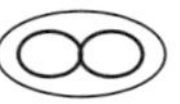

© 2009 Peter Lang Publishing, Inc., New York
29 Broadway, 18th floor, New York, NY 10006
www.peterlang.com

Printed in the United States of America

Table OF Contents

Introduction

During his landmark acceptance speech of the nomination for the presidency of the United States on August 28, 2008, during the Democratic National Convention at Denver, Colorado, the then still Senator Barack Obama spoke eloquently of "The American Promise," presenting his invigorating new vision for a transformed America. As he outlined this promise for change, he made effective use of a number of proverbs and proverbial phrases, adding his very own creation of a quotable phrase or pseudo-proverb to it that has all the makings of one day becoming proverbial. As it was, he called on businesses to "live up to their responsibilities to create American jobs, look out for American workers, and play by the [proverbial] rules of the road." Then he went on to say that the promise of America includes "the idea that we are responsible for ourselves, but that we also rise or fall as one nation; the fundamental belief that I am my brother's keeper; I am my sister's keeper." In this case he changed the questioning Bible proverb "Am I my brother's keeper?" (Genesis 4,9) to an affirmative statement that expresses in gender-free terms that we are all dependent on each other. But as he included women, he was quick to add the proverbial "promise of equal pay for an equal day's work" to it, arguing that women and men of all social, ethnic, and racial backgrounds deserve to be treated equally. There are eight more such preformulated or fixed phrases to be found in this speech, but suffice it to mention only Barack Obama's own creation: "Change happens because the American people demand it – because they rise up and insist on new ideas and new leadership, a new politics for a new time." Interestingly enough, the President-elect never employed his formulaically expressed wisdom again, even though it includes in an easily memorable way his rhetorical leitmotif of change. I had hoped that the newly sworn in President Barack Obama would cite his quotable phrase "A new politics for a new time" in his inaugural address, something that would instantly have changed his pseudo-proverb to a commonly accepted and used proverb. There is, of course, no reason why this might not happen in the future, especially if the President were to cite it again as an obvious piece of wisdom.

But there is no reason to be too concerned, for there are ample other quotable statements that Barack Obama has created with his keen awareness and welcome appreciation of the power of words. His two books, his over two hundred speeches, news conferences, interviews, and radio addresses are replete with concise general statements that might well find their way into dictionaries of quotations. Some of them, as for example "If you invest in America, America will invest in you" or "We cannot have a thriving Wall Street and a struggling Main Street (while Main Street suffers)" should definitely make it into them, especially since Obama used them numerous times during the past few years with thousands of Americans having heard them and in turn quoting them. Yet while the President is perfectly capable of inventing such "truths" that carry the linguistic ring of proverbs with them, he certainly does not reduce his impressive rhetoric to mere sound bites! Not even when he cites proverbs from the Bible or traditional folk proverbs. In fact, he seldom integrates such texts verbatim into his books or oral communications, preferring to alter them slightly in order to make them fit his arguments for change. Naturally he also integrates numerous proverbial expressions, proverbial comparisons, and twin formulas more or less in their traditional wording into his written and oral statements. With their often colorful metaphors they add expressiveness and emotion to his communications, giving people the opportunity to follow his pragmatic or philosophical arguments by way of common language. No matter what Barack Obama writes or speaks about, his prose or speech contains metaphorical language that makes his rhetoric and oratory universally accessible.

My scholarly interest in Barack Obama began when I came across his informative and compelling book *The Audacity of Hope: Thoughts on Reclaiming the American Dream* (2006) about two years ago. Traveling with my wife Barbara, I discovered it, appropriately so, in a bookstore at O'Hare international airport in Chicago. And once I opened it on the flight back to Burlington, Vermont, I was proverbially "hooked" for sure! I literally couldn't put the book down, so fascinated was I by this incredibly well written political and social manifesto by a remarkably young U.S. Senator from Illinois, who was ever more making a name for himself and who, would you believe it, delivered an address on March 10, 2006, on my home campus of the University of Vermont at Burlington, Vermont. As I was reading the various chapters, I became aware not only that Senator Obama's style exhibits an abundance of proverbial language, but also that he is a great admirer of Abraham Lincoln, Frederick Douglass, and Martin Luther King, three great Americans who happen to be my heroes as well. Reading Obama's prose with quotations by these civil rights champions and other important politicians like Franklin D. Roosevelt, Winston S. Churchill, Harry S. Truman, John F. Kennedy, and others, I recognized that his sociopolitical rhetoric was to some degree informed by these renowned historical figures. But not only because he quotes them from time to time, but also because he follows in their "proverbial footsteps", i.e., he clearly recognizes that effective political communication needs to find a linguistic common denominator understandable to all citizens. Part of that accessible language is the employment of folk speech in the form of proverbs and proverbial phrases, with all of the political leaders just mentioned being masters in the art of employing meaningful proverbial language.

Over the years I have shown this in a number of books, among them two earlier ones that I co-authored with my deceased colleague and friend George B. Bryan: *The Proverbial Winston S. Churchill: An Index to Proverbs in the Works of Sir Winston Churchill* (1995) and *The Proverbial Harry S. Truman: An Index to Proverbs in the Works of Harry S. Truman* (1997). After losing my friend, I carried on by myself with two books on the proverbial prowess of Abraham Lincoln: *"A House Divided": From Biblical Proverb to Lincoln and Beyond* (1998) and *The Proverbial Abraham Lincoln: An Index to Proverbs in the Works of Abraham Lincoln* (2000). Then followed my massive study *"No Struggle, No Progress": Frederick Douglass and His Proverbial Rhetoric for Civil Rights* (2001) that led to my decision to become an American citizen after having lived in the United States as an immigrant from Germany since 1960. There were also two more general books with chapters covering John and Abigail Adams, Franklin D. Roosevelt, and others, including a detailed investigation of the proverbs and proverbial phrases cited in all inaugural addresses: *The Politics of Proverbs: From Traditional Wisdom to Proverbial Stereotypes* (1997) and *Proverbs Are the Best Policy: Folk Wisdom and American Politics* (2005). And let me finally also mention my book on *"Call a Spade a Spade": From Classical Phrase to Racial Slur* (2002) which to my regret received very little attention as one of my studies that continues to make me feel just a bit proud. But be that as it may, my interest in proverbial rhetoric by politicians was most certainly reawakened by reading Barack Obama's *The Audacity of Hope* and subsequently becoming fascinated by him as a master of the English language capable of inspiring hope and trust among many Americans and citizens of the world. By now, he is seen and appreciated as the person to bring about change that might lead to a more perfect union here in the United States and an improved sociopolitical existence on this globe.

Barack Obama has learned much from his famous precursors, but rather than copying their ideas and rhetoric, he stands on their shoulders and adapts their insights, vision, and wisdom to his own plan on bringing positive change. All of this is convincingly stated in his political manifesto, as one might call his book *The Audacity of Hope*. The analysis of its proverbial language informs the first chapter of this book. I am starting with his second book, as it were, because I read it first and because it contains such an inclusive picture of what Barack Obama means by such concepts as hope, promise, change, virtue, etc. During 2008, I had the most welcome opportunity to present parts of this chapter at three public lectures, the first at the annual meeting of the American Folklore Society at Louisville, Kentucky; the second, sponsored by the ALANA U.S. Ethnic Studies Program, here on the campus of the University of Vermont; and the third at the first meeting of the International Association of Paremiology (Proverb Studies) at Tavira, Portugal. Locally, nationally, and internationally the reaction to my analysis of Obama's proverbial language in this book met with great interest, and this in turn encouraged me to carry on my work on a much more inclusive scope. Having found 195 phraseologisms on 364 pages, i.e., one idiom, proverbial phrase or proverb for every 1.9 pages of text, I can definitely state that this preformulated language is part of Obama's impressive style, helping him to express his thoughts and hopes regarding such diverse topics as political parties, values, constitutional government, politics, opportunity, faith, race, foreign relations, and the family. By couching his analysis, opinion, and plans at least to some degree in quotations, proverbs, and proverbial phrases, Barack Obama strikes a chord in his readers who identify with these well-known metaphors and are thus well prepared to buy into his strong commitment for necessary change in a time of socioeconomic, environmental, and political crisis.

The second chapter takes a detailed look at Barack Obama's celebrated autobiography *Dreams from My Father: A Story of Race and Inheritance* (1995) that has earned him much recognition as a narrative writer. In fact, most readers here in the United States and abroad (both books have been translated into numerous languages) became spell-bound by this intriguing and revealing account. The first part "Origins" presents a colorful picture of how Obama grew up in Hawaii and Indonesia, while the second part "Chicago" gives readers a very good idea of how Obama as an activist and organizer helped African Americans and other low income people at the South end of that ethnically and racially mixed metropolis. It is here where Obama earned his sociopolitical stripes, preparing him for his later political career. The third part about "Kenya" describes his return to Kenya, the home of his father's side of the family. As Obama searches for and discovers his African roots, he becomes an ethnographer, recording the language and stories of the Luo people. He does the same for the language and slang among the African American community in Chicago, and there are also many linguistic examples of the vocabulary and phrases used by youngsters in the first part of the book. This book, in addition to its high literary value, is proof positive that Barack Obama is indeed very cognizant of various layers of language, clearly differentiating among such sociolects as youth slang, religious language, African American talk, ghetto vocabulary, etc. There is no doubt that Obama, the narrative writer, is a linguistic observer and recorder, and this awareness and knowledge enable him to present an authentic account of his path from childhood to adulthood. With such interest in linguistic matters, it should not be surprising that this personal account is replete with proverbial materials. In fact, this time I located 235 proverbial statements on 447 pages, translating once again to one such formulaic phrase per 1.9 pages. There is, then, an obvious consistency in Obama's use of proverbial language, showing that it is part of his natural and authentic reliance on traditional metaphors.

Turning to the third chapter with its investigation of Obama's oral use of proverbial materials in his many speeches, news conferences, interviews, and radio addresses, I can report that I analyzed 229 such communications that Obama made between 2002 and 2009. Altogether I isolated 1284 proverbial texts, or about 5.6 phraseologisms per event. This shows that Obama's verbal communication is never oversaturated with folk language! It might be remembered that Harry S. Truman, one of the more "folksy" presidents when it comes to oral language (he actually was quite a good writer), was at times ridiculed for his "plain speaking" that included an overdose of colloquialisms and other folk speech in the form of colorful metaphors, proverbial comparisons, and proverbs. This is simply never the case with Barack Obama's rhetoric. His use of proverbs and proverbial expressions is measured and quite deliberate, injecting them to make a point in the case of the wisdom contained in proverbs, and adding imagery to his more abstract policy deliberations in the case of proverbial phrases. This chapter presents a comprehensive analysis of the use, function, and meaning of quotations, pseudo-proverbs, traditional proverbs, frequently and only occasionally appearing proverbial expressions, classical proverbs and phrases, somatic phrases, binary or twin formulas, sport expressions, and maritime phrases. Numerous contextualized examples are cited with many more listed in the large "Index of Proverbs and Proverbial Phrases." As can be imagined, some of these phraseologisms appear numerous times, with the proverbial phrase "To turn the page" as a metaphor for "change" being cited sixty-four times! But most fixed phrases appear only several times, with quite a few of them being used but once or twice. This is a clear indication that Obama possesses a rich repertoire of proverbial language that he employs in highly differentiated ways. There are also times when he amasses three such expressions in one short paragraph, and such statements are often filled with a sense of irony or satire. I certainly recall that Obama delighted his audiences with this type of proverbial cannonades. At times the combination of several metaphors could also result in a bit of humor, as often happened in spontaneous interchanges during so-called town-hall events. And to be sure then, there is a special section on the origin, history, and variants of the proverb "You can put lipstick on a pig, but it's still a pig" in this chapter, and at the end of this long treatise I have also included a discussion of the "Yes We Can" phrasal phenomenon that proved to be Barack Obama's campaign slogan.

While this chapter deals primarily with contextualized examples grouped according to various phraseological genres, metaphors, and themes, the fourth chapter illustrates how proverbial language becomes an extremely important element in the actual message and meaning of a major speech. To accomplish this, I chose seven acclaimed speeches that helped Barack Obama rhetorically – and therefore also proverbially – on his path to the presidency. I begin with his keynote address at the Democratic National Convention on July 27, 2004, at Boston. This is followed by his announcement of candidacy for the presidency of the United States on February 10, 2007, at Springfield, Illinois. Next comes the speech on race on March 18, 2008, at Philadelphia, that saved his political career and that will remain one of the most significant speeches in American history. In order to add an international flavor to this analysis, I chose Obama's address on July, 24, 2008, at Berlin, Germany, as a speech that won him the hearts and minds of people throughout the world. His acceptance speech on August 28, 2008, at the Democratic National Convention at Denver, is analyzed in the next section, followed by his victory speech on election night of November 4, 2008, at Chicago. And then, as the crescendo to this chapter but also to my entire study follows his remarkable inaugural address on January 20, 2009, at Washington, D.C. All seven speeches were major public events, with each of them presenting a giant step towards the presidency. There were many other impressive speeches, interviews, and news conferences, but these seven addresses clearly stand out, and they were listened to and viewed by millions of people. As they heard and watched Barack Obama address them with his sonorous voice, his bright eyes, his confidence, his hope, and his sincere commitment to work towards a more perfect union and a better world, they obviously followed his thoughts and ideas as he expressed them in an oratorical style the type of which we have not witnessed for quite some time. Of course, his politics were convincing, but it took language to bring his promise for change across to the people. Part of that impressive rhetorical power of words came without doubt from his effective use of proverbial language, that common denominator of folk speech that made Barack Obama be one with the people. Chicago's former poet laureate, Carl Sandburg, begins his poem entitled "Good Morning, America" (1928) with the imperative: "Behold the proverbs of a people, a nation." Barack Obama did well in following this advice, and by so doing, his proverbial rhetoric played at least a small part in making him the acknowledged and celebrated first African American President of the United States.

As expected, these four chapters are followed by a long "List of Publications and Speeches," and let me add here that it was a personal and scholarly pleasure to read and analyze all of them. In so doing, I remembered my work on Abraham Lincoln, Frederick Douglass, Martin Luther King, and others, and as I witnessed Barack Obama following in their footsteps, I felt ever more drawn towards this new and shining light on the political stage. What he does achieve rhetorically with proverbial materials in addition to the examples cited in the four chapters can be gathered from the comprehensive "Index of Proverbs and Proverbial Phrases" that registers all 1714 proverbial texts in context! Finally, there is an extensive bibliography dealing with politics and proverbs as well as Barack Obama's rhetoric and oratory.

With this I come to the end of these introductory comments. It should be clear by now that this book, while being a scholarly work, is also a personal statement. In fact, besides my studies on Lincoln and Douglass, I have never been as emotionally involved in a project as with this one. Part of this must be due to the fact that Barack Obama is the first living national political leader whose proverbial language I have investigated. But there is, of course, more than that. Simply stated, it is that I have this image in front of me of President Barack Obama standing on the shoulders of Abraham Lincoln, Frederick Douglass, and Martin Luther King, and by doing so, he can see into the future, he can work on the dream of a more perfect union and world, and he can bring "A new politics for a new time" based on responsible and equitable change.

Finally, it gives me great pleasure to thank all of my colleagues in the Department of German and Russian at the University of Vermont for their constant interest in and support of my work: Gideon Bavly, Theresia Hoeck, Dennis Mahoney, Kevin McKenna, Kenneth Nalibow, Veronica Richel, Helga Schreckenberger, David Scrase, and Beatrice Wood. Let me also thank John Burke from our Political Science Department for supplying me with a number of publications. I owe special thanks to my colleagues Karl Bridges and Janet Sobieski for their help in locating the many speeches on various websites, and to my former student and at times co-author Andreas Nolte for his invaluable help with the voluminous index containing the contextualized proverbs and proverbial phrases. Of course, as always, I would also like to thank Chris Myers and all my friends at Peter Lang Publishing in New York for taking such good care of yet another one of my book projects.

I would like to dedicate this book to my many African and African American colleagues and friends here and abroad. I cannot possibly name all of them here, but let me mention especially Roger Abrahams, Moustapha Diouf, Joseph Healey, Richard Johnson, Fayneese Miller, Mary Rodena-Krasan, Lokangaka Losambe, J.O.J. Nwachakwu-Ogbada, Sw. Anand Prahlad, Aderemi Raji-Oyelade, Sherwood Smith, Patricia Turner, Amani Whitfield, Kwesi Yankah, Yisa Kehinde Ysuf, and Jean-Philippe Zouogbo. As I was working on this book, I often thought of them as well as Barack and Michelle Obama and their lovely daughters Malia and Sasha. This book then is a present for all of them with thanks and the audacity of hope.

Wolfgang Mieder
Winter 2009

"I'm Absolutely Sure ABOUT — THE Golden Rule" Barack Obama's Proverbial Audacity OF Hope

Proverbs, proverbial expressions, and other types of phraseologisms have always played an important role in the world of politics (Mieder 1997, Louis 2000), to wit their effective employment by such varied twentieth-century politicians as Willy Brandt (Eggert 1998), Winston S. Churchill (Mieder and Bryan 1995), Adolf Hitler (Mieder 1997, 9-38), Nikita Khrushchev, Vladimir Ilich Lenin (Breuillard 1984, Viellard 2001), Mao Tse-tung (Schäfer 1983), Franklin D. Roosevelt (Mieder 2005, 187-209), Harry S. Truman (Mieder and Bryan 1997), and others. In American politics proverbial language has long been part of the discourse (Mieder 2005), with former presidents like John Adams (Mieder 2008b, 169-204), Abraham Lincoln (Mieder 2000), and Theodore Roosevelt standing out as particularly proverbial in their rhetoric. Of course, there were also such proverbial giants as Benjamin Franklin (Newcomb 1957, Barbour 1974), Daniel Webster, Frederick Douglass (Mieder 2001), Susan B. Anthony, Elizabeth Cady Stanton (Mieder 2008a, 328-330), and Dr. Martin Luther King (Karabegović 2007) who relied heavily on traditional metaphors and folk wisdom in their oral and written communication with the American people. Modern politicians clearly would do well in taking a look at their reliance on proverbs and proverbial phrases to add some common-sense appeal to their own political messages.

Barack Obama as a major figure on today's American political scene has clearly heeded this advice as is readily apparent from his two best-selling books *Dreams from My Father: A Story of Race and Inheritance* (1995) and *The Audacity of Hope: Thoughts on Reclaiming the American Dream* (2006) as well as his major national addresses, as for example his speech at the Democratic National Convention on July 27, 2004, at Boston, his announcement for the presidency on February 10, 2007, at Springfield, Illinois, his speech on race on March 18, 2008, at Philadelphia, his acceptance speech on having been nominated for the presidency of the United States on August 28, 2008, at Denver, Colorado, and his inaugural address on January 20, 2009, at Washington, D.C. (all references from speeches will be cited from the *Obama News & Speeches* website: http://www.barackobama.com; for a selection of printed speeches see Harrison and Gilbert 2007, and Olive 2008). As one reads his prose or listens to his speeches, it is evident that this extremely well-educated individual is deeply rooted in American political history, with his three heroes being Abraham Lincoln, Frederick Douglass, and Dr. Martin Luther King. There are, of course, other and alive public figures whom Obama respects or admires, but this particular triad stands out, with Thomas Jefferson certainly also deserving a place of honor in his mind.

What is fascinating to the folklorist in general and the paremiologist in particular is the obvious fact that Obama shares a certain predilection to proverbial language with Lincoln, Douglass, and King. He certainly read them, and he must have been impressed and at times moved by some of their deeply felt statements that were quite often couched in proverbial language. Abraham Lincoln's use of the biblical proverb "A house divided against itself cannot stand" (Mark 3,25), Frederick Douglass's use of Jefferson's declaration turned proverb "All men are created equal", and Dr. Martin Luther King's insistence on the golden rule "Do unto others as you would have them do unto you" (also used by Lincoln and Douglass) readily come to mind. There is doubtlessly some direct or indirect rhetorical influence here, which is by no means to say that Obama does not have "a certain talent for rhetoric" (67; sole page numbers in parentheses refer to Barack Obama's *The Audacity of Hope*), as he justifiably points out in *The Audacity of Hope*. And right he is! In this book of 364 pages, a total of 195 phraseologisms have been located, i.e., basically one idiom, proverbial phrase or proverb for every 1.9 pages of text. Merely twenty-two of these are actual proverbs, an indication that Obama, in differentiation to Lincoln, Douglass, and King, is much less the didactic or sermonic rhetorician. This is probably a wise move, since modern readers and audiences would tire quickly of a cannonade of proverbial wisdom. In fact, even when he cites proverbs, they are often used as allusions, as for example, when he speaks of a "'winner-take-all' economy, in which a rising tide doesn't necessarily lift all boats" (146). Being a modern politician, he does not only use such old stand-bys as "Father knows best" (31) and "Look before you leap" (310), but also such modern texts as "Better is not good enough" (233) or "Been there, done that" (312).

Sometimes he doesn't quote the fitting piece of folk wisdom at all and instead adds a bit of indirect proverbial wisdom to a statement by claiming that "conventional wisdom" (see 16, 124, etc.) holds it to be true!

Most of Obama's use of folk speech comes in the form of proverbial phrases without any claim to wisdom or truth. He uses these metaphorical phrases to add a certain expressiveness, emotion, color, imagery, and colloquialism to his writings and speeches. It is here where he shows himself to be part of the general population. He prides himself on listening to and thinking about "the voices of all the people" (356), and consequently he mixes their conventional and proverbial language into his utterances. As an impressive intellectual, he does well to follow in the footsteps of a Woodrow Wilson or John F. Kennedy, who also took to heart the folk speech patterns of their constituents. A few telling examples of Obama's folk speech prowess with very little context are: "I had gotten some taste of how the game had come to be played" (16), "We might've fought like cats and dogs" (35), "If we aren't willing to pay a price for our values" (68), "We have played fast and loose with constitutional principles in the fight against terrorism" (56), "It would have been typical of today's politics for each side to draw a line in the sand" (58), "Simply put, they have an ax to grind" (116), "America's schools are not holding up their end of the bargain" (159), "racial discrimination stays on the front burner" (248), "rid themselves of the instinct to throw their weight around" (306), "she asked me out of the blue if our family was rich" (351), etc.

Of course, various reviews of Barack Obama's personal and political manifesto with its intriguing title of *The Audacity of Hope* have praised him for his obvious writing and rhetorical skills. Thus Michiko Kakutani wrote in *The New York Times* of October 17, 2006, that "Barack Obama [...] is that rare politician who can actually write – and write movingly and genuinely about himself," and he also observed that "Mr. Obama strives in these pages to ground his policy thinking in simple common sense – be it growing the size of our armed forces to maintain reasonable rotation schedules or reining in spending and rethinking tax policy to bring down the nation's huge deficit – while articulating these ideas in level-headed, nonpartisan prose. That, in itself, is something unusual, not only in these venomous pre-election days, but also in these increasingly polarized and polarizing times" (Kakutani 2006). Michael Kazin followed suit in *The Washington Post* of October 22, 2006: "Obama's knack for mixing stirring rhetoric about good and evil with practical policy ideas is rare in the modern history of U.S. politics. At times, Franklin D. Roosevelt, Kennedy, and Reagan managed the feat. But none of these men wrote his own presidential speeches. Nor did Kennedy or Reagan really write the books that carry their names. In contrast, *The Audacity of Hope* is clearly Obama's own creation; the rhythms, the self-deprecating humor and the graceful transitions, all resemble those in his memoir [*Dreams from My Father*]. [...]

In our downbeat, dispiriting era, Obama's talent for proposing humane, sensible solutions with uplifting, elegant prose does fill one with hope. Someday, it may even help him get elected president" (Kazin 2006). Former United States senator Gary Hart, in his review of December 24, 2006, in *The New York Times*, also had the highest praise for Obama's intellectual writing abilities: "In a more perfect world, a graduate program complete with a doctoral thesis might be required of all those seeking the presidency. In certain ways, 'The Audacity of Hope' qualifies as Senator Barack Obama's thesis submission. [...] It presents a man of relative youth yet maturity, a wise observer of the human condition, a figure who possesses perseverance and writing skills that have flashes of grandeur. Obama also demonstrates a wry sense of humor" (Hart 2006). Christopher Hitchens in the *Times* of May 6, 2007, merely mentioned that "Obama's open and engaging style can be found on almost every page" (Hitchens 2007), and the reader is left to wonder what exactly that means.

Even Michael Tomasky's lengthy earlier account entitled "The Phenomenon [of Barack Obama]" in *The New York Review of Books* of November 30, 2006, had nothing more to say about Obama's linguistic and rhetorical skills. He does, however, mention in passing that Obama borrowed the title of his book from the title of a sermon that his minister Reverend Jeremiah Wright Jr. of Trinity United Church of Christ in Chicago had delivered after Mayor Harold Washington's death in 1988. Barack Obama recalls this in his autobiographical *Dreams from My Father*:

> The title of Reverend Wright's sermon that morning was "The Audacity of Hope." He began with a passage from the Book of Samuel – the story of Hannah, who, barren and taunted by her rivals, had wept and shaken in prayer before her God. The story reminded him, he said, of a sermon a fellow pastor had preached at a conference some years before, in which the pastor described going to a museum and being confronted by a painting titled *Hope* [1886, by the nineteenth-century British artist George Frederic Watts].
>
> "The painting depicts a harpist," Reverend Wright explained, "a woman who at first glance appears to be sitting atop a great mountain. Until you take a closer look and see that the woman is bruised and bloodied, dressed in tattered rags, the harp reduced to a single frayed string. Your eye is then drawn to the scene below, down to the valley below, where everywhere are the ravages of famine, the drumbeat of war, a world groaning under strife and deprivation." [...]
>
> "Isn't that ... the world that each of us stands on?"
>
> "Yessuh!"
>
> "Like Hannah, we have known bitter times! Daily, we face rejection and despair!"
>
> "Say it!"
>
> "And yet consider once again the painting before us. Hope! Like Hannah, the harpist is looking upwards, a few faint notes floating upwards towards the heavens. She

> dares to hope. ... She has the audacity ... to make music ... and praise God ... on the one string ... she has left!" (Obama 2004 [1995], 292-293)

And then follows Barack Obama's comment that clearly has never left his keen and compassionate mind during the past twenty years:

> And in that single note – hope! – I heard something else; at the foot of that cross, inside the thousands of churches across the city, I imagined the stories of ordinary black people merging with the stories of David and Goliath, Moses and Pharaoh, the Christians in the lion's den, Ezekiel's fields of dry bones. Those stories – of survival, and freedom, and hope – became our story, my story; [...]. (Obama 2004 [1995], 294)

After this observation Obama returns one more time to the sermon of the preacher, who now uses the phrase that has become Obama's rallying slogan for a better life in this country and elsewhere in the world: "The audacity of hope! I still remember my grandmother, singing in the house, 'There's a bright side somewhere ... don't rest till you find it. ...'" (Obama 2004 [1995], 294). Obama subsequently used "The audacity of hope" as the title of his celebrated keynote address at the Democratic Convention on July 27, 2004, at Boston, which turned him into a national figure literally overnight. It is a shame that Reverend Wright subsequently showed himself to be quite racist in some of his views, causing Obama considerable difficulties in his campaign for the presidency. Nevertheless, he clearly had much positive influence on Obama, and it is understandable that the latter found it very difficult to break with his former pastor and friend. Ultimately this led to Obama delivering his significant speech on race on March 18, 2008, at Philadelphia, entitled "A More Perfect Union."

In any case, the triad of "survival, and freedom, and hope" appears to be solidly engrained in Obama's mind and heart, and it is a definite leitmotif in his many speeches. The same is true for the title "The audacity of hope" that by now has become a popular phrase in the United States and beyond. Little wonder that Peter Preston entitled his review of Obama's *The Audacity of Hope* in *The Observer* of April 29, 2007, with the proverbial "His Hope Springs Eternal" (Preston 2007). And yet, neither in his two books nor in his numerous speeches has Barack Obama despite his constant emphasis on hope ever used the common proverb "Hope springs eternal." Perhaps this piece of folk wisdom is too open-ended for Obama, the political pragmatist. After all, as a visionary politician he wants to get beyond hope, and he certainly does not want to wait an eternity for some sociopolitical hopes to become reality.

But speaking of proverbs or proverbial phrases, none of the reviewers ever refers to the rather obvious fact that Barack Obama's books and speeches are replete with proverbial folk speech. This is also not the case in David Olive's "A Note on Barack Obama's Oratorical Style and Its Impact", who does not go beyond the general observation that "Obama proved words do matter" (Olive 2008, 87-90, here 88). In fact, they really say very little or nothing about his style that combines folk language with a superb literary style, proverbs with quotations, and common sense with intellectualism into a most effective sociopolitical discourse based on a deep sense of humanity and morality (see Rogak 2007). Even though the already mentioned Michael Tomasky has nothing to say about Obama's impressive mastery of this dichotomy, he has unlocked the basic structure of Obama's philosophical and sociopolitical treatise:

> *The Audacity of Hope* hews closely to formula. Each of its nine chapters – on broad, thematic subjects like politics, opportunity, faith, race, and family – begins with an anecdote that suggests the point he wants to make about the subject, then moves on to his ruminations about it, and ends with another anecdote meant to drive the point home. These can tend toward the homiletic (the chapter on faith ends with the sentence "I know that tucking in my daughters that night, I grasped a little bit of heaven"). (Tomasky 2006)

This is quite true, and it is good to see that Tomasky recognizes Obama's fascinating ability at storytelling, from personal narratives to folk tales. But I would argue that his proverbial language is part of all this, especially also in Obama's convincing way of always showing both sides of the political coin. Again Tomasky is absolutely correct in stating that "the book's most interesting aspect is the author's deep ambivalence about contemporary American politics. The chapters boil down to a pattern: here's what the right believes about subject X, and here's what the left believes; and while I basically side with the left, I think the right has a point or two that we should consider, and the left can sometimes get a little carried away" (Tomasky 2006). And yet again, how does Obama manage his attempt of bringing about some convergence of at times diametrically opposed views and standpoints? I will argue again that at least in part it is through his proverbial language that he stylistically finds a common denominator of effective communication, where the metaphors of the proverbial phrases add commonality and common sense for everybody to understand his sociopolitical rhetoric. He is doubtlessly a most skillful communicator (see Obama 2008), having learned much from Lincoln, Douglass, King, and others and also finding his own way to communicate regionally, nationally, and globally with people of very different backgrounds.

"So (and) make no mistake about it," to use one of Barack Obama's favorite phrases from his speeches (for example on July 10, 2008, and on August 4, 2008), his book *The Audacity of Hope* is in addition to all of its other claims to fame also a testimony to the value of proverbial phrases in modern political rhetoric. Right on page two of the "Prologue" Obama uses one of his favorite proverbial expressions to state how he used to argue against the cynicism that is often voiced against a life dedicated to politics and public issues: "I understood the skepticism, but there was – and always had been – another tradition to politics, a tradition that stretched from the days of the country's founding to the glory of the civil rights movement, a tradition based on the simple idea that we have a stake in one another, and that what binds us together is greater than what drives us apart, and that if enough people believe in the truth of that proposition and act on it, then we might not solve every problem, but we can get something meaningful done" (2). And then he continues in relatively simple terms to talk proverbially about the "cutthroat politics and unremitting culture wars" (8), the fact that "we feel in our guts the lack of honesty, rigor, and common sense in our policy debates" (9), and that "if we don't change course soon, we may be the first generation in a very long time that leaves behind a weaker and more fractured America than the one we inherited" (9). Of course, "changing course" is one of Obama's major metaphors for having gotten involved in politics in the first place.

REPUBLICANS AND DEMOCRATS

The first chapter on "Republicans and Democrats" shows that Barack Obama had a clear understanding "of how the [partisan political] game had come to be played" (16) in his home state of Illinois and in Washington. But he maintained his positive attitude during the years in the Illinois legislature, clinging to the refreshing notion "that politics could be different, and that the voters wanted something different; that they were tired of distortion, name-calling, and sound-bite solutions to complicated problems; that if I could reach those voters directly, frame the issues as I felt them, explain the choices in as truthful a fashion as I knew how, then people's instincts for fair play and common sense would bring them around. If enough of us took that risk, I thought, not only the country's politics but the country's policies would change for the better" (18-19). To achieve this change, we must, proverbially speaking, "keep it clean" (18), "take a deep breath" (22), change things "from top to bottom" (22), and "we will need to remind ourselves, despite all our differences, just how much we share: common hopes, common dreams, a bond that will not break" (25).

After these generalities Obama discusses the unsatisfactory *modus operandi* of the two major parties, scolding the Democrats who, for all their social commitment and progress in raising the standard of living in the years following the New Deal, nevertheless cultivated "a certain live-and-let-live philosophy: a philosophy anchored in acquiescence toward or active promotion of racial oppression in the

South; a philosophy that depended on a broader culture in which social norms – the nature of sexuality, say, or the role of women – were largely unquestioned" (26-27). The Republicans likewise adhere to this negative interpretation of the proverb "Live and let live" which only too quickly can undergo the semantic switch from advocating freedom and choice to agreeing with an imperfect status quo. This irresponsible neglect and looking the other way was put into question by "the student protests against the Vietnam War and the suggestion that America was not always right, our actions not always justified – that a new generation would not pay any price to bear any burden that its elders might dictate" (28). The idea of paying the proverbial price for one's actions is yet another leitmotif of Obama's rhetoric (see 48, 68, 98, 119), as can be seen especially in its repetitive use in his speech on "The Cost of War" of March 20, 2008, at Charleston, West Virginia:

> And today, I want to talk about another cost of this war [in Iraq] – the toll it has taken on our economy. Because at a time when we're on the brink of recession – when neighborhoods have For Sale signs outside every home, and working families are struggling to keep up with rising costs – ordinary Americans are paying a price for this war.
>
> When you're spending over $50 to fill up your car because the price of oil is four times what it was before Iraq, you're paying a price for this war.
>
> When Iraq is costing each household about $100 a month, you're paying a price for this war.
>
> When a National Guard unit is over in Iraq and can't help out during a hurricane in Louisiana or with floods here in West Virginia, our communities are paying a price for this war.
>
> And the price our families and communities are paying reflects the price America is paying. The most conservative estimates say that Iraq has now cost more than half a trillion dollars, more than any other war in our history besides World War II. (108; numbers after citations from speeches refer to the list at the end of this book)

And if all this "price paying" is not already clear enough, he adds the following exemplifying paragraph to this leitmotif in the book, driving his point home with two absolutely fitting proverbial expressions:

> And then, with the walls of the status quo breached, every form of "outsider" came streaming through the gates: feminists, Latinos, hippies, Panthers, welfare moms, gays, all asserting their rights, all insisting on recognition, all demanding a seat at the table and a piece of the pie. (28)

Yes, indeed, Americans and their politicians found themselves "in the midst of this topsy-turvy time" (29) that seemed "to be spinning out of control" (30). And now Obama adds, with a somewhat ironic employment of a proverb but with his characteristic honesty, that he has a certain understanding of Ronald Reagan's appeal not only to Republicans:

> As disturbed as I might have been by Ronald Reagan's election in 1980, as unconvinced as I might have been by his John Wayne, *Father Knows Best* pose, his policy by anecdote, and his gratuitous assaults on the poor, I understood his appeal. [...] Reagan spoke to America's longing for order, our need to believe that we are not simply subject to blind, impersonal forces but that we can shape our individual and collective destinies, so long as we rediscover the traditional virtues of hard work, patriotism, personal responsibility, optimism, and faith. (31)

This statement must not be misunderstood as an endorsement of Reagan's Republican policies, especially his mistaken idea of trickle down economics; but taken out of context, some Democrats could well question his political loyalty. Obama knew that "undoubtedly, some of these views will get me into trouble" (11), but he is after "that kernel of truth" (11) in this book, and that must include both ends of the political spectrum. By couching comments like these into proverbial language, he adds an element of metaphorical expressiveness to his bipartisan thoughts that make them more palatable.

In any case, Obama continues his affront against both parties, which ever more looked at the political divide as "a menu of either-or, for-or-against, sound-bite-ready choices. No longer was economic policy a matter of weighing trade-offs between competing goals of productivity and distributional justice, of growing the pie and slicing the pie. You were for either tax cuts or tax hikes, small government or big government. [...] You were with us or against us. You had to choose sides" (33-34). In addition to the proverbial phrase of "slicing the pie," Obama even alludes to the biblical proverb "He that is not with me is against me" (Matthew 12,30) to add extra authority to his correct claim. The remaining pages of this chapter continue in this vein, underscoring the ills of this "ideological deadlock" (34), where "deficit reduction can't take place on the backs of the poor" (37), where "hardball tactics" (39) prevail, and where some "seek to chip away at the very idea of government" (40). Of special interest on these pages is the following statement with its two allusions to the proverbs "War is hell" and "The best-laid plans of mice and men often go astray" (see Mieder et al. 1992, 467 and 640):

> When I ponder the work of a George Kennan or a George Marshall, when I read the speeches of Bob Kennedy or an Everett Dirksen, I can't help feeling that the politics of today suffers from a case of arrested development. For these men, the issues America faced were never abstract and hence never simple. War might be hell and still the right thing to do. Economies could collapse despite the best-laid plans. People could work hard all their lives and still lose everything. (36)

The proverb allusions help Obama to bring his point across that life is full of contradictions and complexities, and "What's needed is a broad majority of Americans – Democrats, Republicans, and independents of goodwill – who are reengaged in the project of national renewal, and who see their own self-interest as inextricably linked to the interests of others" (40). And thus, almost predictably by now for Barack Obama, who shows himself in this book as the grand unifier of opposite views, he concludes his concise review of American government with the following comment:

> Maybe the critics are right. Maybe there's no escaping our great political divide, an endless clash of armies, and any attempts to alter the rules of engagement are futile. Or maybe the trivialization of politics has reached a point of no return, so that most people see it as just one more diversion, a sport, with politicians our paunch-bellied gladiators and those who bother to pay attention just fans on the sidelines: We paint our faces red or blue and cheer our side and boo their side, and if it takes a late hit or cheap shot to beat the other team, so be it, for winning is all that matters.
>
> But I don't think so. They are out there, I think to myself, those ordinary citizens who have grown up in the midst of all the political and cultural battles, but who have found a way – in their own lives, at least – to make peace with their neighbors and themselves. [...] They don't always understand the arguments between right and left, conservative and liberal, but they recognize the difference between dogma and common sense, responsibility and irresponsibility, between those things that last and those that are fleeting.
>
> They are out there, waiting for Republicans and Democrats to catch up with them. (41-42)

Every reader can relate to these comments, and certainly to the phrase of something being a cheap shot and the intentional play with the proverb "Winning isn't everything" with which Obama adds some colloquial spice to his satirical description of those who will not come together for the common good. They believe in the anti-proverb "Winning is all that matters" and its variant "Winning isn't everything, it's the only thing" (see Litovkina and Mieder 2006). The message is clear in its simple proverbiality! In politics, winning is not everything, but compromise, fairness, and the work towards the common good would perhaps create a so-called win-win situation.

VALUES

With these comments Obama has found a natural bridge to his second chapter on "Values" in which he raises the important question: "What are the core values that we, as Americans, hold in common?" (52). After all, he continues, the "shared values – the standards and principles that the majority of Americans deem important in their lives, and in the life of the country – should be the heart of our politics, the cornerstone of any meaningful debate about budgets and projects, regulations and policies" (52-53). Perhaps not surprisingly, he begins with the first few lines of the "Declaration of Independence" with its two proverbial truths that contain the most basic wisdom: "We hold these truths to be self-evident, that all men are created equal, that they are endowed by their Creator with certain unalienable Rights, that among these are Life, Liberty and the pursuit of Happiness" (53). Obama had cited this quotation already in his celebrated speech at the Democratic National Convention on July 27, 2004, at Boston, introducing it as "a very simple premise" and two years later referring to it in his book as being composed of "simple words" (53) but ultimate depth. Perhaps this emphasis on simplicity or his obvious awareness of what has been called Protestant work ethics led him to expand the concepts of equality and liberty to fundamental virtues as they were so clearly expressed by Benjamin Franklin in the middle of the eighteenth century:

> We understand our liberty [...] in the idea of opportunity and the subsidiary values that help realize opportunity – all those homespun virtues that Benjamin Franklin first popularized in *Poor Richard's Almanack* and that have continued to inspire our allegiance through successive generations. The values of self-reliance and self-improvement and risk-taking. The values of drive, discipline, temperance, and hard work. The values of thrift and personal responsibility.
>
> These values are rooted in a basic optimism about life and a faith in free will – a confidence that through pluck and sweat and smarts, each of us can rise above the circumstances of birth. But these values also express a broader confidence that so long as individual men and women are free to pursue their own interests, society as a whole will prosper. Our system of self-government and our free-market economy depend on the majority of individual Americans adhering to these values. (54-55)

Paremiologically speaking, I must admit that I am a bit disappointed that Obama does not at least cite a few of those proverbial gems with which the didactic Franklin bombarded his compatriots, to wit, "The sleeping fox catches no poultry," "Lost time is never found again," "Laziness travels so slowly, that poverty soon overtakes him," "Industry pays debts, while despair increases them," "If you would know the value of money, go and try to borrow some," "Time is money," "It is hard for an empty bag to stand upright," etc. This might especially have been useful in the case of the many translations of the book that by now have appeared in European and Asian languages. Foreign citizens are not necessarily acquainted with this wisdom which for the most part was not created but simply popularized by Benjamin Franklin (see Mieder 2004, 171-180 and 216-218). In all fairness it must be said, however, that Obama might have found a listing of a few proverbs too didactic or better yet unnecessary. But be that as it may, it should be noted here in any case that Barack Obama never uses the word "proverb," and when he uses proverbs, they are more often than not cited as allusions and not full texts. This is nevertheless somewhat surprising, since proverbs traditionally play a major role among African Americans (see Prahlad 1996). It is difficult to know whether Obama consciously refrains from referring to his proverbial language or whether he employs folk speech rather automatically. The latter would, to be sure, go against his clear awareness of his literary style in his speeches and writings.

Perhaps he simply feels that proverbs without a context (and he would be correct!) would not mean much in helping us in "finding the right balance between our competing values" (56), especially since proverbs by themselves often contradict each other, as for example, "Look before you leap" and "He who hesitates is lost." Instead of quoting a proverb, he chooses a less didactic proverbial phrase to describe the virtue of competence, for example: "Nothing brightens my day more than dealing with somebody, anybody, who takes pride in their work or goes the extra mile" (60). In any case, when he reaches the moral value of empathy that he finds himself appreciating more and more, he attains one of the stylistic, proverbial and ethical high points of his *Audacity of Hope* by combining philosophical thought with subjective experience:

> It [empathy] is at the heart of my moral code, and it is how I understand the Golden Rule – not simply as a call to sympathy and charity, but as something more demanding, a call to stand in somebody else's shoes and see through their eyes.
>
> Like most of my values, I learned about empathy from my mother. She disdained any kind of cruelty or thoughtlessness or abuse of power, whether it expressed itself in the form of racial prejudice or bullying in the schoolyard or workers being underpaid. Whenever she saw even a hint of such behavior in me she would look me square in the eyes and ask, "How do you think that would make you feel?" (66)

Four proverbial expressions – "to be at the heart of something," "to stand in somebody else's shoes," "to see something through someone else's eyes," and "to look someone square in the eyes" – form the folk speech underpinning of this short exegesis on the value of empathy, with the actual proverb that has become known as the "golden rule" not being stated explicitly: "Do unto others as you would have them do unto you " (Matthew 7,12). Why not? I would assume that Obama believes that all his readers will know what the golden rule is, and it might be added here that it is not just wisdom from Jesus' "Sermon on the Mount" in the New Testament, but that its idea is similarly expressed in other religions and also in Immanuel Kant's categorical imperative (see Hertzler 1933/34, Burrrell 1997, 235-240). Let us hope that Obama's readers do know the actual text of the golden rule, but with cultural literacy being on a decline, he might just assume a bit too much. Abraham Lincoln and Frederick Douglass, who also used the golden rule several times, usually quoted the proverb as well, even though they could at their time count more on their audience knowing the wisdom from their Bibles.

At the conclusion of his elaboration on a humane value system (see Templeton 1997), Obama argues that "in the end a sense of mutual understanding isn't enough. After all, talk is cheap; like any value, empathy must be acted upon. [...] If we aren't willing to pay the price for our values, if we aren't willing to make some sacrifices in order to realize them, then we should ask ourselves whether we really believe in them at all" (68). And as if the proverb "Talk is cheap" and the proverbial expression of "having to pay the price" were not enough, he drives his point home with yet one more concluding proverb: "Although we recognize that they [our values] are subject to challenge, can be poked and prodded and debunked and turned inside out by intellectuals and cultural critics, they have proven to be both surprisingly durable and surprisingly constant across classes, and races, and faiths, and generations. We can make claims on their behalf, so long as we understand that our values must be tested against fact and experience, so long as we recall that they demand deeds not just words. To do otherwise would be to relinquish our best selves" (69). It might be of interest that the Nobel prize laureate Winston S. Churchill chose the proverb "Deeds, not words" as a rallying battle cry in his relentless fight against Nazi Germany, and in due time he won his military and moral victory against the evil Third Reich with the help of the Allies (see Mieder and Bryan 1995, 192-193). Obama is not fighting such a menace, but his two proverbs of "Do unto others as you would have them do unto you" and "Deeds, not words" certainly qualify as beacons in the rekindling of the basic values of human decency, respect, and compassion.

OUR CONSTITUTION

Just as the somewhat didactic second chapter ends with a proverb, the third more erudite chapter on the Constitution by Barack Obama, the Harvard-educated lawyer, begins with a proverbial comparison coined among U.S. senators: "There's a saying that senators frequently use when asked to describe their first year on Capitol Hill: 'It's like drinking from a fire hose'" (71). This reference represents a wonderful example of Obama as a folkloristic field researcher who records various proverbial phrases, folk narratives, and other traditional matters. In fact, he proves himself to be quite the ethnographer in his *Dreams from My Father* autobiography that is filled with folk speech, anecdotes, stories, etc. In this particular case, the hitherto unrecorded saying serves as an introduction of Obama's ensuing description of his first few months in the U.S. Senate, when, again speaking proverbially, he tried to "get up to speed on the issues" (71) while Republicans wanted "to go in for the kill" as they were "changing the rules in the middle of the game" (82) on a particular issue. This leads him to an insightful analysis of "deliberative democracy" for which the Constitution is not "a fixed blueprint for action" but rather "a framework with rules" (92). And then follows a splendid defense of the Constitution with Obama once again coupling colloquialisms with intellectualism that results in lucid communication:

> I confess that there is a fundamental humility to this reading of the Constitution and our democratic process. It seems to champion compromise, modesty, and muddling through; to justify logrolling, deal-making, self-interest, pork barrels, paralysis, and inefficiency – all the sausage-making that no one wants to see and that editorials throughout our history have often labeled as corrupt. And yet I think we make a mistake in assuming that democratic deliberation requires abandonment of our highest ideals, or of a commitment to a common good. After all, the Constitution ensures our free speech [...] and offers us the possibility of a genuine marketplace of ideas [...]; a marketplace in which, through debate and competition, we can expand our perspective, change our minds, and eventually arrive not merely at agreements but at sound and fair agreements. (94)
>
> [...]
>
> In sum, the Constitution envisions a road map by which we marry passion to reason, the ideal of individual freedom to the demands of the community. And the amazing thing is that it's worked. (95)

True enough, but Obama the keen historian is also well aware of the fact "that it has not always been the pragmatist, the voice of reason, or the force of compromise, that has created the conditions for liberty" (97). This reminds him among others of fighters like William Lloyd Garrison and Frederick Douglass, "who recognized power would concede nothing without a fight" (97) regarding slavery. Quoting Douglass more precisely in a speech on "An Honest Government, A Hopeful Future" on August 28, 2006, at the University of Nairobi in Kenya, Obama said in regard to a better future in Africa: "As Frederick Douglass once stated [August 3, 1857]: 'Power concedes nothing without a demand. It never did, and it never will'" (67).

The thought of slavery reminds Obama of Abraham Lincoln, who grounded his presidency in the most difficult times on pragmatism, compromise, and an adherence to the Constitution, repeatedly basing his arguments on the Bible proverb "A house divided against itself cannot stand" (see Mieder 1998):

> I'm left then with Lincoln, who like no man before or since understood both the deliberative function of our democracy and the limits of such deliberation. We remember him for the firmness and depth of his convictions – his unyielding opposition to

slavery and his determination that a house divided could not stand. But his presidency was guided by a practicality that would distress us today, a practicality that led him to test various bargains with the South in order to maintain the Union without war; to appoint and discard general after general, strategy after strategy, once war broke out; to stretch the Constitution to the breaking point in order to see the war through to a successful conclusion. I like to believe that for Lincoln, it was never a matter of abandoning conviction for the sake of expediency. (97-98)

In an essay entitled "What I See in Lincoln's Eyes" published in *Time* of June 27, 2005, Obama once again alludes to the "house divided" proverb: "In the midst of slavery's dark storm and the complexities of governing a house divided, he somehow kept the moral compass pointed firm and true" (Obama 2005). While this is actually a direct quotation from remarks that Obama had made at the opening of the Abraham Lincoln Presidential Library and Museum in Springfield, Illinois, on April 20, 2005, he also repeated the proverb in a different context on June 16, 2006, during his Northwestern University Commencement Address at Evanston, Illinois: "The class of 1860 would find their country torn apart by civil war in less than a year. Many of them would listen to their President tell them that a house divided cannot stand, and they would answer the call to save a union and free a people" (58). And almost predictably, Obama returned to the proverb during the announcement of his candidacy for the presidency of the United States on February 10, 2007, at Springfield, Illinois:

> It was here, in Springfield, where North, South, East and West come together that I was reminded of the essential decency of the American people – where I came to believe that through this decency, we can build a more hopeful America.
>
> And that is why, in the shadow of the Old State Capitol, where Lincoln once called on a divided house to stand together, where common hopes and common dreams still exist, I stand before you today to announce my candidacy for President of the United States. (76)

Obama's clear preoccupation with Lincoln has led Morgan Meis to the overstated claim that "Obama thinks of himself as Lincoln," beginning her article with the statement that "If platitudes had weight, Barack Obama's *The Audacity of Hope* would be impossible to lift off the table. Still, it's a good book. By the standards of 'writings by politicians' it's in the top percentile. You read it and you like the man" (Meis 2008). This is a strange mixture of innuendo, criticism, and praise, to say the least. Obama is way too humble, just as Lincoln was, to think of himself as the so much admired former president. He looks at him as a hero, and he wants to emulate him the best he can in modern times, and that is a noble cause. As far as platitudes are concerned, there are certainly some (at times perhaps even expressed by elements of folk speech), but Obama's style is too sophisticated to suffer from it. And, to be sure, it is good writing, and not just as far as the writings by politicians are concerned. Obama can well hold his own, just as his three admired precursors Abraham Lincoln, Frederick Douglass, and Martin Luther King could before him.

But Barack Obama deserves the last word regarding his relationship to Lincoln. The thoughts expressed in this conclusion to his deliberations about our constitutional government are anything but platitudinous despite his renewed use of a proverbial leitmotif: "The blood of slaves reminds us that our pragmatism can sometimes be moral cowardice. Lincoln, and those buried at Gettysburg, remind us that we should pursue our own absolute truths only if we acknowledge that there may be a terrible price to pay" (98).

POLITICS

There is no doubt that Barack Obama enjoys politics, and one of his "favorite tasks of being a senator is hosting town hall meetings" (101). In his lively description of how politics work and what people think of political activities, he repeatedly turns to proverbial expressions to add a certain emotional expressiveness to his acute comments, i.e., "They're all [Politicians] in the pockets of special interests" (102), "Things went downhill from there" (106), "I knew in my bones" (106), "But it was too little too late" (107), "people, who have the luxury of licking their wounds" (107), the "campaign plan called for a bare-bones budget" (110), "my dark-horse status protected me from some of the more dangerous pitfalls [taking bribes] of fund-raising" (113), "My staff would shake their head" (117), "you're a typical, two-faced politician" (117), "my status as an underdog" (120), "loses his head with all the publicity" (124), "reporters will go out of their way to stir up the pot" (126), "maintain a straight face during debate" (128), and "they are baptized by fire" (133). The use of somatic phrases, colloquial comparisons to animals, and highly charged idioms with such words as "downhill," "pot," or "fire" add to this account of experiencing politics. And as always, Obama is upbeat about it all, stressing that the frustrations and arguments are well worth it if politicians from both parties come together and actually move things ahead: "Genuine bipartisanship, though, assumes an honest process of give-and-take, and that quality of the compromise is measured by how well it serves some agreed-upon goal, whether better schools or lower deficits" (131).

Throughout this chapter Obama shows himself as a realistic and honest observer of the political scene, especially regarding the pressures of "the need to win, but also the need not to lose" (109). That leads to the so-called money-chase, and "apparently there are still those in Washington who view politics as a means of getting rich, and who, while generally not dumb enough to accept bags of small bills, are perfectly prepared to take care of contributors and properly feather their beds until the time is finally ripe to jump into the lucrative practice of lobbying [...]" (109). So Obama is quite proud of "being something of a stick-in-the-mud when it came to fund-raising, co-authoring the first campaign finance legislation to pass in twenty-five years" (110), as he puts it with a fitting proverbial image. He continues to rely on such proverbial phrases throughout this discussion, as when he describes the pressures that special interest groups put on individuals running for office: "Simply put, they have an ax to grind. And they want you, the elected official, to help them grind it" (116). There are lots of pressures on a politician wanting to be (re)elected, but "as important as money is in campaigns, it's not just fund-raising that puts a candidate over the top. If you want to win in politics – if you don't want to lose – then organized people can be just as important as cash [...]" (115).

All of this reads like a lively textbook on how to make it in politics, with the charm of the account lying in the fact that Obama for the most part includes personal experiences. And he even adds a great bit of proverbial wisdom about the entire election process: "There is a saying in Illinois politics that 'signs don't vote,' meaning that you can't judge a race by how many signs a candidate has" (112). That can easily be translated into solid advice for aspiring politicians. Yet, true to his reluctance of becoming overly didactic or even sermonic, Obama avoids quoting too many such "nuggets of conventional wisdom [that] lodge themselves in our brain without us ever taking the time to examine them" (124). He really is not interested in quick fixes based on proverbs, restricting their use in his own writings and rhetoric to a well-delineated minimum. Proverbs often favor one-sided arguments, and they would deny Obama his constant insistence on bipartisanship, compromise, and the give-and-take necessary in the political process.

OPPORTUNITY

While it is interesting to note that the chapter on primarily economic "Opportunity" with its over fifty pages is the longest of the book, it should not be too surprising that this is the case. After all, opportunity has much to do with Barack Obama's basic theme of hope for a better world. As always, he makes use of a number of very general preformulated phrases that enter automatically into his books and speeches, as for example, "to reduce bureaucracy and red tape" (157), "not holding up their end of the bargain" (159), "when all is said and done" (173), and "the public debate has been deadlocked" (183). But in the excitement of argumentation, Obama is quick in choosing more elaborate proverbial phrases to add some metaphorical spice to his comments, to wit, "anyone who would challenge it [laissez-faire economics] swims against the prevailing tide" (150), "Democratic policy makers [were] more obsessed with slicing the economic pie than with growing the pie" (157), "it was Clinton who would accomplish what Reagan never did, putting the nation's fiscal house in order even while lessening poverty" (158, 175), "will I be able to look squarely in the eyes of those workers in Galesburg and tell them that globalization can work for them and their children?" (172), and "If we're serious about avoiding such a future [with a large national debt], then we'll have to start digging ourselves out of this hole" (188).

To show how the nation got into this proverbial hole and how it might just get out of it again, Obama tries something new in this chapter. Throughout his speeches and writings he is prone to prove some of his points by summarizing them with relatively well-known quotations, of which some have reached a proverbial status of sorts. Others have done this before him, of course. But there is something unique at least to some extent in Obama's quotemanship (for this term see Boller 1967) in that he uses sententious remarks for both positive and negative argumentation:

> Or, as Ronald Reagan succinctly put it: "Government is not the solution to our problem; government is the problem." (147)
>
> Calvin Coolidge once said that "the chief business of the American people is business." (149)
>
> As Ted Turner famously said, in America money is how we keep score. (149)
>
> As he [Franklin D. Roosevelt] would explain in 1944, "People who are hungry, people who are out of a job are the stuff of which dictatorships are made." (155)
>
> Lincoln's simple maxim: that we will do collectively, through our government, only those things that we cannot do as well or at all individually and privately. In other words, we should be guided by what works. (159)

As always, Obama "plays" with these quotations, neither rejecting nor accepting any one of them completely. In fact, as he so often does, he is quick to follow this last quotation by Lincoln up with the honest statement "I won't pretend to have all the answers, and a detailed discussion of U.S. economic policy would fill up several volumes. But I can offer a few examples of where we can break free of our current political stalemate" (159). Later on in this chapter he rephrases the last comment by stating that "It's time we broke the impasse by acknowledging a few simple truths [... that ...] give us a fighting chance" (184 and 187).

And what is it that we are principally fighting against? Obama goes into considerable detail explaining the ills of the socioeconomic situation, but he also couches all of it in a remarkable summary made up of a proverbial expression and an allusion to a proverb. According to his interpretation, we have "what some call a 'winner-take-all' economy, in which a rising tide doesn't necessarily lift all boats" (146). The proverbial phrase of "winner-take-all" refers to an economic policy where the rich get richer and the poor poorer, and the hidden proverb "The rising tide lifts all boats" is negated in light of the fact that only the wealthy rise while leaving the poor stranded. Obama likes this proverb, as can be seen from a positive use of its wisdom in a major speech on "Our Common Stake in America's Prosperity" delivered on September 17, 2007, at New York City. While he praises the American economic system in this address, he also is aware that we need "in FDR's words, a re-appraisal of our values as a nation":

> I believe that America's free market has been the engine of America's great progress. [...] But I also know that in this country, our grand experiment has only worked because we have guided the market's invisible hand with a higher principle. It's the idea that we are all in this together. From CEOs to shareholders, from financiers to factory workers, we all have a stake in each other's success because the more Americans prosper, the more America prospers. That's why we've had titans of industry who've made it their mission to pay well enough that their employees could afford the products they made. That's why employees at companies like Google don't mind the vast success of their CEOs – because they share in that success just the same. And that's why our economy hasn't just been the world's greatest wealth creator – it's been the world's greatest job generator. It's been the tide that has lifted the boats of the largest middle-class in history. [... But] in recent years, we have seen a dangerous erosion of the rules and principles that have made our market to work and our economy to thrive. Instead of thinking about what's good for America or what's good for business, a mentality has crept into certain corners of Washington and the business world that says, "what's good for me is good enough." (89)

The catastrophic result of this deplorable change can be seen today with the economic world crisis that started right here in the United States. Now "we are all in this together," to quote Obama's proverbial phrase at the beginning of the above paragraph. And what will happen with our economy, that according to the proverb, has "been the tide that has lifted the boats"? Interestingly enough, in a speech entitled "Keeping America's Promise" delivered on February 13, 2008 at Janesville, Wisconsin, Obama returned to the "tide"-proverb to underscore his views on the economy of the future:

> Prosperity hasn't always come easily [at Janesville]. [...] But through hard times and good, great challenge and great change, the promise of Janesville has been the promise of America – that our prosperity can and must be the tide that lifts every boat, that we rise or fall as one nation; that our economy is strongest when our middle-class grows and opportunity is spread as widely as possible. And when it's not – when opportunity is uneven or unequal – it is our responsibility to restore the

> balance, and fairness, and keep that promise alive for the next generation. That is
> the responsibility we face right now, and that is the responsibility I intend to meet as
> President of the United States. (105)

In his book chapter, Obama correctly and prophetically writes: "How America's economy performs in the years to come may depend largely on how well we take such wisdom to heart" (163). Playing off the two proverbial expressions "to be in something together" and "to be on one's own", both of which are leitmotifs in his speeches as well (see his speech of March 27, 2008), he summarizes the mess we are in as follows: "If the guiding philosophy behind the traditional system of social insurance could be described as 'We're all in it together,' the philosophy behind the Ownership Society seems to be 'You're on your own'" (178-179). He is, of course, right in concluding that "we rise and fall together" (193), and that we need a new "balancing act between self-interest and community [while we] affirm our bonds with one another" (193). At this point, Obama might well have chosen the proverb "United we stand, divided we fall" as a final word of wisdom, obvious as it might be in its simplicity. As it is, the proverb is also missing in all of his other writings and verbal communications.

FAITH

There is another proverb that Barack Obama, somewhat surprisingly perhaps, has not used in his books and speeches, namely the Biblical claim that "Faith can remove mountains" (1. Corinthians 13,2). But not to worry, he certainly makes biblical wisdom as expressed in folk proverbs the center part of this chapter, while also including emotionally charged proverbial expressions like "churches are growing by leaps and bounds" (202), "to make a way out of no way" (207), and "at the drop of a hat" (210). Obama can become quite colloquial in fact when he amasses such idioms. For example, regarding his 2004 Republican opponent Alan Keyes, Obama recalls the following:

> Alan Keyes was an ideal opponent; all I had to do was keep my mouth shut and start
> planning my swearing-in ceremony. And yet, as the campaign progressed, I found
> him getting under my skin in a way that few people ever have. When our paths
> crossed during the campaign, I often had to suppress the rather uncharitable urge to
> either taunt him or wring his neck. (211)

That is pretty strong proverbial medicine in a chapter on faith, but it once again shows with what honesty and integrity Obama is willing to communicate his feelings, beliefs, frustrations, and anxieties.

This type of proverbial self-characterization is easily transferred to characterize or explain the behavior or beliefs of others. For example, Obama makes an interesting use of the biblical proverb "Render unto Caesar the things which are Caesar's; and unto God the things that are God's" (Matthew 22,21) to describe the attitudes of Southern Christians before they decided to get actively involved in politics: "The reluctance on the part of many evangelicals to be drawn into politics – their inward focus on individual salvation and willingness to render unto Caesar what is his – might have endured indefinitely had it not been for the social upheavals of the sixties" (200). In other words, Obama is arguing with this half of the proverb that these conservative Christians were too quick in acquiescing to governmental politics (Caesar) until the Republican Party mobilized them into a formidable political power house. It might, however, in this case have been only fair for Obama to include the second part of the proverb that emphasizes the religiosity of the evangelicals. He might well have done this upon a closer examination of his text, as can be inferred from a statement that he makes some pages later:

> More fundamentally, the discomfort of some progressives with any hint of religiosity has often inhibited us from effectively addressing issues in moral terms. Some of the problem is rhetorical: Scrub language of all religious content and we forfeit the imagery and terminology through which millions of Americans understand both their personal morality and social justice. Imagine Lincoln's Second Inaugural Address without reference to "the judgments of the Lord," or King's "I Have a Dream" speech without reference to "all of God's children." (214)

This is an absolutely correct observation, but one might add that people of all spiritual persuasions (including agnostics and atheists) do use formulaic religious language, especially proverbial expressions and proverbs stemming from the Bible. They are part of the normal linguistic repertoire, and they are more often than not employed without a conscious awareness of their biblical origin. After all, many proverbs of the Bible have long become true folk proverbs that do not depend on the Bible for their wisdom (see Mieder 1990). In a way Obama is himself a bit guilty of scrubbing language of some of its religious content when he mentions Lincoln's reference to the Lord's judgments in his second inaugural address of March 4, 1865, without including the entire proverbial statement of "The judgments of the Lord are true and righteous altogether" (Psalms 19,9) and failing to mention that a few sentences before this Lincoln cites the better known Bible proverb "Judge not, that you be not judged" (Matthew 7,1) in his memorable address (see Fields 1996, 137-142, Mieder 2005, 154-156).

In any case, there is no doubt that Obama is well versed in religious rhetoric, and while he is aware from his own background that "we are no longer just a Christian nation; we are also a Jewish nation, a Muslim nation, a Buddhist nation, a Hindu nation, and a nation of nonbelievers" (218), he understandably relies primarily on words and passages from the New Testament, notably from "the Sermon on the Mount – a passage so radical that it's doubtful that our Defense Department would survive its application" (218). What incredible irony here, but again, is this mere mentioning of the "Sermon on the Mount" (Matthew, chapters 5-7) enough information to understand what Obama is striving at? Simple allusions are not always effective, and Obama must be careful that he will not be one of those politicians, who, in his own chastising words, "sprinkles in a few biblical citations to spice up a thoroughly dry policy speech" (216). For a lesson of how to be even more engaging with his biblical rhetoric, he might well look especially at his three heroes Frederick Douglass, Abraham Lincoln, and Martin Luther King, who, as "the majority of great reformers in American history – not only were motivated by faith but repeatedly used religious language to argue their causes" (218).

And then follows a barely four-line paragraph towards the end of this chapter on faith that is a personal testimony but also a summary of the entire book, and whose central message serves as the title of my discussion. Having in his usual fair way looked at various issues of faith, including some of his own doubts and his unwillingness to interpret the Bible literally, he states:

> This is not to say that I'm unanchored in my faith. There are some things that I'm absolutely sure about – the Golden Rule, the need to battle cruelty in all its forms, the value of love and charity, humility and grace. (224)

This reminds me of my study on "'Do Unto Others as You Would Have Them Do Unto You': Frederick Douglass's Proverbial Struggle for Civil Rights" (Mieder 2005, 118-146), and a comforting realization how deeply Barack Obama is grounded in the religious, secular, and yes, proverbial wisdom of Douglass, Lincoln, and King, the remarkable triad of truly great Americans.

RACE

These civil rights champions and many others like Rosa Parks, Jesse Jackson, and John Lewis (see 226) have had great influence on Obama's thoughts on race which are, of course, also based on his personal experiences. His own summary says it all:

> When I meet people for the first time, they sometimes quote back to me a line in my speech at the 2004 Democratic National Convention that seemed to strike a chord: "There is not a black America and white America and Latino America and Asian America – there's the United States of America." For them, it seems to capture

a vision of America finally freed from the past of Jim Crow and slavery, Japanese internment camps and Mexican braceros, workplace tensions and cultural conflict – an America that fulfils Dr. King's promise that we be judged not by the color of our skin but by the content of our character. (231)

Yet with all the progress that has been made over the years, Obama is quick to point out that this does not mean "that we have arrived at a 'postracial politics' or that we already live in a color-blind society" (232). In fact, "to suggest that our racial attitudes play no part in these [socioeconomic] disparities is to turn a blind eye to both our history and our experience – and to relieve ourselves of the responsibility to make things right" (233). These two expressive "blind" metaphors are followed up with a forcefully stated proverb that acts as a rallying slogan to keep going with the struggle against racially based inequality: "As much as I insist that things have gotten better, I am mindful of this truth as well: Better isn't good enough" (233). There are still plenty proverbial "hard-nosed" (235) people and "roadblocks" (241) left that keep the steady "pattern of a rising tide lifting minority boats" (246) from moving ahead more swiftly. But Obama warns against concentrating solely on proposals that would benefit only minorities while alienating the white majority. Instead, he stresses the search for "universal appeals around strategies that help all Americans, along with measures that ensure our laws apply equally to everyone and hence uphold broadly held American ideals" (248). In other Obama words, here somewhat surprisingly not used, we are all in this struggle together! This paradigm change is, to be sure, not an easy matter, as Obama explains with a series of proverbial metaphors that add much emotional expressiveness to his comments. He even begins with a very basic proverb underlining the fact that there is much social and political inertia still to overcome on the road to greater equality:

> Such a shift in emphasis is not easy: Old habits die hard, and there is always fear on the part of many minorities that unless racial discrimination, past and present, stays on the front burner, white America will be left off the hook and hard-fought gains may be reversed. I understand these fears – nowhere is it ordained that history moves in a straight line, and during difficult economic times it is possible that the imperatives of racial equality get shunted aside. (248)

Being the eternal optimist filled with unwavering hope, Obama pushes these understandable reservations and doubts aside, arguing that we should be cognizant of the achievements that at least have been made thus far:

> What's remarkable is not the number of minorities who have failed to climb into the middle class but the number who succeeded against the odds; not the anger and bitterness that parents of color have transmitted to their children but the degree to

> which such emotions have ebbed. That knowledge gives us something to build on.
> It tells us that progress can be made. (249)

About two years after this statement, on March 18, 2008, Obama presented his incredible speech on race in Philadelphia (see Garry Wills 2008), basing his title "A More Perfect Union" on the short preamble to the Constitution of the United States: "We, the People of the United States, in order to form a more perfect union, establish justice, insure domestic tranquility, provide for the common defence, promote the general welfare, and secure the blessings of liberty to ourselves and our posterity, do ordain and establish this Constitution for the United States of America." This time, following the upheaval and ramifications of Reverend Jeremiah Wright's racially charged and ill-conceived comments, Obama added much emotional rhetorical power to his argumentation. I would think that his biblically informed proclamation based on the proverb of the golden rule and the slightly changed but wonderfully expanded proverbial interrogative "Am I my brother's keeper" (Genesis 4,9) in the form of a moral imperative explicitly including women will go down in the annals of famous quotations:

> In the end, then, what is called for is nothing less, than what all the world's great religions demand – that we do unto others as we would have them do unto us. Let us be our brother's keeper, Scripture tells us. Let us be our sister's keeper. Let us find that common stake we all have in one another, and let our politics reflect that spirit as well. (107)

I wish that Obama had included this fundamental wisdom in *The Audacity of Hope*, but clearly there is a difference in confronting racial issues intellectually in a book and reacting to it in the heat of political debate with the whole nation listening to every word that comes from a candidate campaigning for the presidency of the United States. For the record it should also be noted that the "brother's/sister's keeper" dyad already appeared in several speeches in 2008 before and after this major address, but without the "golden rule" proverb (see January 20, March 4, April 4, July 8, August 28, 2008). In fact, it had its debut in the 2004 Democratic Convention speech of July 27, 2004: "Alongside our famous individualism, there's another ingredient in the American saga. [...] A belief that we are connected as one people. [...] It's that fundamental belief – I am my brother's keeper, I am my sister's keeper – that makes this country work. It's what allows us to pursue our individual dreams, yet still come together as a single American family. 'E pluribus unum.' Out of many, one" (2; see Aron 2008, 23-25). To be sure, it is at such moments that proverbs, if chosen well and perhaps even modified to be more inclusive, can make a great difference. This also means that each "generation will surely be tested" (269), and as Obama says at the end of this chapter on race, "we are all tested by those voices that would divide us and have us turn on each other" (269). This being said, Barack Obama writes his last sentence on this subject by talking about all Americans, including his two daughters: "America is big enough to accommodate all their dreams" (269).

THE WORLD BEYOND OUR BORDERS

Barack Obama most certainly would agree that this chapter is but a quick overview or lesson on international diplomacy and world affairs as they relate to the American dream. As in previous chapters, Obama employs highly colloquial idioms to pepper up his prose, as for example, "to my heart's content" (274), "the bottom fell out" (277), "the Senate became a hotbed of isolationism" (283), "I had to give the old man [Reagan] his due" (289), "I didn't consider the case against war to be cut-and-dried" (294), "he [Ahmed Chalabi] appeared to have landed on his feet" (299), "Americans have concluded that the United States should mind its own business internationally" (303), "to throw their weight around" (306), "people had shifted their main attention to turning a quick buck" (313), "we want to win the hearts and minds of people" (317), and "whether we just ride the cycles of boom and bust" (322).

But there are also once again several statements in the form of quotations, proverbs, and proverbial expressions that contain actual messages rather than being used as run-of-the-mill phraseologisms. Speaking of Woodrow Wilson's reinterpretation of America's manifest destiny, Obama refers to the president's famous remark that "The world must be made safe for democracy" from his address to the Joint Session of Congress asking for a declaration of war on April 2, 1917: "Making 'the world safe for democracy' didn't just involve winning a war, he argued; it was in America's interest to encourage the self-determination of all peoples and provide the world a legal framework that could help avoid future conflicts. As part of the Treaty of Versailles, which detailed the terms of German surrender, Wilson proposed a League of Nations to mediate conflicts between nations, along with an international court and a set of international laws that would bind not just the weak but also the strong" (283).

Turning to more modern times, Obama writes: "Then came September 11 – and Americans felt their world turned upside down" (290). The consequence was America's misguided war against Iraq, with Obama making the following comments regarding his visit with the American troops and the hope that, proverbially speaking, "at the end of the day our actions would result in a better life for a nation of people we barely knew" (297): "And yet, three conversations during the course of my visit would remind me of just how quixotic our efforts in Iraq still seemed – how, with all the American blood, treasure, and the best of intentions, the house we were building might be resting on quicksand" (297-298). Yet true to his controlled and diplomatic approach to serious issues of world politics, Obama is quick to state proverbially and thus convincingly: "I don't presume to have this grand strategy [for a revised foreign policy framework] in my hip pocket. But I know what I believe" (303). After outlining some of his foreign policy beliefs, he talks of the proverbial "rules of the road" that are part of international cooperation, and this phraseologism has become a major linguistic leitmotif in numerous speeches (see index) as well:

> The growing threat, then, comes primarily from those parts of the world on the margins of the global economy where the international "rules of the road" have not taken hold – the realm of weak or failing states, arbitrary rule, corruption, and chronic violence; lands in which an overwhelming majority of the population is poor, uneducated, and cut off from the global information grid; places where the rulers fear globalization will loosen their hold on power, undermine traditional cultures, or displace indigenous institutions. (305)

Later on he returns to the necessity of following some basic political concepts that he refers to proverbially as the "rules of the road" of international relations:

> Why conduct ourselves in this way? Because nobody benefits more than we do from the observance of international "rules of the road." We can't win converts to those rules if we act as if they apply to everyone but us. When the world's sole superpower willingly restrains its power and abides by internationally agreed-upon standards of conduct, it sends a message that these are rules worth following, and robs terrorists and dictators of the argument that these rules are simply tools of American imperialism." (309)

And then he couches his advice of careful adherence to international diplomatic rules of the road in a well-formulated statement that is based on the wisdom of a straightforwardly expressed proverb: "The painstaking process of building coalitions forces us to listen to other points of view and therefore look before we leap" (310).

Turning to the international financial system, Obama is also quite critical, using proverbial language to underscore his points: "The IMF and World Bank need to recognize that there is no single, cookie-cutter formula for each and every country's development" (318). And yet, as Obama continues, "There is nothing wrong, of course, with a policy of 'tough love' when it comes to providing development assistance to poor countries" (318). But in any case, as Obama continues his proverbial argumentation, we should not be "making political hay over problems at the UN" (320), but instead we should be concentrating on honest assistance, since the world "depends just as much on the work we do in those quiet places [like

Indonesia after the tsunami of 2004] that require a helping hand. [...] I am not naive enough to believe that one episode in the wake of a catastrophe can erase decades of mistrust. But it's a start" (322-323). Being there for each other, and lending a proverbial hand when necessary, is Barack Obama's simple message for international cooperation. He might well have verbalized this concept by the Bible proverb "Love thy neighbor as thyself" (Matthew 19,19) at this point of *The Audacity of Hope* – a proverb that he did, after all, use around the time of the publication of this book in his three speeches of May 11, June 14, and August 7, 2006.

FAMILY

In this quite personal chapter, Obama has the opportunity to give considerable credit to his beloved wife Michelle and also comment upon how important his family life with her and their two lovely daughters Malia (born on the fourth of July!) and Sasha is for him. These reflections and descriptions perhaps do not lend themselves particularly well to proverbial language. There are but a few references, including, for example, the fact that already early in their relationship his future wife was definitely a very engaged and determined woman with plenty of charm: "Oh, Michelle was full of plans that day, on the fast track, with no time, she told me, for distractions – especially men. But she knew how to laugh, brightly and easily, and I noticed she didn't seem in too much of a hurry to get back to the office" (329).

The description of their marriage and family leads Obama quite naturally to some reflections concerning the American family, pointing out proverbially that "by the age of forty-five, 89 percent of women and 83 percent of men will have tied the knot at least once" (332). And yet, Obama observes that the nuclear family is ever more on the verge of collapse, with "the effect of these changes being a mixed bag" (333). With the family structure diminishing, there is a definite increase in unwed mothers bearing children: "Teens still account for almost a quarter of out-of-wedlock births, and teen mothers are more likely to have additional out-of-wedlock births as they get older. Community-based programs that have a proven track record in preventing unwanted pregnancies – both by encouraging abstinence and by promoting the proper use of contraception – deserve broad support" (334). Obama is well aware of the fact that some see in all of this a sinister proof that "civilization itself rests on shifting sands" (335), but being the unrelenting optimist, he feels that advice and help of various groups and programs without government enforcing a rigid concept of sexual morality will be the best way of addressing this situation.

Being a family man, he is also aware of the difficulties of the so-called juggler family (336) in which mother and father both work as they struggle to maintain a meaningful relationship, raise children, and pay the bills: "Keeping all these balls in the air takes its toll on family life" (336), especially regarding the "matter of making ends meet" (337). Doubtlessly these last proverbially expressed comments strike a nerve among the readers of Obama's account. They are clear indications that he understands the joys and worries of American family life and that he himself is blessed with a family that is ready "to make its mark on the world" (341), as Obama phrases it proverbially.

EPILOGUE

It is good that Barack Obama added this short epilogue, since it includes a number of statements, couched once again in proverbial language, that say a great deal about him as a political fighter and survivor. Reflecting on his defeat in the Democratic primary for the Illinois First Congressional District seat in 2000, he quotes a most fitting metaphorical proverb to overcome his disappointment and to muster up the courage to attend the Democratic National Convention of that year at Los Angeles just the same: "The best thing to do after getting thrown off a horse is to get back on right away" (355). Thank God that he did!

Four years later, in 2004, he was asked as a very junior politician to speak at the 2004 Democratic Convention at Boston that was to elevate him to national prominence. As he prepared his unforgettable speech, he "thought about the voices of all the people" (356) he had met during his small political campaign for state office, somewhat like the Illinois poet Carl Sandburg expressed them in his epic poem *The People, Yes* (1931) and in his earlier poem "Good Morning, America" (1928) that includes the lines: "A code arrives; language; lingo; slang; / behold the proverbs of a people, a nation" (Sandburg 1970, 328-330; see also Bryan and Mieder 2003, Mieder 1971, 1973, and 1989, 184-187). Of course, these voices of the people also bring to mind the classical Latin proverb "Vox populi, vox dei" or its English translation "The voice of the people is the voice of God" with its basic democratic meaning that people's opinions expressed in words should count (see Gallacher 1945, Boas 1969, 3-38). Barack Obama might well have used this internationally disseminated proverb here or elsewhere in his sociopolitical rhetoric as he reflects on the trials and tribulations of citizens of all walks of life throughout the country. Be that as it may, he follows his thoughts about the voices of the people with a deeply moving comment that describes his hopeful fight for a better body politics of the land:

> It wasn't just the struggle of these men and women that had moved me. Rather, it was their determination, their self-reliance, a relentless optimism in the face of hardship.

It brought to mind a phrase that my pastor, Rev. Jeremiah A. Wright Jr., had once used in a sermon.

The audacity of hope.

That was the best of the American spirit, I thought – having the audacity to believe despite all the evidence to the contrary that we could restore a sense of community to a nation torn by conflict; the gall to believe that despite personal setbacks, the loss of a job or an illness in the family or a childhood mired in poverty, we had some control – and therefore responsibility – over our own fate.

It was that audacity, I thought, that joined us as one people. It was that pervasive spirit of hope that tied my own family's story to the larger American story, and my own story to those of the voters I sought to represent. (356-357)

Such thoughts concerning humankind inform all of Obama's speeches and writings, and while the common woman and man inspire him in his rhetoric, he clearly draws on the wisdom of some of the great American leaders, mentioning especially Abraham Lincoln and Dr. Martin Luther King once again at the end of *The Audacity of Hope*. In addition, he also alludes one more time to the preamble of the Constitution that urges the American people "to form a more perfect union":

I think about America and those who built it. This nation's founders, who somehow rose above petty ambitions and narrow calculations to imagine a nation unfurling across a continent. And those like Lincoln and King, who ultimately laid down their lives in the service of perfecting an imperfect union. And all the faceless, nameless men and women, slaves and soldiers and tailors and butchers, constructing lives for themselves and their children and grandchildren, brick by brick, rail by rail, calloused hand by calloused hand, to fill in the landscape of our collective dreams. (361-363)

There are no proverbs or proverbial phrases here at the end of Obama's emotionally expressed thoughts. That would perhaps have been too didactic or clichéd. But this folk speech nevertheless serves Obama well throughout the pages of *The Audacity of Hope* whose message is effectively expressed through proverbial language that everyone can understand, relate to, identify with, and descant upon.

PERSONAL POSTSCRIPT

I would like to close with a personal note. As I finished reading *The Audacity of Hope*, I became aware of the fact that Obama uses such words as "struggle" and "progress" quite frequently as he argues for an engaged involvement of people to move ahead to an improved society. This vocabulary can also be found in *Dreams from My Father* and Obama's many speeches, of course. All of this brought to my mind a proverbial utterance made by Frederick Douglass about one hundred fifty years ago that expresses Obama's philosophy of hope in a nutshell. Thus, when I decided that I would prepare a lecture on his proverbial rhetoric, I thought it was time to inform Barack Obama of this proverb, knowing that he has the highest admiration for Frederick Douglass who, just as Lincoln and King, was a masterful speaker and writer with a solid grounding in proverbial lore. So I wrote the following letter and included it in a package with one of my books on proverbs. Did I expect an answer? Of course not, realizing how busy Obama was during his strenuous campaign for the presidency. Had I hoped to get a response? Yes, but I realized that this was unrealistic. I did get a well-worded letter dated May 12, 2008, that indicated to me that my mail had at least arrived among "thousands of personal messages a week from people like me." And who knows, perhaps Barack Obama might actually have read the letter and will, some day, use the proverb "No struggle, no progress" of our hero Frederick Douglass. I will certainly look out for it as I continue my observation of Barack Obama's struggle towards progress. Going yet one step further with my subjective ruminations, let me also state that perhaps Barack Obama will in due time become an equal of Lincoln, Douglass, and King. His effective and sincere communication by way of proverbial language is certainly part of this equation, for, after all, proverbs matter!

April 17, 2008

Dear Senator Barack Obama,

Realizing that you are indeed extremely busy with your campaign activities, I will keep this letter very short. I simply would like to tell you that I am deeply impressed with your work and worldview, and as a recent naturalized citizen, I am very proud of having you as a candidate for the presidency.

As a paremiologist (someone studying proverbs and other forms of folk speech), I am very fascinated in your oratorical and rhetorical skills. In fact, you are clearly one of the most capable public speakers on the modern political scene, comparing well with your heroes Abraham Lincoln, Frederick Douglass, Martin Luther King, and others.

These great Americans happen to be my personal heroes as well. In fact, in the preface to my book *"No Struggle, No Progress". Frederick Douglass and His Proverbial Rhetoric for Civil Rights* (New York: Peter Lang, 2001), I stated that my admiration of this great man helped me to become an American citizen after having lived in this country since 1960. By the way, Douglass's slogan "If there is no struggle, there is no progress" (August 3, 1857) would serve you well in some of your speeches. I have shortened this statement for my book title to "No struggle, no progress".

By now I have read both of your books (at times with tears in my eyes) and all of your speeches that I have been able to find. As far as I can tell, you have not used

Douglass's slogan yet, although you employ the concepts of struggle and progress quite frequently. In any case, I am presently working on a lecture that I will deliver at the annual meeting of the American Folklore Society in late October 2008, at Louisville, Kentucky. The title is: "'I'm Absolutely Sure About — The Golden Rule': Barack Obama's Proverbial Audacity for Hope." Permit me to include an abstract that I submitted for this lecture a couple of weeks ago.

Today I would like to send you a copy of my book *Proverbs Are the Best Policy: Folk Wisdom and American Politics* (Logan, Utah: Utah State University Press, 2005). It is dedicated to Vermont's congressional delegation of three years ago: Patrick Leahy, Jim Jeffords, and Bernie Sanders. You know them all, and I am sure you will agree that we in Vermont can be proud of these politicians.

I hope that you might enjoy parts of the book, especially the chapters on Abraham Lincoln and Frederick Douglass. But the chapter on "Government of the People, by the People, for the People" should also be of interest. Your dear wife might like the chapter on Abigail Adams, etc. Of course, my sales of about 450 copies can't match your well-deserved success!

Here then is wishing you the very best for your campaign. I hope with all audacity that you will become President of the United States. Lincoln, Douglass, and King would be so very proud of you. The same is true for your parents and your family, especially your wife and your two daughters. Above all, millions of Americans and citizens of the world would have hope again that with your struggle there will be progress towards an America of which we can all be proud again.

Good luck, and all best wishes, Sir!

Prof. Wolfgang Mieder

CHAPTER TWO

"Black AS Pitch" AND "White AS Milk"
Barack Obama's Proverbial Autobiography

When Barack Obama as an unknown author published his now celebrated autobiographical narrative *Dreams from My Father: A Story of Race and Inheritance* with Times Books in 1995, it did not, quite expectedly, have a major impact on the rich book market of all types of biographies. That changed dramatically, however, when this unique book was reissued by Crown Publishers as a hardback edition and as a paperback with Three Rivers Press following Obama's stirring speech on July 27, 2004, at the Democratic National Convention at Boston. With his fledgling political career having gained national exposure, there was an immediate surge of interest in this young state senator from Illinois. His book became a best seller almost ten years after its original publication, helping its author to gain such prominence that he won the election for the office of U.S. senator from Illinois later that year. With his characteristic humility and a healthy sense of humor he observes in the preface to the 2004 edition of his autobiography: "It was a difficult race, in a crowded field of well-funded, skilled, and prominent candidates; without organizational backing or personal wealth, a black man with a funny name, I was considered a long shot" (viii). His candidacy for this high office was indeed a far-fetched attempt against considerable odds as metaphorically expressed by the proverbial phrase "to be a long shot." After the presidential election of November 4, 2008, the "long shot" with the basic meaning of having a "remote chance" turned into a "bull's-eye hit" for Barack Obama, to stick with the vivid imagery of marksmanship.

The reaction by various reviewers has been very positive, amounting to high praise both for the content and the style of the intriguing narrative by a young and inexperienced writer fresh out of Harvard's law school. Regarding the stylistic accomplishments, Paul Watkins wrote in his review entitled "A Promise of Redemption" on August 6, 1995, in *The New York Times*: "The scenes describing Mr. Obama's bewilderment at seeing a land [Kenya] he has known only through stories, and at learning of his father's drinking habits, his arrogance and his decline from successful academic to object of pity, are finely written." Dan Holly mentions in his review of November 2004 that "Obama is a deep thinker, a keen observer, an articulate visionary and a vivid storyteller," and about a year later C.D. Rogers speaks of Obama's ability "to tell a story" in a compelling style:

> Obama creates images, many claim the heart of good writing. [...] He uses colors, numbers, names, and vivid verbs. [...] Obama achieves his clarity through basic writing devices [making use of] the extended metaphor [...]. He chooses varied devices to clarify his complex ideas: parallelism, varied punctuation, physical arrangement of words, and active sentences (all emphatic devices) and flexibility with modes for developing ideas. [...] Obama's first book challenges us to take up the gauntlet for good writing.

Joe Klein in his review in *Time* of October 15, 2006, takes his praise of the book even higher, arguing that it "may be the best-written memoir ever produced by an American politician," and Robert McCrum comments in his piece on "A Candidate's Tale" in the British *The Guardian* of August 26, 2007, that "*Dreams from My Father* is a remarkable story, beautifully told, and inspired by its author's divided family history. [...] Many American reviews [...] single out the exceptional grace of Obama's prose, its honesty and freshness. Consciously or not, Obama placed his book in a literary tradition of political prose that goes back to another master of American language: Abraham Lincoln (Obama is the senator from Illinois, Lincoln's home state)." Oona King, in another English review with the title "Obama: A Man with a Dream" in *The Times* (London) of September 15, 2007, makes similar laudatory comments regarding Obama's stylistic prowess:

> Whatever else people expect from a politician, it's not usually a beautifully written personal memoir steeped in honesty. Barack Obama has produced one, possible because he wrote it when he was 33, long before realising any political ambitions. [...] There is an authenticity to the book that makes you think he might really be driven by the quest for common ground; the desire to diagnose the phenomenon of hate, and to come up with a prescription; the desire to prove that what unites us is greater than what divides us. [...] Obama writes candidly about himself as well as about the race divisions that maim America. He delineates people with a rare skill, using individual shortcomings to describe the hurt and failure of a whole society. And he does it in a

language most politicians cannot speak, talking of moon-washed streets, computers that flash emerald messages around the globe, and the dun-coloured plains of the African savannah that seem supple as a lion's back. [...] Obama's background gives him a heightened ability to understand antagonistic world views. He believes in the power of words. "If I could just find the right words, things would change." A decade later he proved this point at the 2004 Democratic Convention when he was chosen as the keynote speaker. The words he picked made him an overnight celebrity and political sensation. [...] What does this book say about Obama the politician? It is proof positive that he is a "listening" politician; he couldn't otherwise have depicted the myriad lives that come off these pages. It also demonstrates his capacity to provide compelling narrative for the human condition.

Finally, thirteen years after its first publication, Dwight D. Murphey sums up these comments on Obama's writing skills in a lengthy review in *The Journal of Social, Political and Economic Studies* (2008): "Stylistically, the book is beautifully written, and thus evokes the tradition of W.E.B. Du Bois's *The Souls of Black Folks* and Claude Brown's *Manchild in the Promised Land*. The flowing, down-to-earth eloquence makes it a pleasure to read. Obama is a master orator on paper just as he is on the stump. His writing is so polished that this reviewer, who has spent a half century writing and editing, is prompted to wonder how much, if any, contribution Obama's editors made to the work. If it was minimal, Obama's literary skill is astonishing. We know that Ted Sorensen produced much of John F. Kennedy's eloquence for him. We would need more information about the internal processes involved in producing this and Obama's later book [*The Audacity of Hope*] to know the true extent of Obama's own literary mastery." I am not certain why Murphey follows his words of praise up with adding speculative doubt to the authenticity of Obama's style. His agent Jane Dystel and his editor Henry Ferris, whom he thanks openly at the end of the introduction to his book (see xvii), doubtlessly had some input, but I would think that this would have been quite limited. Having read and scrutinized both of Obama's books and most of his speeches since 2002, I personally see no major change in his style and can definitely claim that especially his use of metaphorical formulations in the form of proverbs, proverbial expressions, and proverbial comparisons is absolutely consistent, showing that this special aspect of his style is without any doubt authentic.

Nevertheless, since Obama himself believes strongly in looking at different points of view in everything that he confronts, let me at least quickly mention a couple of lengthy critical reviews of *Dreams from My Father* which Jack Cashill has published with the provocative and accusatory titles "Who Wrote *Dreams From My Father?*" and "Evidence Mounts: Ayers Co-Wrote Obama's *Dreams*" in the *American Thinker* of October 9 and October 17, 2008, respectively. His claim is the following: "Shy of a confession by those involved, I will not be able to prove conclusively that Obama did not write this book. As shall be seen, however, there are only two real possibilities: one is that Obama experienced a near miraculous turnaround in his literary abilities; the second is that he had major editorial help, up to and including a ghostwriter" (2008a). Cashill does conveniently ignore the fact that many renowned writers who had not necessarily shown any great literary promise before have been able to write a narrative masterpiece at their first attempt of the craft. Having decided that Bill Ayers, the well-known former political radical of the Weather Underground and now successful professor in the College of Education at the University of Illinois at Chicago, is in fact this ghostwriter, Cashill amasses textual parallels from the writings of Ayers and Obama to prove his point. Interestingly enough, he includes some metaphorical or at least fixed phrases to show that Ayers, who had helped Obama get appointed chairperson of a multimillion dollar challenge grant in Chicago, helped his friend to write his book. Among many parallel textual examples, he also cites the following two short paragraphs from Ayers' own memoir *Fugitive Days* (2001) and Obama's *Dreams*:

> Ayers uses "ship" as a metaphor with some frequency. Early in the book he tells us that his mother is "the captain of her own ship," not a substantial one either but "a ragged thing with fatal leaks" launched into a "sea of carelessness."
>
> Obama too finds himself "feeling like the first mate on a sinking ship." He also makes a metaphorical reference to "a tranquil sea." More intriguing is Obama's use of the word "ragged" as an adjective as in the highly poetic "ragged air" or "ragged laughter."

For the world of me, as a linguist I just don't see how all of this could possibly help to prove that Bill Ayers acted as a ghostwriter for Obama. Looking just at the two proverbial phrases, it should be noted that Ayers' "To be the captain of one's own ship" is a completely different metaphor than Obama's "to be on a sinking ship." Furthermore, a writer does not need to have any maritime experience whatsoever to use either one of them. They belong to the general set of Anglo-American phrases that are in common use. Cashill ends his questionable and inconclusive literary detective work by admitting that "None of this, of course, proves Ayers' authorship conclusively, but the evidence makes him a much more likely candidate than Obama to have written the best parts of the *Dreams*."

One might have thought that Cashill would drop the ridiculous matter with this, but as already mentioned, he followed up with another essay that supposedly offers more evidence for Ayers having "co-written" Obama's *Dreams*. This time he shows that Ayers already used sea metaphors in his book *To Teach* (1993), claiming once again that Obama's employment of similar (not identical) sea references are indications that Ayers was involved in the writing process. Among additional textual pairs from Ayers' *Fugitive Days* and Obama's *Dreams* one finds the following two statements: "Narrative inquiry can be a useful corrective to all of this" (Ayers) and "Truth is usually the best corrective" (Obama). Interestingly enough, I had marked Obama's statement on my reading of his autobiography as possibly being proverbial. When I did a Google search of it, I found 1,130 hits for the sentence fragment "… is the best corrective" with the ellipsis being completed by such concepts as "comedy," "opportunity," "the free market," "traveling," "a nuclear deterrent," "a trade revival," etc. We are dealing here with somewhat of a proverbial structure that is freely used without belonging to any individual. Besides, might one not ask Jack Cashill whether Ayers perhaps reformulated Obama's statement? After all, his memoir appeared six years after Obama! But now I am almost playing Cashill's game, who, after yet another vain attempt to prove his point is once again left to state: "At the end of the day, the observer is left with only two conclusions: either Barack Obama experienced a quantum surge in his writing skills almost overnight; or someone made a major contribution to the writing of his book" (2008b). Having analyzed Cashill's two essays, I see absolutely no reason to decide that Ayers was Obama's ghostwriter. In fact, now ironically speaking, I wonder if Cashill copied his "at the end of the day" from Obama, who has used this proverbial phrase on numerous occasions in his writings and speeches:

> But the American people sent us here [to Washington] to be their voice. They understand that those voices can at times become loud and argumentative, but they also hope that we can disagree without being disagreeable. And at the end of the day, they expect both parties to work together to get the people's business done. (10; numbers after citations from speeches refer to the list of speeches)
> (April 13, 2005, Washington, D.C.)

> But at the end of the day, we aren't the reason you came out and waited in lines that stretched block after block to make your voice heard. You didn't do that because of me or Senator Clinton or anyone else. You did it because you know in your hearts that at this moment – a moment that will define a generation – we cannot afford to keep doing what we are doing. (119)
> (June 3, 2008, St. Paul, Minnesota)

> We will all need to pull our weight because now more than ever, we are all in this together. What this [financial] crisis has taught us is that at the end of the day, there is no real separation between Main Street and Wall Street. There is only the road we're traveling on as Americans – and we will rise or fall on that journey as one nation; as one people. (168)
> (September 30, 2008, Reno, Nevada)

Of course Cashill didn't copy the proverbial phrase from Obama, since this phrase belongs to the stock of clichés frequently used in the Anglo-American language. In any case, as I will most certainly show for Barack Obama's use of proverbial materials, he is very much his own magisterial stylist. And, in any case, let us give the last word on this to Obama himself, who stated in an interview of March 31, 2006, with the *Chicago Tribune*: "I would feel very uncomfortable putting my name to something that was written by somebody else or co-written or dictated. If my name is on it, it belongs to me" (B,166).

To be fair, at least Jack Cashill has looked in considerable detail at Obama's language and style. The other reviewers cited above for the most part simply speak of Obama's narrative and even his metaphorical style without offering any proof to speak of why his use of individual words and phrases makes his writing so compelling, vivid, and emotionally expressive. It is clearly not enough to call Obama's autobiographical narrative "brilliant" and "beautifully written" without an explanation of why these accolades hold true. From my point of view as a paremiologist (proverb scholar), I think I can offer at least a partial explanation for what makes Obama's *Dreams from My Father* so appealing linguistically. Simply put, it is his obvious predilection for proverbial language amounting to 235 such texts on 447 pages, or to be more precise, with 4 proverbial texts in the "Introduction" (xiii-xvii), 97 proverbial statements in the first part entitled "Origins" (1-129), 86 proverbial utterances in the second part of "Chicago" (131-295), 45 proverbial texts in the third part dealing with "Kenya" (297-430), and 3 proverbial references in the "Epilogue" (431-442). This translates into one idiom, proverbial phrase or proverb for every 1.9 pages of text, a figure that is indeed basically the same as in *The Audacity of Hope* (2006). He is thus very consistent in his employment of proverbial folk speech, and this also holds true for the frequent appearance of proverbial language in his many speeches, interviews, and news conferences from 2002 until the beginning of 2009.

PART ONE (CHAPTERS 1-6): ORIGINS

As Barack Obama embarks on his narrative search regarding his complex identity, he couches his status as a person of mixed race in a twice-used proverbial phrase of wanting to be accepted just as he is:

> We have all seen too much, to take my parents' brief union – a black man and a white woman, an African and an American – at face value. As a result, some people have a hard time taking me at face value. When people who don't know me well, black or white, discover my background (and it is usually a discovery, for I ceased to advertise my mother's race at the age of twelve or thirteen, when I began to suspect that by doing so I was ingratiating myself to whites), I see the split-second adjustments they have to make, the searching of my eyes for some telltale sign. They no longer know who I am. Privately, they guess at my troubled heart, I suppose – the mixed

blood, the divided soul, the ghostly image of the tragic mulatto trapped between two worlds. (xv)

These introductory remarks centered on the proverbial phrase "to take at face value" foreshadow Barack's journey towards inner peace with his individual existence and essence. As his grandfather (Gramps) points out to the young Barack in the first chapter of the book, he might well take a lesson from his African father: "'Now there's something you can learn from your dad [...]. *Confidence*. The secret to a man's success" (8). The proverb "Confidence is the secret of success" certainly has served Obama well over the years, especially as he began to struggle with his parents' ethnic background as he grew up. Of course, as he observes with two apt proverbial comparisons, all this did not bother him during his childhood: "That my father looked nothing like the people around me – that he was black as pitch, my mother white as milk – barely registered in my mind" (10). Instead, he learned much from the wisdom of his beloved grandmother (Toot), who was "wise [... and] suspicious of overwrought sentiments or overblown claims, content with common sense" (21). Toot's insistence on "common sense" has long become a leitmotif in Obama's approach to life and politics, with the term appearing frequently in his speeches. And Gramps has had a similar lasting influence by way of his "confidence in the possibility of remaking the world from whole cloth, that proved to be his most lasting patrimony" (22). As the proverbial phrase "from whole cloth" indicates, the grandfather believed in the steady improvement of human existence, and that is, of course, exactly what Barack Obama is trying to do in his role as a world leader. And yet, Obama is perfectly aware that it was not necessarily easy for his grandparents to deal with their daughter marrying a black man, even though it was surely more accepted in Hawaii than on the U.S. mainland:

> In fact, how and when the marriage occurred remains a bit murky, a bill of particulars that I've never quite had the courage to explore. There's no record of a real wedding, a cake, a ring, a giving away of the bride. No families were in attendance; it's not even clear that people back in Kansas were fully informed. Just a small civil ceremony, a justice of the peace. The whole thing seems so fragile in retrospect, so haphazard. And perhaps that's how my grandparents intended it to be, a trial that would pass, just a matter of time, so long as they maintained a stiff upper lip and didn't do anything drastic. (22)

One can't help but feel that Obama has found the perfect proverbial phrase here to characterize his grandparents keeping "a stiff upper lip" in coping with the situation. Of course, as the rest of the autobiography will show, they certainly accepted their grandson with love and care, who in turn has gone to great lengths to express his appreciation of and love for them.

With his father having left the family to study at Harvard and then return to Africa, Obama's mother married another student of the University of Hawaii, an Indonesian named Lolo Soetoro. This took them to Indonesia for several years, where Obama's half sister Maya was born. While his stepfather had a positive influence on young Barack, giving him proverbial advice as "It was a matter of taking life on its own terms" (39), it was his mother who took over as his sole parent after her divorce from Lolo. She clearly was a strong person who worked and brought up her two children with utmost dedication and sacrifice, as can be seen from Obama's comments:

> Five days a week, she came into my room at four in the morning, force-fed me breakfast, and proceeded to teach me my English lessons for three hours before I left for school and she went to work. I offered stiff resistance to this regimen, but in response to every strategy I concocted, whether unconvincing ("My stomach hurts") or indisputably true (my eyes kept closing every five minutes), she would patiently repeat her most powerful defense:
> "This is no picnic for me either, buster." (47-48)

Obama's vivid style is informed by such proverbial metaphors that add life and authenticity to his account. In fact, one can almost hear his mother say that doing English lessons at ungodly hours in the morning is no picnic for anybody.

But his dear mother also had an incredible influence on her son's value system and worldview. Obama describes all of this in a most telling fashion without any pedantic didacticism. But having read the chapter on "Values" in his *The Audacity of Hope*, it becomes clear who instilled these moral convictions in him. There is no doubt that his insistence on human decency and fairness goes back to the teachings of his mother:

> "If you want to grow into a human being," she would say to me, "you're going to need some values."
> Honesty – Lolo should not have hidden the refrigerator in the storage room when the tax officials came, even if everyone else, including the tax officials, expected such things. Fairness – the parents of wealthier students should not give television sets to the teachers during Ramadan, and their children could take no pride in the highest marks they might have received. Straight talk – if you didn't like the shirt I bought you for your birthday, you should have just said so instead of keeping it wadded up at the bottom of your closet. Independent judgment – just because the other children tease the poor boy about his haircut doesn't mean you have to do it too.
> It was as if, by traveling halfway around the globe, away from the smugness and hypocrisy that familiarity had disclosed, my mother could give voice to the virtues of her midwestern past and offer them up in distilled form. [...] My mother's confidence in needlepoint virtues depended on a faith that I did not possess, a faith that

she would refuse to describe as religious; that, in fact, her experience told her was sacrilegious: a faith that rational, thoughtful people could shape their own destiny. In a land where fatalism remained a necessary tool for enduring hardship, where ultimate truths were kept separate from day-to-day realities, she was a lonely witness for secular humanism, a soldier for New Deal, Peace Corps, position-paper liberalism. (49-50)

Giving voice to ethical wisdom "in distilled form" as it was often represented in "needlepoint" proverbs in wooden frames in American households brings to mind that Barack's mother probably also bombarded him with proverbs that continue to be present in his books and speeches. In fact, it is surprising that Obama does not cite the golden rule in this paragraph on values. After all, he has done so repeatedly in other places, arguing that the proverb "Do unto others as you would have them do unto you" (Matthew 7,12) is the ultimate rule for humanity. The world's religions, not just Christianity, proclaim this wisdom as the foundation of social and ethical life, and it is good to know that Barack Obama believes in this very basic principle which Immanuel Kant called the categorical imperative for human relations (see Griffin 1991, 67-69).

After his mother returned with her two children to Hawaii, Barack became a student at the prestigious Punahou Academy. With sadness he comments proverbially on the change that his dear grandparents had undergone during his years in Indonesia: "It was as if they had bypassed the satisfactions that should come with the middle years, the convergence of maturity with time left, energy with means, a recognition of accomplishment that frees the spirit. At some point in my absence, they had decided to cut their losses and settle for hanging on. They saw no more destinations to hope for" (57-58). Little wonder that Obama now speaks so much of rekindling hope for a more fulfilling existence. When he describes a visit by his charismatic birth father in this third chapter, the vanished spirit seems to return to the family. This obviously left a solid impression on the young student that led him later to idealize his distant father in Africa:

Images, and his effect on other people. For whenever he spoke – his one leg draped over the other, his large hands outstretched to direct or deflect attention, his voice deep and sure, cajoling and laughing – I would see a sudden change take place in the family. Gramps became more vigorous and thoughtful, my mother more bashful; even Toot, smoked out of the foxhole of her bedroom, would start sparring with him about politics or finance, stabbing the air with her blue-veined hands to make a point. It was as if his presence had summoned the spirit of earlier times and allowed each of them to reprise his or her old role; as if Dr. King had never been shot, and the Kennedys continued to beckon the nation, and war and riot and famine were nothing more than temporary setbacks, and there was nothing to fear but fear itself. (67)

How very fitting for Obama to cite Franklin Delano Roosevelt's famous utterance "Let me assert my firm belief that the only thing we have to fear is fear itself" from his first inaugural address of March 4, 1933. As Roosevelt promised the country a New Deal after the devastating depression, he brought much hope to the population with this proclamation that has long become proverbial (see Mieder 2005, 166-167). Clearly Obama sees Roosevelt as one of his political mentors, referring to him quite frequently, even if he does not always mention the former president's name directly. For example, at the end of the primary season, he made the following statement on June 3, 2008, at St. Paul, Minnesota: "So it was [...] the Greatest Generation that conquered fear itself, and liberated a continent from tyranny, and made this country home to untold opportunity and prosperity" (119). And on October 10, 2008, at Chillicothe, Ohio, Obama uttered these words: "We have seen our share of hard times. The American story has never been about things coming easy – it's [sic] been about rising to the moment when the moment is hard; about rejecting panicked division for purposeful unity; about seeing a mountaintop from a deepest valley. That's why we remember that some of the most famous words ever spoken by an American came from a President who took office in a time of turmoil – 'The only thing we have to fear is fear itself'" (176). Much has been said about Obama's connections with Abraham Lincoln, but these quotations and others show that he looks at Roosevelt as yet another spiritual father. He will most likely mention Roosevelt even more as he begins his own presidency and offers Americans something like a New Deal to rebuild our socioeconomic foundation. Little wonder that *Time* of November 24, 2008, had as its cover a picture of Obama in a Roosevelt pose offering "The *New* New Deal" to the American nation (see Beinart 2008).

The fourth chapter describing Obama's experiences at his private school in Hawaii is a linguistic and phraseological masterpiece, indicating that he has command over the entire register of the English language, from slang and lingo of the youth culture to the intellectual vocabulary of a highly educated person (see Major 1994). Of course, it is not just authentic language that Obama is after. He is also dealing in a rather direct way with issues of race as confronted by teenagers involved with interracial dating. Here is a charged conversation between Barack and his African American high school friend Ray:

> "Get your hands out of my fries. You ain't my bitch, nigger ... buy your own damn fries. Now what was I talking about?"
>
> "Just 'cause a girl don't go out with you doesn't make her racist."
>
> "Don't be thick, all right? I'm not just talking about one time. Look, I ask Monica out, she says no. I say okay ... your shit's not so hot anyway." Ray stopped to check my reaction, then smiled. "All right, maybe I don't actually say all that. I just tell

her okay, Monica, you know, we still tight [sic]. Next thing I know, she's hooked up with Steve 'No Neck' Yamaguchi, the two of 'em all holding hands and shit, like a couple of lovebirds. So fine – I figure there's more fish in the sea. I go ask Pamela out. She tells me she ain't going to the dance. I say cool. Get to the dance, guess who's standing there, got her arms around Rick Cook. '*Hi, Ray,*' she says, like she don't know what's going down. Rick Cook! Now you know that guy ain't shit. Sorry-assed motherfucker got nothing on me, right? Nothing." (73)

This type of sexual and proverbial talk is contrasted by Obama's reflection on the inner turmoil that he was experiencing during this time: "I was engaged in a fitful interior struggle. I was trying to raise myself to be a black man in America, and beyond the given of my appearance, no one around me seemed to know exactly what that meant" (76). His supportive mother was pursuing a master's degree in anthropology at that time, and the far-between letters from his distant father also did not provide much help: "From time to time he would include advice, usually in the form of aphorisms I didn't quite understand ('Like water finding its level, you will arrive at a career that suits you')" (76).

So Barack and his friend Ray are left to their own devices, trying to figure out the difference between white and black folks. They are aware that things are not quite as racist in multiethnic Hawaii as in New York or Los Angeles: "We were in goddamned Hawaii. We said what we pleased, ate where we pleased; we sat at the front of the proverbial bus. None of our white friends, guys like Jeff or Scott from the basketball team, treated us any differently than they treated each other. They loved us, and we loved them back. Shit, seemed like half of 'em wanted to be black themselves – or at least Doctor J." (82). For the record, this is the only time that Obama uses the adjective "proverbial" in his writings and speeches. In fact, the noun "proverb" never appears, with Obama preferring such terms as aphorism, saying, truth, etc. In any case, he offers the following reflection on his quest for identity:

Perhaps if we had been living in New York or L.A., I would have been quicker to pick up the rules of the high-stake game we were playing. As it was, I learned to slip back and forth between my black and white worlds, understanding that each possessed its own language and customs and structures of meaning, convinced that with a bit of translation on my part the two worlds would eventually cohere. Still, the feeling that something wasn't quite right stayed with me, a warning that sounded whenever a white girl mentioned in the middle of conversation how much she liked Stevie Wonder; or when a woman in the supermarket asked me if I played basketball; or when the school principal told me I was cool. I did like Stevie Wonder, I did love basketball, and I tried my best to be cool at all times. So why did such comments always set me on edge? There was a trick there somewhere, although what the trick was, who was doing the tricking, and who was being tricked, eluded my conscious grasp. (82)

It is fascinating to read how young Barack was trying to understand the proverbial "rules of the game," while constantly being "on edge," as he is quick to point out with yet another proverbial and emotive phrase. The author certainly succeeds in bringing his inner frustrations across that tormented him in his search for belonging. And I would argue that his use of the proverbial expression "to pay the price for something" is perfect to give voice to this struggle for identity: "Without knowing that there might be a price to pay. But was that right? Was there still a price to pay?" (81).

By now this phrase has become a constant leitmotif in Barack Obama's communications. He is always wondering whether there is a price to be paid, and he is more often than not speaking of a monetary price. Here are but a few examples from many such comments employing the expressive metaphor:

> I ask my colleagues to join me in supporting this amendment [Obama's Amendment to Provide Meals and Phone Service to Wounded Veterans]. These are our kids out there, and they're risking their lives for us. When they come home with injuries, the government that asked these kids to serve should provide them with the best possible care and support. This is a small price to pay for those who have sacrificed so much for their country. (11)
> (April 14, 2005, Washington, D.C.)

> And today, I want to talk about another cost of this war [in Iraq] – the toll it has taken on our economy. Because at a time when we're on the brink of recession – when neighborhoods have For Sale signs outside every home, and working families are struggling to keep up with rising costs – ordinary Americans are paying a price for this war. (108)
> (March 20, 2008, Charleston, West Virginia)

> What Washington has done is what Washington always does – it's [sic] peddled false promises, irresponsible policy, and cheap gimmicks that might get politicians through the next election, but won't lead America toward the next generation of renewable energy. And now we're paying the price. Now we've fallen behind the rest of the world. (127)
> (June 24, 2008, Las Vegas, Nevada)

> When special interests put their thumb on the scale [also a proverbial phrase!], and distort the free market, the people who compete by the rules come in last. And when our government fails to meet its obligation – to provide sensible oversight and stand on the side of working people and invest in their future – America pays a heavy price. (148)
> (August 2, 2008, Titusville, Florida)

Such examples indicate a definite consistency in Obama's style, with many other such proverbial leitmotifs to prove the point that he is a skillful writer of prose that is accessible to millions of people in the Anglo-American world and elsewhere.

The many translations of *Dreams from My Father* in languages on all continents are ample proof that readers appreciate not only what Obama has to say but also how he expresses his thoughts in a richly differentiated style of which proverbial elements are not small part.

In the fifth chapter Obama continues with the analysis of his troubled youthful self, expressing with admirable honesty his rebellion: "Like I was somehow responsible for the fate of the entire black race. As if it was me who had kept her [his friend Regina's] grandma on her knees all her life. To hell with Regina. To hell with her high-horse, holier-than-thou, you-let-me-down look in her eyes. She didn't know me. She didn't understand where I was coming from" (92-93). Here the author strings one proverbial phrase to another in order to vent his emotions. And almost predictably, it was his mother, who would listen to her son's ranting with "her face as grim as a hearse" (95), who helped him to spin out of his obsession of "playing" the angry young man:

> "Don't you think you're being a little casual about your future?" she said.
>
> "What do you mean?"
>
> "You know exactly what I mean. One of your friends was just arrested for drug possession. Your grades are slipping. You haven't even started on your college applications [...]."
>
> "Remember what that's like? Effort? Damn it, Bar, you can't just sit around like some good-time Charlie, waiting for luck to see you through."
>
> "A good-time what?"
>
> "A good-time Charlie. A loafer."
>
> I looked at her sitting there, so earnest, so certain of her son's destiny. The idea that my survival depended on luck remained a heresy to her; she insisted on assigning responsibility somewhere – to herself, to Gramps and Toot, to me. I suddenly felt like puncturing that certainty of hers, letting her know that her experiment with me had failed. Instead of shouting, I laughed. "A good-time Charlie, huh? Well, why not? Maybe that's what I want out of life. I mean, look at Gramps. He didn't even go to college." (95)

What a wonderful exchange! His anthropologically and perhaps even folkloristically inclined mother must have enjoyed catching her smart if not smart-aleck son not knowing what a good-time Charlie is. And, of course, this exchange bore exactly the fruit that the mother intended:

> Still, I'd felt bad after that particular episode; it was the one trick my mother always had up her sleeve, that way she had of making me feel guilty. She made no bones about it, either. "You can't help it," she told me once. "Slipped it into your baby food. Don't worry, though," she added, smiling like the Cheshire cat. "A healthy

> dose of guilt never hurt anybody. It's what civilization was built on, guilt. A highly
> underrated emotion." (96)

What a proverbial paragraph with its two fixed phrases and a well-known proverbial comparison! All of this is filled with simple but effective psychology, and sure enough, Barack's guilty conscience got the better of him; he applied to Occidental College at Los Angeles and started upon his successful academic career.

At college Barack Obama lived the life of a typical student, "trying to get laid" (98), drinking, smoking, trying dope, but also putting his keen mind to use and becoming active politically on campus. At this time a marvelous transformation must have occurred in Barack the college student: "I noticed that people had begun to listen to my opinions. It was a discovery that made me hungry for words. Not words to hide behind but words that could carry a message, support an idea" (105). Clearly this statement represents the birth of a political activist, and I would argue that Obama has never lost his "hunger for words," choosing his words and sentences carefully and deliberately, adding proverbial materials wherever suitable to augment his informed rhetoric with the necessary emotional and metaphorical expressiveness.

The account of his first speech on campus regarding the divestment campaign in Africa is very telling: "If I could just find the right words" (106). And as he does now, he succeeded splendidly then:

> "There's a struggle going on," I said. My voice barely carried beyond the first few
> rows. A few people looked up, and I waited for the crowd to quiet.
>
> "I say, there's a struggle going on."
>
> "It's happening an ocean away. But it's a struggle that touches each and every one of
> us. Whether we know it or not. Whether we want it or not. A struggle that demands
> we choose sides. Not between black and white. Not between rich and poor. No – it's
> a harder choice than that. It's a choice between dignity and servitude. Between fair-
> ness and injustice. Between commitment and indifference. A choice between right
> and wrong ..." (106)

This emphasis on struggle (and later also on progress) permeates all of Obama's written and oral communications, and it reminds me of something that the former slave turned abolitionist Frederick Douglass, someone whom Barack Obama admires deeply, had once said in a speech on August 3, 1857:

> The whole history of the progress of human liberty shows that all concessions yet
> made to her august claims, have been born of earnest struggle. [...] If there is no
> struggle[,] there is no progress. [...] This struggle may be a moral one, or it may be a
> physical one, and it may be both moral and physical, but it must be a struggle. Power

concedes nothing without a demand. It never did and it never will. (Blassingame 1985-1992, III, 2004; see also Mieder 2001, 456-457)

It is interesting to note that Obama later in his life quoted the sententious remark "Power concedes nothing without a demand" (see index), but he never used the statement "If there is no struggle, there is no progress" or the shortened version "No struggle, no progress" that I created for the title of my book on Frederick Douglass. Both "struggle"-statements follow traditional proverb structures, and it remains my hope that Barack Obama will use them in the future.

Be that as it may, Obama realized that words alone will not bring change, or, as he puts it, "Pretty words don't make it so" (108). This too might just become a proverb some day, somewhat reminiscent of the old English saw "Fair words butter no cabbage." But he is also so very much aware that proverbial wisdom alone will not bring change:

> Look at yourself before you pass judgment. Don't make someone else clean up your mess. It's not about you. They were such simple points, homilies I had heard a thousand times before, in all their variations, from TV sitcoms and philosophy books, from my grandparents and from my mother. [...] Except now I was hearing the same thing from black people I respected, people with more excuses for bitterness than I might ever claim for myself. (110)

Such thoughts lead the student Barack to "the determination to resist the easy or the expedient" (111), to accept "responsibilities" (111), to get actively involved and thus to find himself: "My identity might begin with the fact of my race, but it didn't, couldn't, end there. At least that's what I would choose to believe" (111). And he has steadfastly held on to this belief and conviction that he could effectively combine the black and white worlds just as they are one in himself. He continues to have the admirable "willingness to endure. Endure – and make music that wasn't there before" (112) but which will sound the trumpets of social progress.

The following sixth chapter concludes the first section of Obama's autobiography dedicated to his "Origins." He transfers to Columbia University in New York, continuing his quest for the deeper meaning of humanity, including such basic questions as the proverbially phrased "How could we judge other men until we had stood in their shoes?" (117). I would think that the biblical proverb "Judge not, lest ye be judged" (Mathew 7,1) is part of this question and its proverbial phrase "to stand in someone else's shoes." Abraham Lincoln used the proverb in his second inaugural address of March 4, 1865, to warn against too hasty a judgment against the secessionist South (Basler 1953, VIII, 333; see also Mieder 2000, 5-6), and Obama will surely have come across it in his reading of the Bible and Lincoln.

In any case, Obama is very concerned about people being able and willing to put themselves in the position of others, as the following references based on the proverbial expression "to stand in someone else's shoes" bring to light:

> From the earliest days of our founding, they [questions of strategy and tactics, leadership and power] have been asked and then answered by Americans who have stood in your shoes and shared your concerns about the future. (25)
> (July 25, 2005, Chicago, Illinois)

> You know, there's a lot of talk in this country about the federal deficit. But I think we should talk more about our empathy deficit – the ability to put ourselves in someone else's shoes; to see the world through the eyes of those who are different from us – the child who's hungry, the steelworker who's [sic] been laid-off, the family who lost the entire life they built together when the storm came to town. (66)
> (August 11, 2006, New Orleans, Louisiana)

> Like no other illness, AIDS tests our ability to put ourselves in someone else's shoes – to empathize with the plight of our fellow man. (72)
> (December 1, 2006, Lake Forest, California)

> It's not easy to stand in somebody else's shoes. It's not easy to see past our differences. We've all encountered this in our own lives. But what makes it even more difficult is that we have a politics in this country that seeks to drive us apart – that puts up walls between us. (99)
> (January 20, 2008, Atlanta, Georgia)

> The change we seek will not just come from overcoming the ingrained and destructive habits of Washington, it will require overcoming our own fears and our own doubts. It will require each of us to do our part in closing the moral deficit – the empathy deficit – that exists in this nation. It will take standing in one another's shoes and remembering that we are our brother's keeper, we are our sister's keeper. (103)
> (January 29, 2008, El Dorado, Kansas)

This is truly powerful rhetoric, linking the proverbial phrase with the moral value of empathy that is lacking in the modern world, where people do not heed the biblical proverb "Am I my brother's keeper?" (Genesis 4,9) which Obama expands to include women as well. What a difference one senses in these comments from a statement by an acquaintance in New York who reduces the egocentricity of people in the metropolis to a number of aggressive proverbs and phrases: "'Everybody looking out for number one. Survival of the fittest. Tooth and claw. Elbow the other guy out of the way. That, my friend, is New York'" (119). But this most certainly is not Obama's worldview or value system upon his graduation from Columbia University in 1983 with a major in Political Science and a specialization in International Relations. And thus, after a short employment in New York City he decides to get actively involved as a community organizer in the South end of Chicago.

PART TWO (CHAPTERS 7-14): CHICAGO

The second part of the book with its eight chapters has the title "Chicago" and presents a lively picture of Barack Obama's work from 1985 to 1988 for the Developing Communities Project, a church-based organization helping people to cope in some of the poorest areas of Chicago. Having dealt with community work in New York already, Obama was well aware of what awaited him in Chicago. But instead of explaining the challenges in normal prose, he has a fellow Chicago community organizer verbalize them in direct speech peppered with three proverbial phrases:

> "Most of our work is with churches," he [Marty Kaufman] said. "If poor and working-class people want to build real power, they have to have some sort of institutional base. With the unions in the shape they're in, the churches are the only game in town. That's where the people are, and that's where the values are, even if they've been buried under a lot of bullshit. Churches won't work with you, though, just out of the goodness of their hearts. They'll talk a good game – a sermon on Sunday, maybe, or a special offering for the homeless. But if push comes to shove, they won't really move unless you can show them how it'll help them pay their heating bill." (141)

Obama makes solid use of such direct discourse in order to add verbal authenticity to his account, spicing the dialogues up with proverbial metaphors that reflect the impoverished existence in the South end of Chicago. Wilbur (Will) Milton, a member of the Calumet Community Religious Conference, couches the struggle that community organizers like Obama faced in a telling proverbial statement: "It's a long road we're traveling, but tonight showed me what we can do when we put our minds to it. That good feeling you got right now, we got to keep it going until we get this neighborhood back on its feet'" (154). Getting people back on their feet, i.e., becoming independent professionally and financially, is what it is really all about in rebuilding poor neighborhoods. The use of this phrase has certainly stuck with Obama as he has commented on getting Americans moving towards a society that watches out for those less fortunate. He returns to the image of getting back on one's feet again and again, thereby conjuring up a picture of people facing up to realities and mustering the strength to move ahead. A few references from his speeches show this proverbial leitmotif as an effective rhetorical device:

> He [Franklin D. Roosevelt] understood that the freedom to pursue our own individual dreams is made possible by the promise that if fate causes us to stumble or fall, our larger American family will be there to lift us up. That if we're willing to share even a small amount of life's risks and rewards with each other, then we'll have the chance to make the most of our God-given potential. And because Franklin Roosevelt had

> the courage to act on this idea, individual Americans were able to get back on their feet and build a shared prosperity that is still the envy of the world. (14)
> (April 26, 2005, Washington, D.C.)

> We all know what happened to the families on the Gulf Coast due to Hurricane Katrina, and it will be a long time before these families can rebuild their lives. Many of the families in the affected states were evacuated to other areas, and many of them cannot even afford to get back. And the federal response so far has been inadequate to get these families effectively back on their feet. (40)
> (February 1, 2006, Washington, D.C.)

> When I'm President, we'll reform our bankruptcy laws so that we give Americans who find themselves in debt a second chance. We'll make sure that if you can demonstrate that you went bankrupt because of medical expenses, you can relieve that debt and get back on your feet. (122)
> (June 9, 2008, Raleigh, North Carolina)

> I've seen the flood damage here in Iowa and I've visited communities that have been devastated in my home state of Illinois. Now is the time for America to stand by those who have suffered so much, while helping them get back on their feet. (143)
> (July 31, 2008, Cedar Rapids, Iowa)

> For those responsible homeowners in danger of losing their homes, I've proposed a three-month moratorium on foreclosures so that we give people the breathing room they need to get back on their feet. (179)
> (October 15, 2008, Londonderry, New Hampshire)

In addition to such emotive proverbial leitmotifs that permeate Obama's narrative and discourse, he also includes stories that he has heard or experienced himself and remembers. Reflecting in the eighth chapter on people losing their homes, he links them with his own experiences and constructs a telling contrast that is intensified by way of a proverbial comparison describing For Sale signs appearing like dandelions:

> Often, as I listened to these stories [of blacks moving into white neighborhoods], I would find myself reminded of the stories that Gramps and Toot and my mother had told – stories of hardship and migration, the drive for something better. But there was an inescapable difference between what I was now hearing and what I remembered, as if the images of my childhood had been run in reverse. In these new stories, For Sale signs cropped up like dandelions under a summer sun. Stones flew through windows and the strained voices of anxious parents could be heard calling children indoors from innocent games. Entire blocks turned over in less than six months; entire neighborhoods in less than five years. (156)

While recalling stories – a sign of a good listener – Obama delights in supplying them with proverbial comparisons or similes to add imagery and expressiveness to the accounts, reflecting a keen awareness of colloquial folk speech. Here are at least a few examples of this effective stylistic device, with some of them being quite drastic in their intended authenticity:

> "That's why he (Gramps] can come over here and drink my whiskey and fall asleep in that chair you're sitting in right now. Sleep like a baby. See, that's something I can never do in his house." (90)

> His white girlfriend was probably waiting for him up in his room, listening to country music. He was happy as a clam, and I wanted nothing more than for him to go away. (102)

> I sat there, roasting like a pig on a spit, as the pastors went on to discuss a joint Thanksgiving service in the park across the street. (161)

> About halfway through the meeting, Marty arrived. After it was over, he came up and put a hand on my shoulder. "Feels like shit, huh?" It did. He helped me clean up, then took me out for coffee and pointed out some of my mistakes. (162)

> In the parking lot afterward, Marty looked stunned. "They're not interested," he told me, shaking his head. "Like a bunch of lemmings running towards a cliff." I had felt bad for Marty. (169)

> "They [Korean merchants] understand business, what it means to cooperate. They pool their money. Make each other loans. We don't do that, see. The black merchants around here, we're all like crabs in a bucket." (182)

> "When I [Johnnie] was in high school, I got to feeling ashamed of him. My old man, I mean. Working like a dog. Sitting there, getting drunk with his brothers. I swore I'd never end up like that." (260)

> "I don't care how many mouths you have to feed, you cannot treat your own people like dogs. Here ..." Auma snapped open her purse and took out a crumpled hundred-shilling note. "You see!" she shouted. "I can pay for my own damn food." (313)

> "What about Yusuf?" Auma asked. "Couldn't he do more?" Sayid shook his head. "My brother, he talks like a book, but I'm afraid he does not like to lead by example." (381)

> "Look at you now! Well-fed, like a prize bull! You must be enjoying yourself in the States." "It's okay," Roy said. (385)

> Old faces and young faces all glow like jack-o'-lanterns in the shifting lamplight, laughing and shouting, slumped in dark corners or gesticulating wildly for cigarettes or another drink, anger or joy pitching up to a crest, then just as quickly ebbing away [...]. (389)

> "She [Granny] said that often the women needed to be beaten, because otherwise they would not do everything that was required of them. You see how we are? We complain, but still we encourage men to treat us like shit." (405)

As can be seen from these isolated and minimally contextualized similes, Obama describes a tough and difficult world in this book with people struggling to survive in an adverse environment. His use of proverbial expressions also mirrors this troubling situation in colloquial images that add much emotion to the descriptions or conversations:

> Frank's shoulders slumped, and he fell back in his chair with a sigh. "No. I didn't say that. You've got to go [to college]. I'm just telling you to keep your eyes open. Stay awake." (97)

> In fact, that whole first year [in college] seemed like one long lie, me spending all my energy running around in circles, trying to cover my tracks. (102)

> "How old are you anyway?" "Twenty-two." "See there, Don't waste your youth, Mr. Barack. Wake up one morning, an old man like me, and all you gonna be is tired, with nothing to show for it." (136)

> "I told you Chicago's polarized and that politicians use it to their own advantage. That's all [Reverend] Smalls is − a politician who happens to wear a collar. Anyway, it's not the end of the world. You should just be glad you learned your lesson early." Yes, but what lesson? (162)

> "So," I said, taking a seat on the windowsill. "Why all the long faces?" "We're quitting," Angela said. "Who's quitting?" Angela shrugged. "Well ... I am, I guess. I can't speak for everybody else." (170-171)

> I knew I was on precarious ground; I wasn't close enough to any of them to be sure my plan wouldn't backfire. At that particular moment, though, I had no other hand to play. (172)

> "These mixed-up Negroes inside St. Catherine's ain't never gonna do nothing," he [Will] said. "If we wanna get something done, we gonna have to take it to the streets!" He pointed out that many of the people who lived in the immediate vicinity of St. Catherine's were jobless and struggling [...]. (173-174)

> Two weeks of preparation and yet, the night of the meeting, my stomach was tied up in knots. At six forty-five only three people had shown up [...]. (184)

> "Can't think about this thing in isolation ... got to look at the big picture. You don't understand the forces at work out here. Is big, man. All kinds of folks ready to stab you in the back." (195)

> "Listen, Barack, your loyalty is admirable. But right now you need to worry about your own development. Stay here and you're bound to fail. You'll give up organizing before you gave it a real shot." (228)

> The receptionist looked up with an icy stare, but we stood our ground. "Have a seat," she said finally. The parents sat down, and everyone fell into silence. (239)

> Such concessions helped to lift the spirits of some of the parents, and after a few weeks of licking our wounds, we started meeting again [...]. (247)

As far as they were concerned, my color had always been a sufficient criterion for community membership, enough of a cross to bear. Was that all that had brought me to Chicago, I wondered – the desire for such simple acceptance? (278)

"I'll try to help you if I can," he [Reverend Jeremiah Wright] said. "But you should know that having us involved in your effort isn't necessarily a feather in your cap." "Why's that?" Reverend Wright shrugged. "Some of my fellow clergy don't appreciate what we're about. They feel like we're too radical. Others, we ain't radical enough." (283)

"If you have something, then everyone will want a piece of it. So you have to draw the line somewhere. If everyone is family, no one is family. Your father, he never understood this, I think." (337)

"He [Obama's African grandfather] would never allow himself to be beaten by a white man. This is how he lost many jobs. If the white man he worked for was abusive, he would tell the man to go to hell and leave to find other work." (407)

Little wonder then, that he also talks of a "young man who lived in the crumbling apartment a few blocks away and was trying to make ends meet by mixing records at dance parties" (158). The old proverbial phrase of "making ends meet" financially is yet another image on which Obama has continued to rely as he tries to help citizens make it in the harsh reality of the world, to wit, these segments from his speeches:

> The teacher who works another shift at Dunkin Donuts after school just to make ends meet – she needs us to reform our education system so that she gets better pay, and more support, and her students get the resources they need to achieve their dreams. (100)
> (January 26, 2008, Columbia, South Carolina)

> We need to significantly extend unemployment insurance and expand it to include folks who are currently left out. That way, we can help them make ends meet while they're out of work, and make sure they're still spending money so we can keep the wheels of our economy turning. (111)
> (April 10, 2008, Gary, Indiana)

> It's something [juggling jobs and parenting] I hear all the time from working parents, especially working women – many of whom are working more than one job to make ends meet. And then there are the jobs you have once the workday ends: whether it's cleaning the house or paying the bills or buying the groceries, helping with that science project or enforcing those bedtimes. The jobs you don't get paid for, but that hold our families together. Jobs that still, even in the year 2008, far too often fall to women. (134)
> (July 10, 2008, New York, New York)

> With job losses mounting, prices rising, increased turbulence in our financial system, and a growing credit crunch, we need to do more. [...] The main risk we face today is

> doing too little in the face of our growing economic troubles. That's why today, I'm announcing a two-part emergency plan to help struggling families make ends meet and get our economy back on track. (144)
> (August 1, 2008, St. Petersburg, Florida)

"Making ends meet" is the one proverbial phrase that Obama employs convincingly to argue for assistance of different types to people trying their level best to succeed under difficult circumstances. But there is a second expression that is one of his favorites, namely "to get a fair shot", with the meaning of having a chance to succeed. In the ninth chapter Obama talks of his tough job in Chicago, where at times he had to muster all his strength "to face the music" (170) when confronted with inertia or despair in trying to change things around:

> I looked out of the window and saw a group of young boys gathered across the street. They were tossing stones at the boarded-up window of a vacant apartment, their hoods pulled over their heads like miniature monks. One of the boys reached up and started yanking at a loose piece of plywood nailed across the apartment door, then stumbled and fell, causing the others to laugh. A part of me suddenly felt like joining them, tearing apart the whole dying landscape, piece by piece. Instead, I turned back toward Angela [one of his co-workers].
>
> "Let me ask you something," I said, pointing out the window. "What do you suppose is going to happen to those boys out there?"
>
> "Barack ..."
>
> "No, I'm just asking you a question. You say you're tired, the same way most folks out here are tired. So I'm just trying to figure out what's going to happen to those boys. Who's going to make sure they get a fair shot? The alderman? The social workers? The gangs?" (171-172)

Luckily, this conversation led Obama to renewed action rather than mere words, and it is exactly this engaged and proactive approach to life's challenges that makes him so appealing in his words and deeds. Perhaps remembering this paragraph from his *Dreams from My Father*, he said on July 8, 2008, in Washington, D.C.: "It's [the election] about giving all Americans a fair shot at the American dream. That's what most Americans are looking for. It's not a lot. Americans don't need government to solve all their problems, and they don't want it to. They just want to know that if they put in the work that's required, they'll be able to build a better life not just for themselves, but for their children and grandchildren. It's the idea that in this country, the only limit to success is how big you're willing to dream and how hard you're willing to work" (133).

How rough things could get for a community organizer in the South end of Chicago, can be seen in the ninth chapter from the use of such proverbs and proverbial expressions as "Once a thug, always a thug" (181, a variant of "Once a thief, always a thief"), "we shouldn't have to break our backs just to survive" (182), and "punk-ass motherfucker ... try to tell me shit" (186). But it is the tenth chapter where the author once again shows himself as a linguistic and cultural ethnographer (see Major 1970, Smitherman 1977 and 1994), stressing in particular the importance of the stories that people had to tell: "Stories full of terror and wonder, studded with events that still haunted or inspired them. Sacred stories" (190). And as he shared his stories of finding his place with the common people of Chicago, he felt uplifted and part of a larger social network: "Then they'd offer a story to match or confound mine, a knot to bind our experiences together – a lost father, an adolescent brush with crime, a wandering heart, a moment of simple grace. As time passed, I found that these stories, taken together, had helped me bind my world together, that they gave me the sense of place and purpose I'd been looking for" (190). And then he tells the stories of the poor African Americans, dealing not only with racial issues as expressed by whites but also with the fact, as someone states, "'That black people still hate themselves'" (192). But to this Obama offers an insightful response:

> Since my first frightening discovery of bleaching creams in *Life* magazine, I'd become familiar with the lexicon of color consciousness within the black community – good hair, bad hair; thick lips or thin; if you're light, you're all right, if you're black, get back. In college, the politics of black fashion, and the questions of self-esteem that fashion signified, had been a frequent, if delicate, topic of conversation for black students, especially among the women, who would smile bitterly at the sight of the militant brother who always seemed to be dating light-skinned girls – and tongue-lash any black man who was foolish enough to make a remark about black women's hairstyles. (192-193)

Such stereotypical self-characterizations, as expressed in particular in the proverb "If you're light, you're all right, if you're black, get back," are obviously painful for the author to discuss, but the fact that he does mention such matters shows the sincerity of his narrative (see Daniel 1973, Prahlad 1996). This is also evident from such proverbial comments as when he hears a young black mother telling her child that "he wasn't worth shit" (195), when a black man states that "'All kinds of [black] folks [are] ready to stab you in the back'" (195), and when he is told that "all the black people [are] willing to sell their people down the river" (196). Such proverbial utterances draw a very drastic picture of deep-rooted anxieties, and obviously "black folks needed a chance to let off a little steam every once in a while" (203), as Obama puts it proverbially. The conclusion is also couched in proverbial terms: "Desperate times called for desperate measures, and for many blacks, times were chronically desperate" (200).

Not to be discouraged, Obama and his co-organizers kept up "the continuing struggle to align word and action" (204), with Obama reminding himself in moments of faltering of his father's rebuke: "You do not work hard enough, Barry. You must help in your people's struggle. Wake up, black man!" (220). And hard he worked, in fact so much so, that after a year of having arrived in Chicago, Obama is able to write proverbially in chapter twelve that their "labor had finally begun to bear fruit" (226). Another co-organizer had used a proverb in the following statement to keep Obama's spirit up: "'Life is short, Barack. If you're not trying to really change things out here, you might as well forget it'" (229). It is indeed amazing to realize what emotional role such proverbs play in this powerful narrative, with the organizers always trying to see the positive in people. So Obama is absolutely correct when he reaches the conclusion that he "wasn't a fool chasing pipe dreams" (230) with his mission of bringing change to the area and its people. All of this is beautifully summarized by "a poster of a young black boy that read 'God Don't Make No Junk'" (232). I must admit that I did not know this proverb when I marked it as such in the novel. A Google search convinces me that it is in fact a proverb, making me wonder where I have been! It is usually cited as "God does not make junk," but in this particular poster the proverb is given in the African American variant and as such serves as a slogan for positive self-esteem and "a reservoir of hope" (242) that dreams will result in actual social change.

But Barack Obama the intriguing proverbialist has yet another proverb up his sleeve that I was not aware of before. In fact, he begins his thirteenth chapter by citing it twice:

> "I'm telling you, man, the world is a *place*."
> "Say, the world is a place, huh."
> "That's just what I'm saying." (249)

This interchange between his friend Johnnie and Obama is followed by the former giving the account of a recent suicide of a young white girl ("one of these punk rock types, with blue hair and a ring through her nose") who jumped from a high building. Johnnie concludes his account like this:

> Johnnie stamped out his cigarette. "So that's what I'm saying, Barack. Whole panorama of life out there. Crazy shit going on. You got to ask yourself, is this kinda stuff happening elsewhere? Is there any precedent for all this shit? You ever ask yourself that?"
> "The world's a place," I repeated.
> "See there! It's serious, man." (251)

Perhaps this proverb is a modern variant of "The world is a stage" or "The world is what people make it" (see Mieder et al. 1992, 678). In any case, it expresses the idea that "crazy" things go on that are beyond our control and comprehension. But far be it for Obama and his colleagues to despair, because the "most radical of ideas – survival, and freedom, and hope" (272) or those "stubborn ideas – survival, and freedom, and hope" (273), as the author is quick to repeat, will persist and make the struggle for change and progress go on. And so Obama finishes the center part of his book on "Chicago" with a discussion of Reverend Jeremiah Wright's sermon on "The Audacity of Hope" (see 291-295, discussed in my first chapter), remembering also his grandmother Toot "singing in the house, 'There's a bright side somewhere ... don't rest till you find it ...'" (294). This traditional song brings to mind the proverb "Always look on the bright side," and for Obama this is encapsulated in "those stories – of survival, and freedom, and hope" (294) that he continues to tell the people in America and elsewhere as he dares to hope for better times.

PART THREE (CHAPTERS 15-19): KENYA

But life goes on, and by 1988 Barack Obama had decided to apply to Harvard for further study. Before starting Law School, however, he decided to travel to Kenya to trace his African roots and to visit the grave of his father who had died there in an automobile accident in 1982. Appropriately, he calls his account of this journey "Kenya," providing his readers with a fascinating account of his African family and their Luo culture and tradition. Its five chapters are a treasure trove of linguistic, folkloristic, cultural, and social observations while at the same time showing how Barack Obama adds the African component to his already multiethnic identity. After the experience of this trip, he has come to terms with his amazingly diverse background that enables him to deal with people of different ethnicities, faiths, cultures, languages, and traditions. He describes his sojourn in colorful images, paying once again special attention to language, including stories and proverbial matters. In fact, he begins the fifteenth chapter by stating that he set out on his journey hoping "that the truth would somehow set me free" (302). Adding the missing link of his African heritage to his persona is understood as a catharsis, as expressed in the Bible proverb "The truth shall make you free" (John 8,32). This is exactly what happened to Barack Obama, giving him the spiritual, psychological, and intellectual freedom to pursue his legal studies, to return to Chicago, and eventually start his meteor-like political career.

Already at Kenyatta International Airport, Obama had a revealing first experience when an African British Airways employee recognizes his last name being that of his father Dr. Obama. This gave the author the immediate feeling that he had come home to his roots: "I felt the comfort, the firmness of identity that a name might provide. [...] My name belonged and so I belonged" (305). Then his half sister Auma and Auntie Zeituni, their father's sister, appear and when they drop the aunt off at her work, Obama registers his first new proverbial expression, showing his keen interest in traditional folk speech:

> "You [Auma] take good care of Barry now," she [Zeituni] said. "Make sure he doesn't get lost again."
>
> Once we were back on the highway, I asked Auma what Zeituni had meant about my getting lost. Auma shrugged.
>
> "It's a common expression here," she said. "Usually, it means the person hasn't seen you in a while. 'You've been lost,' they'll say. Or 'Don't get lost.' Sometimes it has a more serious meaning. Let's say a son or a husband moves to the city, or to the West, like our Uncle Omar, in Boston. They promise to return after completing school. They say they'll send for the family once they get settled. At first they write once a week. Then it's just once a month. Then they stop writing completely. No one sees them again. They've been lost, you see. Even if people know where they are." (307)

And Obama learns fast! At the end of the chapter he uses the expression regarding his deceased father, whom Auma refers to as the Old Man:

> "Who are your relatives? Who[m] do you know? If you don't know somebody, you can forget it. That's what the Old Man never understood, you see. He came back here thinking that because he was so educated [Ph.D. from Harvard] and spoke his proper English and understood his charts and graphs everyone would somehow put him in charge. He forgot what holds everything together here."
>
> "He was lost," I said quietly. (322)

There are other such linguistic, folkloristic, and cultural comments in this Kenyan account. Obama clearly did his ethnographic homework, including the Luo tribe and its language to which his family belongs. He even registers the proverbial stereotypes that continue to be present among the various tribes of the country:

> The country's forty black tribes [...] were a fact. You didn't notice the tribalism so much among Auma's friends, younger university-educated Kenyans who'd been schooled in the idea of nation and race; tribe was an issue with them only when they were considering a mate, or when they got older and saw it help or hinder careers. But they were the exceptions. Most Kenyans still worked with older maps of identity, more ancient loyalties. Even Jane or Zeituni could say things that surprised me. "The Luo are intelligent but lazy," they would say. Or "The Kikuyu are money-grubbing but industrious." Or "The Kalenjins – well, you can see what's happened to the country since they took over."
>
> Hearing my aunts traffic in such stereotypes, I would try to explain to them the error of their ways. "It's thinking like that that holds us back," I would say. "We're all part of one tribe. The black tribe. The human tribe. Look what tribalism has done to places like Nigeria or Liberia."

And Jane would say, "Ah, those West Africans are all crazy anyway. You know they used to be cannibals, don't you?"

And Zeituni would say, "You sound just like your father, Barry. He also had such ideas about people."

Meaning he, too, was naive; he, too liked to argue with history. Look what happened to him ... (348)

It is interesting to note that Barack Obama already in 1995 is going beyond emphasizing only his black identity by his insistence that black and white and by extension people of all colors and ethnic backgrounds belong to "the human tribe." In any case, life is full of challenges as it is, as the use of a number of proverbs by various characters in the narrative brings to light: "Life's hard enough without all excess baggage" (344), "Sins of the father" (355, an allusion to the Bible proverb "The sins of the fathers are visited on the children" [Exodus, 20,5]), "You can't make money unless you spend money" (360), and "Mind your own business" (365).

In chapter eighteen Obama includes another fine piece of ethnographic and social analysis that is summarized by a fitting African proverb. He is discussing the hardship of life with his uncle Sayid, who is struggling in the belief "that persistence would eventually pay off" (381), even if lawyers dealing with their father's estate stand in the way of honest progress:

"To get a job these days, even as a clerk, requires that you know somebody [...]. Or you must grease the palm of some person very heavily. That's why I would like to start my own business. Something small only. But mine. That was your father's error, I think. For all his brilliance, he never had something of his own. [...] Of course, there's no point wasting time worrying about the mistakes of the past, am I correct? Like this dispute over your father's inheritance. From the beginning, I have told my sisters to forget this thing. We must get on with our lives. They do not listen to me, though. And in the meantime, the money they fight over goes where? To the lawyers. The lawyers are eating very well off this case, I believe. How does the saying go? When two locusts fight, it is always the crow who feasts."

"Is that a Luo expression?" I asked. Sayid's face broke into a bashful smile.

"We have a similar expression in Luo," he said, "but actually I must admit that I read this particular expression in a book by Chinua Achebe. The Nigerian writer. I like his books very much. He speaks the truth about Africa's predicament. The Nigerian, the Kenyan – it is the same. We share more than divides us." (382)

The proverb does not appear in Achebe's novel *Arrow of God* (1964), as claimed on the Internet. The novel does include, however, a proverbial reference that expresses its basic idea: "It looks like the saying of our ancestors that when brothers fight to death a stranger inherits their father's estate" (Achebe 1967 [1964], 275). In fact, the "locust"-proverb seems to be absent from any novels by Achebe, since it is not listed in a collection of his proverbs and in studies dealing with his use of proverbial language (see Lindfors 1970-1971, and the twelve studies listed in Mieder and Bryan 1996, 30). I have also not been able to locate this precise proverb in my numerous African proverb collections. However, there is the Kenyan variant "War among grasshoppers delights the crow" which expresses the same idea in very close language (Mieder 1986, 513; Scheven 1981, 484). But more important than tracing the proverb is the fact that Obama does a superb job in integrating proverbial wisdom into his narrative, where it adds much colloquial and metaphorical authenticity. Obama is certainly interested in picking up the local customs and folklore, as can be seen from a later conversation with his Uncle Sayid who is philosophizing about getting married and what that would mean:

> Sayid caught himself suddenly and smiled. "Of course, I have not even one wife, so I shouldn't carry on so. Where there is no experience, I believe the wise man is silent."
> "Achebe?" I asked.
> Sayid laughed and clutched my hand. "No, Barry. That one was only me." (386)

Sayid definitely has his ways with proverbial formulations. This becomes perfectly clear at the end of this chapter, when he is lecturing his nephew Bernard on proper behavior towards adults:

> "You must respect your elders. They clear the way for you so that your path is easier. But if you see them falling into a pit, then you must learn what?"
> "Step around," Bernard said.
> "You are right. Diverge from that path and make your own." (391)

One can't help but feel that Barack Obama, by telling these proverbial stories, has also stored them away in his own consciousness, drawing on their wisdom as he continues to find his own way and identity. By integrating such basic wisdom into casual dialogues, he avoids being overly didactic, letting the message appear rather naturally without putting on a sermonic voice.

In the nineteenth and last chapter of the book there is one more proverbial exchange of this type. It is a conversation among Granny (Obama's African grandmother), Auma, and Obama about Luo marriage customs that included the bride to be to pretend that she refuses her suitor. The man's friends then capture her, take her to his hut, and then the marriage ceremony would follow. This explanation is followed by a humorous rinterchange in Luo that employs a proverb with a clear sexual implication:

> Auma turned to ask Granny something, and whatever it was that Granny said in response made Auma hit Granny – only half playfully – on the arm.

"I asked her if the man would force the girl to sleep with him the night of the capture," Auma explained, "and she told me that no one knew what went on in a man's hut. But she also asked me how a man would know if he wanted the whole bowl of soup unless he first had a taste." (404-405)

This humorous interchange is followed by a more serious discussion of arranged marriages and the wife-beating that takes place by men who make all the decisions. Especially Auma is incensed about such bad treatment of women, but Granny explains her own experiences of these traditions with the proverbs "If one is a fish, one does not try to fly" and "One only knows what one knows":

"Much of what you say is true, Auma," she [Granny] said in Luo. "Our women have carried a heavy load. If one is a fish, one does not try to fly – one swims with other fish. One only knows what one knows. Perhaps, if I were young today, I would not have accepted these things. Perhaps I would only care about my own feelings, and falling in love. But that's not the world I was raised in. I only know what I have seen. What I have not seen doesn't make my heart heavy."

I [Obama] leaned back on the mat and thought about what Granny had said. There was a certain wisdom there, I supposed; she was speaking of a different time. But I also understood Auma's frustration. (406)

There is indeed proverbial wisdom in these comments by Granny, based on social traditions that are changing. Barack Obama, as is his predictable reaction, is willing to see both sides of the coin, the old and the new, hoping that the conscious struggle with these conflicts will lead to progress. At the end of his compelling narrative, Obama exclaims convincingly that he considers himself to be a partner in this struggle. Sitting at his father's grave weeping, he describes how his trip to Kenya has brought closure to his long search for identity:

When my tears were finally spent, I felt a calmness wash over me. I felt the circle finally close. I realized that who I was, what I cared about, was no longer just a matter of intellect and obligation, no longer a construct of words. I saw that my life in America – the black life, the white life, the sense of abandonment I'd felt as a boy, the frustration and hope I'd witnessed in Chicago – all of it was connected with this small plot of earth an ocean away, connected by more than the accident of my name or the color of my skin. The pain I felt was my father's pain. My questions were my brothers' questions. Their struggle, my birthright. (429-430)

The word "struggle" has long become a leitmotif for Obama, and it should not be surprising that he also speaks of the continuing "struggles" (437) facing the American people in the short "Epilogue" to his autobiography.

Referring to Jefferson, Lincoln, Douglass and others, he then quotes the words from the "Declaration of Independence" that represent the basic goals for humanity: "We hold these truths to be self-evident" (437). He knows, of course, that every American can add by heart: "that all men are created equal; that they are endowed by their Creator with certain inalienable rights; that among these are life, liberty and the pursuit of happiness." And when he adds "I hear the voices of the people" (437), he is looking not so much for what separates them but for "what ties us together" (438). Returning one more time to the proverbial "words put to paper over two hundred years ago" (439) with their claim for human and civil rights, he states with conviction: "Black and white, they make their claim on this community we call America. They choose our better history" (439). And he remembered these thoughts when he gave his memorable keynote address on July 27, 2004, at the Democratic National Convention in Boston:

> I stand here today, grateful for the diversity of my heritage, aware that my parents' dreams live on in my precious daughters. I stand here knowing that my story is part of the larger American story, that I owe a debt to all of those who came before me, and that, in no other country on earth, is my story even possible. Tonight, we gather to affirm the greatness of our nation, not because of the height of our skyscrapers, or the power of our military, or the size of our economy. Our pride is based on a very simple premise, summed up in a declaration made over two hundred years ago, "We hold these truths to be self-evident, that all men are created equal. That they are endowed by their Creator with certain inalienable rights. That among them are life, liberty and the pursuit of happiness." That is the true genius of America, a faith in the simple dreams of the people, the insistence on small miracles. (2)

Barack Obama could not have found a better proverb than "All men are created equal" to bring his personal narrative to a close. By also reaffirming the proverbial triad of "life, liberty and the pursuit of happiness," he makes his own discovered and confirmed identity part of all the people. He most certainly is doing his proverbial best in "reversing the tide" (438) that moves counter to these high principles and values. Writing his autobiography obviously had a cathartic effect on Barack Obama. Looking at his life thus far, he found his identity and can now stand self-assured in front of the American people and the rest of the world as he confronts the challenges of his leadership role. And as he communicates with millions of people, he might be wise to maintain his rhetorical skills that definitely include the measured use of proverbs and proverbial expressions. They have consistently been part of his written and spoken words, and they will doubtlessly serve him well in the future as he listens as president of the United States to the voices of the people and responds to their needs and dreams.

CHAPTER THREE

"I Am My Brother's AND My Sister's Keeper"
The Proverbial Speeches AND Media Events

More than two thousand years ago the Roman statesman Marcus Cato observed that "Speech is a gift of all, but the thought of few," and it certainly behooves modern speakers to reflect upon this ancient proverbial wisdom that continues to have some currency in modern languages (Stevenson 1948, 2183; Mieder 1992, 557). The proverb is an apt reminder of the power of language as a means of communication not just among individuals but also on the world stage of the mass media and especially politics. It is of utmost importance to pay attention to how politicians couch their thoughts and plans in words, and they in turn ought to be conscious of the effects which their words might have on the people whom they serve (see Tulis 1987). The great political communicators clearly have thought deeply about their written and oral choice of language, with Barack Obama proving himself to be among those world leaders who reflect long and hard about the nature and influence of their speech. But in doing so, he is also very much committed not to misuse language as a manipulative tool. After arriving at the nation's capital as the junior Senator of Illinois, he expressed this view in an interview on "Morning Edition" of July 14, 2006: "One of the wonderful things about coming to Washington is realizing that everything you do is perceived as calculation. So I can't really spend a lot of time worrying how my words are interpreted. All I can do is make those words as true as possible" (Rogak 2007, 161). A few months later he made a related statement on "Talk of the Nation" of November 2, 2006: "One of the things that I'm always battling – and I've only been on the national stage for a couple of years now – is that tendency to edit yourself so much that, at a certain point, you stop sounding like a regular person and you start taking on the persona of those bad politicians" (Rogak 2007, 88). Authenticity of speech based on truth and common sense, as he repeatedly mentions in his political oratory, informs his impressive and memorable rhetoric. Of course, his way of dealing with and trying to solve the pressing needs of an American and world crisis is what convinced so many voters to elect him as the 44th president of the United States. But make no mistake, to use one of Obama's favorite phrases, his linguistic prowess had ample to do with it all.

There have been numerous comments on Obama's oratorical style, with David Olive as the editor of some of his speeches speaking of his "soaring rhetoric":

> Obama proved words do matter, as Marc Antony, Churchill, FDR, and Nelson Mandela had done before him. He toppled Hillary Clinton, the heavily financed, nationally known prohibitive favorite for the 2008 Democratic presidential nomination with erudite speeches that somehow touched the everyday American – with hope backed by facts, a futuristic vision of a better America grounded in the nation's earlier triumphs, and a convention-breaking decision to showcase his intellectual gifts rather than hide them for fear of giving offense. "He seems to be actually thinking about what he is saying," one U.S. political strategist said early in 2008. Obama's decision not to dumb down his message for widespread consumption prompted a somewhat amazed British newspaper columnist to write last spring that Obama "treats the American people as adults." (Olive 2008b, 88)

A few months before these introductory remarks to his volume of Obama's speeches, Olive had made a similar comment in the *Toronto Star* of February 9, 2008: "If he becomes the first black head of state of a major industrial nation in November, Obama, 47, will have done it largely on the strength of his oratory. He will be credited with reviving a political skill long moribund in the modern era of drive-by rhetoric" (Olive 2008a). Interestingly, he entitled his complimentary essay as "Does Obama Talk the Talk? Will Senator's Smooth Delivery Spark a Renaissance in Political Oratory? Only if He Takes the White House. Lend Us Your Ears," obviously playing off the African American proverb "If you want to talk the talk, you have to walk the walk" (Doyle 1996, 80; Major 1994, 466). Perhaps Olive knew that Obama had used a similar truncated version of this proverb in his speech at a Labor Day rally on September 3, 2007, at Manchester, New Hampshire, that is not in his book of speeches:

> So let's be clear – there are a lot of people who have been in Washington longer than me; who have better connections and go to the right dinner parties and know how to talk the Washington talk. Well I might not have the experience Washington likes,

but I believe I have the experience America needs right now. Hope and change are not just the rhetoric of a campaign for me. Hope and change have been the causes of my life. Hope and change are the story of our country. And we're here today to continue that story. (88; numbers in parentheses refer to the list of speeches at the end of this book)

And to turn this hope into change means quite naturally "to walk the walk", as the complete proverb has it. But the agenda towards new goals also needs to be verbalized and made palatable for the general population, and it is here where "Obama and the Power of Words" come in, as Stephen F. Hayes expressed it in the title of an essay in *The Wall Street Journal* of February 26, 2008. It is, however, not enough to speak of Obama's rhetorical skills in flowery language without presenting at least some explicit reasons and examples that explain and illustrate Barack Obama's unique ways with words.

One of them is without doubt his magisterial use of formulaic and often metaphorical language in the form of quotations, pseudo-proverbs, folk proverbs, proverbial expressions, and twin formulas. In the 229 speeches, news conferences, radio addresses, and interviews that form the basis of this chapter, Barack Obama has employed 1284 such phraseologisms or about 5.6 phrases per event. While this is not a staggering number, it is a clear indication that Obama uses preformulated sayings deliberately without letting his rhetoric suffer from an overabundance of clichés. In fact, having looked at his books and other writings as well as his oratory, it can be said that his written and oral language use is very consistent regarding the choice of vocabulary and fixed phrases. The important point here is that Obama communicates today very much in the same way as he did when he was a little known politician in Illinois.

It is a known fact that he wrote his essays and two books by himself, and this is also true for his early speeches and his celebrated Democratic National Convention speech of July 27, 2004, at Boston. As time progressed and the all-consuming campaign for the presidency began, Obama had no choice but to solicit help for his numerous addresses. As Richard Wolffe reported in *Newsweek* on January 6, 2008: "Barack Obama is more than a little busy campaigning across Iowa and New Hampshire right now. So it was [Jon] Favreau who led the team that wrote Obama's victory speech in Des Moines last week [on January 3, 2008] – a moment that prompted the TV pundits to drop months of skepticism about Obama's candidacy to make breathless comparisons with the Kennedy era" (Wolffe 2008). By now Jon Favreau, a twenty-seven year old staffer from Obama's senate office and a graduate of Holy Cross College, has gained considerable media attention just as Theodore C. Sorensen or William Gershon, the chief speechwriters for John F. Kennedy and George W. Bush, had before him. He is assisted by Adam Frankel and Ben Rhodes, and doubtlessly this rhetorical team will grow in the future. The question for these aids is simply "What Would Obama Say?", as they work on a rough draft for a speech to be delivered by Obama. This question was the title of an article of January 20, 2008 by Ashley Parker, in *The New York Times* that describes the speechwriter's *modus operandi* as follows: "Mr. Favreau used time to master Mr. Obama's voice. He took down almost everything the senator said and absorbed it. Now, he said, when he sits down to write, he just channels Mr. Obama – his ideas, his sentences, his phrases" (Parker 2008). As it is, Favreau and his helpers become their "master's voice," who, as other presidents before him, is involved in various stages and certainly puts the finishing touches on the final document.

All of this is well explained in Jay Newton-Small's article on "How Obama Writes His Speeches" in *Time* of August 28, 2008, showing clearly that he takes ownership in his oratory:

> Obama takes an unusually hands-on approach to his speech-writing, more so than most politicians. His best writing time comes late at night when he's all alone, scribbling on yellow legal pads. He then logs these thoughts into his laptop, editing as he goes along. This is how he wrote both of his best selling books – *Dreams from My Father* and *The Audacity of Hope* – staying up after Michelle and his two young daughters had long gone to bed, reveling in the late night quiet. For this speech [his acceptance speech at the Democratic National Convention at Denver on August 28, 2008] Obama removed himself from the distractions at home and spent many nights in a room in the Park Hyatt Hotel in Chicago. These late-night sessions produced long, meandering texts that were then circulated to a close group of advisors, including [Obama's top strategist David] Axelrod and Obama's speechwriter Jon Favreau – a 27-year-old wunderkind wordsmith. "When you're working with Senator Obama the main player on a speech is Senator Obama," Axelrod said. "He is the best speechwriter in the group and he knows what he wants to say and he generally says it better than anybody else would." (Newton-Small 2008)

But time is of the essence, and by now Jon Favreau has made himself indispensable, as Jeff Zeleny reported on November 26, 2008, in his article "Obama's Speechwriter Moves to the White House" in "The Caucus Blog" of the *The New York Times*: "In his latest round of White House staff announcements, Mr. Obama said Wednesday that he was naming Jon Favreau as his director of speechwriting. Mr. Favreau, 27, has had a hand in practically every speech that the president-elect has delivered over the last four years, following Mr. Obama from his Senate Office to the presidential campaign. While legend has it that Mr. Obama writes his own speeches longhand on a legal pad, a better historical account will show that he offers input and Mr. Favreau crafts them" (Zeleny 2008). On the same day there appeared an interesting response by a person "Nic" on this blog: "Like most legends, this one about Obama is not entirely untrue either. Obama did write his famous 2004 speech and had a very significant role in his early speeches in the campaign. After Jon [Favreau] started growing accustomed to Obama's style, the candidate started gives [i.e., to give] him more leeway in his writing. Even through the last week [of the campaign], however, Obama edited every last speech, something most other candidates do not do."

All of this frenzy about the authorship of speeches by major political figures is nothing new, especially in light of the fact that "political consciousness is dependent upon language" and that "political language must function to mobilize society and stimulate social action" (Denton and Hahn 1986, 5 and 7). Two revealing summaries of how more recent presidents have dealt with the vexing problem of giving a speech almost every day (!) can be found in Kurt Ritter's and Martin J. Medhurst's edited volume on *Presidential Speechwriting: From the New Deal to the Reagan Revolution and Beyond* (2003) and very recently in Robert Schlesinger's comprehensive study *White House Ghosts: Presidents and Their Speechwriters* (2008). While presidents from George Washington on have received help with their speeches and other types of communication, it was Franklin D. Roosevelt who made a multi-person institution out of the necessity of speechwriting. When all is said and done, the following summary concerning the myths about presidential speeches will also fit Barack Obama's situation:

> While it is true that different presidents have been involved to very different degrees in the speechwriting process, it has seldom been the case that a president simply mouthed the words penned for him by someone else. [...] While presidents seldom do a first draft of their speeches, they are often highly involved in both the subsequent drafting and editing processes. [...] At the presidential level, there is simply no truth to the charge that words are being put into the president's mouth. The presidents are too involved and the staffing process is too rigorous for anything like that to happen. The typical presidential speech – if there is such a thing as a typical speech – is vetted by anywhere from five to twenty people before it is finalized. Given such a process, it is hard for any one individual to dictate what the president will say. (Medhurst 2003, 8-9)

With his inaugural address of January 20, 2009, now behind him, all of this will take effect in earnest for Barack Obama. But since my analysis stops with that date, it can be said that these speeches are as authentic "Obama" as possible with some of them being written completely by him and others drafted by Jon Favreau and his colleagues with considerable editing by Obama. Furthermore, when it comes to his proverbial rhetoric, my analysis of his news conferences, radio addresses, and interviews shows that they parallel the use of such fixed phrases in the speeches and his writings. This is ample proof that Barack Obama's reliance on proverbial metaphors is his personal style that permeates his entire communicative corpus thus far.

QUOTATIONS

This said, it is time to take a look at his use of relatively well-known quotations that stem more from the political than the literary world, unless one were to consider Bible quotations also as literature. It certainly is not surprising that Obama included the following quotation in his speech on "The America We Love" on June 30, 2008, in Independence, Missouri, but in addition to parts of this quotation having long turned proverbial in America, there is the charm of remembering it from his childhood years abroad: "I remember, when living four years in Indonesia as a child, listening to my mother reading me the first lines of the Declaration of Independence – We hold these truths to be self-evident, that all men are created equal. That they are endowed by their Creator with certain inalienable rights, that among these are Life, Liberty and the pursuit of Happiness" (129). Just as he quotes Thomas Jefferson here and elsewhere, he cites a number of other former American presidents, especially Franklin D. Roosevelt and John F. Kennedy, to underscore his economic, social, or political points (see Safire 1978; Frost 1988):

> That's why we remember that some of the most famous words ever spoken by an American came from a President [FDR] who took office in a time of turmoil – "The only thing we have to fear is fear itself." (176)
> (October 10, 2008, Chillicothe, Ohio)
>
> President Kennedy said it best: "Let us never negotiate out of fear, but let us never fear to negotiate." Only by knowing your adversary can you defeat them or drive wedges between them. (85)
> (August 1, 2007, Washington, D.C.)

By his own admission, there is no doubt that Abraham Lincoln is Obama's favorite historical person, whose words and works represent "an extraordinary inspiration" (198) for him. In fact, during his CBS "60 Minutes" interview with Steve Kroft on November 16, 2008, he said, "I've been spending a lot of time reading Lincoln. There's a wisdom there and a humility about his approach to government, even before he was president, that I just find very helpful" (201). His repeated use of the Bible proverb "A house divided against itself cannot stand" (Mark 3:25) in his speeches with reference to its frequent employment by Lincoln (see Mieder 1998) has already been discussed in the first chapter. He used the Bible quotation turned proverb the first time at the opening of the Abraham Lincoln Presidential Library and Museum on April 20, 2005, at Springfield, Illinois: "In the midst of slavery's dark storm and the complexities of governing a house divided, he kept his moral compass pointed firm and true" (12). This mere allusion to the quotation-proverb suffices in this instance to help the listeners recall its actual message. But Obama goes on from here to argue that Lincoln's "moral compass" is exactly what is needed for America to move forward in the present day crisis: "It serves us then to reflect on whether that element of Lincoln's character, and the American character – that aspect which makes tough choices, and speaks the truth when least convenient, and acts while still admitting doubt – remains with us today." Lincoln once said that "character is like a tree and reputation like its shadow. The shadow is what we think of it; the tree is the real thing" (12). Here Obama cites a less known statement by Lincoln, but by doing so he adds considerable authority to his call for an America based on the moral values of the folkloric "Honest Abe."

Obama also quotes Lincoln's friend Frederick Douglass, the former slave turned abolitionist and social reformer, quite often. He used the latter's "Power concedes nothing without a demand. It never did, and it never will" (in a speech on August 3, 1857) with reference to its originator in a speech on August 28, 2006, in Nairobi, Kenya. More than two years later, on October 25, 2008, at Canton, Ohio, he alluded to this significant quotation in the first delivery of his closing argument speech "One Week" (before the election night on November 4), repeating it verbatim during the next four days: "Don't believe for a second this election is over. Don't think for a minute that power concedes. We have to work like our future depends on it in this last week [of the election], because it does" (190-194). Then, two days before the election, on November 2 and 3, he made some minor adjustments, changing his "power concedes" leitmotif to a count-down of sorts:

> Don't believe for a second this election is over. Don't think for a minute that power concedes. We have to work like our future depends on it in these last few days [of the election], because it does. (195)

> Don't believe for a second this election is over. Don't think for a minute that power concedes. We have to work like our future depends on it in the next twenty-four hours [of the election], because it does. (196)

Personally I feel, however, that Obama went a bit far with his truncation of the original quotation. It might have been better to keep "Power concedes nothing without a demand" as it is or changing it somewhat fitting the excitement of the election to something like "Power concedes nothing without a struggle." Frederick Douglass would have liked it, since he formulated the proverbial quotation "If there is no struggle, there is no progress" in the same August speech just mentioned (Mieder 2001, 456-457). And most likely Obama himself would have subscribed to this change, since the word "struggle" and by the way also the word "progress" clearly are his favorite terms. As it stands, "power concedes" appears awkward and devoid of the rhetorical power that Douglass's formulation carries with it.

But speaking of struggling for change, Barack Obama came up with his own "Douglassesque" slogan close to the end of the presidential campaign. On October 20, 2008, at Tampa Bay, Florida, he declared: "We were thrilled yesterday when a great American statesman, General Colin Powell, joined our cause. But we cannot let up. And we won't. Because one thing we know is that change never comes without a fight" (183). He repeated it as part of his stump speech three more times in identical fashion during the next few days, and on October 25, 2008, at Reno, Nevada, he employed it without reference to Powell one more time just over a week before the election: "We're going to have to work, and struggle, and fight for every single one of those 10 days to move our country in a new direction. We cannot let up. And we won't. Because one thing we know is that change never comes without a fight" (189). There is no reason why the phrase "Change never comes without a fight" might not become proverbial, especially as America and the rest of the world is struggling with bringing the global economy back on the right track.

Another major rhetorical model for Barack Obama is without doubt Dr. Martin Luther King, whose oratory in the cause of civil rights is legendary. Obama has the greatest respect and admiration for this outstanding American, dedicating a number of speeches to him in which he describes him as a great moral force. To do so, he relies on a powerful quotation by King, using it in its precise formulation for the first time in a speech on February 21, 2005, at Washington, D.C., at the 65th birthday gala of Representative John Lewis, who marched together with Martin Luther King for civil rights:

> You know, two weeks after Bloody Sunday, when the march finally reached Montgomery, Martin Luther King Jr. spoke to the crowd of thousands and said "The arc of the moral universe is long, but it bends towards justice." He's right, but you know what? It doesn't bend on its own. It bends because we help it bend that way. (3)

The quotation appears in five more speeches in various mutations, the last time being in his emotional victory speech on November 4, 2008, at Chicago: "It's [Obama's election] the answer that led those who have been told for so long by so many to be cynical, and fearful, and doubtful of what can be achieved to put their hands on the arc of history and bend it once more toward hope of a better day" (197). The "bending arc" metaphor might have been a bit difficult to grasp in this mere allusion to King's original thought, but it certainly added a celestial element to the hope for a better world. Such a world would have to continue striving towards racial and economic equality, or as King put it so convincingly: "The inseparable twin of racial justice is economic justice." And Obama did well in his speech of August 2, 2008, at Orlando, Florida, to make use of this utterance as he argued for socioeconomic improvements for minorities: "Because you know that civil rights and equal treatment under the law are necessary, but not sufficient, to seize America's promise – as Dr. King once said, 'the inseparable twin of racial justice is economic justice'" (145).

There are many other memorable quotations that Obama employed in his speeches, as for example the one of Robert Kennedy's insight that Obama put to effective use in his campaign against John McCain in his speech on "The Cost of War" on March 20, 2008, at Charleston, West Virginia: "So we know what this war has cost us – in blood and in treasure. But in the words of Robert Kennedy, 'past error is no excuse for its perpetuation'. And yet, John McCain refuses to learn from the failures of the Bush years" (108). And there is also his use of former Prime Minister Tony Blair's apt summary of what it takes to be successful in a changing world in his speech on "Our Common State in America's Prosperity" delivered on September 17, 2007, at New York City: "Tony Blair once said that 'Talent is the 21st century wealth,' and I believe we all have a stake in nurturing that talent if we hope to prosper in this century. Ensuring our competitive edge also means investing more in the science and technology that has fueled so much of our nation's economic growth" (89). But above all, there is Obama's predilection for Ralph Waldo Emerson's quotation "Hitch your wagon to a star" that has long become a proverb that is normally cited without any reference to its originator (see Mieder 2007, 338). Obama used the proverb in six commencement speeches with only slight changes. In fact, once there are two references that are absolutely identical but separated by one calendar year, something that should not be that surprising. Busy as Obama has been during the past four years, he clearly was forced into recycling parts of (but not entire) speeches:

> You [graduating students] need to take up the challenges that we face as a nation and make them your own. [...] You need to take on the challenge because you have an obligation to yourself. Because our individual salvation depends on collective salvation. Because it's only when you hitch your wagon to something larger than yourself that you will realize your true potential. And if we're willing to share the risks and the rewards this new century offers, it will be a victory for each of you, and for every American. (19)
> (June 4, 2005, Galesburg, Illinois: Knox College)

> You need to take on the challenges that your country is facing because you have an obligation to yourself. Because our individual salvation depends on collective salvation. Because it's only when you hitch your wagon to something larger than yourself that you will realize your true potential. (21, 51)
> (June 10, 2005, Chicago, Illinois: Pritzker School of Medicine; May 20, 2006, Springfield, Illinois: Southern Illinois University of Medicine)

> I hope you choose to broaden, and not to contract, your ambit of concern. [...] It's because you have an obligation to yourself. Because our individual salvation depends on collective salvation. And because it's only when you hitch your wagon to something larger than yourself that you will realize your true potential – and become full-grown. (58)
> (June 16, 2006, Evanston, Illinois: Northwestern University)

> I ask you to take it [the harder path] because you have an obligation to yourself. Because our individual salvation depends on our collective salvation. And because it's only when you hitch your wagon to something larger than yourself that you will realize your true potential. (66)
> (August 11, 2006, New Orleans, Louisiana: Xavier University)

> Because it's only when you hitch your wagon to something larger than yourself that you realize your true potential and discover the role you'll play in writing the next great chapter in America's story. (116)
> (May 25, 2008, Middletown, Connecticut: Wesleyan University)

What is of special interest is that Obama never cites the quotation-proverb in its usual wording. Instead, once having rephrased it as "It's only when you hitch your wagon to something larger than yourself that you realize your true potential," he sticks to it for the next three years, making it his own piece of advice that he wants to give to the graduates. And his wisdom does put another spin on Emerson's admonition. The latter tells people to reach for the stars, somewhat reminiscent of the classical Latin proverb "Per aspera ad astra." But while these imperatives encourage the individual person to go after high goals, Obama explains to young people that they must not only look out for the proverbial "number one" but that they should get involved in social issues that concern everybody.

It is almost surprising that Barack Obama does not add the Bible proverb "Am I my brother's keeper?" (Genesis 4,9) with its appropriate expansion "Am I my sister's keeper?" to this moral statement. After all, he used this egalitarian combination fifteen times starting with his unforgettable speech at the Democratic National Convention on July 27, 2004, at Boston, all the way to his remarks for the Congressional Hispanic Caucus on September 10, 2008, at Washington, D.C. These references, as all other proverbial utterances, are listed in their context in the proverb index of this book, and so I will cite only one specific employment of this new proverbial formula here that Obama cited identically in three speeches:

> We know that we've been called in churches and mosques, synagogues and Sunday schools to love our neighbors as ourselves; to be our brother's keeper; to be our sister's keeper. That we have individual responsibility, but we also have collective responsibility to each other. (50, 57, 65)
> (May 11, 2006, Washington, D.C.; June 14, 2006, Washington, D.C.; August 7, 2006, Chicago, Illinois)

The reasons for singling out this particular text must be obvious. First of all, it illustrates Obama's willingness to recognize various religions while also stressing the fact that they do preach similar ethical values. He even adds the universal proverb "Love thy neighbor as thyself" (Leviticus 19,18; Matthew 22,39) to the "keeper" proverb, thereby adding the love component to the social obligation of caring for each other. And then he moves on to the idea of collective responsibility that is part of his reformulation of the "wagon" proverb as well. Of course, the "golden rule" proverb "Do unto others as you would have them do unto you" (Matthew 7,12) enters into this equation, but Obama's emphasis on its humane message has already been discussed in the first chapter. With his use of Biblical quotations and proverbs Obama is following in the rhetorical footsteps of his three heroes Lincoln, Douglass, and King, but as a secular politician of the modern age, his verbal communication is less invested in religious oratory. Just the same, his proverbial dyad "I am my brother's keeper and my sister's keeper" will certainly be remembered from his compassionate speeches. It overcomes the gender bias of the old wisdom, it adapts its message to the modern age, and it should best be cited the Obama way henceforth.

PSEUDO-PROVERBS

These comments beg the question whether Barack Obama has coined some other memorable phrases that might just have "the stuff" to become proverbial in due time? Everybody remembers John F. Kennedy's famous remark "Ask not what your country can do for you, ask what you can do for your country" from his inaugural address on January 20, 1961. Obama alludes to this quotation with its proverbial ring four times in his speeches, with the statement at the Northwestern University commencement on June 16, 2006, at Evanston, Illinois, being especially noteworthy to get the young graduates to think about America's social history and their role in shaping the future: "The class of 1960 would find themselves at the beginning of a decade where social and racial strife threatened to tear apart the very fabric of the nation. They would hear a young President [Kennedy] urge them to ask what they could do for their country. And they would answer the call to sit at lunch counters and take those Freedom Rides; they would march for justice and live for equality" (58). Perhaps mindful of Kennedy's message, Obama came up with his own rephrasing: "You invest in America, America will invest in you." Between June 16 and October 25, 2008, Obama used this slogan ten times. At its first occurrence during a speech on "Renewing American Competitiveness" on June 16, 2008, at Flint, Michigan, the mentioning of the Peace Corps certainly brings to mind the Kennedy years. And the wording "America invests in you, and you invest in America" mirrors rather closely Kennedy's "Ask not what your country can do for you, ask what you can do for your country" and its basic message:

> I want to give tax breaks to young people, in the form of an annual $4,000 tax credit that will cover two-thirds of the tuition at an average public college, and make community college completely free. In return, I will ask students to serve, whether it's by teaching, joining the Peace Corps, or working in your community. And for those who serve in our military, we'll cover all of your tuition with an even more generous 21st Century GI Bill. The idea is simple – America invests in you, and you invest in America. That's how we're going to ensure that America succeeds in this century. (124)

Three weeks later, in a speech on "An Agenda for Middle-Class Success" of July 7, 2008, at St. Louis, Missouri, Obama reversed the order of the bipartite structure of his "catchy" slogan, putting the stress squarely on the college students to do something for the country:

> To make a college education affordable for every American family, I'll make this promise to every student – your country will offer you $4,000 a year of tuition if you offer your country community or national service when you graduate. If you invest in America, America will invest in you. (132)

It took until October 17, 2008, during a speech on the economy at Roanoke, Virginia, for Obama to return to this proverbial message, dropping the preposition "if" in order to give the statement a more definitive if not imperative nature:

> If you [college students] commit to serving your community or your country, we will make sure you can afford your tuition. No ifs, ands, or buts. You invest in America, America will invest in you, and together, we will move this country forward. (180)

And now Obama was on a roll, citing this precise paragraph in seven more speeches. And it did not hurt to add the well-known triadic formula "No ifs, ands, or buts (the seven later references do not have the comma) to it to underscore that this is not an empty campaign promise as far as Obama is concerned. It would seem to me that this slogan should be continued as the new president strives to help out college students. In turn it will doubtlessly take on a proverbial character and might be remembered as one of Obama's famous phrases.

There are numerous other original statements by Barack Obama that follow the parallel structure, the stylistic characteristics (i.e., alliteration, rhyme, brevity, memorability, etc.), and the often metaphorical nature of folk proverbs (see Mieder 2004, 4-9). Especially in those cases, where Obama used these formulaic statements repeatedly during his campaign, many people heard them and they were also spread by the mass media of newspapers, radio, and television. Sticking with "America" for a moment longer, there is Obama's civil rights message that "In America, separate can never be equal" (15) used the first time at an NAACP event on May 1, 2005, at Detroit, Michigan, with three additional occurrences later. And there is also the more patriotic claim that "America prospers when all Americans prosper" that first appeared in remarks at a meeting of the National Association of Latino Elected and Appointed Officials on June 28, 2008, at Washington, D.C.: "America can only prosper when all Americans prosper – brown, black, white, Asian, and Native American. That's the idea that lies at the heart of my campaign, and that's the idea that will lie at the heart of my presidency. Because we are all Americans" (128). In this case, Obama directs his remarks especially at the search for prosperity among minorities. In later speeches, as the one on "Confronting an Economic Crisis" of September 16, 2008, at Golden, Colorado, Obama applies his formulaic wisdom to the economic well-being of all Americans: "The American economy has worked in large part because we have guided the market's invisible hand with a higher principle – that America prospers when all Americans can prosper. That is why we have put in place rules of the road to make competition fair, and open, and honest" (156).

But speaking of economics, this presidential campaign will certainly be remembered for the talk about the terrible effects the financial collapse has had on the people of "Main Street" and "Wall Street" here in the United States and throughout the world. Little wonder that Obama came up with two slogan-like structures that describe the interrelationship of these two "streets" or spheres. The first could be phrased as a general lemma as "What's good (bad) for Main Street, is good (bad) for Wall Street" with two contextualized examples being:

> When all is said and done, losses will be in the many hundreds of billions. What was bad for Main Street was bad for Wall Street. Pain trickled up. (109)
> (March 27, 2008, New York, New York)

> Even as we are doing whatever's required to stabilize the financial system [...] we [must] also recognize that a strong Main Street will reinforce and help a strong Wall Street, and that we can't separate those two things. (203)
> (November 24, 2008, Chicago, Illinois)

The final wording of this modern wisdom appears not to have been solidified as yet, but due to its parallel structure and the imagery of the two streets it could reach proverbial status some day. In any case, Obama also reversed the two street names and came up with the insight that "We cannot have a thriving Wall Street and a struggling Main Street (while Main Street suffers)." He used this pattern with some variations eight times between July 30 and November 25, 2008, as can be seen from the following two examples:

> In the past few years, we have relearned the essential truth that in the long run, we cannot have a thriving Wall Street and a struggling Main Street. When wages are flat, prices are rising and more and more Americans are mired in debt, the economy as a whole suffers. When a reckless few game the system, as we've seen in this housing crisis, millions suffer and we're all impacted. (142)
> (July 30, 2008, Springfield, Missouri)

> If this financial crisis has taught us anything, it's that we cannot have a thriving Wall Street while Main Street suffers – in this country, we rise and fall as one nation; as one people. And that is how we will meet the challenges of our time – together. (200)
> (November 15, 2008, radio address)

Again, I would argue that this piece of modern wisdom couched in a proverbial structure has a good chance to become a general proverb. There are numerous other such memorable quotations in the speeches that due to their linguistic formulation and metaphorical nature could perhaps be called "pseudo-proverbs." Only time will tell whether they might "catch on" or "click" with the general population. If Obama were to continue using them, their chance of entering quotation dictionaries is very good, and eventually they might find their way into modern proverb dictionaries as well. Of course, in the following representative list of a few additional "pseudo-proverbs" it is not absolutely clear whether Barack Obama, Jon Favreau, or another wordsmith might have penned them. My gut reaction, however, especially in those cases where Obama has used them in press conferences or interviews, is that they stem from him personally. After all, he "invented" some of them in his two books *Dreams from My Father* (1995) and *The Audacity of Hope* (2006) as well, and we know that he wrote those without the help of speechwriters. Here then are a few proverb-like utterances to watch out for to see whether they will last beyond Obama's use:

> "Ballot boxes don't make a democracy."
> We must understand that setting up ballot boxes does not a democracy make – that real freedom and real stability come from doing the hard work of helping to build a strong police force, and a legitimate government, and ensuring that people have food, and water, and electricity, and basic services. (81)
> (March 21, 2007, Washington, D.C.)

> "Countries that out-teach us today will out-compete us tomorrow."
> I don't accept that we can't give every single child in America a world-class education. We know countries that out-teach us today will out-compete us tomorrow. But it's

bigger than that. The America we believe in isn't a country where millions of children are robbed of their opportunity by failing schools. And the answer isn't just a snappy slogan. (88)
(September 3, 2007, Manchester, New Hampshire)

"Opportunity doesn't come easy."
We believe that there is a place in the American economy for every American's dream. And we know when we extend that dream of opportunity to more Americans, all of us gain. Americans know that opportunity doesn't come easy. You have to work for it. (90)
(September 18, 2007, Washington, D.C.)

"One man cannot make a movement."
And I will stand up for you, and fight for you, and wake up every day thinking about how to make your lives better. But the truth is, one man cannot make a movement. (91)
(September 28, 2007, Washington, D.C.)

"The government that people count on most is the one that's closest to the people."
But when a disaster strikes – a Katrina, a shooting, or a six-alarm blaze – it's City Hall we lean on. It's City Hall we call first, and City Hall we depend on to get us through tough times. Because whether it's a small town or a big city, the government that people count on most is the one that's closest to the people. (125)
(June 21, 2008, Miami, Florida)

"A new politics for a new time."
Change comes to Washington. Change happens because the American people demand it – because they rise up and insist on new ideas and new leaders, a new politics for a new time. (152)
(August 28, 2008, Denver, Colorado)

"You can't change direction with a new driver who follows the same old map."
But another thing I know is this – we can't steer ourselves out of this crisis by heading in the same, disastrous direction. We can't change direction with a new driver who wants to follow the same old map. And that's what this election is all about. (158)
(September 18, 2008, Espanola, New Mexico)

By adding such introductory formulas as "Americans know" and "the truth is" to these common sense statements, Obama adds a certain claim of authority to them, implying that they are general truisms. And as already mentioned, they might have a chance to become new proverbs in due time.

TRADITIONAL PROVERBS

Of course, as far as traditional proverbs are concerned, they are by definition authoritative generalizations based on experiences and observations common to existence (see Mieder 2004, 2-9). Some of these proverbs go back to classical antiquity, the Bible, or the Middle Ages, but proverbs have also been coined during later centuries. Above all, proverbs are still created today, and they are most certainly in common use in all modes of human communication, as I have shown in my book *Proverbs Are Never Out of Season: Popular Wisdom in the Modern Age* (1993). Just as all presidents before him, among the more recent ones Franklin D. Roosevelt, Harry S. Truman, and Ronald Reagan in particular (see Mieder 2005), Barack Obama includes proverbs in his various verbal communications without ever using them to that extent that he might sound "folksy." In fact, strange as it might seem, Obama appears not to know the word "proverb," or at least he has never used it in the large corpus of speeches, news conferences, radio addresses, and interviews that served as the basis for this study. When he introduces a proverb in its traditional wording or as an intentionally varied statement with a linguistic marker, he uses words like saying, truth, etc., thereby pointing to the sapiential and at times didactic nature of the traditional phrase. My personal feeling would be that it would do no harm for him to include the word "proverb" in these introductory formulas from time to time, since this would add considerable rhetorical emphasis to the wisdom he wishes to express.

Be that as it may, Obama's oral communications do not contain an overabundance of *bona fide* folk proverbs. Perhaps in keeping with not identifying any of this traditional wisdom with the term "proverb," he often merely alludes to them, leaving it up to his listeners to recall the actual text. Obviously Obama avoids being overly didactic or sermonic by this method of integrating folk wisdom, but since he uses actual proverbs rather sparingly, I don't think that it would do any harm to cite a few more common proverbs in their traditional wording. The following contextualized references will illustrate this point, with the second one about "half a loaf" almost making no sense if people don't recall the entire proverb:

> "Time heals all wounds."
> Well, lessons can be just as easily unlearned as they are learned. Time may heal, but it can also cloud the memory and remove us further from that initial core of concern. And so what this all means is that today and every day, you have a responsibility to remember what happened here in New Orleans. (66)
> (August 11, 2006, New Orleans, Louisiana)

> "Half a loaf (of bread) is better than none."
> If I look at an issue or if I look at how I approach campaigning, if it's something that is consistent with my broader values and is just a matter of tactics – having to take half a loaf – then that's something I'm comfortable with, and that's sort of the nature of the process. If it's something that violates my core beliefs, then it's not worth it. (B,59)
> (November 2, 2006, "Talk of the Nation" interview)

"History repeats itself."
Iran's President Ahmadinejad's regime is a threat to all of us. His words contain a chilling echo of some of the world's most tragic history. Unfortunately, history has a terrible way of repeating itself. (77)
(March 2, 2007, Chicago, Illinois)

"Heaven helps those who help themselves."
We shouldn't help those in need without helping them help themselves. That's why I'll partner with the private sector in creating a new fund for Small and Medium Enterprise, so we're investing in ideas that can create growth and jobs in the developing world. (164)
(September 25, 2008, New York, New York)

An especially telling case in point appears in Barack Obama's tribute to the American cartoonist Herblock (Herbert Block) on April 11, 2005, at Washington, D.C., where he alludes to the modern American proverb "A picture is worth a thousand words" that has gained an international currency in English and in translation since its origin as an advertising slogan in 1921 (see Mieder 1993, 135-151): "People like Herblock and Tony Auth and others jolt us awake from our political cynicism with a few ingenious images and a clever phrase that can often speak more truth than a thousand words. And this is the kind of wake-up call our politics need today more than ever" (8). Obama is right on the mark in stating that cartoons or even better political caricatures can say a great deal by way of a simple illustration. In fact, the mass media has already come up with quite a few striking caricatures of Obama before his inauguration. It will definitely serve Obama well to pay attention to these messages and to appreciate their humorous or satirical intent.

Of course, Barack Obama also employs proverbs without any alterations. This is especially the case with the three-word proverb "Enough is enough" which is nothing more than a non-metaphorical tautology, but which served the presidential candidate extremely well as a leitmotif in thirteen speeches during the campaign. It gave him a precise formulation to say that the failed political and economic policies of the Bush administration should not go on. He began using the short proverb on May 2, 2005, during a floor statement in the U.S. Senate on his "Amendment to Stop No-Bid Contracts for Gulf Coast Recovery and Reconstruction": "So the amendment we're offering today is our effort to say enough is enough. Our amendment requires all federal agencies to follow competitive bidding procedures for any Katrina-related contracts exceeding $500,000" (49). As a more general observation, he employed the following paragraph in four stump speeches during the week of September 24–29, 2008: "At this defining moment, we have the chance to finally stand up and say: enough is enough! We can do this because Americans have done this before. Time and again, we've battled back from adversity by recognizing that common stake that we have in each other's success" (161, 163, 166, 167). And then, on October 23, 2008, he repeated it a final time as a direct slam against John McCain and George Bush in Indianapolis, Indiana, during his remarks on the economy: "We've tried it John McCain's way. We've tried it George Bush's way. And we're here [in Indianapolis] today to say enough is enough. We can't afford four more years of their 'fundamental economics'" (188). The remaining texts (see the index) all show how this seemingly simplistic proverb can be used to express utter frustration with the sociopolitical *status quo*, making it, despite its lack of metaphor, a most effective tool during the presidential campaign.

This is also true for his three-time citation of the American proverb "Government of the people, by the people, and for the people." Even though Abraham Lincoln did not originate this triadic definition of democracy, his use of it in his famous Gettysburg Address of November 19, 1863 ("that this nation, under God, shall have a new birth of freedom – and that government of the people, by the people, for the people, shall not perish from the earth"), has led to the identification of the proverb with him in the American psyche (Mieder 2005, 15-55). Clearly Obama with his love and respect for Lincoln is aware of this, and when he cites the proverb, he knows that he speaks with the trusted voice of Lincoln:

> It's time for us to stand up and tell George Bush that the government in this country is not based on the whims of one person, the government is of the people, by the people and for the people. (92)
> (October 2, 2007, Chicago, Illinois)

> George Washington is rightly revered for his leadership of the Continental Army, but one of his greatest acts of patriotism was his insistence on stepping down after two terms [as president], thereby setting a pattern for those who would follow, reminding future presidents that this is a government of and by and for the people. (129)
> (June 30, 2008, Independence, Missouri)

> It [Obama's campaign] grew strength from the young people who rejected the myth of their generation's apathy; who left their homes and their families for jobs that offered little pay and less sleep; from not-so-young people who braved the bitter cold and scorching heat to knock on the doors of perfect strangers; from the millions of Americans who volunteered, and organized, and proved that more than two centuries later, a government of the people, by the people and for the people has not perished from this Earth. This is our victory. (197)
> (November 4, 2008, Chicago, Illinois)

Not surprisingly for someone so deeply steeped in American history and its presidents, Obama also has committed himself to the proverb that "The buck stops here" which, although once again not having been coined by Harry S. Truman ("and there's a sign on my desk which says, 'The Buck Stops Here'"), certainly has long become associated with his name (Mieder and Bryan 1997, 62-63). And in keeping with Truman's insistence that the ultimate responsibility of the actions of the government rests with the president, Barack Obama has used the well-known proverb to state categorically that he will follow in Truman's footsteps in this regard. He even goes so far as to exchange the final word "here" with the personal pronoun "me," thereby emphasizing his personal accountability:

> We need to ensure that our ability to respond to threats around the world is never compromised. And I will always respect – and not ignore – the advice of military commanders. But I will also make clear that when I am President, the buck will stop in the Oval Office. (87)
> (August 21, 2007, Kansas City, Missouri)

> But understand, I will be setting policy as president. I will be responsible for the vision that this team carries out, and I expect them to implement that vision once decisions are made. So, as Harry Truman said, the buck will stop with me. And nobody who's standing here, I think, would have agreed to join this administration unless they had the confidence that in fact that vision was one that would help secure the American people and our interests. (207)
> (December 1, 2008, Chicago, Illinois: fifth news conference as President-elect)

It should not be a surprise that Obama also likes the related proverbial expression "To pass the buck," as can be seen from at least this one reference during an appearance at the National Press Club on April 26, 2005, at Washington, D.C.: "Taking responsibility for oneself and showing individual initiative are American values we all share. Frankly, they're values we could stand to see more of in a culture where the buck is too often passed to the next guy. They are values we could use more of here in Washington too" (14). The proverb as well as the proverbial expression, while frequently used in American parlance and writing, actually present a considerable semantic problem regarding the noun of the "buck". Some might think of "buck" in terms of money or a male deer, but this would in fact make little sense. As it turns out, "buck" refers to a marker in the game of poker which can be passed on to another player by someone who does not wish to deal the cards. And as can be seen from Obama's use of the proverbial metaphor, it has taken on the meaning of passing on a problem or responsibility. The proverbial phrase has been known since the nineteenth century, with the proverb gaining currency during the first half of the twentieth century.

Many more proverbs could be discussed along these lines, but it is also true that their meaning in Barack Obama's speeches is rather self-evident. Being aware that generally people have no problems in understanding proverbs, Obama usually integrates them without marking them as such. In other words, he incorporates them so naturally into his rhetorical flow that they become his own words of wisdom without coming across like time-worn clichés. A few more examples in the context of the presidential campaign will underscore this stylistic procedure, also illustrating that Obama often adds just a word or two to break up the formulaic nature of proverbs and giving them a less apparent didactic tone. Of course, the message of a deeper insight is carried forth nevertheless:

> "Knowledge is power."
> See, in this new world, knowledge really is power. A new idea can lead not just to a new product or a new job, but [to] entire new industries and a new way of thinking about the world. And so you need to be the Idea Generation. The generation who's always thinking on the cutting edge, who's wondering how to create and keep the next wave of American jobs and American innovations. (16)
> (May 7, 2005, Rockford, Illinois)

> "The rich get richer and the poor get poorer."
> It is social [sic] Darwinism, a view of America that says there is not a problem that cannot be solved by making sure that the rich get richer and the poor get poorer. It requires no sacrifice on the part of those of us who have won life's lottery and does not consider who our parents were or the education received or the right breaks that came at the right time. (20)
> (June 8, 2005, Washington, D.C.)

> "A promise made is a promise kept."
> We'll never rise together if we allow medical bills to swallow family budgets or let people retire penniless after a lifetime of hard work, and so today we must demand that when it comes to commitments made by working men and women on health care and pensions, a promise made is a promise kept. (25)
> (July 25, 2005, Chicago, Illinois)

> "Time will tell."
> Time will tell. You [graduating students] will be tested by the challenges of this new century, and at times you will fail. But know that you have it within your power to try. That generations who have come before you faced these same fears and uncertainties in their own time. (58)
> (June 16, 2006, Evanston, Illinois)

> "Numbers don't lie."
> The numbers don't lie. At a time when income inequality is growing sharper, the Bush tax cuts gave the wealthiest 1 percent of Americans a tax cut that was twice as large as the middle class. (90)
> (September 18, 2007, Washington, D.C.)

> "Let the chips fall where they may."
> It's a course that further divides Wall Street from Main Street; where struggling families are told to pull themselves up by their bootstraps because there's nothing

government can do or should do – and so we should give more to those with the most
and let the chips fall where they may. (106)
(March 4, 2008, San Antonio, Texas)

"Pay as you go."
It's time to put an end to the run-away spending and the record deficits – it's not how
you would run your family budget, and it must not be how Washington handles your
tax dollars. It's time to return to the fiscal responsibility and pay as you go budgeting
that we had in the 1990s. (169)
(October 1, 2008, La Crosse, Wisconsin)

"Use it or lose it."
Well [We'll] invest your precious tax dollars in new and smarter ways, and well [we'll]
set a simple rule – use it or lose it. If a state doesn't act quickly to invest in roads and
bridges in their communities, theyll [they'll] lose the money. (210)
(December 6, 2008: radio address)

There are two more proverbs used by Obama that need a comment before turning to his massive use of proverbial expressions that give his speeches a considerable metaphorical flavor without any claim to any particular insights. There is
first of all his change of the proverb "Beauty is in the eye of the beholder" to a
strikingly satirical anti-proverb in an interview of November 2006 in *Harper's*:
"Pork is in the eye of the beholder. The recipients don't tend to think it's pork,
especially if it's a great public-works project" (B,123). Such deliberate changes
of proverbs have become very popular during the twentieth century. By altering
traditional proverbs into humorous, ironical, or satirical statements, the ensuing
proverb expresses a new insight or truth in the form of an easily understood and
memorable message. Little wonder that they are frequently found in newspaper
headlines, advertising slogans, and political rhetoric (see Litovkina and Lindahl
2007; Litovkina and Mieder 2006; Mieder and Sobieski 2006). It is, therefore, a
bit surprising that Obama shies away from them. Creating an anti-proverb from
time to time could well spice up his rhetoric even more, since his audience would
clearly enjoy the instantaneous juxtaposition of the new anti-proverb with the
old folk proverb.

LIPSTICK ON A PIG

Finally, then, there was the campaign event on September 9, 2008, at Lebanon,
Virginia, that was blown way out of proportion by the Republicans and especially the mass media. As it were, Barack Obama was commenting spontane-
ously on John McCain's economic plan, peppering his remarks with the by now
famous "lipstick" proverb while adding a second colloquially expressed thought

based on a similar structure to it:

> John McCain says he's about change too, and so I guess his whole angle is, "Watch
> out George Bush – except for economic policy, health care policy, tax policy, educa-
> tion policy, foreign policy and Karl Rove-style politics – we're really going to shake
> things up in Washington." That's not change. That's just calling something [that's]
> the same thing something different. You know you can put lipstick on a pig, but it's
> still a pig. You know you can wrap an old fish in a piece of paper called change, it's
> still going to stink after eight years. We've had enough of the same old thing. (no
> speech number, just this remark)

As can be seen, this statement definitely was directed at John McCain and not
at his vice-presidential running mate Sarah Palin. However, in light of the fact
that Palin had spoken of lipstick, hockey moms, and pit bulls in her speech of
September 3, 2008, at the Republican Convention in Minneapolis ("I was just
your average hockey mom. I love those hockey moms, you know, they say, what
is the difference between a hockey mom and a pit bull? Lipstick."), it was easy to
attack Obama's colorful remarks as being directed at Sarah Palin as an ill-chosen
sexist remark. Having listened carefully to the statement on YouTube, I can state
categorically that this claim is utterly absurd. But in the heat of the vigorous
campaign this accusation gave Obama and his staff a few days of anxiety, to be
sure. Luckily there were a number of journalists who very quickly helped to set
the record straight by proving that the proverb or parts of it has a solid standing in
American politics. Using paremiographical tools, they pointed out that the "lipstick" proverb has a 16th century precursor in the form of "You can't make a silk
purse from a sow's ear." Similar proverbs are "A hog in armor [a person of strange
appearance] is still a hog" (18th century) and "A hog in a silk waistcoat is still a
hog" (19th century; Zimmer 2008). From the twentieth century there are also such
variants as "A pig in a palace is still a pig," "A pig with feathers behind its ears is
still a pig," "The pig may have a tuxedo on, but he is still a pig," "A pig painted gold
is still a pig," and "A pig in a parlor is still a pig." Since the word "lipstick" dates
only from about 1880, its appearance in proverbial language also had to wait until
more recent times. In fact, the earliest reference found thus far is from November
16, 1985, in the *Washington Post*: "The board of commissioners [of San Francisco],
reluctant to commit to such a project [building a new downtown stadium for the
Giants], asked if they couldn't use the money to renovate Candlestick Park. 'That,'
replied KNBR personality Ron Lyons, 'would be like putting lipstick on a pig'."
Two months later the *Dallas Morning News* of January 8, 1986, had the following reference: "'It's like putting lipstick on a pig. It can't hide its ugliness,' said
[Jim] Hightower, a self-styled 'progressive' Democrat [...]." As can be seen from
these two texts, the proverb also exists as the proverbial phrase "to put lipstick on

a pig" that might or might not have been the precursor to the proverb for which the earliest citation thus far is from the *Virginian-Pilot* of October 16, 1992: "She [a character on the TV series 'Designing Women'] speaks her mind and tosses around such Bubba-isms as this one: 'You can put lipstick on a pig and call it Mathilda. But it's still a pig" (this information comes from the manuscript of the *Yale Dictionary of Modern Proverbs* being edited by Charles Doyle, Fred Shapiro, Jane Garry, and me).

The relatively new proverb variant "You can put lipstick on a pig, but it's still a pig" caught on quickly and it has certainly been used in the political arena to great effect both by Democrats and Republicans. Ben Zimmer, a day after Obama's remark, came to Obama's "rescue" with a splendid piece of detective work on "Who First Put 'Lipstick on a Pig': The Origins of the Porcine Proverb" in *Slate Magazine* of September 10, 2008, citing a number of examples of how Ann Richards as the Democratic governor of Texas has made repeated use of the "lipstick" expression:

> Ann Richards did much to boost the saying's political popularity when she used a number of variations while governor of Texas in the early '90s. In 1991, in her first budget-writing session, she said, "This is not another one of those deals where you put lipstick on a hog and call it a princess." The next year, at a Democratic barbecue in South Dakota, she criticized the George H.W. Bush administration for using warships to protect oil tankers in the Middle East, which she considered a hidden subsidy for foreign oil. "You can put lipstick on a hog and call it Monique, but it is still a pig," she said. Richards returned to the theme in her failed 1994 gubernatorial race against the younger Bush, using the "call it Monique" line to disparage her opponent's negative ads. (Zimmer 2008)

Dennis Baron in his blog-essay on "Pig-Gate: Any Way You Spin It, Lipstick on a Pig Is Politics as Usual" of September 10, 2008, as well as Marti Covington and Maya Curry in "A Brief History of: 'Putting Lipstick on a Pig'" in *Time* of September 11, 2008, followed suit one and two days later respectively (amazingly quick and good work!), showing how the proverb has definitely gained a certain momentum as a politically employed piece of wisdom. Having these references now makes it abundantly clear that Obama was doing nothing more than citing a highly metaphorical proverb to get his point across with a bit of humor (the audience broke out in laughter!) or better satire added to it. Here are the telling references:

> They're [Republicans] going to try every way they know to put lipstick on this pig [lackluster job-creation numbers]. But you know when you put lipstick on a pig, at the end of the day, it's still a pig.
> (John Edwards, September 2004)

> He's [John Kerry] trying every which way to cover up his record of weakness on national defense [by talking tough]. But he can't do that. It won't work. As we like to say in Wyoming, you can put all the lipstick you want on a pig, but at the end of the day it's still a pig.
> (Dick Cheney, November 2004)

> I think they put some lipstick on the pig [Hillary Clinton's revamped health care plan], but it's still a pig.
> (John McCain, October 2007)

> I don't like to use this term, but the latest proposal [Hillary Clinton's health care plan] I see is putting lipstick on a pig.
> (John McCain, May 2008)

There are more examples, but suffice it to end this enumeration by also referring to Torie Clarke's book entitled *Lipstick on a Pig: Winning in the No-Spin Era by Someone Who Knows the Game* (2006) in which this former Republican administrator argues that sugarcoating bad policy decisions doesn't make them any more applicable. But in any case, when McCain and his staffers went after Obama for having used the proverb, it might have been well to have remembered that he had used it twice against Hillary Clinton's health plan, and nobody accused him of sexism! Be that as it may, the modern proverb "You can put lipstick on a pig, but it is still a pig" is now solidly established in American speech and beyond, as can be seen from mass media reports about the hoopla around Obama's use in the foreign press. In the German newspaper *Süddeutsche Zeitung* of September 16, 2008, it was reported in translation as "Ein Schwein bleibt ein Schwein, selbst wenn man es mit Lippenstift schminkt" (see Klüver 2008). The proverb, with all of its shades of meaning that can be reduced to the simple statement that facts are facts, is here to stay, but its association with Obama will surely fade away over time. He will instead be remembered for another and much shorter proverb, but that discussion will have to wait as a bit of a suspense builder until the end of this chapter.

FREQUENT PROVERBIAL EXPRESSIONS

For now, the time has come to take a look at a sampling of the over thousand proverbial expressions that Barack Obama has integrated into his various writings, speeches, and interviews. As can be seen from the attached contextualized index, he has definite favorites that have appeared so frequently in his communications during the past few years that they can be considered as proverbial leitmotifs. The following phrases are among Obama's most liked ready-made idioms, appearing at least eleven times and in the case of "to turn the page" being cited sixty-four times! Regarding this "page-turning" phrase that varies Obama's constant use of the word "change," its employment in his speech on "A New Beginning" delivered on October 2, 2007, at Chicago, Illinois, is especially revealing. It appears there six times as a leitmotif to underscore the idea of change and a new beginning. With much rhetorical skill, Obama finds ever new ways of making use of this metaphor:

> When I said that as President I would lead direct diplomacy with our adversaries, I was called naive and irresponsible. But how are we going to turn the page on the failed Bush-Cheney policy of not talking to our adversaries if we don't have a President who will lead that diplomacy? [...]
>
> In 2009, we will have a window of opportunity to renew our global leadership and bring our nation together. If we don't seize that moment, we may not get another. This election is a turning point. The American people get to decide: are we going to turn back the clock, or turn the page? [...]
>
> I'll turn the page on a growing empire of classified information, and restore the balance we've lost between the necessarily secret and the necessity of openness in a democratic society by creating a new National Declassification Center. [...]
>
> And I'll turn the page on the imperial presidency that treats national security as a partisan issue – not an American issue. I will call for a standing, bipartisan Consultative Group of congressional leaders on national security. I will meet with this Consultative Group every month, and consult with them before taking major military action. The buck will stop with me. But these discussions have to take place on a bipartisan basis, and support for these decisions will be stronger if they draw on bipartisan counsel. We're not going to secure this country unless we turn the page on the conventional thinking that says politics is just about beating the other side.
>
> It's time to unite America, because we are at an urgent and pivotal moment.
>
> There are those who suggest that there are easy answers to the challenges we face. We can look, they say, to Washington experience – the same experience that got us into this war. Or we can turn the page to something new, to unite this country and to seize this moment. (92)

It is important to note as well, as is quite common for Obama's rhetoric, that he adds the proverb "The buck stops here" and the proverbial phrase "To turn back the clock" to his proverbial leitmotif in order to underscore his message with the expressive power of additional metaphors.

Following this example of the six-time use of "To turn the page" in various paragraphs of the same speech, let me add just one small section from Obama's important speech on "The Cost of War" that he delivered on March 20, 2008, at Charleston, West Virginia, where the proverbial phrase "To pay the price for something" appears in rapid succession a total of five times:

> And today, I want to talk about another cost of the war – the toll it has taken on our economy. Because at a time when we're on the brink of recession – when neighborhoods

have For Sale signs outside every home, and working families are struggling to keep up with rising costs – ordinary Americans are paying a price for this war.

When you're spending over $50 to fill up your car because the price of oil is four times what it was before Iraq, you're paying a price for this war.

When Iraq is costing each household about $100 a month, you're paying a price for this war.

When a National Guard unit is over in Iraq and can't help out during a hurricane in Louisiana or with floods here in West Virginia, our communities are paying a price for this war.

And the price our families and communities are paying reflects the price America is paying. The most conservative estimates say that Iraq has now cost more than half a trillion dollars, more than any other war in our history besides World War II. Some say the true cost is even higher and that by the time it's over, this could be a $3 trillion war. (108)

What Obama is doing here with a proverbial phrase is quite similar to his rhetorical device of creating a sequence of enumerations by repeating each statement with the same phrasal unit, to wit "Real reform means ..." (39, four times), "I've had enough of ..." (50, four times), "Let this be the day that ..." (79, three times), "The sacrifices of war are ..." (81, three times), "This is the moment when we must ..." (141, eight times!), "We can choose to ..." (146, 5 times), and "Now is the time to ..." (153, 4 times). He also likes such standard phrases as "Let me be (crystal, perfectly, very) clear ..." and "Make no mistake ..." that appear again and again, and perhaps Obama should refrain from using these two rather meaningless and somewhat tedious formulas. Of course, it was wonderfully effective when he closed four paragraphs of his primary night speech of May 6, 2008, at Raleigh, North Carolina, with that self-assured and perfectly appropriate leitmotif "That's why I'm running for President" (113).

Alas, it is not possible to cite as many texts as I would like to for all the frequently employed proverbial phrases. But what follows is at least one expressive contextualized example for twelve more high frequency expressions that helped Obama to add a certain everyday tone to his at times demanding statements. Some of the multiple references are, of course, due to the fact that Barack Obama did not vary certain parts of his different stump speeches very much, but this still does not negate the fact that he has some definite favorites among traditional phrases:

"To be in something all together." (41 times)
Yes, our greatness as a nation has depended on individual initiative, on a belief in the free market. But it has also depended on our sense of mutual regard for each other, of mutual responsibility. The idea that everybody has a stake in the country, that we're all in it together and everybody's got a shot at opportunity. (65)
(August 7, 2006, Chicago, Illinois)

"To obey the rules of the road." (37 times)
We have not come this far because we practice survival of the fittest. America is America because we believe in creating a framework in which all can succeed. Our free market was never meant to be a free license to take whatever you can get, however you can get it. And so from time to time, we have to put in place certain rules of the road to make competition fair, and open, and honest. (89)
(September 17, 2007, New York, New York)

"To get back on one's feet." (31 times)
When I'm President, we'll reform our bankruptcy laws so that we give Americans who find themselves in debt a second chance. We'll make sure that if you can demonstrate that you went bankrupt because of medical expenses, you can relieve that debt and get back on your feet. (122)
(June 9, 2008, Raleigh, North Carolina)

"To pay a (the) price for something." (28 times)
And while we pay a heavy price in Iraq – and Americans pay record prices at the pump – Iraq's government is sitting on a $79 billion dollar budget surplus from windfall oil profits. (150)
(August 19, 2008, Orlando, Florida)

"To be (get back) on track." (25 times)
I am absolutely confident that if we take the right steps over the coming months, that not only can we get the economy back on track, but we can emerge leaner, meaner, and ultimately more competitive and more prosperous. (212)
(December 7, 2008, seventh news conference as President-elect)

"To be on one's own." (23 times)
After a lifetime of hard work and contributions to this country, do we tell our seniors that they're on their own, or that we're here for them to provide a basic standard of living? Is the dignity of life in their latter years their problem, or one we all share? (14)
(April 26, 2005, Washington, D.C.)

"To have a shot at something." (21 times)
We can restore a sense of fairness and balance that will give ever[y] American a fair shot at the American dream. And above all, we can restore confidence – confidence in America, confidence in our economy, and confidence in ourselves. (178)
(October 13, 2008, Toledo, Ohio)

"To be (stand, put oneself) in someone else's shoes." (15 times)
It's not easy to stand in somebody else's shoes. It's not easy to see past our differences. We've all encountered this in our lives. But what makes it even more difficult is that we have a politics in this country that seeks to drive us apart – that puts up walls between us. (99)
(January 20, 2008, Atlanta, Georgia)

"To tighten one's belt." (15 times)
Right now, our economy is trapped in a vicious cycle: The turmoil on Wall Street means a new round of belt-tightening for families and businesses on Main Street, and

as folks produce less and consume less, that just deepens the problems in our financial markets. (203)
(November 24, 2008, Chicago, Illinois; second news conference as President-elect)

"To open the door(s) to someone or something." (14 times)
We should all be grateful where opportunity has opened the doors of success for Americans of every background. [...] I think it is wonderful that Asian Americans, Latinos, African Americans, and others are represented in all parties and across the political spectrum. When such representation exists, then those [minority] groups are less likely to be taken for granted by any political party. (20)
(June 8, 2005, Washington, D.C.)

"To make ends meet." (12 times)
So we need to significantly extend unemployment insurance and expand it to include folks who are currently left out. That way, we can help them make ends meet while they're out of work. (111)
(April 10, 2008, Gary, Indiana)

"To be on the cutting (leading) edge of something." (11 times)
And to ensure that America stays on the cutting edge, we'll expand broadband access, expand funding for basic research, and pass comprehensive immigration reform so that we continue to attract the best and the brightest to our shores. (109)
(March 27, 2008, New York, New York)

There are a few more frequently used proverbs and proverbial expressions, and in these cases they are even bundled into a multiple-phrase statement! Here, for example, is a very short statement that Obama cited in exactly this wording in a series of five stump speeches between September 30 and October 9, 2008, that contains the three fixed phrases "To pull one's weight," "To be in something all together," and "at the end of the day":

We will all need to sacrifice and we will all need to pull our weight because now more than ever, we are all in this together. What this crisis has taught us is that at the end of the day, there is no real separation between Main Street and Wall Street. (168, 170, 171, 174, 175)

With a very minor change Obama reemployed this proverbial sequence, which he reduced to two phrases, an additional five times between October 10 and 18, 2008:

We will all need to sacrifice and we will all need to pull our weight because now more than ever, we are all in this together. This country and the dream it represents are being tested in a way that we haven't seen in nearly a century. (176, 177, 179, 180, 181)

And finally there is a third statement along these lines, but this time Obama is back to three phrases by adding the new proverbial expression "To tighten one's belt" in five more deliveries of his stump speech between October 20 and 25, 2008:

> Now, make no mistake: the change we need won't come easy or without cost. We will all need to tighten our belts, we will all need to sacrifice and we will all need to pull our weight because now more than ever, we are all in this together. (183, 184, 187, 188, 189)

Each of these variants of basically the same message was used in five speeches during three consecutive weeks towards the end of the campaign. It is not immediately apparent why they were altered at all. After all, delivered throughout this giant country, Obama did not need to worry about being accused of recycling his speeches. Furthermore, journalists traveling with him from stump stop to stump stop are perfectly aware of the fact that no candidate could possibly deliver a new speech every day! Nor is there any need to do so, of course.

Obama never tired arguing that in hard times it is absolutely necessary for people to realize that, proverbially speaking, "we are all in this together." As we have hope for better times and as we struggle to "make ends meet," it behooves us to show empathy for each other's fate. Empathy belongs to one of Barack Obama's core values, and as he argues for an increased awareness of the suffering around us, he turns to the two proverbial phrases "To put oneself in someone else's shoes" and "To see something through someone else's eyes" to make his plea abundantly clear through these traditional metaphors. He used this dyad in slightly varied statements six times between June 2, 2006, and June 15, 2008, with the following statement being representative for all the others:

> You know, there's a lot of talk in this country about the federal deficit. But I think we should talk more about our empathy deficit – the ability to put ourselves in someone else's shoes; to see the world through the eyes of those who are different from us – the child who's hungry, the steelworker who's been laid off, the family who lost the entire life they built together when the storm came to town. (66)
> (August 11, 2006, New Orleans, Louisiana)

Finally, there is also this somewhat longer critical paragraph about the ownership society that occupied Barack Obama in eight speeches between June 4, 2005, and August 28, 2008. The first time Obama spoke of this ill-conceived approach to life was in his commencement address at Knox College on June 4, 2005, at Galesburg, Illinois. He characterizes this selfish attitude by the proverb "Everyone for himself," and he cites the proverb "Life is not fair" to show how people who are successful use it to push less fortunate citizens aside. As can be seen, both proverbs are put to use in a highly questionable way to rationalize the inhumane neglect of others. This is also true for the proverbial expression "To pull oneself up by one's bootstraps" that Obama cites with bitter irony here:

> In Washington, they call this the Ownership Society. But in our past there has been another term for it – Social Darwinism, every man and woman for him or herself. It's a tempting idea, because it doesn't require much thought or ingenuity. It allows us to say to those whose health care or tuition may rise faster than they can afford – tough luck. It allows us to say to the Maytag workers who have lost their job – life isn't fair. It let's us say to the child born into poverty – pull yourself up by your bootstraps. (19)

In a speech of May 11, 2006, at Washington, D.C., Obama rephrased this paragraph very slightly and then repeated it two more times verbatim on June 14, 2006, in his speech "Take Back America" at Washington, D.C., and again on August 7, 2006, at Chicago. But what is remarkable is that he now had added the fixed phrase "To be on your own" to this proverbially "crowded" statement:

> It's called the Ownership Society in Washington. But in our past there has been another term for it – Social Darwinism – every man or woman for him or herself. It allows us to say to those whose health care or tuition may rise faster than they can afford – life isn't fair. It allows us to say to the child who didn't have the foresight to choose the right parents or be born in the right suburb – pick yourself up by your bootstraps. It lets us say to the guy who worked twenty or thirty years in the factory and then watched his plant move out to Mexico or China – we're sorry, but you're on your own. (50)

And finally, there is this somewhat truncated version that Barack Obama included in his magnificent acceptance speech entitled "The American Promise" on August 28, 2008, at Denver, Colorado. The proverbs "Everyone for himself" and "Life isn't fair" have been dropped, and instead the short statement is framed by the twice cited proverbial phrase "To be on your own" that encapsulates the dire straights in which many people find themselves. And sandwiched in between is an incredibly ironic manipulation of the proverbial expression "To pull yourself up by your bootstraps" that Obama changes to an imperative that is absurdly put into question by the image of not having any shoes in the first place due to utter poverty:

> In Washington, they call this the Ownership Society, but what it really means – you're on your own. Out of work? Tough luck. No health care? The market will fix it. Born into poverty? Pull yourself up by your own bootstraps – even if you don't have boots. You're on your own. (152)

Would a pedantic teacher or professor of English have put this utterance into question by writing in think red ink "clichés" next to it? Somehow I fear that this might well have happened. And yet, having listened to this emotional speech and now reading these sentences, I know that Obama was very sincere, that he meant every word, and that these fixed phrases in the greater context of the address were absolutely perfect. All of this reminds me of some of the finest examples of the use of proverbs and proverbial phrases by such great politicians and social reformers as John Adams, Thomas Jefferson, Theodore Parker, Abraham Lincoln, Frederick Douglass, Susan B. Anthony, Elizabeth Cady Stanton, Franklin D. Roosevelt, Harry S. Truman, John F. and Robert Kennedy, Dr. Martin Luther King, and many others. Of course, that great British statesman Winston S. Churchill also belongs to this august group of great orators who knew very well when a proverbial phrase would hit the nail squarely on the head, as it were (Mieder and Bryan 1995). But Barack Obama, at the very beginning of his presidency, has surely "hit the ground running" with his numerous "proverbial" speeches during his presidential campaign and deserves a seat at the round table of great rhetorical proverbialists.

OCCASIONAL PROVERBIAL PHRASES

So let us now look at a few more isolated speech references that illustrate Barack Obama's proverbial prowess, who is always mindful, I would point out, not to oversaturate his oratory with these folk metaphors. There are numerous instances where he refers to powerful metaphors to add emotive expressiveness to his argumentation, with the proverbial expression mirroring the negative situation that he happens to be dealing with. As such, his listeners will have absolutely no difficulty to get a solid mental image of what is going on, and they will follow Obama with keen attention as he moves from the negative description on to a possible solution in the future in the ensuing comments:

> "To wear something on one's sleeve."
> I don't think it's healthy for public figures to wear religion on their sleeves as a means to insulate themselves from criticism or dialogue with people who disagree with them. (B,93)
> (April 5, 2004, interview in the *Chicago Sun-Times*)

> "To have an ax to grind."
> Everybody has got an ax to grind when it comes to the press. My attitude is, let the press do its job. (B,89)
> (June 28, 2006, interview on "Hannity & Colmes" of the Fox News channel)

> "To be (nothing but) baloney."
> We were told this war would cost $50 to $60 billion, and that reconstruction would pay for itself out of Iraq oil profits. We were told higher estimates were nothing but "baloney." Like so much else about this war, we were not told the truth. (108)
> (March 20, 2008, Charleston, West Virginia)

"To be a bad apple."
Let me be perfectly clear. The fact that we are in this mess is an outrage. It's an outrage because we did not get here by accident. This was not a normal part of the business cycle. This was not the actions of a few bad apples. This financial crisis is a direct result of the greed and irresponsibility that has dominated Washington and Wall Street for years. (168, 169)
(September 30, 2008, Reno, Nevada; October 1, 2008, La Crosse, Wisconsin)

"To hit the ground running."
And so what I can assure you is that my team is very active in reviewing what's already been done, to ensure that when we hit the ground running on January 20th, that any taxpayer money is going to be properly spent. (209)
(December 3, 2008, Chicago, Illinois, sixth news conference as President-elect)

This procedure of citing proverbial expressions to have their metaphors help to illustrate a negative situation is, of course, much intensified when such statements add a second fixed phrase to it, as for example in this case that connects the phrases "To pull the carpet (rug) out from under someone" and "To be left out in the cold" used in a speech on the economy on October 17, 2005, at Roanoke, Virginia: "When you've worked hard your whole life, and paid into the system, and done everything right, you shouldn't have the carpet pulled out from under you when you least expect it and can least afford it. Health care shouldn't be some kind of either-or tradeoff where our seniors get left out in the cold" (180). And as expected by now, Obama is perfectly capable of linking three phraseologisms into a short two-sentence observation as well, to wit another speech on the economy two weeks earlier on October 3, 2008, at Abington, Pennsylvania: "So to Democrats and Republicans in the House who are now on the fence, let me say this: do not make the same mistake twice. For the sake of our families, our economy, and our country, step up to the plate and pass this [rescue] plan" (171). There is first of all the critical metaphor of "sitting on the fence" that is followed by the didactic proverbial imperative "Do not make the same mistake twice." But having said this, Obama goes on by changing the syntax of the proverbial expression "To step up to the plate" from the world of baseball to yet another imperative: "Step up to the plate!" This then is a perfect example of how Barack Obama employs proverbial material to move from critical analysis to hopeful improvement.

Of special interest is also Obama's reliance on the proverbial phrase "To break (hit, shatter) the glass ceiling" in discussions of women's rights. Having a professional wife, two beautiful little girls, and a grandmother who experienced job discrimination first hand, he is definitely committed to help women achieve true equality in the work force. The "ceiling" phrase appears in seven speeches between November 10, 2005, and September 20, 2008, vividly showing Obama's concern with this matter. In general terms he had this to say in his first use of the metaphor at the National Women's Law Center in Washington, D.C.: "At its heart, this has always been the essence of the women's movement in America – the quest to ensure that our daughters will have the same opportunities as our sons. Now, I realize that one day, my girls will discover that this journey is not over – that there are doors left to be open[ed] and glass ceilings yet to be shattered" (34). As can be seen, he added the proverbial phrase "To open the door to someone or something" for good measure, an expression that appears another thirteen times in other speeches to express his goals for positive change. Of course, he also goes from the abstract to the person in this statement by referring to his beloved daughters Sasha and Malia, something that he very much enjoys doing as a proud father. But he also used this phrase three times to express his admiration for his grandmother who helped raise him and who was a pioneer in the advancement of professional women. At a joint event with Hillary Clinton on July 10, 2008, at New York, and on the same day during remarks at a town hall event concerning women's economic security at Fairfax, Virginia, he said the following: "I saw my grandmother, who helped raise me, work her way up from a secretary at a bank to become one of the first women bank vice presidents in the state. But I also saw how she ultimately hit a glass ceiling – how men no more qualified than she was kept moving up the corporate ladder ahead of her" (134, 135). And it was also kind and collegial of Barack Obama to acknowledge Hillary Clinton's definite achievements in the field of women's rights by mentioning her together with his daughters in a speech of September 20, 2008, at Daytona Beach, Florida: "That's why all of us are here today – because of women who came before us. [...] Women like my friend Hillary Clinton who put those 18 million cracks in that glass ceiling so that my daughters – and all our sons and daughters – could dream a little bigger and reach a little higher" (160). And who could be surprised that Obama also used the proverb "Equal pay for an equal day's work (for equal work)" four times between November 10, 2005, and August 28, 2008. How much more direct and proverbial could he possibly have expressed his commitment to equal treatment of women than he did in the following personal vow stated in his speech on "An Agenda for Middle-Class Success" on July 7, 2008, at St. Louis, Missouri: "I'll make sure that women get equal pay for an equal day's work, because that's what's right and that's what families need to get ahead" (132).

The expression of the "glass ceiling" as the invisible barrier that especially women and minorities can see through but not penetrate as they try to advance in their profession is of modern vintage (Room 2000, 282), to be sure, but there is yet another proverbial expression that Obama used once that is even newer and that has, to my knowledge, not yet been registered in phraseological dictionaries. It stems from the world of computers, with its basic form being "To have something (available) at the click of a mouse." Speaking of the need of modern technology in the medical field, Obama made this statement at the Pritzker School of Medicine graduation ceremony on June 10, 2005, at Chicago, Illinois: "Yet, because we haven't updated technology in the rest of the health care industry, a single transaction still costs up to twenty-five dollars – not one dime of which goes toward improving the quality of our health care. Doctors are forced to fumble through paperwork and don't have all of the information about each patient at the click of a mouse" (21). I must admit that I had not heard this phrase before, but a Google search definitely confirms its proverbiality. Young people will surely know it, but at the same time I wonder how they feel about the old phrase "To keep the wolf from knocking on the door" to which Obama obviously alluded in yet another commencement address at Knox College on June 4, 2005, at Galesburg, Illinois: "As a peasant in 11th century China, you knew that no matter how hard you worked, the local warlord might take everything you had – and that famine might come knocking on your door any day" (19). As he looked back in history in this part of the speech, Obama did well to draw on an archaic phrase, but it was a definite stroke of genius to exchange the traditional "wolf" with the clearer noun "famine" to make sure that his message was not lost.

CLASSICAL PROVERBS AND PHRASES

Since Obama in his speeches is intent to communicate with the entire population of various social and educational backgrounds, it is understandable that he stays away from proverbs and phrases in foreign languages as well as expressions that might not be clear to the greatest common denominator of his audience. When he wanted to mention the credo on the American seal (see Fields 1996, 1-4; Aron 2008, 23-25) during his speech of July 27, 2004, at the Democratic National Convention at Boston, he therefore cited it in its original Latin but was quick to add the English equivalent to it: "It's that fundamental belief – I am my brother's keeper, I am my sister's keeper – that makes this country work. It's what allows us to pursue our individual dreams, yet still come together as a single American family. 'E pluribus unum.' Out of many, one" (2). The following three occurrences of allusions to Greek mythology in phrases are of such wide currency throughout the world that people should not have had any problems in understanding them (see Dibbley 1993; Macrone 1992; Burrell

1997). But again, Obama is wise in keeping these more challenging expressions to a minimum:

> "To be the Achilles heel."
> More than anything else, these comments [by Osama bin Laden on America's dependency on foreign oil] represent a realization of American weakness shared by the rest of the world. It's a realization that for all of our military might and economic dominance, the Achilles heel of the most powerful country on Earth [sic] is the oil we cannot live without. (43)
> (February 28, 2006, Washington, D.C.)
>
> "To be a Herculean task."
> We know how hard Kenyans are willing to work, the tremendous sacrifices that Kenyan mothers make for their children, the Herculean efforts that Kenyan fathers make for their families. (67)
> (August 28, 2006, Nairobi, Kenya)
>
> "To be a Trojan horse."
> I know there are those who dismiss such beliefs [in a common effort to improve life] as happy talk. They claim that our insistence on something larger, something firmer and more honest in our public life is just a Trojan horse for higher taxes and the abandonment of traditional values. (152)
> (August 28, 2008, Denver, Colorado)

Things were, of course, perfectly clear when Barack Obama most likely unconsciously alluded to the classical proverb "A dwarf on a giant's shoulders sees further of the two" which has long been reduced to the proverbial expressions "To stand on the shoulders of giants" and "To stand on someone's shoulders" in English and other languages (Wilson 1970, 209). The variant with the noun "giants" as the older one was used by Obama in a tribute to several civil rights leaders in a speech of July 20, 2006, at Washington, D.C.: "Dr. King told a gathering of organizers and activists and community members that they should not despair because the arc of the moral universe is long, but it bends towards justice. That's because of the work that each of us do to bend it towards justice. It's because of people like John Lewis and Fannie Lou Hamer and Coretta Scott King and Rosa Parks, all the giants upon whose shoulders we stand that we are beneficiaries of that arc bending towards justice" (63). In another speech of November 2, 2007, at Manning, South Carolina, Obama returned to the same theme, but he used the younger variant of the expression without any reference to the giants: "And I know that I stand on their shoulders [of civil rights advocates], that their courage and sacrifice six decades ago makes it possible for me to run today for President of the United States" (93). It is indeed telling to see Obama use this proverbial phrase to express with sincere humility his indebtedness to all those who stood up against racism and other social ills before him and thus prepared the ground for him to become the first African American president of the United States.

SOMATIC PHRASES

But speaking of "shoulders" to stand on, it should also be pointed out that Obama has a definite predilection for somatic phrases that abound in all languages. By referring to parts of the human body, they add emotive metaphors to Obama's rhetoric of compassion, empathy, and hope. For example, citing the proverbial expression "To put (push) one's shoulder to the wheel" gives Obama the opportunity to say in one metaphorical sentence what is needed to rescue this nation from its socioeconomic malaise: "It's this sense of mission that has compelled Americans of all backgrounds and beliefs to put aside their differences and push their shoulder against the wheel of history in search of a better day" (88). Many additional somatic statements could be mentioned here, but the following isolated examples must suffice with all others being registered in the index for easy perusal:

"To cram (shove) something down one's throat."
I don't oppose all wars. [...] What I am opposed to is a dumb war. What I am opposed to is a rash war. What I am opposed to is the cynical attempt by Richard Perle and Paul Wolfowitz and other armchair, weekend warriors in this administration to shove their own ideological agendas down our throats, irrespective of the costs in lives lost and in hardships borne. (1)
(October 2, 2002, Chicago, Illinois)

"To bring to one's knees."
You must choose: Will the groundbreaking [medical] miracles you discover over the next generation reach only the luckiest few? Or will history look back at this moment as the time when we finally made care available at a cost that won't bring the world's largest economy to its knees? (21)
(June 10, 2005, Chicago, Illinois)

"To take something to heart."
History will not judge the architects of this war kindly. But the books have yet to be written on our efforts to right the wrongs we see in Iraq. The history has yet to be told about how we turned from this moment, found our way out of the desert, and took to heart the lessons of war that too many refused to heed back then. (81)
(March 21, 2007, Washington, D.C.)

"To turn one's back on someone or something."
But, we cannot weaken the very essence of what America is by turning our backs on immigrants who want to reunite with their family members, or immigrants who have a willingness to work hard but who may not have the right graduate degrees. (82)
(June 2, 2007, Washington, D.C.)

"To turn a blind eye towards something."
If the last few months have taught us anything, it's that we can all suffer from the excesses of a few. Turning a blind eye to the cronyism in our midst can put us all in jeopardy. And we cannot accept that in the United States. (89)
(September 17, 2007, New York, New York)

"To (not) lift a finger."
They [school children in South Carolina] are overwhelmingly black and Latino and poor. And when they look around and see that no one has lifted a finger to fix their school since the 19th century; when they are pushed out the door at the sound of the last bell – some into a virtual war zone – is it any wonder they don't think their education is important? (96)
(November 20, 2007, Manchester, New Hampshire)

"To feel (know) something in one's bones."
So Dr. King had been to the mountaintop. He had seen the Promised Land. And while he knew somewhere deep in his bones that he would not get there with us, he knew that we would get there. (110)
(April 4, 2008, Fort Wayne, Indiana)

"To throw up one's hands."
We need to fix and improve our public schools, not throw our hands up and walk away from them. We need to uphold the ideal of public education, but we also need reform. (138)
(July 14, 2008, Cincinnati, Ohio)

"To drag one's feet."
We know that cyber-espionage and common crime is already on the rise. And yet while countries like China have been quick to recognize this change, for the last eight years we have been dragging our feet. (140)
(July 16, 2006, West Lafayette, Indiana)

"To put one's head in the sand."
History shows us that there is no substitute for presidential leadership in a time of economic crisis. FDR and Harry Truman didn't put their heads in the sand, or hand accountability over to a Commission. Bill Clinton didn't put off hard choices. (156)
(September 16, 2008, Golden, Colorado)

"To put the thumb on the scales."
Instead of allowing interests to put their thumbs on the economic scales and CEOs run off with excessive golden parachutes, we're going to ensure openness, accountability and transparency in our markets so that people can trust the value of the financial product they're buying. (217)
(December 18, 2008, Chicago, Illinois; twelfth news conference as President-elect)

This last example of Obama's much larger repertoire of somatic phrases is of special interest historically. It has a precursor in the old English proverbial phrase of the miller having a golden thumb, i.e., he would put his thumb on the scales in order to gain an advantage over the farmers bringing their grain to the mill. Already Geoffrey Chaucer in the *Canterbury Tales* spoke around 1386 of "the Miller's thumb of gold" with plenty of irony (see Mieder 2004, 46-48). Even though one still hears people refer to this "golden" metaphor from time to time, if it is used today at all, it is usually cited in the way that Obama has it. What a coincidence, however, that he happens to bring the concept of "gold" into play by also integrating the proverbial phrase "To give (have) a golden parachute" in this short rhetorical slam at the greed of certain high-level business people. Obama is quite fond of this not particularly well-known phrase that can be found four more times in his speeches, of which this additional text, this time with the proverbial phrase "To pay the price for something" added to it, may serve as another example: "When special interests put their thumb too heavily on the scale, and distort the free market, those who compete by the rules come in last. And when government fails to meet its obligation – to provide sensible oversight and stand on the side of working people and invest in their future – America pays a heavy price" (142). It might well be that if Barack Obama continues to employ this phrase, it will gain in currency and popularity again.

BINARY OR TWIN FORMULAS

Before leaving this discussion of somatisms, it should be noted that Obama's speeches also contain so-called binary or twin formulas as a subcategory of proverbial phrases. They are basically two often alliterative or rhyming words joined by a conjunction that have developed into standard formulas over time. One of them is "to risk life and limb," which can express a high level of emotion as in the following text in Obama's floor statement in support of the Voting Rights Act on July 20, 2006, at Washington, D.C.: "But to me, the most striking evidence of our progress [in voting rights] can be found right across this building, in my dear friend, Congressman John Lewis, who was on the front lines of the civil rights movement, risking life and limb for freedom" (63). Another somatic binary formula frequently heard is "heart and soul," and Obama made good use of it in an important speech at the AFL-CIO National Convention on July 25, 2005, at Chicago: "The real job of organizing working America – politics and policy, vision and mission, heart and soul – belongs to each of you. And if you have the courage to succeed, labor will rise again. And hope will rise again" (25). As the workers listened to this statement, they clearly could identify themselves with these proverbially expressed remarks. Many more twin formulas do appear in the speeches, to wit, "slice and dice" (2), "tit for tat" (27), "cut and run" (36), "hard and fast" (59), "bells and whistles" (68), "hit and run" (77), "loud and clear" (94), "wait and see" (116), "ups and downs" (153), "bait and switch" (172), "sooner or later" (198), and "part and parcel" (201). Simple as they seem, they can nevertheless add a certain expressive element to a speech. Let this last example of Obama's double use of the twin formula "sick and tired" illustrate, how this rang true in the minds of his listeners as he delivered his significant speech on "Reclaiming the American Dream" on November 7, 2007, at Bettendorf, Iowa: "We're tired of more Americans going without health care, of more Americans falling into poverty, of more American kids who have the brains and the drive to go to college – but can't – because they can't afford it. We're ready for the Bush Administration to end, because we are sick and tired of being sick and tired" (95).

SPORT EXPRESSIONS

Quite naturally the hundreds of proverbial phrases listed in the index could be arranged into several groups according to their origin, subject, or theme. Two such groupings stand out, the first being from the world of sports. Realizing that Barack Obama is an accomplished athlete, one can well understand that he feels drawn towards this type of metaphorical phrases, many of which Christine Ammer has collected and explained in her book *Southpaws &Sunday Punches and Other Sporting Expressions* (1992). As one would expect, traditional phrases from sports add a certain physical aspect to the speeches, and since these metaphorical expressions are extremely well known in the country, they add much spice to Obama's political rhetoric. Here are but a few examples to illustrate this point:

"To step up to the plate."
Although we have begun to step up to the plate in the Senate, it is unfortunate that none of the avian flu bills that have been introduced have passed into law. Frankly, there's been a lot of talk, but not enough action. And this isn't just true of the Congress. (28)
(October 18, 2005, Washington, D.C.)

"To throw one's hat in the ring."
Well, I thought about it [running for the state Senate], and then I did what every wise man does when faced with a difficult decision: I prayed, and I asked my wife. And after consulting with these higher powers, I threw my hat in the ring and I did what every person on a campaign does – I talked to anyone who'd listen. (50, 57)
(May 11, 2006, Washington, D.C.; June 14, 2006, Washington, D.C.)

"To level the playing field."
They [people] know we can't go back to yesterday or wall off our economy from everyone else. Their problem is not that the world is flat. It's that our playing field isn't level. It's that opportunity is no longer equal. And that's something we cannot accept anymore. (89)
(September 17, 2007, New York, New York)

"To sit on the sidelines."
But we always knew that hope is not blind optimism. It's not ignoring the enormity of
the task ahead or the roadblocks that stand in our path. It's not sitting on the sidelines
or shrinking from a fight. (98)
(January 3, 2008, Des Moines, Iowa)

"To pinch-hit for someone."
I have the distinct honor today of pinch-hitting for one of my personal heroes – and a
hero to this country, Senator Edward Kennedy. Teddy wanted to be here very much,
but as you know, he's had a very long week and is taking some much-needed rest. He
called me up a few days ago and I said that I'd be happy to be his stand-in, even if there
was no way I could fill his shoes. (116)
(May 25, 2008, Middletown, Connecticut)

"To pull no punches."
He [Paul Volcker] has served under both Republicans and Democrats, and is held in
the highest esteem for his sound and independent judgment. He pulls no punches.
He seems fairly opinionated. He has a long and distinguished record of service to our
nation. (205)
(November 26, 2008, Chicago, Illinois; fourth news conference as President-elect)

Before moving on to one last group of proverbial phrases, let me just state that at
this moment everybody in America knows that the Obama family will get a puppy
for the two girls once the inauguration is passed, but I have the feeling that thus
far the experience for all four family members with animals has been relatively
small. Perhaps this explains why Obama does not use many animal expressions
in his speeches.

MARITIME PHRASES

But this is different for maritime phrases, not surprising for someone who has
lived in Hawaii and Indonesia. And yet, I don't want to overstate the lack or
abundance of either animal or sea expressions. After all, they belong to the common expressions used by all speakers, as can be seen from Robert Hendrickson's
collection *Salty Words* (1984) and my *Salty Wisdom: Proverbs of the Sea* (1990). But
here are at least a few textual examples of traditional phrases relating to the water
and boats:

"To be in the same boat."
I have been feeling that many of you might be in a similar boat when it comes to politics and organizing and activism after college, and so today I'd just like to offer you a
few pieces of advice that might be able to help you on your way. (61)
(July 12, 2006, Washington, D.C.)

"To turn back the tide."
As President, I will make it a focus of my foreign policy to roll back the tide of hopelessness that gives rise to hate. Freedom must mean freedom from fear, not the freedom of anarchy. (85)
(August 1, 2007, Washington, D.C.)

"To stay above water."
You're trying to pay your bills every week and stay above the water – you can't ignore it [the economy]. You're worrying about whether your job will be there a month from now – you can't ignore it. You're worrying about whether you can pay your mortgage and stay in your house – you can't turn the page. (173)
(October 5, 2008, Ashville, North Carolina)

"To be at the helm."
Steven [Chu] is uniquely suited to be our next secretary of Energy, as we make this pursuit a guiding purpose of the Department of Energy as well as a national mission. The scientists at our national labs will have a distinguished peer at the helm. His appointment should send a signal to all that my administration will value science [...]. (214)
(December 15, 2008, Chicago, Illinois; ninth news conference as President-elect)

"To have all hands on deck."
The pursuit of a new energy economy requires a sustained, all-hands-on deck effort, because the foundation of our energy independence is right here in America, in the power of wind and solar and new crops and new technologies, in the innovation of our scientists and entrepreneurs and the dedication and skill of our workforce. (214)
(December 15, 2008, Chicago, Illinois; ninth news conference as President-elect)

Such maritime references in the speeches, including the proverb "A rising tide lifts all boats" discussed in the first chapter, can certainly be taken as solid proof that Barack Obama uses them quite naturally as part of his personal linguistic repertoire. This fact can therefore serve as a rebuttal of Jack Cashill's unfounded claim that Obama received help from Bill Ayers in adding sea expressions to his *Dreams from My Father* (see the beginning of the previous chapter).

"YES WE CAN"

In any case, the last "all-hands-on deck" proverbial metaphor in the previous list, appearing five more times in speeches from December 1, 2006, to August 6, 2008, is the perfect transition to the last proverbial statement to be discussed in this section. As hinted earlier, it is indeed a very short piece of wisdom that suggests that if we do get all hands on deck, if we all work together, our struggle for a better tomorrow will succeed. The main thing is that we follow our dreams, believe in hope, and hitch our wagon to something larger than ourselves. All of this rhetoric, proverbs and proverbial phrases included, was summarized by Barack Obama in one of his early speeches on April 11, 2005, at Washington, D.C., by the three-word proverb "Yes we can":

> It's hard to imagine that there are hundreds of thousands of parents every year who are forced to turn to kids who've worked hard and studied hard all through school and tell them "No, we can't send you to college." But it's harder to imagine that any of us could rest until those parents can start saying "yes we can" to their kids. (8)

That was the start of the proverbial slogan that carried Barack Obama to the presidency and that he used many more times in speeches until the evening of November 4, 2008, at Chicago, when he employed it as a proverbial leitmotif seven times in his victory speech that will be analyzed in the next chapter. In a primary victory speech on January 26, 2008, at Columbia, South Carolina, he appears to acknowledge the fact that this campaign slogan is not of his invention: "Where we are met with cynicism, and doubt, and those who tell us that we can't, we will respond with that timeless creed that sums up the spirit of a people in three simple words: Yes. We. Can." (100). And he did in fact not coin the triad, as has been explained by the well-known phraseological sleuth Nigel Rees (also citing Allegra Stratton) in a short article on "Yes We Can" in his *"Quote ... Unquote" Newsletter* of January 2009. Among some other references of a later date, one learns that "Obama is also on record as loving the Pointer Sisters. And in 1973 they sang Yes We Can Can, with its suitably uplifting sentiment: 'Now's the time for all good men to get together with one another'." Well, here are the surprising lyrics of the song:

> Now's the time for all good men
> to get together with one another.
> We got to iron out our problems
> and iron out our quarrels
> and try to live as brothers.
> And try to find a piece of land
> without stepping on one another.
> And do respect the women of the world.
> Remember you all have mothers.
> We got to make this land a better land
> than the world in which we live.
> And we got to help each man be a better man
> with the kindness that we give.
> I know we can make it.
> I know darn well we can work it out.
> Oh yes we can, I know we can can

> Yes we can can, why can't we?
> If we wanna get together we can work it out.
>
> And we gotta take care of all the children,
> the little children of the world.
> 'cause they're our strongest hope for the future,
> the little bitty boys and girls.
>
> We got to make this land a better land
> than the world in which we live.
> And we got to help each man be a better man
> with the kindness that we give.
> I know we can make it.
> I know darn well we can work it out.
> Oh yes we can, I know we can can
> yes we can can, why can't we?
> If we wanna, yes we can can.

Realizing that Obama likes the formula "Now is the time," that he uses the word "together" often, including his frequent employment of the proverbial phrase "To be in something together," that he repeatedly speaks of being "our brother's and our sister's keeper," that he talks of children, and that he always refers to making the world a better place, it might just be that this popular song had some subconscious influence on his rhetoric. But be that as it may, obviously the proverb "Yes we can" is absolutely nothing new, but that is also the case with many other proverbs that former presidents used and that then became attached to their names, to wit, Abraham Lincoln's "Government of the people, by the people, and for the people" and Harry S. Truman's "The buck stops here." Things will be no different for the proverb "Yes we can" and Barack Obama. Straight forward, honest, hopeful proverbial rhetoric like this last minute citation from his speech of November 2, 2008, at Columbus, Ohio, just two days before his election to the presidency of the United States, makes this perfectly clear: "We can prove that the one thing more powerful than the politics of anything goes is the will and determination of the American people. We can change this country. Yes we can" (195). There is no doubt that his effective proverbial rhetoric helps Obama to communicate "on the same wavelength" with all Americans for whom the name Barack Obama is equivalent to "Yes we can!"

PERSONAL POSTSCRIPT

As I was nearing the end of my work on this book on the freezing evening (minus 20 degrees) of January 15, 2009, in Williston, Vermont – anxiously awaiting the inaugural address in five days – my wife Barbara informed me that the renowned Vermonter ice-cream maker "Ben & Jerry's" had just announced a new flavor for that special inauguration. Keeping with their tradition of unique names, the ice-cream in honor of Barack Obama is called – did you guess it? – "Yes Pecan!"

"At A Crossroads IN America's History"
The Proverbial Rhetoric TO THE Presidency

It is one thing to deliver dozens of more or less repetitive stump speeches, press conferences, and interviews where not every word and sentence is scrutinized for its rhetorical and political import. Clearly Barack Obama is very much at ease in these situations, and this was, of course, also the purpose of holding so-called town hall meetings during the campaign. The situation is, however, quite different in those cases when a particular speech is billed from the outset as a major national address. It is where Obama labored hard on his words and message, sometimes for days on end late at night at home or in a lonely hotel room. Especially in his earlier speeches of this sort he was indeed the single author, but as we know, as time went on, he had no choice but to rely at least in part on the drafting and wordsmithing skills of his major speechwriter Jon Favreau and a number of colleagues. But as has already been argued in the previous chapter, these nationally and even worldwide broadcasted addresses are in fact Barack Obama's own speeches, since he is always deeply involved in the language and content of the final version that he verbalizes in front of giant audiences. And what is amazing from a proverbial point of view is that no matter when, where, or about what he speaks, his oratory is incredibly consistent in its vocabulary, syntax, and fixed phrases. Formulaic language in the form of traditional proverbs, proverbial phrases, and twin formulas is simply part of his natural speech pattern, and since he is determined to communicate with the people in an authentic fashion, these phraseological units also appear in what must be considered his most eloquent and thoughtful speeches that have been compared to the political addresses by such rhetorical power houses as Abraham Lincoln, Franklin D. Roosevelt, and John F. Kennedy. And yes, they too interspersed famous quotations and proverbial utterances into their communications in order to add a certain emotional and metaphorical expressiveness to their sociopolitical oratory (see Frost 1988; Harnsberger 1964; Jay 1996; Miller 1989). Being the excellent writer and speaker that Barack Obama is, he is very well aware of these and other great American communicators, and he has clearly been a good student of their rhetorical call to fame. But while he cites or alludes to some of their famous statements long having become quotations or even proverbs, he also very much goes his own self-assured, natural, and authentic way. All of his major speeches are informed by a humanity, sincerity, and empathy that resonate in his audiences as they look with hope, trust, and determination to a brighter future together with Barack Obama.

Let us then in the following pages take a more detailed look at Obama's seven universally acclaimed speeches that not only were of major importance in his campaign for the presidency but which also set the tone for the national rebirth of this country: his keynote speech at the Democratic National Convention (July 27, 2004), his announcement of candidacy for the presidency of the United States (February 10, 2007), his speech on race and "A More Perfect Union" (March 18, 2008), his speech in Berlin on "A World That Stands as One" (July 24, 2008), his acceptance speech at the National Democratic Convention on "The American Promise" (August 28, 2008), his victory speech on election night (November 4, 2008), and his inaugural address (January 20, 2009). As Obama spoke of the hope for change so that the American dream of carving out a life based on moral values and hard work could once again be obtained, he took on the voice of the nation with its economic, social, and racial diversity. All of this illustrates that political language at its best "serves as the agent of social integration; as the means of cultural socialization; as the vehicle for social interaction; as the channel for the transmission of values; and as the glue that bonds people, ideas, and society together" (Denton and Woodward 1998, 45). Being a person of compromise who is able to look at problems and issues from various points of view, he very quickly struck a chord with the American people. He uses a political language that finds a balance between the popular and the intellectual, coming from the heart and reaching across all divides in an attempt to reunite a nation for the common purpose of leaving an economic crisis, an unjustified war, and many social problems behind. There is no doubt that Barack Obama by now has taken political rhetoric to new heights, definitely reversing what Elvin T. Lim describes in his fascinating book as *The Anti-Intellectual Presidency: The Decline of Presidential Rhetoric from*

George Washington to George W. Bush (2008). There are clearly not just better days ahead politically but also linguistically for the United States.

KEYNOTE SPEECH AT THE DEMOCRATIC NATIONAL CONVENTION

As will be remembered, Barack Obama's rhetorical call to fame started with his incredibly significant address on July 27, 2004, at the Democratic National Convention in Boston. At the time, it was an unexpected honor for the young and relatively unknown state senator from Illinois to be invited to give this keynote speech, but crafting his remarks by himself, he did more than rise to the challenge and the occasion by electrifying participants at the convention and via the mass media the nation as well. Obama has gone on record stating that he is the sole author of this remarkable speech, with *USA Today* quoting him accordingly on the very day of the speech: "I like writing my own stuff. So I made a rare intelligent decision to start writing immediately after I was asked to deliver the speech. And so I actually had a draft completed before it was publicly announced, which was helpful, because if I'd known it was such a big deal, I might have gotten nervous and gotten writer's block" (B,82). And as Jay Newton-Small reports in his article on "How Obama Writes His Speeches" in *Time* of August 28, 2008, "Obama spent months writing the convention speech that would catapult him onto the national stage. Even though he was busy with his day job in the Illinois State Senate and was running for the U.S. Senate, Obama would find time to scribble thoughts, often sneaking off the State Senate floor to the men's room to jot down ideas, or writing in the car as he campaigned across southern Illinois. It took him months to gather all those fleeting ideas and craft his acclaimed keynote speech." Obviously a lot of time and effort went into this speech, but it was all worth it, for Obama continues to this day to draw on various parts of this speech in one way or another.

About a year or so after the speech, David A. Frank, Professor of Rhetoric at the University of Oregon, and Mark Lawrence McPhail, Professor of Interdisciplinary Studies at Miami University, published their fascinating article on "Barack Obama's Address to the 2004 Democratic National Convention: Trauma, Compromise, Consilience, and the (Im)possibility of Racial Reconciliation" (2005). It is a masterfully crafted essay in which the two scholars present their opposing views, with Frank taking the position that Obama's speech deals with racial healing while McPhail contends that it presents the old argument of racelessness. In their joint conclusion, the two scholars come around to agreeing that Obama's speech reflects this tension with a lot of work still having to be done from both sides of the color line for actual racial reconciliation. Of course, it must be remembered that race was not the sole topic of this speech for which both rhetoric scholars have considerable respect. McPhail goes so far as to say that "Obama's rhetoric, while stylistically appealing, nonetheless ignores the historical and social realities of American racism" (583). Be that as it may, it might have been helpful to find a few words about what exactly is meant by "stylistically appealing." Since he refers to Obama's use of the Latin proverb "E pluribus unum" (581) and even cites the paragraph with the extended Biblical proverb "I am my brother's keeper, I am my sister's keeper" (581), one might be justified to argue that Obama's "appealing style" is due at least in part to these proverbs. In fact, Frank also includes quotations and proverbial materials in his part of the essay. He quotes Obama's citation of the beginning of the Declaration of Independence (578) and also refers to passages in which Obama employs such traditional phrases as "To slice and dice" (579), "To sense something deep in one's bones" (580), and "To have a shot at something" (580). And yet, there is no linguistic or rhetorical comment by either author on these proverbial phrases which, as has been shown throughout this book, are a consistent and significant part of Obama's oral and written communication. Just as I am not primarily concerned here with the questions of race in my analysis, Frank and McPhail could argue that they are not at all interested in proverbial language. True, but I honestly feel that as we analyze political language, more attention should be paid to linguistic matters in general and the use of phraseologisms in particular.

Altogether Obama cites thirteen quotations, proverbs, and proverbial expressions in this relatively short speech. Mentioning his own diverse racial background in a rather subjective statement in the early part of the speech, he links his own life with the credo of the country as it is expressed in the Declaration of Independence that includes the proverb "All men are created equal" and the proverbial triad "Life, liberty and the pursuit of happiness":

> I stand here today, grateful for the diversity of my heritage, aware that my parents' dreams live on in my precious daughters. I stand here knowing that my story is part of the larger American story, that I owe a debt to all those who came before me, and that, in no other country on earth, is my story even possible. Tonight, we gather to affirm the greatness of our nation, not because of the height of our skyscrapers, or the power of our military, or the size of our economy. Our pride is based on a very simple premise, summed up in a declaration made over two hundred years ago. "We hold these truths to be self-evident, that all men are created equal. That they are endowed by their Creator with certain inalienable rights. That among these are life, liberty and the pursuit of happiness." (2; numbers in parentheses refer to the list of speeches at the end of this book)

This is rhetoric in the tradition of Abraham Lincoln and Frederick Douglass, who both cited this section of the Declaration of Independence on numerous occasions (see Mieder 2000, 146-150; Mieder 2001, 353-359). Knowing Obama's respect and admiration for these two men, I can well imagine that their writings might have influenced Obama here. But again, his own use is unique in that he also mentions his parents and his little daughters, endearing himself to his audience as a person with a story to tell, a self-made man like Lincoln and Douglass and as so many other men and women in this country.

Later in the speech, when Obama talks about these Americans who are perfectly willing to stand on their own two feet, he employs the three proverbial phrases "To sense something deep in one's bones," "To have a shot at something," and "To open the door for someone" to give expression to the idea that while they are not waiting for the government to solve all their problems, changes are definitely needed: "No, people don't expect government to solve all their problems. But they sense, deep in their bones, that with just a change in priorities, we can make sure that every child in America has a decent shot at life, and that the doors of opportunity remain open to all" (2). The three metaphors add much emotional emphasis to this statement, with the entire audience being able to identify with their message.

Throughout the speech, Obama is referring to not just one group of Americans, not just blacks or whites, not just rich or poor, not just old or young, but all the people of the country. He speaks as the great unifier and compromiser, and what could be more natural than to cite the classical Latin proverb "E pluribus unum" with its English translation and the expanded Bible proverb "Am I my brother's keeper?" (Genesis 4,9) to express this unity that includes taking care of each other. But notice, in order to make his proverbial argument for compassion and interdependence, he changes the interrogative Biblical original to an affirmative statement that includes women! That is absolutely effective rhetoric, leaving no doubt about Obama's commitment to this approach to life:

> A belief that we are connected as one people. If there's a child on the south side of Chicago who can't read, that matters to me, even if it's not my child. If there's a senior citizen somewhere who can't pay for her prescription and has to choose between medicine and the rent, that makes my life poorer, even if it's not my grandmother. If there's an Arab American family being rounded up without benefit of an attorney or due process, that threatens my civil liberties. It's that fundamental belief – I am my brother's keeper, I am my sister's keeper – that makes this country work. It's what allows us to pursue our individual dreams, yet still come together as a single American family. "E pluribus unum." Out of many, one. (2)

Once again Obama is general as well as personal in his argumentation, showing that he cares even about people whom he does not know. People must have sensed during this speech that here is a person talking to them who practices what he preaches, and so he did as an organizer in the South end of Chicago. This work clearly awakened him to the need of being our brother's and sister's keeper, as the variation of the old proverb puts it. With that attitude based on a solid moral value system, Americans as a family would indeed live up to the credo on the country's seal that with its "E pluribus unum" admonishes us to be united as one big family.

But Obama is by no means naive, and as already mentioned, he is perfectly aware of racial issues, economic problems, political divisions, and all the other social ills that tear this unity apart. In yet another powerful paragraph he deals with these aspects, characterizing them by the negative proverb "Anything goes" and the equally destructive twin formula "Slice and dice":

> Yet even as we speak, there are those who are preparing to divide us, the spin masters and negative ad peddlers who embrace the politics of anything goes. Well, I say to them tonight, there's not a liberal America and a conservative America – there's the United States of America. There's not a black America and white America and Latino America and Asian America; there's the United States of America. The pundits like to slice-and-dice our country into Red States and Blue States; Red States for Republicans, Blue States for Democrats. But I've got news for them, too. [...] We are one people, all of us pledging allegiance to the stars and stripes, all of us defending the United States of America. (2)

And then Obama sums his positive outlook for the future of the country and its people up with an early use of the phrase "The audacity of hope!" which was to become the title of his book two years later that contains his political manifesto. Having thus expressed his fundamental belief in hope, he adds a proverbial definition to it, and by also citing the proverbial phrase "To be at (on) the crossroads," he states metaphorically that positive change is coming:

> In the end, that is God's greatest gift to us, the bedrock of this nation; the belief in things not seen; the belief that there are better days ahead. I believe we can give our middle class relief and provide working families with a road to opportunity. I believe we can provide jobs to the jobless, homes to the homeless, and reclaim young people in cities across America from violence and despair. I believe that as we stand on the crossroads of history, we can make the right choices, and meet the challenges that face us. (2)

And to reiterate his hope and optimism for the immediate political future at the time of the convention, he ends his rousing speech with an expected political prophecy and a final rephrasing of the proverb "There are brighter (better) days ahead":

> Tonight, if you feel the same energy I do, the same urgency I do, the same passion I do, the same hopefulness I do – if we do what we must do, then I have no doubt

that all across the country, from Florida to Oregon, from Washington to Maine, the people will rise up in November, and John Kerry will be sworn in as president, and John Edwards will be sworn in as vice president, and this country will reclaim its promise, and out of this long political darkness a brighter day will come. (2)

The politics of the day turned out differently with President George W. Bush and his Vice President Dick Cheney being reelected. But the torch for change had been lit, and a new promising African American was on his way to transform the political scene during the next four years until his own election as the president of the United States. Many Americans can still see and hear Barack Obama delivering his inspiring speech at the Fleet Center in Boston, and for me personally it started my fascination with his proverbial rhetoric. Of course, he had a lot on his proverbial plate that eventful evening, but there is no doubt that the thirteen fixed phrases discussed here had much to do with his speech being such an unforgettable rhetorical success.

ANNOUNCEMENT OF CANDIDACY FOR THE PRESIDENCY OF THE UNITED STATES

As Barack Obama announced his bid for the presidency on the steps of the state capital in Springfield, Illinois, on the cold day of February 10, 2007, he did well to recall that state's and America's most celebrated president, Abraham Lincoln, in his speech on unification and hope for the country. Lincoln repeatedly called for a better union and nation, notably in his Gettysburg Address (Wills 1992), and as Obama he was very much aware of the preamble of the Constitution calling for the formation of "a more perfect union." And so Obama sets the tone of his speech about bringing Americans back together by alluding to this credo: "In the face of a politics that's shut you out, that's told you to settle, that's divided us for too long, you believe we can be one people, reaching for what's possible, building that more perfect union." The call for a perfected union certainly rings very familiar in the American mind, and it was ingenious of Obama to frame his speech through this metaphor by repeating it at the end. And how could it be different after what has been said throughout this book, he eagerly includes nine proverbs and proverbial phrases as well to add traditional wisdom and an element of colloquial speech to his compelling remarks.

As he continues to talk of compromise and the construction of a revitalized America, he turns to the simple proverbial phrase "To have a seat at the table" to give voice to the people in front of him who wish to be part of this drive to a better union, reminding them that he had originally come to this capital city as their state Senator to lend a helping hand (one of his favorite phrases): "It was here, in Springfield, where I saw all that is America converge – farmers and teachers, businessmen and laborers, all of them with a story to tell, all of them seeking a seat at the table, all of them clamoring to be heard" (76). And with this he is ready to make his candidacy announcement with a well-chosen allusion to Lincoln's repetitive use of the Bible proverb "A house divided against itself cannot stand" (Mark 3, 25) which has become associated with the president's name in the folk's mind (Mieder 1998):

> It was here, in Springfield, where North, South, East and West come together that I was reminded of the essential decency of the American people – where I came to believe that through this decency, we can build a more hopeful America.
>
> And that is why, in the shadow of the Old State Capitol, where Lincoln once called on a divided house to stand together, where common hopes and common dreams still [exist?], I stand before you today to announce my candidacy for President of the United States. (76)

What follows is a short history lesson of sorts to describe that Americans have always had the audacity to push for change to the better, where he adds a certain colloquial flavor by way of the proverbial expression "To bring to one's knees" and plenty of ethics by quoting another Bible proverb (Amos 5,24) used on several occasions by Dr. Martin Luther King:

> The genius of our founders is that they designed a system of government that can be changed. And we should take heart, because we've changed this country before. In the face of tyranny, a band of patriots brought an Empire to its knees. In the face of secession, we unified a nation and set the captives free. In the face of Depression, we put people back to work and lifted millions out of poverty. We welcomed immigrants to our shores, we opened railroads to the west, we landed a man on the moon, and we heard a [Marin Luther] King's call to let justice roll down like water, and righteousness like a mighty stream. (76)

With this sweeping statement covering the past, Obama can move on to some of the problems facing the country now. He does so quite effectively, for example, in employing the two fixed phrases "To play games" with its negative connotation and "To turn the page" that in a positive way implies the change that must come: "As people have looked away [from a government gone astray] in disillusionment and frustration, we know what's filled the void. The cynics, and the lobbyists, and the special interests who've turned our government into a game only they can afford to play. They write the checks and you get stuck paying the bills, they get the access while you get to write a letter, they think they own this government, but we're here today to take it back. The time for that politics is over. It's time to turn the page" (76). It might be interesting to note here that this is the first time that Obama spoke of "turning the page," a phrase that has proven itself to be his most favorite. By now he has cited it sixty-three additional times, making it a proverbial leitmotif in his political rhetoric of change.

Of course, Obama is also very much aware of the continued threat to this country by terrorists, whom he intends to pursue vigorously. The descriptive phrase "To tighten the net" is perfect to illustrate how he will deal with this life threatening menace: "We can work together to track terrorists down with a stronger military, we can tighten the net around their finances, and we can improve our intelligence capabilities" (76). And having been an outspoken critic of the Iraq war from the start, it should not be surprising that he includes some remarks on this catastrophic undertaking as well. Relying on the emotive value of the somatic phrase "To break someone's heart," he expresses his sincere compassion for those Americans who have lost someone in this war: "Today we grieve for the families who have lost loved ones, the hearts that have been broken, and the young lives that could have been. America, it's time to start bringing our troops home" (76). With this said, he can move on to what is to be done in Iraq, drawing one more time on the common phrase "To come to the table" as a metaphor for getting appropriate communication started to resolve this costly conflict: "That's why I have a plan that will bring our combat troops home by March of 2008. Letting the Iraqis know that we will not be there forever is our last, best hope to pressure the Sunni and Shia to come to the table and find peace" (76).

With this Obama reaches the crescendo of his speech at Springfield by returning to his idol Abraham Lincoln. The following paragraph, though not proverbial, is a true rhetorical masterpiece in structure and expressive power, enhanced by Obama's typical use of a phrasal leitmotif, in this case "He [Lincoln] tells us":

But the life of a tall, gangly, self-made Springfield lawyer [reminiscent of Barack Obama] tells us that a different future is possible.

He tells us that there is power in words.

He tells us that there is power in conviction.

That beneath all the differences of race and religion, faith and station, we are one people.

He tells us that there is power in hope.

As Lincoln organized the forces arrayed against slavery, he was heard to say: "Of strange, discordant, and even hostile elements, we gathered from the four winds, and formed and fought to battle through."

This is our purpose here today.

That's why I am in this race.

Not just to hold office, but to gather with you to transform a nation.

> I want to win that next battle – for justice and opportunity.
>
> I want to win that next battle – for better schools, and better jobs, and health care for all.
>
> I want us to take up the unfinished business of perfecting our union, and building a better America.

There can be no doubt that Obama has Abraham Lincoln and especially the end of his Gettysburg Address ("that this nation, under God, shall have a new birth of freedom – and government of the people, by the people, for the people, shall not perish from the earth") in mind, when he closes his speech with his rallying call to the American people: "Together, starting today, let us finish the work that needs to be done, and usher in a new birth of freedom on this Earth [sic]." Lincoln and Obama, what a rhetorical combination, and yet, personally I still wish that he had included Frederick Douglass's quotation turned proverb "If there is no struggle, there is no progress" with the attached proverbial comment that "Power concedes nothing without a demand" (see Mieder 2001, 456-457). As Obama's occasional use of the proverbial expression "To stand on the shoulders of giants" shows us, he is very well aware of his indebtedness for some of his ideas and rhetorical abilities. Yes, he stands on the shoulders of Lincoln, but also on those of Douglass from the same time and on King's later on. Speaking proverbially then, we have black and white combined in Barack Obama as a person and as an orator who knows well the power of words.

SPEECH ON RACE AND "A MORE PERFECT UNION"

These comments form a fitting transition to Obama's much anticipated and appreciated speech on racial issues that he very appropriately delivered in Philadelphia, the city of brotherly (he would add "sisterly") love, on March 18, 2008. This particular speech entitled more broadly "A More Perfect Union" was partly but certainly not only scripted as a response to the racially motivated remarks by his pastor Jeremiah Wright. It was awaited with much expectation, and it earned Barack Obama lasting laurels as a sincere, compassionate, fair, and conciliatory person of stature who is well aware of the power of words that can be an ambiguous blessing depending on the use or misuse of this verbal tool. Much has been said about this address, with the Lincoln scholar Garry Wills's detailed article on "Two Speeches on Race" in *The New York Review of Books* of May 1, 2008, comparing Lincoln's Cooper Union speech of February 27, 1860, to that by Obama some hundred fifty years later. Both men presented their speeches motivated by campaign matters relating to race, but, as Wills points out so convincingly at the end of his intriguing interpretation, "Both used a campaign occasion to rise to a higher vision of America's future. Both argued intelligently for closer union in the cause of progress" (Wills 2008). But as is customary in such discussions, there is once again no analysis of the "power of words" of these gifted orators. Regarding proverbial matters, Wills merely points out in passing that Lincoln liked the works of the abolitionist Theodore Parker, "especially his often used formula for democracy – government of the people, by the people, and for the people" (see Mieder 2005, 15-55). But Lincoln did not incorporate it into his Cooper Union address and chose instead to end his speech with a powerful proverb that goes back to the sixteenth century: "Neither let us be slandered from our duty by false accusations against us [by anti-abolitionists], nor frightened from it by the menaces of destruction to the Government [John Brown's attack] nor of dungeons to ourselves. *Let us have faith that right makes might, and in that faith, let us, to that end, dare to do our duty as we understand it*" (Basler 1953, III, 550; for a discussion of this reference see Mieder 2000, 25-27). What an incredible idea to close this significant speech with the proverb that "Right makes might!" that belonged to Lincoln's traditional wisdom as he guided the nation beyond slavery. But let us now look at how Barack Obama fares in comparison with his widely praised speech that once again contains nine proverbial utterances.

The speech has as its appropriate motto the first sentence of the Constitution: "We the people, in order to form a more perfect union." Its beginning is somewhat of a short history lesson, stating that this unique document "was stained by this nation's original sin of slavery," with racism still dividing us. Returning one more time to his general theme of perfecting the union, Barack Obama declares: "I chose to run for the presidency at this moment in history because I believe deeply that we cannot solve the challenges of our time unless we solve them together – unless we perfect our union by understanding that we may have different stories, but we hold common hopes; that we may not look the same and we may not have come from the same place, but we all want to move in the same direction – towards a better future for our children and our grandchildren." By speaking in general terms of not looking the same, he is clearly being much more inclusive in his views on race than just dividing the American population into blacks and whites. More than ten years earlier in an interview of October 1995 in the magazine *Crisis*, at the time of the publication of his autobiography *Dreams from My Father* (1995), he had expressed this a bit more drastically by employing the proverbial phrase "To throw something out the window" as a metaphor for overcoming racial division: "America is getting more complex. The color line in America being black and white is out the window. That does break down barriers. People can come together around values and not just race" (B,94). He now backs this up by referring to his own mixed background, and as expected, he distances himself from the divisive and racially motivated comments by Reverend Jeremiah Wright that prompted this particular speech. And yet, he is honest and fair enough to acknowledge that his pastor had a lasting influence on him. In fact, he quotes an entire paragraph from his *Dreams* in which he recalls how the first service he listened to in Wright's church influenced him. At that time, he began to think about the famous Biblical stories of overcoming obstacles through struggle and hope, including the proverbial account of "Daniel in the lion's den":

> People began to shout, to rise from their seats and clap and cry out, a forceful wind carrying the reverend's voice up into the rafters ... And in that single note – hope! – I heard something else; at the foot of that cross, inside the thousands of churches across the city, I imagined the stories of ordinary black people merging with the stories of David and Goliath, Moses and Pharaoh, the Christians in the lion's den, Ezekiel's field of dry bones. Those stories – of survival, and freedom, and hope – became our story, my story; the blood that had spilled was our blood, the tears our tears; until this black church, on this bright day, seemed once more a vessel carrying the story of a people into future generations and into a larger world. Our trials and triumphs became at once unique and universal, black and more than black; in chronicling our journey, the stories and songs gave us a means to reclaim memories that we didn't need to feel ashamed about ... memories that all people might study and cherish – and with which we could start to rebuild. (107)

Words like survival, freedom, hope, and triumph speak of how far this country has come in battling racism, and by adding comments like "unique and universal" and "black and more than black," Obama wants to look into a future where people of all races can have their identities and live together in a world based on universal understanding and compassion for each other. But to be sure, Obama is not just a dreamer and compromiser, and he is well aware of the fact that blatant racism must be confronted and dealt with vigorously. He says as much by putting a negative spin on the proverbial expression "To fade into the woodwork" and by acknowledging this imperfection of the nation by using his "more perfect union" leitmotif for a third time in a subsequent paragraph:

> Some will see this [his acknowledged indebtedness to Reverend Wright] as an attempt to excuse comments that are simply inexcusable. I can assure you it is not. I suppose the politically safe thing would be to move on from this episode [the controversial remarks by Rev. Jeremiah Wright] and just hope that it fades into the woodwork. [...] But race is an issue that I believe this nation cannot afford to ignore right now. [...] The fact is that the comments that have been made and the issues that have surfaced over the last few weeks reflect the complexities of race in this country that we've never really worked through – a part of our union that we have yet to perfect. And if we

walk away now, if we simply retreat into our respective corners, we will never be able to come together and solve challenges like health care, or education, or the need to find good jobs for every American. (107)

Obama is perfectly aware that "even for those blacks who did make it ["to get a piece of the American Dream"], questions of race, and racism, continue to define the worldview in fundamental ways." And as a striking example, he cites an "old truism" (he might have said "proverb" for once) that I personally have never heard, but which obviously reflects a certain reality still today: "The fact that so many people are surprised to hear that anger in some of Reverend Wright's sermons simply reminds us of the old truism that the most segregated hour in American life occurs on Sunday morning. That anger is not always productive; indeed, all too often it distracts attention from solving real problems; it keeps us from squarely facing our own complicity in our condition, and prevents the African-American community from forging the alliances it needs to bring about real change" (107). Having said this, Obama switches sides, arguing that such anger also exists in the white community. Many Americans of the working and middle class don't feel that they have fared any better than their black neighbors, and life seems a proverbial game without any progress: "They [middle-class white Americans] are anxious about their futures, and feel their dreams slipping away; in an era of stagnant wages and global competition, opportunity comes to be seen as a zero sum game" (107).

Having outlined some of the vexing racial issues, Obama interjects a short uplifting paragraph in which he once again stresses the necessity of working together in the struggle of overcoming racial problems, and, as expected perhaps, he adds his leitmotif of perfecting the union that gives his address a structural unity: "But I have asserted a firm conviction – a conviction rooted in my faith in God and my faith in the American people – that working together we can move beyond some of our old racial wounds, and that in fact we have no choice if we are to continue on the path of a more perfect union." Having now dealt with the "black and white color line," Obama is ready to move on to issues that face all Americans who despite their racial, gender, and socioeconomic differences, are tied together by a bond of humanity. And this "means binding our particular grievances – for better health care, and better schools, and better jobs – to the larger aspirations of all Americans – the white woman struggling to break the glass ceiling, the white man whose [who's] been laid off, the immigrant trying to feed his family" (107). By not mentioning black women wanting to break the proverbial glass ceiling here, Obama is not being discriminatory. He just happens to be talking about the white segment of the society at this moment of his speech. This is also the case with this next statement and its allusion to the proverb "Deeds, not words" as well as the reappearance of the "perfection" leitmotif: "In the white community, the path to a more perfect union means acknowledging that what ails the African-American community does not just exist in the minds of black people; that the legacy of discrimination – and current incidents of discrimination, while less overt than in the past – are real and must be addressed. Not just with words, but with deeds – by investing in schools and our communities; by enforcing our civil rights laws and ensuring fairness in our criminal justice system" (107).

With that said, Obama has reached the climax of his speech, and he couches his thoughts about a unified and compassionate America in the two Bible proverbs that have been part of his entire public life, the universal golden rule and the idea of being each other's keeper: "In the end then, what is called for is nothing more, and nothing less, than what all the world's great religions demand – that we do unto others as we would have them do unto us. Let us be our brother's keeper, Scripture tells us. Let us be our sister's keeper. Let us find that common stake we all have in one another, and let our politics reflect that spirit as well" (107). This statement is reminiscent of Lincoln's inspirational rhetoric, and it rang loud and clear through the American population on the day that Obama spoke in Philadelphia. Even though he mentions the religions and the Bible, this is not so much a religious proclamation but a call for fairness, compassion, and understanding for each other.

This might have been a good point to bring his speech to a close, but instead Obama decided to make a few additional comments regarding the immediate political scene of the presidential campaign. It was the race issue that had flared up at this moment, but Obama argues that Americans have a choice of not letting this divisiveness overshadow other important political issues. Changing the proverbial phrase "To play one's trump (best) card" to urging people to refrain from "playing the race card" (107), he argues for coming together to move ahead in a united front in order to, yes you guessed it, perfect the nation: "This union may never be perfect, but generation after generation has shown that it can always be perfected." To carry on the struggle towards this goal, supported by the Biblical triad of "faith, hope, and charity (love)" (1 Corinthians 13,13), is what Barack Obama advocates in this speech and promises to continue as president.

SPEECH IN BERLIN ON "A WORLD THAT STANDS AS ONE"

As a German American I will never forget President John F. Kennedy's symbolic declaration on June 26, 1963, at the Berlin Wall: "All free men, wherever they may live, are citizens of Berlin. And therefore, as a free man, I take pride in the words 'Ich bin ein Berliner.'" And I shall also forever recall Ronald Reagan's statement at the Brandenburg Gate in West Berlin on June 12, 1987: "General Secretary Gorbachev, if you seek peace, if you seek prosperity for the Soviet Union and Eastern Europe, if you seek liberalization: Come here to this gate! Mr. Gorbachev, open this gate! Mr. Gorbachev, tear down this wall" (Mieder 1997, 100-101 and 114). Parts of these statements have entered the major dictionaries of quotations, and as I have shown in my book chapter on "'Raising the Iron Curtain': Proverbs and Political Cartoons of the Cold War" (1997, 99-137), they have reached a certain proverbial status by now. So when I heard that Barack Obama was going to travel to Germany in order to give a major foreign policy address, I was indeed very excited. And so were the Germans! And not just the Germans either! Obama has been an absolute "hit" in Europe and elsewhere in the world. So there was much anticipation for this speech, with thousands of people attending the event itself, while millions experiencing it on their televisions. The leading German weekly newspaper *Die Zeit* dedicated an entire page to Obama's upcoming remarks, impressively written by the German literary author Peter Schneider. In memory of Kennedy's words of forty-five years ago he chose the perfectly appropriate title "Noch ein Berliner" for his essay that speaks of the hope for a renewed world that the possible presidency of this young African American politician would signify.

The speech took place on July 24, 2008, at the "Siegessäule" (victory column commemorating the war of 1870/71 with France) in the center of Berlin. As Obama was welcomed and applauded as a folk hero, he charmed the Berliners, the Germans, and especially the Europeans with his thoughtful and eloquent remarks on "A World That Stands as One," beginning his address with a touching personal comment: "I come to Berlin as so many of my countrymen have come before. Tonight, I speak to you not as a candidate for President, but as a citizen – a proud citizen of the United States, and a fellow citizen of the world." As he presents a short historical overview of the fate of this city with its destruction during the Second World War, the blockade after the war, the airlift, the division, and finally the reunification, he also mentions the Marshall Plan that helped rebuild Germany and provided food and clothing for youngsters like me. Having said all of this and much more, he won the hearts of the Berliners and other citizens of the world by saying: "People of the world – look at Berlin, where a wall came down, a continent came together, and history proved that there is no challenge too great for a world that stands as one." With this statement he has reached the basic theme of his talk: breaking down walls and building togetherness so that a new era of European-American cooperation may begin:

> Yes, there have been differences between America and Europe. No doubt there will be differences in the future. But the burdens of global citizenship continue to bind us together. A change of leadership in Washington will not lift this burden. In this

> new century, Americans and Europeans alike will be required to do more – not less. Partnership and cooperation among nations is not a choice; it is the one way, the only way, to protect our common security and advance our common humanity.
>
> That is why the greatest danger of all is to allow new walls to divide us from one another.
>
> The walls between old allies on either side of the Atlantic cannot stand. The walls between the countries with the most and those with the least cannot stand. The walls between races and tribes; natives and immigrants; Christian and Muslim and Jew cannot stand. These now are the walls we must tear down. (141)

This is without doubt one of Obama's rhetorical masterpieces. People were overwhelmed by these sentences, with some German friends writing to me the next day that they sensed a real new beginning for America and its relation to Germany, Europe, and beyond. And perhaps they recognized behind the refrain "The walls ... cannot stand" Abraham Lincoln's favorite proverb "A house divided against itself cannot stand" that plays into this formulation. Especially in the United States, in part because of Lincoln, this proverb from the Bible (Mark 3,25) has become a folk proverb, while the same Bible passage in its German translation never gained currency. But, and this is an important point that Obama almost certainly did not know, the Germans had learned about the English proverb through the former mayor of West Berlin and later German chancellor Willy Brandt. He had cited the proverb in an English speech that he delivered on the occasion of the sesquicentennial celebration of Abraham Lincoln's birthday on April 12, 1959, at Springfield, Illinois. And when thirty years later Germany was undergoing its reunification process, Brandt remembered the proverb and used it in English and with his own very good German translation "Ein in sich gespaltenes Haus hat keinen Bestand" at numerous political rallies. The Germans heard and read these speeches in the mass media, and by now Lincoln and Brandt, more than the Bible, have helped to establish a certain proverbiality for this wisdom in Germany as well (see Mieder 1998, 115-125). So the Germans for the most part could understand this important proverbial leitmotif spoken in English, even though it contained but an allusion to the proverb itself. The same, of course, is true for the final sentence of "the walls we must tear down" which clearly is a reference to Reagan calling upon Gorbachev to tear the Berlin Wall down. From a paremiological point of view, Barack Obama shows himself in these few proverbial lines as an incredibly astute stylist and rhetorician, who most definitely uses the power of words to a most positive effect.

It is absolutely amazing to see how Barack Obama continues from here. He stays with his motif of "tearing down walls," and then quite logically moves on to the proverbial idea of building bridges: "So history reminds us that walls can be torn down. [...] That is why America cannot turn inward. That is why Europe cannot turn inward. America has no better partner than Europe. Now is the time to build new bridges across the globe as strong as the one that bound us across the Atlantic" (141). This is followed by eight consecutive paragraphs each beginning with "This is the moment ...," a structural procedure that he has used numerous times in his speeches. The individual paragraphs are relatively short, and two contain proverbial phrases that add metaphors and emotion to his points. In the following short excerpt the phrase "To dry up the well" provides a clear image of what needs to be done: "This is the moment when we must defeat terror and dry up the well of extremism that supports it. This threat is real and we cannot shrink from our responsibility to combat it" (141). The same is true in the case of a second paragraph where the somatic expression "To extend a hand to someone" underscores the need for cooperation: "This is the moment when every nation in Europe must have the chance to choose its own tomorrow free from the shadows of yesterday. In this century, we need a strong European Union that deepens the security and prosperity of this continent, while extending a hand abroad. In this century – in this city [Berlin] of all cities – we must reject the Cold War mind-set of the past, and resolve to work with Russia when we can, to stand up to our values when we must, and to seek a partnership that extends across this entire continent" (141). In fact, after the eight "This is the moment ..." paragraphs, he more or less repeats this formula one more time in the following statement while also returning to the "hand extending" metaphor: "Now the world will watch and remember what we do here – what we do with this moment. Will we extend our hand to the people in the forgotten corners of this world who yearn for lives marked by dignity and opportunity; by security and justice? Will we lift the child in Bangladesh from poverty, shelter the refugee in Chad, and banish the scourge of AIDS in our time?" (141). As can be seen, Obama now moves beyond Europe to concerns in the rest of the world: "People of Berlin – people of the world – this is our moment. This is our time."

Towards the end of the speech, Obama very acutely brings the United States back into focus, reminding his German and European audience that his country remains dedicated to the idea of self-improvement (perfecting the union!) as it serves others:

> But I also know how much I love America. I know that for more than two centuries, we have strived – at great cost and great sacrifice – to form a more perfect union; to seek, with other nations, a more hopeful world. Our allegiance has never been to any particular tribe or kingdom – indeed, every language is spoken in our country; every culture has left its imprint on ours; every point of view is expressed in our public squares. What has always united us – what has always driven our people; what drew my father to America's shores – is a set of ideals that speak to aspirations shared by all people: that we can live free from fear and free from want; that we can speak our minds and assemble with whomever we choose and worship as we please.

This is an impressive and compact statement of what America stands for, and what Obama rightfully argues should be the case for every country in the world. And so, in a final use of a proverbial expression, he calls on people and their countries everywhere "to make their mark" in this world, a mark guided by the principles of civility, compassion, and courage: "These are the aspirations that joined the fates of all nations in this city. These aspirations are bigger than anything that drives us apart. It is because of these aspirations [for freedom, prosperity, etc.] that all free people – everywhere – became citizens of Berlin. It is in the pursuit of these aspirations that a new generation – our generation – must make our mark on the world" (141). By speaking of "becoming citizens of Berlin," Obama is even alluding to Kennedy's famous declaration "Ich bin ein Berliner," and most Germans in his audience would have caught this reference. Yes, indeed, Barack Obama reminds us of Lincoln, but there is quite a bit of Kennedy in him as well. He certainly conquered Berlin through the positive power of his words, his demeanor, his honesty, and his sincere belief in wanting to build a more perfect world beyond the United States.

ACCEPTANCE SPEECH ON "THE AMERICAN PROMISE"

By the time of his acceptance of the nomination for the presidency on August 28, 2008, at the Democratic National Convention in Denver, Colorado, Obama had delivered over one hundred fifty speeches that are part of my study. But there were many other events, such as town hall meetings and remarks at smaller events, at which he was asked to make at least some remarks. Clearly by this time he was an extremely busy man, and he did not have as much time to prepare this speech as he had for the convention speech he delivered at Boston four years earlier. In fact, his top strategist David Axelrod made the following remarks concerning the preparation of this second convention speech to reporters on Obama's flight to Denver: "The difference here is, you know, he's got a few other things going. It's hard to find the quality time to do this." And as the reporter Jay Newton-Small of *Time* continues to comment in his report on "How Obama Writes His Speeches" on August 28, 2008, it became rather frantic at the end to get the final version of this significant address into shape: "The first draft wasn't finished until last week, and as of Wednesday his staff couldn't say how long the speech was running or when it might be finished. The looming deadline [Thursday!] has led to a lot of late nights and bleary-eyed mornings for Obama, who instead of practicing delivery has been focused on his writing, even during his walk-through of Invesco Field Wednesday night." Despite all the frenzy, these comments once again clearly demonstrate Obama's involvement and ownership of the major addresses that he present to the American people. While there is help from his major speechwriter Jon Favreau and his colleagues, Barack Obama is heavily involved to the very end until he is thoroughly satisfied with the final product.

And his speech with the uplifting title "The American Promise" was a smashing success watched by millions of people in this country and abroad. Once again Obama was able to electrify his audience at Denver and elsewhere on the television screen by his ideas and words, even though, as reported by Newton-Small, Obama had said that "This is going to be a more workmanlike speech. I'm not aiming for a lot of high rhetoric, I'm much more concerned with communicating how I intend to help middle-class families live their lives." But, make no mistake (to use one of Obama's favorite phrases) and let me make it perfectly clear (yet another of his often repeated expressions), Barack Obama is well aware of the power of words, and so it is not surprising that he came across as the great orator that people have become accustomed to over the past few years. And, as expected by now, this speech contains once again nine proverbial phrases to add a certain amount of colloquial rhetoric to this major address.

Barack Obama begins with these simple but sincere words of thanks: "With profound gratitude and great humility, I accept your nomination for the presidency of the United States." After shortly reviewing how he and his family got to this exciting moment, he turns quickly to the socioeconomic problems at hand: "We meet at one of those defining moments – a moment when our nation is at war, our economy is in turmoil, and the American promise has been threatened once more." What follows are short paragraphs about what ails America and how the government has failed to fulfill its obligations to the people. But there is also the claim: "America, we are better than these last eight years. We are a better country than this." One of the examples contains the somatic expression "To sit on one's hands" that adds much metaphorical import to this reprimand of the government: "We are more compassionate than a government that lets veterans sleep on our streets and families slide into poverty; that sits on its hands while a major American city drowns before our eyes" (152). With just these few words and a proverbial phrase Obama is able to address the unfortunate neglect of veterans, the alarming increase of poverty, and the failure of reacting effectively to the destruction in New Orleans caused by the hurricane Katrina.

As one would expect from a speech at a political convention, Obama also takes a direct swipe at his opponent Senator John McCain, before he moves on to chastise the government of George W. Bush in general. He had used very similar wording in seven earlier speeches between June 4, 2005, and August 7, 2006, with the main difference being that they include the proverb "Life isn't fair" in addition to the two proverbial phrases "To be on one's own" and "To pull oneself up by one's bootstraps" that appear two years later in this particular address:

> It's not because John McCain doesn't care [about the various problems]. It's because John McCain doesn't get it.
>
> For over two decades, he's subscribed to that old, discredited Republican philosophy – give more and more to those with the most and hope that prosperity trickles down to everyone else. In Washington, they call this the Ownership Society, but what it really means is – you're on your own. Out of work? Tough luck. No health care? The market will fix it. Born into poverty? Pull yourself up by your own bootstraps – even if you don't have boots. You're on your own.
>
> Well it's time for them to own their failure. It's time for us to change America. (152)

This is strong rhetorical and proverbial medicine, even though this utterance represents a considerable recycling from previous speeches. The people at Denver did not read all the speeches as I have done in my scholarly "obsession" to find as many proverbial statements as possible in Obama's writings and speeches. For most of them, this paragraph was "new" and effective, and I remember well how much I enjoyed his innovative twist with the "bootstrap" phrase: "Pull yourself up by your own bootstraps – even if you don't have any boots." The audience loved this satirical use of the metaphor, and it earned Obama definite points in the rhetorical and emotive evaluation of his speech.

As is typical of the structure of Obama's speeches, the time has come at this point to turn from the review of negative matters to the definitely positive "American Promise," as the title of this speech indicates. Here too, owing to the polyfunctionality of proverbial metaphors, these fixed phrases are perfectly suited to enable Obama to add considerable expressiveness to his description of a better government. Proverbially speaking, the promise that he is making will "play by the rules of the road" and will be based on a positive answer to the Bible proverb "Am I my brother's keeper?" that with its expansion to include women functions as a moral leitmotif in numerous speeches since his 2004 convention address:

> What is that promise?
>
> It's a promise that says each of us has the freedom to make of our lives what we will, but that we also have the obligation to treat each other with dignity and respect.
>
> It's a promise that says the market should reward drive and innovation and generate growth, but that businesses should live up to their responsibilities to create American jobs, look out for American workers, and play by the rules of the road.
>
> Ours is a promise that says government cannot solve all our problems, but what it should do is that which we cannot do for ourselves – protect us from harm and provide every child a decent education; keep our water clean and our toys safe; invest in new schools and new roads and new science and technology.

> Our government should work for us, not against us. It should help us, not hurt us. It should ensure opportunity not just for those with the most money and influence, but for every American who's willing to work.
>
> That's the promise of America – the idea that we are responsible for ourselves, but that we also rise or fall as one nation; the fundamental belief that I am my brother's keeper; I am my sister's keeper.
>
> That's the promise we need to keep. That's the change we need right now. (152)

This is a definite highpoint of this acclaimed speech, with Obama then outlining some of the changes that he plans to initiate if elected as president. In the ensuing list he begins each paragraph with the structural formula "Now is the time ..." that is part of his speech pattern in general, with the last statement as his "sister's keeper" stressing equal treatment of women in the workforce with a modern American proverb from the women's movement: "And now is the time to keep the promise of equal pay for an equal day's work, because I want my daughters to have exactly the same opportunities as your sons" (152). What a fantastic paragraph! Instead of giving long explanations and discussing the unfair treatment of working women, he simply quotes the "equal pay" proverb and then brings his daughters Sasha and Malia as women of the future on equal footing with other people's sons into play. The effect of such rhetoric is heartwarming in its subjectivity and by way of the proverb also demandingly didactic and programmatic for the necessary change.

With all the ideas for change expressed with his healthy optimism for the future, Obama returns expectedly to the upcoming debates with his opponent John McCain, expressing his desire to make the process fair and free of invalid accusations: "One of the things that we have to change in our politics is the idea that people cannot disagree without challenging each other's character and patriotism. The times are too serious, the stakes are too high for this same partisan playbook. So let us agree that patriotism has no party. I love this country, and so do you, and so does John McCain" (152). The stakes of this campaign were indeed high, as the proverbial phrase has it, and it made a lot of sense for Obama to make this statement. And while he is at it, he adds yet another concern to it, this time making use of the classical expression "To be a Trojan horse." He is well aware of the claim by McCain and others that he presents too much hope and optimism for change that would cost the electorate plenty in taxes if he were to become president: "I know there are those who dismiss such beliefs [in a common effort to improve life] as happy talk. They claim that our insistence on something larger, something firmer and more honest in our public life is just a Trojan horse for higher taxes and the abandonment of traditional values" (152). But, with utmost consistency, Barack Obama sticks to his "American Promise," claiming with his own pseudo-proverb "A new politics for a new time," that has all the makings to become a new proverb, that "Change comes to Washington. Change happens because the American people demand it – because they rise up and insist on new ideas and new leaders, a new politics for a new time" (152). This said, he concludes his speech with an allusion to a verse in the Bible that my colleague and friend Dennis Mahoney found in Hebrews 10,23, and that results in numerous Google hits: "Let us hold fast the profession of our faith without wavering; for he is faithful that promised." It does not belong to the large set of well-known Bible references, however, having not even entered Burton Stevenson's massive compilation *The Home Book of Bible Quotations* (1949). Yet Obama obviously is acquainted with it and by mentioning "Scripture" assumes that others know it as well: "Let us keep that promise – that American promise – and in the words of Scripture hold firmly, without wavering, to the hope that we confess." But since it does not appear in any of the major quotation dictionaries either, I would argue that this closing statement was perhaps not the best from a cultural literacy point of view, and more subjectively expressed, from the viewpoint of someone interested in traditional phrases from the Bible, literature, or the folk that have general currency in American parlance. But be that as it may, Obama again proves himself to be an acute innovator in his adaptation of this Bible passage. While the quotation speaks of the promise of Christian faith, Obama takes it out of its religious context and applies it in a secular sense to the hope and promise of the United States in the years to come. As such, the Bible allusion serves Obama well, and yet I wonder, why he might not have used Alexander Pope's well-known quotation "Hope springs eternal in the human breast" from 1733 that has long been reduced to the common proverb "Hope springs eternal." And, even stranger yet, I remain utterly perplexed by the fact that Barack Obama with his constant emphasis on hope has never used this so appropriate proverb.

VICTORY SPEECH ON ELECTION NIGHT

On November 4, 2008, late at night in Chicago, the end of the long and hard road towards the presidency came to end, and Barack Obama stood in front of thousands of people, with millions watching the long-awaited event on television, and declared his well-earned election victory. After yet another hectic week of non-stop campaigning, he confronted his giant audience here and abroad with his typical winning smile, his contagious charisma, and his eloquent oratory based on magisterial rhetoric and uplifting ideals. Already the first sentence sets the tone and vision of the rest of the speech, and I consider it another remarkable feat that

Obama accomplishes this by citing the universal proverb "All things are possible" and claiming its truth factor especially for the United States:

> If there is anyone out there [at Chicago on election night] who still doubts that America is a place where all things are possible, who still wonders if the dream of our founders is alive in our time; who still questions the power of democracy, tonight is your answer. (197)

This is a fantastic proverbial opening, with Obama then listing some aspects of this answer, starting each paragraph in typical leitmotif- fashion with "It's the answer ...," among them this universal statement:

> It's the answer spoken by young and old, rich and poor, Democrat and Republican, black, white, Latino, Asian, Native American, gay, straight, disabled and not disabled – Americans who sent a message to the world that we have never been a collection of Red States and Blue States: we are, and always will be, the United States of America.

Knowing that Obama does quite frequently refer back to former speeches, I was surprised at this point of listening and watching his speech on television that he did not repeat the proverbial sentence "It's what allows us to pursue our individual dreams, yet still come together as a single American family. 'E pluribus unum.' Out of many, one" (2) used so effectively in his first convention speech on July 27, 2004, at Boston. Instead he recalls a quotation from Dr. Martin Luther King's speech entitled "Where Do We Go From Here?" that he delivered on August 16, 1967, at Atlanta, Georgia (see Karabegovic 2007). This is exactly the question that Obama attempted to answer throughout his campaign, and in five speeches from between February 21, 2005 and April 4, 2008, he quoted King's insistence on morality and justice that the civil rights champion had verbalized by way of a powerful metaphor: "The arc of the moral universe is long, but it bends towards justice." And so Obama returns in his victory speech to this wisdom for a sixth time, but as we have seen so often by now, he appropriates the almost proverbial quotation into a freely altered statement of his own, thereby empowering people to bend the arc of history towards hope – a truly innovative rephrasing of King's statement: "It's [Obama's election] the answer that led those who have been told for so long by so many to be cynical, and fearful, and doubtful of what can be achieved to put their hands on the arc of history and bend it once more toward hope of a better day" (197).

Further on in his speech he deals somewhat similarly with the democratic proverb "Government of the people, by the people, and for the people" that he used twice before in his speeches of October 2, 2007, at Chicago, and of June 30, 2008, at

Independence, Missouri. In both cases he did not mention that Abraham Lincoln, who did not coin it, was quite fond of this proverbial triad. He does not refer to Lincoln in the present scenario either, and yet, by adding the phrasal segment "shall not perish from this earth," he most certainly has the end of Lincoln's Gettysburg Address on his mind. The small change from Lincoln's "the earth" to "this Earth" is of no consequence here, unless Obama means to emphasize the United States by using a demonstrative pronoun and a capitalized noun. In any case, the majority of his audience will have felt Lincoln's voice when Obama said: "It [my campaign] grew strength from the young people who rejected the myth of their generation's apathy; who left their homes and their families for jobs that offered little pay and less sleep; from not-so-young people who braved the bitter cold and scorching heat to knock on the doors of perfect strangers; from the millions of Americans who volunteered, and organized, and proved that more than two centuries later, a government of the people, by the people and for the people has not perished from this Earth. This is our victory" (197). With calling the successful election "our victory," Obama makes a welcome link between himself and the government of the people that he represents, knowing proverbially, as he so often said during the campaign, that "we are all in this together."

Of course, there is much work to do, and as the American people approach challenging changes, Obama encourages them to keep the following principles in mind:

> So let us summon a new spirit of patriotism; of service and responsibility where each of us resolves to pitch in and work harder and look after not only ourselves, but each other. Let us remember that if this financial crisis taught us anything, it's that we cannot have a thriving Wall Street while Main Street suffers – in this country, we rise or fall as one nation; as one people. (197)

The argument for unity and a common purpose comes through loud and clear, and it is brought into focus in light of the economic crisis by the statement that "We cannot have a thriving Wall Street while Main Street suffers." This formulation is of particular paremiological interest, since it can show us a possible proverb in the making. In four previous speeches, Obama cited this new wisdom as "We cannot have a thriving Wall Street and a struggling Main Street" (142, 144-146). After his victory speech under discussion here, he used the new variant "We cannot have a thriving Wall Street while Main Street suffers" (200) in a subsequent radio address on November 15, 2008. But then, during his second news conference as President-elect of November 24, 2008, he employed the third variant "We cannot have a thriving Wall Street without a thriving Main Street" (203). And yet, only one day later, he came up with a fourth variant during his third news conference: "Wall Street cannot thrive so long as Main Street is struggling" (204). The basic structure with its references to Wall Street and Main Street in each segment is solidly established, and it is now a question which variant will eventually become the dominant standard form. If Obama continues to cite his "pseudo-proverb," it will doubtlessly become current in our society and over time be considered a proverb with, at least for some period, Barack Obama's name attached to it.

After this short excurse on the creation of a proverb, I can turn to the final climax of this magnificent victory speech. It is to a large degree attained by Obama citing his proverbial campaign slogan "Yes We Can" six times in a row! The background to this three-word proverb has been dealt with already at the end of the previous chapter, explaining that Obama might well have picked it up from the popular song "Yes We Can Can" (1973) by the Pointer Sisters. What remains to be done here is to show that Obama accomplished an unforgettable *tour de force* with this proverb as an electrifying leitmotif. It all starts with Obama singling out Ann Nixon Cooper, a 106 year-old African American, as a positive symbol for all changes on all fronts that she has experienced as a representative of all Americans during her long life: "And tonight, I think about all that she's seen throughout her century in America – the heartache and the hope; the struggle and the progress; the times we were told that we can't, and the people who pressed on with that American creed: Yes we can" (197). I can't help but interject one more time here, with Obama having chosen the word combination "the struggle and the progress," how exciting it would have been for him to include Frederick Douglass's "Where there is no struggle, there is no progress." I have to assume that he has not come across it, and my letter to him mentioning this proverb quite obviously did not reach him (see the letter at the end of the first chapter). But be that as it may, once Barack Obama has used the "Yes we can" proverb, he is on a definite proverbial roll. And do notice, how he even succeeds in bringing Franklin D. Roosevelt's "We have nothing to fear but fear itself" and Martin Luther King's "We shall overcome" into play in this fantastic crescendo:

> At a time when women's voices were silenced and their hopes dismissed, she [Ann Nixon Cooper] lived to see them stand up and speak out and reach for the ballot. Yes we can.
>
> When there was despair in the dust bowl and depression across the land, she saw a nation conquer fear itself with a New Deal, new jobs and a new sense of common purpose. Yes we can.
>
> When the bombs fell on our harbor and tyranny threatened the world, she was there to witness a generation to rise to greatness and a democracy was saved. Yes we can.
>
> She was there for the buses in Montgomery, the hoses in Birmingham, a bridge in Selma, and a preacher from Atlanta who told a people "We Shall Overcome." Yes we can.
>
> A man touched down on the moon, a wall came down in Berlin, a world was connected by our science and imagination. And this year, in this election, she touched

> her finger to a screen, and cast her vote, because after 106 years in America, through the best of times and the darkest of hours, she knows how America can change. Yes we can. (197)

It would be hard to equal this history lesson with the centenarian Ann Nixon Cooper as a living symbol and the proverb "Yes we can" as an affirmation! Through struggle to progress, that is the fundamental message, as Obama explains it by linking this old woman to his young children and thus the future: "America, we have come so far. We have seen so much. But there is so much more to do. So tonight, let us ask ourselves – if our children should live to see the next century; if my daughters should be so lucky to live as long as Ann Nixon Cooper, what change will they see? What progress will we have made?"

With this Barack Obama is at the end of his uplifting victory speech which contains no sign of hubris but instead is filled with humility and humanity. It is a statement of the vision and the hope for a more perfect union with proverbial open doors and the vindication of the proverb "that out of many, we are one" (imagine my delight when I heard this that election night!):

> This is our moment. This is our time – to put our people back to work and open doors of opportunity for our kids; to restore prosperity and promote the cause of peace; to reclaim the American Dream and reaffirm that fundamental truth – that out of many, we are one; that while we breathe, we hope, and where we are met with cynicism, and doubt, and those who tell us that we can't, we will respond with that timeless creed that sums up the spirit of a people: Yes We Can. (197)

With this seventh appearance of the "Yes we can" proverb, a beaming and confident Barack Obama closed his unforgettable victory speech with the typically American forward-looking vision (Dundes 2004) that he can handle the challenges facing the nation if we all work together for our common goals. The other seven proverbs and proverbial expressions underscore this fundamental belief in improving the imperfect union, for after all, "America is a place where all things are possible" with "a government of the people, by the people, and for the people."

THE INAUGURAL ADDRESS

With Barack Obama's inaugural address of January 20, 2009, just having been delivered two days ago, I can write this last section of my book on his proverbial rhetoric. With millions of other Americans and the rest of the world I had eagerly awaited this great moment at the beginning of the twenty-first century, and I can honestly state as a citizen and scholar that I was again deeply moved by the remarks of the brand-new President of the United States Barack Obama! Of course, the pressures and expectations for Obama to give a most memorable speech were enormous, and there was much talk and speculation about what he would include and how he would verbalize this address. This also led to a series of reviews of previous inaugural addresses, with Jill Lepore's essay of January 12, 2009, on "The Speech: Have Inaugural Addresses Been Getting Worse" in *The New Yorker* standing out as a solid piece of historical scholarship. It begins with the statement that "Barack Obama has been studying up, reading Abraham Lincoln's speeches, raising everyone's expectations for what just might be the most eagerly awaited inaugural" (Lepore 2009, 49), and the author goes on to explain how previous presidents received plenty of help from friends and speechwriters in the formulation of their inaugurals, with James Garfield and Jimmy Carter most likely being the only presidents who wrote this particular address completely on their own. As has been pointed out repeatedly by presidential historians and rhetorical studies, the ritual of the inauguration of the president has turned the speech into somewhat of a formulaic event, making it very difficult to deviate from various traditional expectations:

> From a generic perspective, then, a presidential inaugural reconstitutes the people as an audience that can witness the rite of investiture, rehearses communal values from the past, sets forth the political principles that will guide the new administration, and demonstrates that the president can enact the presidential persona appropriately. Still more generally, the presidential inaugural address is an epideictic [rhetorically demonstrative] ritual that is formal, unifying, abstract, and eloquent. At the core of this ritual lies epideictic timelessness − the fusion of the past and future of the nation in an eternal present in which we reaffirm what Franklin Roosevelt called "our covenant with ourselves," a covenant between the executive and the nation that is the essence of democratic government. (Campbell and Jamieson 2008, 56)

Having looked at previous inaugural addresses that are easily accessible in a number of anthologies (see Hunt 1997; Lott 1961; Remini and Golway 2008), Barack Obama was very well aware of their uplifting purpose that is certainly different from speeches given during political campaigns. And yet, especially his major speeches discussed in this chapter at least in part exhibit this epideictic character. So Obama, the impressive rhetorician and orator, did well to decide to write his speech himself, receiving only minor editorial or factual help, as reported by Mary Kate Cary, former speechwriter for President George H.W. Bush:

> Earlier this morning [January 20, 2009], aides to Mr. Obama told reporters that the president-elect had consulted historian David McCullough (presumably to double-check the references to Valley Forge); Lincoln biographer Doris Kearns Goodwin (he mentioned the Gettysburg address, and his homage to those who endured the "lash

of the whip" was a reference to a line in Lincoln's second inaugural) and the dean of the White House speechwriters, Kennedy speechwriter Ted Sorensen. I'm sure Mr. Sorensen liked the litany "To the Muslim world ... To those leaders around the globe ... To those who cling to power through corruption ... To the people of poor nations ..." which clearly echoed a similar litany in Kennedy's inaugural address. (Cary 2009)

And yet, one of the big surprises of the speech was in fact that Obama, breaking with his own predilection to doing so, did not include any of the well-known quotations by such great Americans as Abraham Lincoln, Franklin D. Roosevelt, John F. Kennedy, and others. Gerard Baker put it somewhat negatively this way in his comments on "The Speech That Failed to Fly" one day after its delivery in the London *Times*:

> There were few truly memorable pieces of phraseology – no Kennedyesque, or Rooseveltian quotations for the ages.
>
> He [Obama] laboured hard to echo the tone and cadence of his biggest campaign performances. And there was more than a hint of a self-conscious echo – distractingly – of the speeches of his hero and fellow Illinoisan, Abraham Lincoln.
>
> The language in particular sounded decidedly 19th century in parts – all those commands to "know" some or other intent of US policy, all those glancing biblical references.
>
> But it wasn't up to Lincoln's standards – which perhaps is asking too much. In fact, it may not have been really memorable at all. It's unlikely that most people will remember a phrase from it a few weeks from now, let alone a century.
>
> In fairness it was a speech more obviously measured to the practical immensity of the immediate challenges. It was directed at two audiences: a hopeful but anxious one at home, and an uncertain but hopeful one overseas. (Baker 2009)

It is true, I must confess that at first I was also a little dismayed by Obama not having employed any of his "favorite" quotations, many of which have turned into proverbs, to wit Abraham Lincoln's use of "A house divided against itself cannot stand" and "Government of the people, by the people, and for the people," "Frederick Douglass's "Power never concedes without a demand," Franklin D. Roosevelt's "We have nothing to fear but fear itself," John F. Kennedy's "Don't ask what your country can do for you, ask what you can do for your country," etc. Of course, I liked Obama's allusion to Winston S. Churchill's title *The Gathering Storm* (1948) of the first volume of his celebrated six-volume history of *The Second World War* (1948-1954) by speaking of the fact that "every so often, the [presidential] oath is taken amidst gathering clouds and raging storms" (see Sanger 2009). His variation, at the end of the inaugural address, of William Shakespeare's proverbial line "Now is the winter of our discontent" (1594, *Richard III*), popularized by John Steinbeck's last novel *The Winter of Our Discontent* (1961), was clearly also very effective as a follow-up comment to the unexpected and little known quotation of a statement made by George Washington at Valley Forge:

> In the year of America's birth, in the coldest of months, a small band of patriots huddled by dying campfires on the shores of an icy river. The capital was abandoned. The enemy was advancing. The snow was stained with blood. At a moment when the outcome of our revolution was most in doubt, the father of our nation ordered these words to be read to the people:
>
> "Let it be told to the future world ... that in the depth of winter, when nothing but hope and virtue could survive ... that the city and the country, alarmed at one common danger, came forth to meet [it]."
>
> America. In the face of our common dangers, in this winter of our hardship, let us remember these timeless words. With hope and virtue, let us brave once more the icy currents, and endure what storms may come.

This quotation by the father of the American nation marks the beginning of Obama's emotional peroration of his magisterial address that speaks not of the "discontent" of the American people but rather of the "hardship" that they can and will conquer: "Let it be said by our children's children that when we were tested, we refused to let this journey end, that we did not turn back, nor did we falter; and with the eyes fixed on the horizon and God's grace upon us, we carried forth that great gift of freedom and delivered it safely to future generations." This is inaugural speech at its best at the end, and upon reflection I am thoroughly convinced that Barack Obama was wise to finish with Washington's insistence on hope, virtue, and freedom couched not in a quotable phrase but rather in a verbal image of striving towards a better future.

Before moving on to an analysis of the proverbial language of Obama's inaugural address, let me present a few additional comments by journalists and former presidential speechwriters concerning the relationship between rhetoric and content in these remarks. Michael Gerson, who basically wrote George W. Bush's first inaugural address in 2001, was quite harsh in his criticism, claiming that "too many of his [Obama's] words were platitudes" and that "heading into this inaugural address, many expected the speech to be rhetorically masterful but perhaps ideologically shallow. Instead, we heard a speech that was rhetorically flat and substantively interesting. On his first day in office, President Obama has managed to surprise." In fact, Gerson goes on to argue that "like Lincoln or Martin Luther King Jr., Obama positioned himself as a conservative revolutionary – attempting to re-create our country by reasserting the traditional moral principles that gave it birth" (Gerson 2009). I am not certain whether all of these leaders would agree with the "conservative revolutionary" label, but, to look at it positively, it might help Obama to bring more Republican conservatives on board of the changing ship of state.

Tom Brune, writing in *Newsday*, is a bit more balanced in his analysis of the epideictic nature of Obama's speech, stressing in all fairness that the address had to be almost somewhat anti-climactic in view of all the incredible "noise" that the media had created around this event:

> Barack Obama didn't always soar in his inaugural address yesterday, but he scored the points he needed to satisfy the legion of hopeful supporters eagerly listening to the new president here and around the world.
>
> Looking out over a sea of people from the Capitol's west steps on a cold, sunny midday, Obama delivered a confident, almost somber speech, rooted in history and aimed at the future, with the primary themes of responsibility and change.
>
> After all the hype leading up to the ceremony yesterday, Obama's address almost seemed anti-climactic, but it still hit every marker he needed to hit in a strong speech that lasted just about 20 minutes. (Brune 2009)

And here then is a third view, this time from abroad, by Fintan O'Toole of *The Irish Times*, who to my way of thinking hits the proverbial nail on the head with his analysis. Yes, there definitely was a change of Obama's rallying campaign rhetoric with its use of preformulated language based on emotive expressiveness to a more sober and content-rich communicative approach. On January 20, 2009, with the oath of office and the inaugural speech, the candidate and President-elect Barack Obama changed to President Barack Obama, and this giant step is, appropriately so, reflected in a noticeable change of language:

> The shift from candidate to president was obvious to a degree that may have disappointed some of his hearers.
>
> It was not just that Obama's eloquence was less fluent, less dazzling, less of a performance, than the electrifying speeches that previously defined him, the address to the Democratic Party convention in 2004 that marked him out, or the brilliant discourse on race that saved his candidacy last year.
>
> His body language was certainly more constrained, his cadences less dramatic, his rhythms less mesmeric. (O'Toole 2009)

I have to admit that from a purely rhetorical point of view I also was somewhat disappointed with the inaugural address by missing some of the quotations, pseudo-proverbs, proverbs, proverbial phrases and twin formulas that had been the trademark of Obama's writings and speeches. Upon reflection, I came around to thinking that Obama, wanting this speech to be his very own, must have consciously decided to stay away from some of those expected quotations by former presidents and time-worn proverbs. However, I am still wondering why he did not use some of his own phraseological creations from previous speeches that by their structures and metaphors have a good chance to become quotable or proverbial. I referred to such statements as "pseudo-proverbs" in the previous chapter, among them:

"America prospers when all Americans prosper." (128, 133, 156, 157, 163, 217; numbers in parentheses refer to the list of speeches at the end of the book)

"If you invest in America, America will invest in you." (124, 132, 180, 181, 182, 183, 184, 187, 188, 189)

"In America, separate can never be equal." (15, 30, 46, 96)

"Ballot boxes don't make a democracy." (81, 85)

"Countries that out-teach us today will out-compete us tomorrow." (88, 89)

"You can't change direction with a new driver who follows the same old map." (158, 160)

"The government that people count on most is the one that's closest to the people." (125)

"One man cannot make a movement." (91)

"Opportunity doesn't come easy." (90)

"A new politics for a new time." (152)

"We cannot have a thriving Wall Street and a struggling Main Street (while Main Street suffers)." (142, 144, 145, 146, 197, 200, 203, 204)

Obviously not every one of these quotable creations in the form of pseudo-proverbs by Barack Obama would have been suitable for the inaugural address, but his formulation "A new politics for a new time" would have fit, at least in my opinion. As mentioned earlier in this chapter, he had used it in his acceptance speech on "The American Promise" at the Democratic National Convention on August 28, 2008, at Denver, Colorado, with millions of Americans witnessing its creation as they watched and heard Obama on television. Strangely enough, he never used his pseudo-proverb again, and he missed the opportunity to make it into a truly memorable phrase at the time of his inauguration when he said:

That we are in the midst of crisis is now well understood. Our nation is at war, against a far-reaching network of violence and hatred. Our economy is badly weakened, a consequence of greed and irresponsibility on the part of some, but also our collective failure to make hard choices and prepare the nation for a new age. Homes have been lost; jobs shed; businesses shuttered. Our health care is too costly; our schools fail too many; and each day brings further evidence that the ways we use energy strengthen our adversaries and threaten our planet.

At the end of this enumeration, I believe that Barack Obama might well have interspersed his quotable, memorable, and proverb-like invention "A new politics for a new time." I am convinced that critics of the inaugural address would have interpreted its use positively. But instead, Obama moved on with a short but powerful paragraph, employing the first of eighteen proverbs, pseudo-proverbs, and proverbial phrases that are part of this speech:

> These are the indicators of crisis, subject to data and statistics. Less measurable but no less profound is a sapping of confidence across our land – a nagging fear that America's decline is inevitable, and that the next generation must lower its sights. Today I say to you that the challenges we face are real. They are serious and they are many. They will not be met easily or in a short span of time. But know this, America: They will be met. (229)

This is vintage Obama rhetoric, with first applying the negative proverbial phrase "To lower one's sights" and then immediately pushing it aside in favor of meeting the challenges facing the country with courage, hope, and optimism. By now Obama is on a proverbial roll, even though his use of the Biblical phrase "To set aside childish things" (I Corinthians 13,11) and the allusion to the proverb "All men are created equal" and the triad "Life, liberty, and the pursuit of happiness" from the Declaration of Independence are much more subtle than their employment during the campaign:

> We remain a young nation, but in the words of Scripture, the time has come to set aside childish things. The time has come to reaffirm our enduring spirit; to choose our better history; to carry forward that precious gift, that noble idea, passed on from generation to generation: the God-given promise that all are equal, all are free, and all deserve a chance to pursue their full measure of happiness. (229)

It is here where I can show that Barack Obama consciously tuned down his use of quotations and proverbs as he was gearing up for his inaugural address. It will be remembered that three days before his inauguration, on Saturday, January 17, 2009, Barack Obama and Joe Biden and their families embarked on a whistle-stop train trip from Philadelphia to Washington, in part retracing the trip that Abraham Lincoln had taken to his inauguration. In two basically identical speeches at Philadelphia and Baltimore on that day Obama said:

> And yet, they [early patriots] were willing to put all they were and all they had on the line – their lives, their fortunes and their sacred honor – for a set of ideals that continue to light the world. That we are equal. That our rights to life, liberty and the pursuit of happiness come not from our laws, but from our maker. And that government of, by and for the people can endure. It was these ideals that led us to declare independence and craft our constitution, producing documents that were imperfect but had within them, like our nation itself, the capacity to be made more perfect. (226, 227)

Already here he has changed the proverb "All men are created equal" to the shorter and gender-free statement "We are all equal." However, he still maintains the proverbial triad "Life, liberty, and the pursuit of happiness," and he also at least alludes to the proverbial definition of democracy by stating that "government of, by and for the people can endure." Personally I wish he would not have dropped this proverb in its shortened form. In fact, I think this entire paragraph with its reference to making the union more perfect is better formulated than its counterpart in the inaugural address. But I can also understand Barack Obama's predicament. He clearly was working on his whistle-stop and inaugural speech at the same time, and he did not want to have them be identical! So he edited a bit more, weakening his key address ever so slightly from a rhetorical and proverbial vantage point.

But to return to the speech at hand, Obama next turns to a major theme of his, i.e., the basic greatness of the American nation. And it is here where he includes the statement "Greatness is never a given. It must be earned" that in its wording, form, and structure is memorable and that consequently might, in due time, find its way into quotation dictionaries:

> In reaffirming the greatness of our nation, we understand that greatness is never a given. It must be earned. Our journey has never been one of shortcuts or settling for less. It has not been the path for the fainthearted – for those who prefer leisure over work, or seek only the pleasures of riches and fame. Rather it has been the risk-takers, the doers, the makers of things – some celebrated, but more often men and women obscure in their labor – who have carried us up the long, rugged path toward prosperity and freedom. (229)

Using such favorite words as "struggle" and "work," Obama continues to argue that America and its people need to be steadfast in dealing with the socioeconomic crisis at hand, once again amassing three proverbial phrases, namely "To stand pat," "To pick oneself up," and "To dust oneself off," thereby adding some colloquial color to his plea:

> This is the journey we continue today. We remain the most prosperous, powerful nation on Earth. Our workers are no less productive than when this crisis began. Our minds are no less inventive, our goods and services no less needed than they were last week or last month or last year. Our capacity remains undiminished. But our time of standing pat, of protecting narrow interests and putting off unpleasant decisions – that time has surely passed. Starting today, we must pick ourselves up, dust ourselves off, and begin again the work of remaking America. (229)

Not being a poker player, I must admit that I did not know the phrase "To stand pat" with the meaning of "to stick by a decision, to refuse to budge" (Wilkinson 1993, 486). Obama, on the other hand, appears to be well versed in the phrases relating to this card game, as can be seen from his use of the expression "To maintain a poker face" in his autobiography *Dreams from My Father* (1995): "Roy maintained a poker face, as if the conversation didn't concern him. Both he and Amy had the sheen of too many beers, and I saw Jane sneak an anxious look at Kezia. I decided to change the subject, and asked Zeituni if she'd been to Garden Square before" (D,363). The *New York Times* columnist and former speechwriter for President Richard Nixon, William Safire, in his quite negative review of this speech – "[it] fell short of the anticipated immortality" – includes a fascinating comment regarding the idea of standing pat that plays off the first name of Pat Nixon:

> He [Obama] got into good rhythm with a cheer-up paragraph, reminding us of America's productive workers and inventive minds, our capacity undiminished, setting up his warning against "standing pat." (I once wrote a line for Nixon, "America cannot stand pat," which got a glare from the First Lady – we never used the phrase again.) Obama topped that passage with a warmly familiar metaphor: "Starting today, we must pick ourselves up, dust ourselves off, and begin again the work of remaking America." That worked. (Safire 2009)

Great comment by the acute language observer William Safire! Yet, he does not know everything, for that "warmly familiar metaphor," which I had identified as a combination of the two proverbial phrases "To pick oneself up" and "To dust oneself off," is actually two lines from "a Hollywood musical," as the unsigned editorial "Inaugural Address Sounds Notes of Optimism and Reality" in the *Los Angeles Times* reminded its readers (Editorial 2009). When I asked our administrative assistant Janet Sobieski of the Department of German and Russian at the University of Vermont about these lines and a possible song, she recalled it instantly and subsequently located it by way of a Google search. The song is in fact called "Pick Yourself Up" (lyrics by Dorothy Fields, music by Jerome Kern) and was part of the film *Swing Time* (1936), staring Fred Astaire and Ginger Rogers. The following four stanzas appear twice in the popular song:

> Nothing's impossible I have found,
> For when my chin is on the ground,
> I pick myself up,
> Dust myself off,
> Start all over again.
>
> Don't lose your confidence if you slip,
> Be grateful for a pleasure trip,
> And pick yourself up,
> Dust yourself off,
> Start all over again.

> Work like a soul inspired,
> Till the battle of the day is won.
> You may be sick and tired,
> But you'll be a man, my son!
>
> Will you remember the famous men,
> Who had to fail to rise again?
> So take a deep breath,
> Pick yourself up,
> Dust yourself off,
> Start all over again.

For the record, there was also Jeff Shesol, deputy speechwriter for President Bill Clinton, who should have done a bit more checking before writing the following comment a few hours after President Obama finished his address:

> The speech was well written, structured and paced. To the credit of Mr. Obama and his speechwriters [he basically wrote it himself!], there was no swinging for the rhetorical fences. They did not yield to temptation. They did not strain to etch a new line in granite somewhere or in Bartlett's [*Familiar Quotations*] or the collective memory. Perhaps as a result, there were memorable passages but few memorable phrases. What appears (at least for now) to be the most quoted line was one of the most colloquial: "pick ourselves up, dust ourselves off" may not be poetry, but it well describes a nation that's been knocked to the ground and kicked around for eight years. (Shesol 2009)

These well-known lines by the American songwriter Dorothy Field (1905-1974), with famous songs like "On the Sunny Side of the Street" (1930) and "I'm in the Mood for Love" (1935) to her credit, have still not made it into the most recent edition of John Bartlett's *Familiar Quotations* (2002), but Fred Shapiro's exquisite new *Yale Book of Quotations* (2006) does finally include several memorable lines from four of her songs – alas not yet from the "Pick Yourself Up" lyrics (Shapiro 2006, 255-256). Now that Barack Obama has revitalized the lines by changing "yourself" to the more inclusive "ourselves," new editions of Bartlett, Shapiro, and other quotation dictionaries are bound to list them. The new "proverb" might even become associated with Barack Obama's name just as the "Government of, by, and for the people" will forever be linked with Abraham Lincoln. Jeff Shesol is certainly correct in claiming that Obama's slightly modified lines from Dorothy Field are already the most frequently cited from his inaugural address (see Brune 2009; Cary 2009; Stewart 2009).

But speaking of quotable passages in President Obama's inaugural address, I would think that his statement "[It] is not whether our government is too big or too small, but whether it works" might reach a certain currency, even though it appears to be somewhat of a rephrasing of President Ronald Reagan's famous maxim that Obama quotes in *The Audacity of Hope* (2006): "Or, as Ronald Reagan succinctly put it: 'Government is not the solution to our problem; government is the problem'" (H,147). In any case, here is Obama's own formulation in context:

> What the cynics fail to understand is that the ground has shifted beneath them – that the stale political arguments that have consumed us for so long no longer apply. The question we ask today is not whether our government is too big or too small, but whether it works – whether it helps families find jobs at a decent wage, care they can afford, a retirement that is dignified. Where the answer is yes, we intend to move forward. Where the answer is no, programs will end. And those of us who manage the public's dollars will be held to account – to spend wisely, reform bad habits, and do our business in the light of day – because only then can we restore the vital trust between a people and their government. (229)

It is interesting to note that Obama adds the proverbial metaphor "To do something in the light of day" at the end of this paragraph to underscore his intent of conducting the nation's business in a fair and open fashion. No matter how pragmatic or philosophical his remarks might be, he usually resorts to some fixed phrase to add an easily understood image to his rhetoric.

And he strikes an impressive balance between quotable statements in the form of his own pseudo-proverbs and traditional folk expressions. Consequently, he continues with a well formulated paragraph that includes yet another statement that could catch on in common political parlance, namely "A nation cannot prosper long when it favors only the prosperous":

> Nor is the question before us whether the market is a force for good or ill. Its power to generate wealth and expand freedom is unmatched, but this crisis has reminded us that without a watchful eye, the market can spin out of control – and that a nation cannot prosper long when it favors only the prosperous. The success of our economy has always depended not just on the size of our gross domestic product, but on the reach of our prosperity; on our ability to extend opportunity to every willing heart – not out of charity, but because it is the surest route to our common good. (229)

Let me here return one more time to William Safire, who agrees with my assessment of this quotable statement, and who also mentions a number of other proverbial utterances by Obama that I wish to comment upon as well:

> To his oratorical credit, the president did not strain for quotable quotes. "A nation cannot prosper when it favors only the prosperous" was a nice insertion with an eye toward Bartlett's, and I liked "the lines of tribe shall soon dissolve," though it is not in the league with "the mystic chords of memory" [in the last paragraph of Lincoln's first inaugural address of March 4, 1861]. Obama's "know that you are on the wrong side of history" message to Muslim extremists concluded with "we will extend a hand

if you are willing to unclench your fist"; that is quotable if it is original, but I think I've seen it before. His "this winter of our hardship" is a well-turned phrase about discontent, even if not as Shakespeare punned it, "made glorious summer by this sun of York." (Safire 2009)

First of all, I actually think that President Obama strained at least a bit "for quotable quotes," especially since he knew very well that his entire audience – from general citizen to erudite scholar – wanted him to deliver at least two or three memorable phrases! For example, Safire misses an incredibly important statement in the very paragraph that he is discussing, namely "People will judge you on what you can build, not what you can destroy." The audience liked this pseudo-proverb, and they also could relate to Obama's extension of the proverbial phrase "To be on the wrong side" to include human history in general:

> To the Muslim world, we seek a new way forward, based on mutual interest and mutual respect. To those leaders around the globe who seek to sow conflict, or blame their society's ills on the West: Know that your people will judge you on what you can build, not what you destroy. To those who cling to power through corruption and deceit and the silencing of dissent, know that you are on the wrong side of history; but that we will extend a hand if you are willing to unclench your fist. (229)

Regarding the other memorable sentence in this "loaded" proverbial paragraph, i.e., "We will extend a hand if you are willing to unclench your fist," I have to admit that my comprehensive search in numerous dictionaries of quotations and also on the internet have not resulted in any identification of an earlier use. Thus, at least for now, my conclusion is that Obama has simply taken the proverbial phrase "To extend a hand to someone" (see speeches 141, 176, 179) and expanded it by the somatic image of an "unclenched fist" into a memorable statement.

And how about Obama's sententious "The world has changed, and we must change with it" that summarizes his entire presidential campaign for change in one sentence that he had not used before? This formulaic phrase might also be remembered:

> To the people of poor nations, we pledge to work alongside you to make your farms flourish and let clean waters flow; to nourish starved bodies and feed hungry minds. And to those nations like ours that enjoy relative plenty, we say we can no longer afford indifference to suffering outside our borders; nor can we consume the world's resources without regard to effect. For the world has changed, and we must change with it. (229)

Of course, the necessity for change was always just one side of the equation in the struggle for progress, as far as Obama is concerned. The other side is clearly the return to a solid value system based on rigorous work ethics, where all Americans give their proverbial all to perfect the union and by extension the world:

> Our challenges might be new. The instruments with which we meet them may be new. But those values upon which our success depends – hard work and honesty, courage and fair play, tolerance and curiosity, loyalty and patriotism – these things are old. These things are true. They have been the quiet force of progress throughout our history. What is demanded then is a return to these truths. What is required of us now is a new era of responsibility – a recognition, on the part of every American, that we have duties to ourselves, our nation and the world; duties that we do not grudgingly accept but rather seize gladly, firm in the knowledge that there is nothing so satisfying to the spirit, so defining of our character, than giving our all to a difficult task. This is the price and the promise of citizenship. (229)

That last sentence is a fitting reminiscence of Barack Obama's frequent use of that seemingly so mundane proverbial expression "To pay a (the) price for something" that he cites twenty-nine times in his books and speeches. One of these appears in his book *The Audacity of Hope*, where Obama uses the phrase in connection with his hero Abraham Lincoln having done his utmost to save a house divided and to perfect the union through ethical struggle: "Lincoln, and those buried at Gettysburg, remind us that we should pursue our own absolute truths only if we acknowledge that there may be a terrible price to pay" (H,98). This severe statement would not have been in the spirit of an epideictic inaugural address, in which the new President of the United States wants to be positive and optimistic. By relying on quotable new pseudo-proverbs of his own and traditional proverbs as well as proverbial phrases, Obama followed in the footsteps of previous presidents, as I have shown in my study "'It's Not a President's Business to Catch Flies': Proverbial Rhetoric in Presidential Inaugural Addresses" (Mieder 2005, 147-186). And uplifting as this speech and other major addresses might have been in language and content, Obama's political rhetoric is characterized by such important ingredients as "'practical wisdom,' 'practical knowledge,' 'practical reason,' [and] 'practical judgment'" that are part of quotations and proverbs in particular (Nichols 1996, 687). With his most recent address behind him, President Barack Obama has once again illustrated that proverbial language is a significant part of the inauguration of the presidents of the United States. Quotations, pseudo-proverbs, proverbs, and proverbial phrases certainly do their metaphorical part in making the inaugural addresses "timeless words," to use two final words from President Barack Obama's memorable inaugural address. But, as I have tried to show in this study on the president's proverbial rhetoric, such folk speech together with innovative variations and new formulations assures a colorful, meaningful, and comprehensible communication with the American people.

PERSONAL POSTSCRIPT

It might be recalled that I finished my first chapter with a postscript that includes a letter that I had written to then presidential candidate Barack Obama. Well, as the President-elect was approaching the time of his inauguration, I decided to write to him once again on December 10, 2008, primarily to send him a copy of my book *The Proverbial Abraham Lincoln* (2000) and also to encourage him to write his very own inaugural address. As expected perhaps, he never received my letter or my book. They were returned unopened with the following comment taped on the outside of my original package: "Thank you for your interest in sharing this parcel with President-elect Obama. Unfortunately, to enhance security and aid in compliance, we are unable to accept gifts or packages. In addition, the campaign is no longer able to process constituent mail. To contact the Obama-Biden Presidential Transition, please go to: http://change.gov/page/content/cointact/. Sincerely, Obama for America Operations Team." Obviously I was once again disappointed that my mail did not reach Barack Obama, especially since he admires Abraham Lincoln so much. But as the proverb says, "All good things come in threes," and so I will try again when this book on his own proverbial rhetoric will appear in print. Perhaps one of our only three congressional delegates from Vermont – Senator Patrick Leahy, Senator Bernie Sanders, and Representative Peter Welsh – will be able to deliver the book to President Barack Obama. In any case, here then is my letter:

December 10, 2008

Dear President-elect Barack Obama,

A few months ago, on April 17, 2008, I had the audacity to write to you and also send you a copy of my book *Proverbs Are the Best Policy: Folk Wisdom and American Politics* (Logan, Utah: Utah State University Press, 2005). On May 12, 2008, you answered with a most kind form letter, and I certainly appreciated this response. Obviously I am aware of the fact that you receive literally thousands of messages each day. In any case, I am attaching a copy of my letter for you once again, wishing to remind you also that my book includes a chapter (pp. 147-186) on all the inaugural speeches of American presidents. You might find this chapter of interest as you prepare your first inaugural address. I can hardly wait to hear it and comparing it to all the others from a rhetorical point of view. I told my students that I hope that you will write it completely alone without the assistance of your staff. You are such a superb master of the English language, and it would be absolutely fantastic if you and we could say that this is your very own speech!

I would venture the guess that you will mention Abraham Lincoln in your inaugural address, perhaps also Frederick Douglass and Dr. Martin Luther King.

They are clearly three of your heroes, and I can honestly tell you that we share this respect and admiration for these three great Americans. You will ever more be mentioned together with them, and there is no doubt in my mind that you deserve this honor.

Knowing that you enjoy reading Abraham Lincoln's works and also books about him, I would like to send you my book on this great American president who will be smiling down on you on January 20th. Lincoln, just like you, was a master linguist and rhetorician, and I think that you might find some of the utterances included in my book most meaningful.

Suffice it to tell you that I am currently hard at work on a book similar to my enclosed Lincoln book that studies your proverbial rhetoric in your two books, your speeches, interviews, radio addresses, etc. Once you have given your inaugural address, I will finish my study and hope that the book will appear in print in the summer. It will be a pleasure and honor at that time to send you a copy, and perhaps you will place it on your shelf next to *The Proverbial Abraham Lincoln*. You belong next to Lincoln, and people everywhere will mention both of you together more and more.

Here is wishing you and your wonderful family the very best for the coming years as you serve this country as its President and the world as a person bringing hope for a better life everywhere. Good luck with your inaugural speech – it will be your proverbial best!

Sincerely yours,

Prof. Wolfgang Mieder

List OF Publications AND Speeches

References from printed publications have been identified throughout the book by a letter and page number in parentheses. Speeches, news conferences, interviews, and radio addresses are followed by a simple number in parentheses that refers to this list with precise dates, places, and titles. These oral communications were located on the following websites:

http://www.obama.senate.gov/
http://www.barack.obama.com/
http://www.obamaspeeches.com/

LIST OF PUBLICATIONS

O = "Why Organize? Problems and Promise in the Inner City." In Peg Knoepfle (ed.), *After Alinsky: Community Organizing in Illinois*. Springfield, Illinois: Sangamon State University, 1990. 35-40 (roundtable discussion with remarks by Barack Obama on pp. 123-152). This essay was first published in August/September 1988 in *Illinois Issues*.

D = *Dreams from My Father. A Story of Race and Inheritance*. New York: Three Rivers Press, 2004 (originally published 1995).

L = "What I See in Lincoln's Eyes." *Time Magazine* (June 27, 2005), p. 74.

H = *The Audacity of Hope. Thoughts on Reclaiming the American Dream*. New York: Three Rivers Press, 2006.

B = Rogak, Lisa (ed.). *Barack Obama in His Own Words*. New York: Carroll & Graf, 2007. (A collection of short quotations from 2002 to 2007).

W = (editor not listed!). *Barack Obama. What He Believes in From His Own Works. Resolutions and Bills Sponsored & Co-Sponsored by Senator Barack Obama During the 110th Session (First Half) of the U.S. Congress January 4, 2007 to December 19, 2007*. Rockville, Maryland: Arc Manor, 2008. (A collection of actual documents).

LIST OF SPEECHES, NEWS CONFERENCES, INTERVIEWS, AND RADIO ADDRESSES

2002

1. October 2, 2002, Chicago, Illinois: Speech against the war with Iraq.

2004

2. July, 27, 2004, Boston, Massachusetts: Speech at the Democratic National Convention.

2005

3. February 21, 2005, Washington, D.C.: John Lewis's 65th birthday gala.
4. February 28, 2005, Washington, D.C.: Floor statement in the U.S. Senate on the Bankruptcy Abuse and Prevention Act of 2005.
5. March 8, 2005, Silicon Valley, California: Remarks at TechNet.
6. March 11, 2005, no place listed: CURE keynote address.
7. March 28, 2005, Washington, D.C.: Remarks to the American Legion legislative rally.
8. April 11, 2005, Washington, D.C.: Remarks at the Herblock Foundation annual lecture.
9. April 11, 2005, Washington, D.C.: Opening statement at the confirmation hearing of John Bolton.
10. April 13, 2005, Washington, D.C.: Floor statement in the U.S. Senate on the nuclear option.
11. April 14, 2005, Washington, D.C.: Floor statement in the U.S. Senate about his amendment to Provide Meals and Phone Service to Wounded Veterans.

12. April 20, 2005, Springfield, Illinois: Remarks at the opening of the Abraham Lincoln Presidential Library and Museum.
13. April 23, 2005, Carbondale, Illinois: SIUC College of Agriculture's 50th anniversary.
14. April 26, 2005, Washington, D.C.: Remarks at the National Press Club: "A Hope to Fulfill."
15. May 1, 2005, Detroit, Michigan: Remarks at the NAACP Fight for Freedom Fund Dinner.
16. May 7, 2005, Rockford, Illinois: Remarks at the *Rockford Register Star* Young American Awards.
17. May 26, 2005, Washington, D.C.: Remarks about America's nuclear non-proliferation policy.
18. May 30, 2005, Elwood, Illinois: Remarks at the Abraham Lincoln National Cemetery.
19. June 4, 2005, Galesburg, Illinois: Remarks at the Knox College commencement.
20. June 8, 2005, Washington, D.C.: Remarks on the nomination of Justice Janice Rogers Brown.
21. June 10, 2005, Chicago, Illinois: Remarks at the Pritzker School of Medicine commencement.
22. June 27, 2005, no place listed: Addressing the American Library Association: "Literacy and Education in a 21st-Century Economy."
23. July 16, 2005, Springfield, Illinois: Remarks at the American Legion conference.
24. July 19, 2005, Washington, D.C.: Remarks on the Foreign Operations Appropriation Bill and the Avian Flu.
25. July 25, 2005, Chicago, Illinois: Remarks at the AFL-CIO National Convention.
26. September 15, 2005, Washington, D.C.: Speech on "Securing Our Energy Future."
27. September 22, 2005, Washington, D.C.: Remarks on the confirmation of Judge John Roberts.
28. October 18, 2005, Washington, D.C.: Floor statement in the U.S. Senate on the Avian Flu.
29. October 25, 2005, Washington, D.C.: Floor statement in the U.S. Senate on the death of Rosa Parks.
30. October 25, 2005, no place listed: Speech at the Center for American Progress on "Teaching Our Kids in a 21st-Century Economy."
31. October 27, 2005, Washington, D.C.: Floor statement in the U.S. Senate on the Chicago White Sox.

32. November 1, 2005, Washington, D.C.: Speech at the Council on Foreign Relations on "Non-Proliferation and Russia: The Challenges Ahead."
33. November 9, 2005, Washington, D.C.: Remarks at the Kaiser Family Foundation regarding the "Sex on TV 4" report.
34. November 10, 2005, Washington, D.C.: Remarks at the National Women's Law Center.
35. November 16, 2005, Washington, D.C.: Remarks at the Robert F. Kennedy Human Rights Award Ceremony.
36. November 22, 2005, Chicago, Illinois: Speech at the Chicago Council on Foreign Relations on "Moving Forward in Iraq."
37. December 15, 2005, Washington, D.C.: Floor statement in the U.S. Senate on the "Patriot Act."

2006

38. January 26, 2006, Washington, D.C.: Floor statement in the U.S. Senate on the confirmation of Judge Samuel Alito, Jr.
39. January 26, 2006, Washington D.C.: Remarks at the Lobbying Reform Summit.
40. February 1, 2006, Washington, D.C.: Floor statement in the U.S. Senate on the Hurricane Katrina Child Assistance Amendment.
41. February 9, 2006, Washington, D.C.: Opening statement at the Foreign Relations Committee regarding Lugar-Obama legislation S.1949.
42. February 16, 2006, Washington, D.C.: Floor statement in the U.S. Senate on S.2271 – USA Patriot Act Reauthorization.
43. February 28, 2006, Washington, D.C.: Speech for the Governor's [Governors'?]Ethanol Coalition on "Energy Security Is National Security."
44. March 7, 2006, Washington, D.C.: Opening floor statement in the U.S. Senate on the debate on ethics reform.
45. March 8, 2006, Washington, D.C.: Floor statement in the U.S. Senate on the Meals Amendment.
46. March 13, 2006, Chicago, Illinois: Speech on "21st Century Schools for a 21st Century Economy."
47. April 3, 2006, Washington, D.C.: Floor statement in the U.S. Senate on immigration reform.
48. April 3, 2006, Chicago, Illinois: Speech on "Energy Dependence and the Safety of Our Planet."

49. May 2, 2006, Washington, D.C.: Floor statement in the U.S. Senate on his Amendment to Stop No-Bid Contracts for Gulf Coast Recovery and Reconstruction.
50. May 11, 2006, Washington, D.C.: Remarks at Emily's List annual luncheon.
51. May 20, 2006, Springfield, Illinois: Southern Illinois University of Medicine commencement address.
52. May 23, 2006, Washington, D.C.: Floor statement in the U.S. Senate on his Employment Verification Amendment for the Immigration Bill.
53. May 24, 2006, Washington, D.C.: Floor statement in the U.S. Senate in opposition to the Amendment Requiring a Photo ID to Vote.
54. May 25, 2006, Washington, D.C.: Floor statement in the U.S. Senate concerning the General Michael Hayden nomination.
55. June 2, 2006, Amherst, Massachusetts: University of Massachusetts commencement address.
56. June 5, 2006, Washington, D.C.: Floor statement in the U.S. Senate on the Federal Marriage Amendment.
57. June 14, 2006, Washington, D.C.: Speech on "Take Back America."
58. June 16, 2006, Evanston, Illinois: Northwestern University commencement address.
59. June 21, 2006, Washington, D.C.: Floor statement in the U.S. Senate on Iraq Debate.
60. June 28, 2006, Washington, D.C.: June 28, 2006: "Call to Renewal" keynote address.
61. July 12, 2006, Washington, D.C.: Remarks at the Campus Progress annual conference.
62. July 17, 2006, Washington, D.C.: Floor statement in the U.S. Senate in support for Stem Cell Research.
63. July 20, 2006, Washington, D.C.: Floor statement in support of H.R. 9, the Voting Rights Act.
64. August 1, 2006, Washington D.C.: Statement on his vote against the Gulf of Mexico Energy Bill.
65. August 7, 2006, Chicago, Illinois: Remarks at the AFSCME national convention.
66. August 11, 2006, New Orleans, Louisiana: Xavier University commencement address.
67. August 28, 2006, Nairobi, Kenya: Speech at the University of Nairobi on "An Honest Government, A Hopeful Future."

68. September 27, 2006, Washington, D.C.: Floor statement in the U.S. Senate on the Habeas Corpus Amendment.
69. September 28, 2006, Washington, D.C.: Floor statement in the U.S. Senate on the Military Commission Legislation.
70. November 13, 2006, no place given: Remarks at the Dr. Martin Luther King Jr. National Memorial groundbreaking ceremony.
71. November 20, 2006, Chicago, Illinois: Speech at the Chicago Council on Global Affairs on "A Way Forward in Iraq."
72. December 1, 2006, Lake Forest, California: Speech at the Global Summit on Aids and the Church on "Race Against Time."

2007

73. January 19, 2007, Washington, D.C.: Floor statement in the U.S. Senate on President's decision to increase troops in Iraq.
74. January 25, 2007, Washington, D.C.: Speech at the Families USA Conference on "The Time Has Come for Universal Health Care."
75. January 30, 2007, Washington, D.C.: Floor statement in the U.S. Senate on the Iraq War De-escalation Act of 2007.
76. February 10, 2007, Springfield, Illinois: Announcement of candidacy for the presidency of the United States.
77. March 2, 2007, Chicago, Illinois: Remarks at the AIPAC Policy Forum.
78. March 8, 2007, Washington, D.C.: Floor statement in the U.S. Senate on Latin America.
79. March 13, 2007, Washington, D.C.: Floor statement in the U.S. Senate on New Leadership Resolution on Iraq.
80. March 15, 2007, Washington, D.C.: Floor statement in the U.S. Senate on Zimbabwe.
81. March 21, 2007, Washington, D.C.: Floor statement in the U.S. Senate on the Iraq War.
82. June 6, 2007, Washington, D.C.: Floor statement in the U.S. Senate on an amendment to the Immigration Reform Bill.
83. July 15, 2007, Chicago, Illinois: Remarks on Chicago violence.
84. July 26, 2007, Columbia, South Carolina: Speech at the University of South Carolina on "College Democrats of America."
85. August 1, 2007, Washington, D.C.: Speech at the Wilson Center on "The War We Need to Win."
86. August 2, 2007, Washington, D.C.: Floor statement in the U.S. Senate on the need of ethics reform.

87. August 21, 2007, Kansas City, Missouri: Speech to the Veterans of Foreign Wars of the United States on "A Sacred Trust."

88. September 3, 2007, Manchester, New Hampshire: Remarks at a Labor Day rally.

89. September 17, 2007, New York, New York: Speech on "Our Common Stake in America's Prosperity."

90. September 18, 2007, Washington, D.C.: Speech on "Tax Fairness for the Middle Class."

91. September 28, 2007, Washington, D.C.: Remarks at the Howard University convocation.

92. October 2, 2007, Chicago, Illinois: Speech on "A New Beginning."

93. November 2, 2007, Manning, South Carolina: Speech on "A Challenge for Our Times."

94. November 3, 2007, Spartanburg, South Carolina: Speech on "A Change We Can Believe In."

95. November 7, 2007, Bettendorf, Iowa: Speech on "Reclaiming the American Dream."

96. November 20, 2007, Manchester, New Hampshire: Speech on "Our Kids, Our Future."

97. December 18, 2007, Des Moines, Iowa: Speech on "Foreign Policy."

2008

98. January 3, 2008, Des Moines, Iowa: Victory speech on Iowa Caucus Night.

99. January 20, 2008, Atlanta, Georgia: Speech on "The Great Need of the Hour."

100. January 26, 2008, Columbia, South Carolina: Primary victory speech.

101. January 28, 2008, Washington, D.C.: Remarks at Kennedy endorsement event.

102. January 28, 2008, Washington, D.C.: Response to President Bush's State of the Union Address.

103. January 29, 2008, El Dorado, Kansas: Speech on "Reclaiming the American Dream."

104. January 30, 2008, Denver, Colorado: Speech on "The Past Versus the Future."

105. February 13, 2008, Janesville, Wisconsin: Speech on "Keeping America's Promise."

106. March 4, 2008, San Antonio, Texas: Remarks on March 4th primary night.

107. March 18, 2008, Philadelphia, Pennsylvania: Speech on "A More Perfect Union."
108. March 20, 2008, Charleston, West Virginia: Speech on "The Cost of War."
109. March 27, 2008, New York, New York: Speech on "Renewing the American Economy."
110. April 4, 2008, Fort Wayne, Indiana: Speech on "Remembering Dr. Martin Luther King, Jr."
111. April 10, 2008, Gary, Indiana: Remarks on the economy.
112. April 22, 2008, Evansville, Indiana: Remarks on Pennsylvania primary night.
113. May 6, 2008, Raleigh, North Carolina: Primary victory speech.
114. May 12, 2008, Charleston, West Virginia: Remarks to veterans.
115. May 20, 2008, Des Moines, Iowa: Speech on "Forging a New Future for America."
116. May 25, 2008, Middletown, Connecticut: Wesleyan University commencement address.
117. May 26, 2008, Las Cruces, New Mexico: Remarks on Memorial Day.
118. June 2, 2008, Troy, Michigan: Remarks at Troy High School.
119. June 3, 2008, St. Paul, Minnesota: Remarks on the final primary night.
120. June 4, 2008, Washington, D.C.: Remarks at the AIPAC Policy Conference.
121. June 5, 2008, Bristol, Virginia: Remarks at a town hall event concerning health care.
122. June 9, 2008, Raleigh, North Carolina: Speech on "Change That Works for You."
123. June 15, 2008, Chicago, Illinois: Remarks at the Apostolic Church of God.
124. June 16, 2008, Flint, Michigan: Speech on "Renewing American Competitiveness."
125. June 21, 2008, Miami, Florida: Speech on "A Metropolitan Strategy for America's Future."
126. June 23, 2008, Albuquerque, New Mexico: Remarks on working women.
127. June 24, 2008, Las Vegas, Nevada: Speech on "A Serious Energy Policy for Our Future."
128. June 28, 2008, Washington, D.C.: Remarks to the National Association of Latino Elected and Appointed Officials.

129. June 30, 2008, Independence, Missouri: Speech on "The America We Love."
130. July 1, 2008, Zanesville, Ohio: Remarks to the Council for Faith-Based and Neighborhood Partnerships.
131. July 3, 2008, Fargo, North Dakota: Remarks to veterans.
132. July 7, 2008, St. Louis, Missouri: Speech on "An Agenda for Middle-Class Success."
133. July 8, 2008, Washington, D.C.: Remarks to the League of United Latin American Citizens.
134. July 10, 2008, New York, New York: Remarks at a joint event with Senator Hillary Clinton.
135. July 10, 1008, Fairfax, Virginia: Remarks at a town hall event concerning women's economic security.
136. July 11, 2008, Dayton, Ohio: Speech on "A Secure Energy Future."
137. July 13, 2008, Chicago, Illinois: Remarks at the 80th Convention of the American Federation of Teachers.
138. July 14, 2008, Cincinnati, Ohio: Remarks at the 99th Annual Convention of the NAACP.
139. July 15, 2008, Washington, D.C.: Speech on "A New Strategy for a New World."
140. July 16, 2008, West Lafayette, Indiana: Remarks at the Summit on Confronting New Threats.
141. July 24, 2008, Berlin, Germany: Speech on "A World That Stands as One."
142. July 30, 2008, Springfield, Missouri: Remarks at a town hall event concerning the economy.
143. July 31, 2008, Cedar Rapids, Iowa: Remarks at a town hall event concerning energy.
144. August 1, 2008, St. Petersburg, Florida: Remarks at a town hall event concerning the economy.
145. August 2, 2008, Orlando, Florida: Remarks to the Urban League.
146. August 2, 2008, Titusville, Florida: Remarks at a town hall event on the economy.
147. August 4, 2008, Lansing, Michigan: Speech on "New Energy for America."
148. August 5, 2008, Youngstown, Ohio: Remarks at a town hall event concerning energy.
149. August 6, 2008, Elkhart, Indiana: Remarks at a town hall event concerning energy.

150. August 19, 2008, Orlando, Florida: Remarks at the VFW National Convention.

151. August 23, 2008, Springfield, Illinois: Announcement of Senator Joe Biden as his Vice Presidential running mate.

152. August 28, 2008, Denver, Colorado: Acceptance speech for the presidency of the United States on "The American Promise" at the Democratic National Convention.

153. September 6, 2008, no place given: Remarks at the AARP Life@50+ National Expo.

154. September 10, 2008, Washington, D.C.: Remarks at the Congressional Hispanic Caucus Institute Gala.

155. September 12, 2008, Dover, New Hampshire: Speech "On Taxes."

156. September 16, 2008, Golden, Colorado: Speech on "Confronting an Economic Crisis."

157. September 17, 2008, Elko, Nevada: Speech on "The Change We Need."

158. September 18, 2008, Espanola, New Mexico: Remarks on the economy and need for change.

159. September 19, 2008, Miami, Florida: Remarks on the Fed/Treasury Plan.

160. September 20, 2008, Daytona Beach, Florida: Remarks on the economy and need for change.

161. September 21, 2008, Charlotte, North Carolina: Remarks on the economy and need for change.

162. September 23, 2008, Tampa, Florida: Remarks on a plan to protect taxpayers and homeowners.

163. September 24, 2008, Dunedin, Florida: Remarks on the economy and other issues facing America.

164. September 25, 2008, New York, New York: Speech on "The Clinton Global Initiative."

165. September 27, 2008, Greensboro, North Carolina: Remarks on the economy and other issues facing America.

166. September 28, 2008, Detroit, Michigan: Remarks on the economy and other issues facing America.

167. September 29, 2008, Westminster, Colorado: Remarks on the economy and other issues facing America.

168. September 30, 2008, Reno, Nevada: Remarks on the economy and other issues facing America.

169. October 1, 2008, La Crosse, Wisconsin: Remarks on the economy and other issues facing America.

170. October 2, 2008, Grand Rapids, Michigan: Remarks on the economy and other issues facing America.
171. October 3, 2008, Abington, Pennsylvania: Remarks on the economy and other issues facing America.
172. October 4, 2008, Newport News, Virginia: Speech on "Health Care."
173. October 5, 2008, Asheville, North Carolina: Remarks on the economy and other issues facing America.
174. October 8, 2008, Indianapolis, Indiana: Remarks on the economy and other issues facing America.
175. October 9, 2008, Dayton, Ohio: Remarks on the economy and other issues facing America.
176. October 10, 2008, Chillicothe, Ohio: Remarks on the economy and other issues facing America.
177. October 11, 2008, Philadelphia, Pennsylvania: Remarks on the economy and other issues facing America.
178. October 13, 2008, Toledo, Ohio: Speech on "A Rescue Plan for the Middle-Class."
179. October 15, 2008, Londonderry, New Hampshire: Remarks on the economy and other issues facing America.
180. October 17, 2008, Roanoke, Virginia: Remarks on the economy and other issues facing America.
181. October 18, 2008, St. Louis, Missouri: Remarks on the economy and other issues facing America.
182. October 19, 2008, Fayetteville, North Carolina: Remarks on the economy and other issues facing America.
183. October 20, 2008, Tampa Bay, Florida: Remarks on the economy and other issues facing America.
184. October 21, 2008, Miami, Florida: Remarks on the economy and other issues facing America.
185. October 21, 2008, Lake Worth, Florida: Remarks at the Growing American Jobs Summit.
186. October 22, 2008, Richmond, Virginia: Speech on "National Security Avail."
187. October 22, 2008, Richmond, Virginia: Remarks on the economy and other issues facing America.
188. October 23, 2008, Indianapolis, Indiana: Remarks on the economy and other issues facing America.
189. October 25, 2008, Reno, Nevada: Remarks on the economy and other issues facing America.

190. October 27, 2008, Canton, Ohio: Closing argument speech "One Week" before the election (begin of the final count-down to the election).
191. October 28, 2008, Chester, Pennsylvania: Remarks on the economy, change, and the election.
192. October 29, 2008, Raleigh, North Carolina: Remarks on the economy, change, and the election.
193. October 30, 2008, Sarasota, Florida: Remarks on the economy, change, and the election.
194. October 31, 2008, Des Moines, Iowa: Remarks on the economy, change, and the election.
195. November 2, 2008, Columbus, Ohio: Remarks on the economy, change, and the election.
196. November 3, 2008, Jacksonville, Florida: Remarks on the economy, change, and the election.
197. November 4, 2008, Chicago, Illinois: Victory speech on election night.
198. November 7, 2008, Chicago, Illinois: First news conference as President-elect.
199. November 8, 2008: Radio address.
200. November 15, 2008: Radio address.
201. November 16, 2008: CBS "60 Minutes" interview with Steve Kroft.
202. November 22, 2008: Radio address.
203. November 24, 2008, Chicago, Illinois: Second news conference as President-elect.
204. November 25, 2008, Chicago, Illinois: Third news conference as President-elect.
205. November 26, 2008, Chicago, Illinois: Fourth news conference as President-elect.
206. November 29, 2008: Radio address.
207. December 1, 2008, Chicago, Illinois: Fifth news conference as President-elect.
208. December 2, 2008, Washington, D.C.: Remarks to the National Governors' Association.
209. December 3, 2008, Chicago, Illinois: Sixth news conference as President-elect.
210. December 6, 2008: Radio address.
211. December 7, 2008, Chicago, Illinois: NBC "Meet the Press" interview with Tom Brokaw.
212. December 7, 2008, Chicago, Illinois: Seventh news conference as President-elect.

213. December 11, 2008, Chicago, Illinois: Eighth news conference as President-elect.
214. December 15, 2008, Chicago, Illinois. Ninth news conference as President-elect.
215. December 16, 2008, Chicago, Illinois: Tenth news conference as President-elect.
216. December 17, 2008, Chicago, Illinois: Eleventh news conference as President-elect.
217. December 18, 2008, Chicago, Illinois: Twelfth news conference as President-elect.
218. December 19, 2008, Chicago, Illinois: Thirteenth news conference as President-elect.
219. December 29, 2008: Interview of "Person of the Year Barack Obama" in *Time* (December 29, 2008-January 5, 2009), 66-68 and 70.
220. January 7, 2009, Washington, D.C.: News conference as President-elect (not numbered any longer).
221. January 8, 2009, Washington, D.C.: Speech on "American Recovery and Reinvestment Plan."
222. January 8, 2009, Washington, D.C.: Announcement of Governor Tim Kaine as Chairman of the Democratic National Convention.
223. January 9, 2008, Washington, D.C.: News conference as President-elect to announce his intelligence team.
224. January 15, 2009: Barack Obama's letter to his daughters: "Dear Malia and Sasha" in *New York Post* (January 15, 2009), 7.
225. January 17, 2009: Radio address.
226. January 17, 2009, Philadelphia, Pennsylvania: Remarks at the beginning of Barack Obama's whistle stop train trip to Washington, D.C.
227. January 17, 2009, Baltimore, Maryland: Remarks at a stop on Barack Obama's train trip to Washington, D.C.
228. January 18, 2009, Washington, D.C.: Speech at the Lincoln Memorial "We Are One" concert.
229. January 20, 2009, Washington, D.C.: Barack Obama's inaugural address as the 44th President of the United States.

Index OF Proverbs AND Proverbial Phrases

This index includes all of Barack Obama's proverbial statements in their actual context. There are 430 texts from his two books and 1284 texts from his speeches and other verbal communications for a total of 1714 proverbial references. Standard proverb collections usually do not list such detailed information. However, proverbial speech becomes meaningful only when it is cited in textual passages that show the use and function of this metaphorical language. The numerous references from Barack Obama are preceded by a standard version of the proverbial text being cited. The key-word of the proverbial statement appears in bold type and the entire material is arranged alphabetically according to these key-words. Under each key-word the citations are arranged chronologically. A letter plus a page number or simply a number that follow the contextualized citations in parentheses refer to Barack Obama's written works and speeches, news conferences, interviews, and radio addresses. Some citations are followed by up to ten numbers, indicating that Barack Obama repeated these statements verbatim during a series of more or less identical stump speeches. For detailed bibliographical information and dates see the "List of Publications and Speeches."

To clean up one's **act**.

So you know, I want a more proactive Interior Department. I also want an Interior Department that very frankly cleans up its act. There have been too many problems and too much, too much emphasis on big-time lobbyists in Washington and not enough emphasis on what's good for the American people. (216)

In politics, there may be second **acts**, but there is no second place.

Like most men and women who followed the path of public life, Gore knew what he was getting himself into the moment he decided to run. In politics, there may be second acts, but there is no second place. (H,108)

To be (either) with someone or **against** someone.

In his Manichean struggle, compromise came to look like weakness, to be punished or purged. You were with us or against us. You had to choose sides. It was Bill Clinton's singular contribution that he had tried to transcend this ideological deadlock. (H,34)

To put on **airs**.

"Despite all our troubles, he would never admit to Roy or myself that anything was wrong. I think that's what hurt the most – the way he still put on airs about how we were children of Dr. Obama. We would have empty cupboards, and he would make donations to charities just to keep up appearances!" (D,216)

All for one and one for all.

All for one and one for all. It's the idea that's at the heart of LULAC [League of United Latin American Citizens]. It's the idea that's at the heart of America. And it's what this election is all about. It's about the future we can build together. (133)

It goes back to the idea that's at the heart of LULAC [League of United Latin American Citizens] – that it's all for one and one for all. That's the idea we need to reclaim in this country. And that's the idea that we can reclaim in this election. (133)

America is great because Americans are good.

Make this a nation that is worthy of the sacrifices of so many of its citizens, and in doing so, make real the observation made by a visitor to our country so many centuries ago: "America is great because Americans are good." (66)

America prospers when all Americans prosper.

Because America can only prosper when all Americans prosper – brown, black, white, Asian, and Native American. That's the idea that lies at the heart of my campaign, and that's the idea that will lie at the heart of my presidency. Because we are all Americans. (128)

It [the danger to the American way of life] will come [...], if we stand idly by as our problems grow, as more and more Americans go without quality jobs, affordable health care, or skills they need to get ahead in the 21st century. Because America can only prosper if all Americans prosper. (133)

But the American economy has worked in large part because we have guided the market's invisible hand with a higher principle – that America prospers when all Americans can prosper. That is why we have put in place rules of the road to make competition fair, and open, and honest. (156, 157)

But the American economy has worked in large part because we have guided the market's invisible hand with a higher principle – that America prospers when all Americans can prosper. That's the change we need right now. (163)

But the American economy has worked in large part because we've guided the market's invisible hand with a higher principle: that America prospers when all Americans prosper. That principle is why we put in place common-sense rules of the road to regulate our market, and it's why we need to restore and renew those rules today. (217)

If you invest in **America**, America will invest in you.

I want to give tax breaks to young people, in the form of an annual $4,000 tax credit that will cover two-thirds of the tuition at an average public college, and make community college completely free. In return, I will ask students to serve, whether it's by teaching, joining the Peace Corps, or working in your community. And for those who serve in our military, we'll cover all of your tuition with an even more generous 21st Century GI Bill. The idea is simple – America invests in you, and you invest in America. That's how we're going to ensure that America succeeds in this century. (124)

To make a college education affordable for every American family, I'll make this promise to every student – your country will offer you $4,000 a year of tuition if you offer your country community or national service when you graduate. If you invest in America, America will invest in you. (132)

If you [college students] commit to serving your community or your country, we will make sure you can afford your tuition. No ifs, ands, or buts. You invest in America, America will invest in you, and together, we will move this country forward. (180)

If you [college students] commit to serving your community or your country, we will make sure you can afford your tuition. No ifs, ands or buts. You invest in America, America will invest in you, and together, we will move this country forward. (181, 182, 183, 184, 187, 188, 189)

Each **American** does better when all Americans do better.

As I said at the NASDAQ last September: the core of our economic success is the fundamental truth that each American does better when all Americans do better;

that the well being of American business, its capital markets, and the American people are aligned. (109)

To run amuck (**amok**).

We know it was George Bush's Washington that let the banks and financial institutions run amok and take our economy down this dangerous road. (102)

To play the **angles**.

He hadn't cut corners, though, or played all the angles. He was diligent and honest, no matter what it cost him. He had led his life according to principles that demanded a different kind of toughness, principles that promised a higher form of power. (D,50)

To bite one's **ankle**.

Iran is a classic case of something biting us on the ankle, when we assisted in overthrowing the democratically elected regime that was replaced by the Shah. (B,64)

To have **ants** in one's pants.

It is said of him that he had ants up his anus, because he could not sit still. He would wander off on his own for many days, and when he returned he would not say where he had been. [Granny's story] (D,397)

Anything goes.

Yet even as we speak, there are those who are preparing to divide us, the spin masters and negative ad peddlers who embrace the politics of anything goes. Well, I say to them tonight, there's not a liberal America and a conservative America — there's the United States of America. (2)

Unfortunately, instead of establishing a 21st century regulatory framework, we simply dismantled the old one. [...] We encouraged a winner take all, anything goes environment that helped foster devastating dislocations in our economy. (109)

It's a [recovery] plan that represents not just new policy, but a whole new approach to meeting our most urgent challenges. For if we hope to end this crisis, we must end the culture of anything goes that helped create it — and this change must begin in Washington. (221)

To keep up **appearances**.

"Despite all our troubles, he would never admit to Roy or myself that anything was wrong. I think that's what hurt the most — the way he still put on airs about how we were children of Dr. Obama. We would have empty cupboards, and he would make donations to charities just to keep up appearances!" (D,216)

To be a bad **apple**.

This bill does a great job protecting credit card companies from the few bad apples who try to escape their debt, but what does it do to protect the American public from the credit card companies who try to take advantage of them? (4)

We did not arrive at this moment by some accident of history. This was not a normal part of the business cycle. This was not just a few bad apples on Wall Street. This crisis is a direct result of a philosophy that folks running Washington have been following for decades. (167)

Let me be perfectly clear. The fact that we are in this mess is an outrage. It's an outrage because we did not get here by accident. This was not a normal part of the business cycle. This was not the actions of a few bad apples. This financial crisis is a direct result of the greed and irresponsibility that has dominated Washington and Wall Street for years. (168, 169)

Now, let me be perfectly clear. The fact that we are in this mess is an outrage. It's an outrage because we did not get here by accident. This was not a normal part of the business cycle. This did not happen because of a few bad apples. This financial crisis is a direct result of the greed and irresponsibility that has dominated Washington and Wall Street for years. (170, 171)

The **arc** of the moral universe is long, but it bends towards justice.

You know, two weeks after Bloody Sunday, when the march finally reached Montgomery, Martin Luther King Jr. spoke to the crowd of thousands and said "The arc of the moral universe is long, but it bends towards justice." He's right, but you know what? It doesn't bend on its own. It bends because we help it bend that way. (3)

You know, two weeks after Bloody Sunday, when the march reached Montgomery, Martin Luther King Jr. spoke to the crowd of thousands and said "The arc of the moral universe is long, but it bends towards justice." He's right, but you know what? It doesn't bend on its own. It bends because we help it bend that way. (15)

Dr. King told a gathering of organizers and activists and community members that they should not despair because the arc of the moral universe is long, but it bends towards justice. That's because of the work that each of us do to bend it towards justice. It's because of people like John Lewis and Fannie Lou Hamer and Coretta Scott King and Rosa Parks, all the giants upon whose shoulders we stand that we are beneficiaries of that arc bending towards justice. (63)

I would not be in the United States Senate had it not been for the efforts and courage of so many parents and grandparents and ordinary people who were willing to reach up and bend that arc in the direction of justice. (63)

You know, Dr. King once said that the arc of the moral universe is long but that it bends toward justice. But what he also knew was that it doesn't bend on its own. It bends because each of us puts our hands on that arc and bends it in the direction of justice. [...] Let's bend that arc toward justice. Let's bend that arc toward opportunity. Let's bend that arc toward prosperity for all. (110)

It's [Obama's election] the answer that led those who have been told for so long by so many to be cynical, and fearful, and doubtful of what can be achieved to put their hands on the arc of history and bend it once more toward hope of a better day. (197)

To twist someone's **arm**.

They [lobbyists] got what they paid for when their friends in Congress broke the rules and twisted arms to push through a prescription drug bill that actually made it illegal for our own government to negotiate with the pharmaceutical companies for cheaper drug prices. (86)

To have more than one **arrow** to one's bow.

But when the Democrats lost their Senate majority in 2002, they had only one arrow left in their quiver, a strategy that could be summed up in one word, the battle cry around which the Democratic faithful now rallied: *Filibuster!* (H,80)

To be an (sorry) **ass**.

The secretary shook her head, and Dr. Collier frowned. "Hold all calls," she said as I followed her into her office, "except for that good-for-nothing building engineer. I want to tell him just what I think of his sorry ass." (D,231)

To have an **ax** to grind.

Instead, they [interest groups] are focused on a narrow set of concerns – their pensions, their crop supports, their cause. Simply put, they have an ax to grind. And they want you, the elected official, to help them grind it. (H,116)

Everybody has got an ax to grind when it comes to the press. My attitude is, let the press do its job. (B,89)

To sleep like a **baby**.

"That's why he [Obama's grandfather] can come over here and drink my whiskey and fall asleep in that chair you're sitting in right now. Sleep like a baby. See, that's something I can never do in his house." (D,90)

To break someone's **back**.

"As people, we're not willing to do that anymore [working sixteen hours each day]. I guess we worked so long for nothing, we feel like we shouldn't have to break our backs just to survive. That's what we tell our children anyway." (D,182)

As important as moral exhortation was in changing hearts and minds of white Americans during the civil right era, what ultimately broke the back of Jim Crow and ushered in a new era of race relations were the Supreme Court cases. (H,62)

To do something behind someone's **back**.

Blacks had no real power to act on the occasional slips into anti-Semitism or Asian-bashing, people would tell me; and anyway, black folks needed a chance to let off a little steam every once in a while – man, what do you think those folks say about us behind our backs? (D,203)

In Onyango's presence, he [Barack Obama] appeared well-mannered and obedient, and never answered back when his father told him to do something. But behind the old man's back, Barack did as he pleased. [Granny's story] (D,414)

To put something on someone's **back**.

Men and women who recognize that piling up debt to finance tax cuts for the wealthy is irresponsible, that deficit reduction can't take place on the backs of the poor, that the separation of church and state protects the church as well as the state. (H,37)

We can't afford an economy where folks keep working harder for less. We can't let the women in our workforce get paid even less for doing the same work. And we can't keep pushing more and more of the burden on the backs of working parents who are struggling to balance their jobs and their family. (126)

To stab someone in the **back**.

"We gotta talk, Barack [...]. Can't think about this thing in isolation [...] got to look at the big picture. You don't understand the forces at work out here. Is big, man. All kinds of folks ready to stab you in the back." (D,195)

To turn one's **back** (to something or someone).

It is my hope that the President will break his practice of touting the importance of the Americas during his travels only to turn his back upon his return. Each stop on the President's trip presents an opportunity to move beyond rhetoric, to renew relations in the hemisphere. (78)

But, we cannot weaken the very essence of what America is by turning our backs on immigrants who want to reunite with their family members, or immigrants who have a willingness to work hard but who may not have the right graduate degrees. (82)

Above all, I will send a clear message: we will not repeat the mistake of the past, when we turned our back on Afghanistan following Soviet withdrawal. (85)

We're going to have to reclaim in our lives the belief that I am my brother's keeper; I am my sister's keeper. It's the belief that led folks in Clarendon [South Carolina] not to turn their backs on Harry Briggs and his fellow foot soldiers [for civil rights]. (93)

To be the **backbone** (of something).

Our rural communities are the backbone of Illinois. Yet, factories have closed, jobs have disappeared, and homes and farms have been foreclosed upon. Effective federal programs are necessary to protect the rural economy. (B,142)

But no law can force a Congress to stand up to the President. No law can make Senators read the intelligence that showed the President was overstating the case for war. No law can give Congress a backbone if it refuses to stand up as the co-equal branch the Constitution made it. (92)

We take it for granted that women are the backbone of our families, but we too often ignore the fact that women are also the backbone of our middle class. And we won't truly have an economy that puts the needs of the middle class first until we ensure that when it comes to pay and benefits at work, women are treated like the equal partners they are. (134, 135)

And when the guns [of World War II] fell silent, America stood by them [the veterans], because they had a government that didn't just ask them to win a war – it helped them to live their dreams in peace, and to become the backbone of the largest middle class that the world has ever known. (150)

Our young men and women in uniform have proven that they are the equal of the Greatest Generation on the battlefield [of World War II]. Now we must ensure that our brave troops serving abroad today become the backbone of our middle class at home tomorrow. (150)

The auto industry is the backbone of American manufacturing and a critical part of our attempt to reduce our dependence on foreign oil. I would like to see the administration do everything it can to accelerate the retooling assistance that Congress has already enacted. (198)

The auto industry historically has been the backbone of America's manufacturing base. And it's not just the auto industry. It's not just the Big Three. It's also all the suppliers, all the businesses that in one way or another are part of our auto industry that are at stake here. (203)

To strengthen our economy, we must also strengthen the small businesses that are its backbone. I can think of no one better to lead this effort as an administrator of the Small Business Administration than Karen Mills. With Karen at the helm, America's small businesses will have a partner in Washington, helping them create jobs and spur growth in communities across this country. (218)

To take a **backseat**.

We cannot let enforcement of existing trade agreements take a backseat to the negotiation of new ones. Put simply, we need tougher negotiators on our side of the table – to strike bargains that are good not just for Wall Street, but also for Main Street. And when I am President, that's what we will do. (124)

To be a mixed **bag**.

For adults, at least, the effect of these changes is a mixed bag. Research suggests that on average, married couples live healthier, wealthier, and happier lives, but no one claims that men and women benefit from being trapped in bad or abusive marriages. (H,333)

To be left holding the **bag.**

The recklessness of some of these executives has helped cause this mess, even as they walk away with multimillion dollar golden parachutes while taxpayers are left holding the bag. (159)

A **bait** and switch.

So when you read the fine print, it's clear that John McCain is pulling an old Washington bait and switch. It's a shell game. He gives you a tax credit with one hand – but raises your taxes with the other. (172)

He [Senator McCain] talks about giving every family a $5,000 credit to buy health care, but he didn't mention last night that he'll also tax your benefits for the first time in history. It's an old Washington bait and switch. He gives you a tax credit with one hand, but raises your taxes with the other. (174)

To take the **bait**.

Democrats, for the most part, have taken the bait. At best, we may try to avoid the conversation about religious values altogether, fearful of offending anyone and claiming that – regardless of our personal beliefs – constitutional principles tie our hands. (60)

To drop the **ball** on something/someone.

Charities that invested in Madoff [Investment Securities] could end up losing savings on which millions depend, a massive fraud that was made possible in part because regulators who were assigned to oversee Wall Street dropped the ball. (217)

To have a **ball**.

Zeituni grabbed my hand, and [...] soon we were all dancing into a sweat, arms and hips and rumps swaying softly; tall, ink-black Luos and short, brown Kikuyus, Kamba and Meru and Kalenjin, everyone smiling and shouting and having a ball. (D,364)

To (not) have a crystal **ball**.

Well, I want to be completely honest with the American people. I don't have a crystal ball. What I have control of is making the good, smart decisions that lead to long-term sustainable economic development and growth. (214)

I don't have a crystal ball, and economists are all over the map on this. I think we should anticipate that 2009 is going to be a tough year. And if we make some good choices, I'm confident that [...] we can start seeing an upward trajectory on the economy. (219)

Ballot boxes don't make a democracy.

We must understand that setting up ballot boxes does not make a democracy – that real freedom and real stability come from doing the hard work of helping to build a strong police force, and a legitimate government, and ensuring that people have food, and water, and electricity, and basic services. (81)

We do need to stand for democracy. And I will. But democracy is about more than a ballot box. America must show – through deeds as well as words – that we stand with those who seek a better life. (85)

To keep (many) **balls** in the air.

The result has been what [...] Karen Kornbluh calls "the juggler family," in which parents struggle to pay the bills, look after their children, maintain a household, and maintain their relationship. Keeping all these balls in the air takes its toll on family life. (H,336)

To be (nothing but) **baloney**.

We were told this war would cost $50 to $60 billion, and that reconstruction would pay for itself out of Iraq oil profits. We were told higher estimates were nothing but "baloney." Like so much else about this war, we were not told the truth. (108)

To put a **band-aid** on something.

This is not a time for window-dressing or putting a band-aid on a problem just to score political points. This is a time for real reform, and I think the Democrats' Honest Leadership and Open Government Act does this by including provisions that so far the Republican proposals do not. (39)

This is not a time for window-dressing or putting a band-aid on a problem just to score political points. This is a time for real reform. I think the Honest Leadership and Open Government Act, which has 41 cosponsors, established the right marker for reform. (44)

To jump on the **bandwagon**.

The American people weren't just failed by a President – they were failed by much of Washington. By a media that too often reported spin instead of facts. By a foreign policy elite that largely boarded the bandwagon for war. And most of all by the majority of Congress. (92)

To lead the **bandwagon**.

She [Michelle Obama] cares more about whether I'm a good father and a good husband than she does about whether I'm a U.S. senator. As she likes to say, she would be my Number 1 political supporter – she'd make calls and raise money – if we I were her neighbor. She would be leading the bandwagon for me to run for President if I was married to somebody else. (B,87)

To set the **bar**.

So in January, I came back with Senator Feingold and we set a high bar for reform. And I am pleased to report that the bill before us today comes very close to what we proposed. (86)

I think it is very important just to look at the history when it comes to the regulation of emission in California. Consistently, California has hit the bar, and then the rest of the country has followed. (214)

To hold up one's end of the **bargain**.

And in a world where knowledge determines value in the job market, where a child in Los Angeles has to compete not just with a child in Boston but also with millions of children in Bangalore and Beijing, too many of America's schools are not holding up their end of the bargain. (H,159)

And even when our government refused to hold up its end of the bargain [to educate everybody], ordinary people marched and bled, they took to the streets and fought in the courts, they stood up and spoke out until the day when the arrival of nine little children at a school in Little Rock made real the decision that in America separate could never be equal. (30)

And even when our government refused to hold up its end of the bargain [to educate everybody], ordinary people stood up and spoke out until the day when the arrival of nine little children at a school in Little Rock made real the decision that in America, separate could never be equal. (46)

But even though they've held up their end of the bargain, many seniors are struggling to keep pace with costs. And as so many Americans know, their worry becomes an entire family's worry. (90)

To pass the **baton** (to someone).

So George Bush may be in an undisclosed location, but Dick Cheney's out there on the campaign trail because he'd be delighted to pass the baton to John McCain. (195)

Beauty is in the eye of the beholder.

Pork is in the eye of the beholder. The recipients don't tend to think it's pork, especially if it's a great public-works project. (B,123)

To feather one's **bed**.

Apparently there are still those in Washington who view politics as a means of getting rich, and who, while generally not dumb enough to accept bags of small bills, are perfectly prepared to take care of contributors and properly feather their beds until the time is financially ripe to jump into the lucrative practice of lobbying on behalf of those they once regulated. (H,109)

Been there, done that.

I looked behind me and noticed Lugar standing toward the back of the room. "You don't want a closer look, Dick?" I asked, taking a few steps back myself. "Been there, done that," he said with a smile. (H,312)

At this point I turned around and said "Hey, where's [Dick] Lugar? Doesn't he want to see this?" I found him standing about fifteen feet away, all the way in the back of the room. He looked at me and said, "Been there, done that." Of course, Dick has been there and he has done that, and thanks to the Cooperative Threat Reduction Programs he co-founded with Senator Sam Nunn, we've made amazing progress in finding, securing, and guarding some of the deadliest weapons that were left scattered throughout the former Soviet Union after the Cold War. (32)

The **beginning** of the end.

It's the same approach George W. Bush floated a few years ago. It was dead on arrival in Congress. But if Senator McCain were to succeed where George Bush failed, it very well could be the beginning of the end of our employer-based health care system. (172)

It's the same approach President Bush floated a few years ago. And it could be the beginning of the end of our employer-based health care system. In fact, studies show that under the McCain plan, at least 20 million Americans will lose the insurance you rely on from your workplace. (173)

With all the **bells** and whistles.

The irony of the underlying bill [Habeas Corpus Amendment] as it is written is that someone like Khalid Shaikh Mohammed is going to get basically a full military trial, with all the bells and whistles. He will have counsel, he will be able to present evidence, and he will be able to rebut the Government's case. (68)

To tighten one's **belt**.

Now, I won't pretend that any of this will come easy or without cost. We will all need to tighten our belts, we will all need to sacrifice and we will all need to pull our weight because now more than ever, we are all in this together. (182)

Now, make no mistake: the change we need won't come easy or without cost. We will all need to tighten our belts, we will all need to sacrifice and we will all need to pull our weight because now more than ever, we are all in this together. (183, 184, 187, 188, 189)

The cost of this economic crisis, and the cost of the war in Iraq, means that Washington will have to tighten its belt and put off spending on things we can afford to do without. (190, 191, 192)

And we saw the largest decline in consumer spending in 28 years as wages failed to keep up with the rising cost of living, and folks have been watching every penny and tightening their belts. (193, 194, 195, 196)

Right now, our economy is trapped in a vicious cycle: The turmoil on Wall Street means a new round of belt-tightening for families and businesses on Main Street, and as folks produce less and consume less, that just deepens the problems in our financial markets. (203)

Government at every level will have to tighten its belt, but we'll help struggling states avoid harmful budget cuts, as long as they take responsibility and use the money to maintain essential services like police, fire, education, and health care. (221)

To place a **bet** on someone or something.

The oil companies have placed their bet on Senator McCain, and if he wins, they will continue to cash in while our families and our economy suffer and our future is put in jeopardy. [...] We can make a different bet – a bet on the ingenuity, industry and determination of the American people. (148)

Better isn't good enough.

I have witnessed a profound shift in race relations in my lifetime. I have felt it as surely as one feels a change in temperature. [...] But as much as I insist that things have gotten better, I am mindful of this truth as well: Better isn't good enough. (H,233)

For **better** or worse.

In 1960, though, my grandfather had not yet been tested; the disappointments would come later, and even then they would come slowly, without the violence that might have changed him, for better or worse. (D,16-17)

To do someone one **better**.

But we can do them [the auto companies] one better. If they install flexible-fuel tanks in their cars before the decade's up, we will provide them a $100 tax credit to do it – so there's no excuse for delay. (48)

To foot the **bill**.

Bankruptcy laws should be amended to move pension beneficiaries to the front of the creditor line so that companies can't just file for Chapter 11 to stiff workers. Moreover, new rules should force companies to properly fund their pension funds, in part so taxpayer don't end up footing the bill. (H,182)

Bits and pieces.

And I knew that the father was absent, although Mary never mentioned him. Only in bits and pieces, over the course of many months, would I learn that she had grown up in a small Indiana town, part of a big, working-class Irish family. (D,175)

As **black** as pitch; pitch-black.

That my father looked nothing like the people around me – that he was black as pitch, my mother white as milk – barely registered in my mind. In fact, I can recall only one story that dealt explicitly with the subject of race. (D,10)

Black and white.

The issues facing the [Supreme] Court are rarely black and white, and all advocacy groups who have a legitimate and profound interest in the decisions that are made by the Court should try to make certain that their advocacy reflects that complexity. (27)

To bring something (someone) under one **blanket**.

There have always been Americans who [...] said we're going to keep on dreaming, and we're going to keep on building, and we're going to keep on marching, and we're going to keep on working because that's who we are. Because we've always fought to bring all of our people under the blanket of the American Dream. (57)

In the **blink** of an eye.

For in the end laws are just words on a page – words that are sometimes malleable, opaque, as dependent on context and trust as they are in a story or poem or promise to someone, words whose meanings are subject to erosion, sometimes collapsing in the blink of an eye. (H,77)

Terrorist networks can spread their doctrines in the blink of an eye; they can probe the world economic system's weakest links, knowing that an attack on London or Tokyo will reverberate in New York or Hong Kong. (H,306)

To smell **blood**.

The press, smelling blood, discovered that another South Side project contained pipes lined with rotting asbestos. Aldermen began calling for immediate hearings. Lawyers called about a class-action suit. (D,242)

To appear out of the **blue**.

Once, when she [daughter Malia] was just six years old and we were taking a walk together along the lake, she asked me out of the blue if our family was rich. I told her that we weren't really rich, but that we had a lot more than most people. (H,351)

To be a **blueprint**.

According to this conception, the genius of Madison's design is not that it provides us a fixed blueprint for action, the way a draftsman plots building's construction. It provided us with a framework and with rules. (H,92)

To be on **board**.

It's an honor to be here with the hundreds of dedicated librarians who make up the American Library Association. Before we begin, I'd like to say a special hello to ALA member Nancy Gibbs, who is the mother of my communications director, Robert Gibbs. Believe me, I have no idea how the biggest mouth in our office came from a family of two librarians, but we're proud to have him on board and I'm sure you are too. (22)

To be in the same **boat**.

I have been feeling that many of you might be in a similar boat when it comes to politics and organizing and activism after college, and so today I'd just like to offer you a few pieces of advice that might be able to help you on your way. (61)

To miss the **boat**.

And for us to simply recreate what existed back in the '30s in the 21st century, I think would be missing the boat. We've got to come up with solutions that are true to our times and true to the moment. And that's going to be our job. (201)

To be a (time-) **bomb**.

Another area where we can make significant progress in prevention is by removing the stigma that goes with getting tested for HIV-AIDS. The idea that in some places, nine in ten people with HIV have no idea they're infected is more than frightening – it's a ticking time bomb waiting to go off. (72)

As bare as a **bone**; bare-bones.

Our campaign plan called for a bare-bones budget, a heavy reliance on grassroots support and "earned media" – that is, an ability to make our own news. Still, David

[Axelrod] informed me that one week of television advertising in the Chicago media market would cost approximately half a million dollars. (H,110)

To feel (know) in one's **bones**.

And so, less than halfway into the campaign, I knew in my bones that I was going to lose. Each morning from that point forward I awoke with a vague sense of dread, realizing that I would have to spend the day smiling and shaking hands and pretending that everything was going according to plan. (H,106)

No, people don't expect government to solve all their problems. But they sense, deep in their bones, that with just a change in priorities, we can make sure that every child in America has a decent shot at life, and that the doors of opportunity remain open to all. (2)

So Dr. King had been to the mountaintop. He had seen the Promised Land. And while he knew somewhere deep in his bones that he would not get there with us, he knew that we would get there. (110)

To make no **bones** about something.

Still, I'd felt bad after that particular episode; it was the one trick my mother always had up her sleeve, that way she had of making me feel guilty. She made no bones about it, either. "You can't help it," she told me once. "Slipped it into your baby food. Don't worry, though," she added, smiling like the Cheshire cat. "A healthy dose of guilt never hurt anybody. It's what civilization is built on, guilt. A highly underrated emotion." (D,96)

To be the oldest trick in the **book**.

Just today, Senator McCain offered up the oldest Washington stunt in the book – you pass the buck to a commission to study the problem. But here's the thing – this isn't 9/11. We know how we got into this mess. What we need now is leadership that gets us out. (156)

The other side trots out this attack [against liberal ideas] every year, in every election. It's a scare tactic. It's the oldest trick in the book. And it's what you do when you are out of ideas, out of touch, and running out of time. (182)

To hit the **books**.

Our kids will have to turn off the TV sets and put away the video games and start hitting the books. We will have to reform institutions, like our public schools, that were designed for an earlier time. (19)

Boom and bust.

I wonder, sometimes, whether men and women in fact are capable of learning from history – whether we progress from one stage to the next in an upward course or whether we just ride the cycles of boom and bust, war and peace, ascent and decline. (H,322)

To pull oneself up by one's **bootstraps**.

In Washington, they call this the Ownership Society. But in our past there has been another term for it – Social Darwinism, every man and woman for him or herself. It's a tempting idea, because it doesn't require much thought or ingenuity. It allows us to say to those whose health care or tuition may rise faster than they can afford – tough luck. It allows us to say to the Maytag workers who have lost their job – life isn't fair. It let's [sic] us say to the child born into poverty – pull yourself up by your bootstraps. (19)

In Washington, they call this the Ownership Society. But in our past there has been another term for it – Social Darwinism, every man and woman for him or herself. It's a tempting idea, because it doesn't require much thought or ingenuity. It allows us to say to those whose health care or tuition may rise faster than they can afford – tough luck. It allows us to say to the factory workers who have lost their job – life isn't fair. It let's [sic] us say to the child born into poverty – pull yourself up by your bootstraps. (25)

In Washington, they call this the Ownership Society. But in our past there has been another term for it – Social Darwinism, every man and woman for him or herself. It allows us to say to those whose health care or tuition may rise faster than they can afford – tough luck. It allows us to say to the women who lose their jobs when they have to take care for a sick child – life isn't fair. It let's [sic] us say to the child born into poverty – pull yourself up by your bootstraps. (34)

We know this as the Ownership Society. But in our past there has been another term for it – Social Darwinism – every man or woman for him or herself. It allows us to say to those whose health care or tuition may rise faster than they can afford – tough luck. It allows us to say to the child who was born into poverty – pull yourself up by your bootstraps. It let's [sic] us say to the workers who lose their job when the factory shuts down – you're on your own. (35)

It's called the Ownership Society in Washington. But in our past there has been another term for it – Social Darwinism – every man or woman for him or herself. It allows us to say to those whose health care or tuition may rise faster than they can afford – life isn't fair. It allows us to say to the child who didn't have the fore-sight to choose the right parents or be born in the right suburb – pick yourself up by your bootstraps. It lets us say to the guy who worked twenty or thirty years in the factory and then watched his plant move out to Mexico or China – we're sorry, but you're on your own. (50, 57, 65)

It's a course that further divides Wall Street from Main Street; where struggling families are told to pull themselves up by their bootstraps because there's nothing government can do or should do – and so we should give more to those with the most and let the chips fall where they may. (106)

In Washington, they call this the Ownership Society, but what it really means is – you're on your own. Out of work? Tough luck. No health care? The market will fix it. Born into poverty? Pull yourself up by your own bootstraps – even if you don't have boots. You're on your own. (152)

The **bottom** falls out of something.

Then, in 1997, the bottom fell out. A run on currencies and securities throughout Asia engulfed an Indonesian economy already corroded by decades of corruption. The rupiah's value fell 85 percent in a matter of months. (H,277)

To be (live) in a **box**.

I met a woman a few weeks ago in New Mexico who told me she works two jobs […] but the last time she saw a doctor was ten years ago, because she didn't have insurance, and couldn't afford an appointment. She later said, "This is a pretty hard life, I just want to figure out how we get out of this box." (135)

To be one's **bread** and butter.

Bill Clinton's Third Way, a scaled-back welfare state without grand ambition but without sharp edges, seemed to describe a broad, underlying consensus on bread-and-butter issues, a consensus to which even George W. Bush's first campaign, with its "compassionate conservatism," would have to give a nod. (D,ix-x)

To get a **break**.

"I'm saying yeah, I might not get the breaks on the team that some guys get, but they play like white boys do, and that's the style the coach likes to play, and they're winning the way they play. I don't play that way." (D,74)

To put on the **breaks**.

Now, when it came to rescuing Wall Street, Washington didn't waste a minute. But now that auto-workers are suffering, Washington's put on the breaks. It turns out it could take a year for the auto industry to get the loan guarantees we passed a few weeks ago. (188)

To hold one's **breath**.

There's […] the millions of waitresses and temp secretaries and nurse's assistants and Wal-Mart associates who hold their breath every single month in the hope that they'll have enough money to support the children that they did bring into the world. (H,42)

To take a deep **breath**.

When Democrats rush up to me at events and insist that we live in the worst of political times, that a creeping fascism is closing its grip around our throats, I may mention the internment of Japanese Americans under FDR, the Alien and Sedition Acts under John Adams, or a hundred years of lynching under several dozen administrations as having been possibly worse, and suggest we all take a deep breath. (H,22-22)

To build a **bridge**.

That is why America cannot turn inward. That is why Europe cannot turn inward. America has no better partner than Europe. Now is the time to build new bridges across the globe as strong as the one that bound us across the Atlantic. (141)

To cross a **bridge**.

And where will our courage come from to speak these truths? When we stand on our own Edmund Pettus Bridge, what hope will sustain us? I believe it is the hope of knowing that people like John Lewis have stood on that same bridge and lived to cross it. (3)

I'm sure you'll all agree that we have songs left to sing and bridges left to cross. And if there's anything we can learn from this living saint [John Lewis] sitting beside me, it is that change is never easy, but always possible. That it comes not from violence or militancy or the kind of politics that pits us against each other [...]; but from a strong message of hope, and from the courage to turn against the tide so that the tide eventually may be turned. (3)

If you told Dick [Durbin] thirty years ago that he – the son of Lithuania[n] immigrants [...] – would be returning to Cairo [Illinois] as a sitting United States Senator, and that he would have in tow a black guy born in Hawaii with a father from Kenya and a mother from Kansas named Barack Obama, no one would have believed it. But it happened. And it happened because John Lewis and scores of brave Americans stood on that bridge and lived to cross it. (3)

How can we cut through the apathy and the partisanship and the business-as-usual culture in Washington? When we wonder this, we need to rediscover the hope that people have been in our shoes and they've lived to cross those bridges. (15)

If you told Dick [Durbin] thirty years ago that he – the son of Lithuania[n] immigrants [...] – would be returning to Cairo [Illinois] as a sitting United States Senator, and that he would have in tow a black guy born in Hawaii with a father from Kenya and a mother from Kansas named Barack Obama, no one would have believed it. And it happened because John Lewis and scores of brave Americans stood on that bridge and lived to cross it. (15)

Am I my **brother's** keeper?

It's that fundamental belief – I am my brother's keeper, I am my sister's keeper – that makes this country work. It's what allows us to pursue our individual dreams, yet still come together as a single American family. "E pluribus unum." Out of many, one. (2)

We know that we've been called in churches and mosques, synagogues and Sunday schools to love our neighbors as ourselves; to be our brother's keeper; to be our sister's keeper. That we have individual responsibility, but we also have collective responsibility to each other. (50, 57, 65)

What holds this country together is this fundamental belief that we all have a stake in each other – that I am my brother's keeper; that I am my sister's keeper. And that must express itself not only in our churches and synagogues or in our personal lives, but in our government too. (88)

We're going to have to reclaim in our lives the belief that I am my brother's keeper; I am my sister's keeper. It's the belief that led folks in Clarendon [South Carolina] not to turn their backs on Harry Briggs and his fellow foot soldiers [for civil rights]. (93)

America is the sum of our dreams. And what binds us together, what makes us one American family, is that we can stand up and fight for each other's dreams, that we reaffirm that fundamental belief – I am my brother's keeper, I am my sister's keeper – through our politics, our policies, and in our daily lives. (95)

I'm talking about a moral deficit. I'm talking about an empathy deficit. I'm taking [sic] about an inability to recognize ourselves in one another, to understand that we are our brother's keeper; we are our sister's keeper; that, in the words of Dr. King, we are all tied together in a single garment of destiny. (99)

It [change] will require each of us to do our part in closing the moral deficit – the empathy deficit – that exists in this nation. It will take standing in one another's shoes and remembering that we are our brother's keeper; we are our sister's keeper. (103)

But we also believe that there is a larger responsibility we have to one another as Americans. We believe that we rise or fall as one nation – as one people. That we are our brother's keeper. That we are our sister's keeper. (106)

In the end then, what is called for is nothing more, and nothing less, than what all the world's great religions demand – that we do unto others as we would have them do unto us. Let us be our brother's keeper, Scripture tells us. Let us be our sister's keeper. Let us find that common stake we all have in one another, and let our politics reflect that spirit as well. (107)

We all have a stake in one another, we are our brother's keeper, we are our sister's keeper, and "either we go up together, or we go down together." (110)

It [his work as a community organizer] was one of the most meaningful experiences of my life – because it showed me that what holds this country together is that fundamental belief that we all have a stake in each other; that I am my brother's keeper; I am my sister's keeper; and in this country, we rise and fall together. (133)

That's the promise of America – the idea that we are responsible for ourselves, but that we also rise or fall as one nation; the fundamental belief that I am my brother's keeper; I am my sister's keeper. (152)

And at that darkest moment [September 11], we understood that here in America, we all have a stake in each other; I am my brother's keeper, I am my sister's keeper; and we rise and fall as one nation. (154)

Bubble and bust.

No longer can we allow Wall Street wrongdoers to slip through regulatory cracks. No longer can we allow special interests to put their thumbs on the economic scales. No longer can we allow the unscrupulous lending and borrowing that leads only to destructive cycles of bubble and bust. (221)

The **buck** stops here.

We need to ensure that our ability to respond to threats around the world is never compromised. And I will always respect – and not ignore – the advice of military commanders. But I will also make clear that when I am President, the buck will stop in the Oval Office. (87)

And I'll turn the page on the imperial presidency that treats national security as a partisan issue – not an American issue. I will call for a standing, bipartisan Consultative Group of congressional leaders on national security. I will meet with this Consultative Group every month, and consult with them before taking major military action. The buck will stop with me. (92)

But understand, I will be setting policy as president. I will be responsible for the vision that this team carries out, and I expect them to implement that vision once decisions are made. So, as Harry Truman said, the buck will stop with me. And nobody who's standing here, I think, would have agreed to join this administration unless they had the confidence that in fact that vision was one that would help secure the American people and our interests. (207)

To pass the **buck**.

Taking responsibility for oneself and showing individual initiative are American values we all share. Frankly, they're values we could stand to see more of in a culture where the buck is too often passed to the next guy. They are values we could use more of here in Washington too. (14)

Remember what happens when responsibilities are ignored and bucks are passed – when the White House blames FEMA and FEMA blames the state of Louisiana and pretty soon no one's fixing the problem because everyone thought somebody else would. (66)

Just today, Senator McCain offered up the oldest Washington stunt in the book – you pass the buck to a commission to study the problem. But here's the thing – this isn't 9/11. We know how we got into this mess. What we need now is leadership that gets us out. (156)

To turn (make) a (quick) **buck**.

They [military personnel] had made careers, had been honored, for perfecting the tools of war. Now they found themselves presiding over remnants of the past, their institutions barely relevant to nations whose people had shifted their main attention to turning a quick buck. (H,313)

There's no silver **bullet**.

There's no silver bullet. A solution to our energy dilemma won't come overnight. But we don't have to accept the wait-and-see attitude anymore. It flies in the face of our history and our founding principles. (26)

As I have said before, there are no magic [silver] bullets for a good outcome in Iraq. I am not the Chairman of the Joint Chiefs of Staff, the Secretary of State, or the Director of National Intelligence. I have neither the expertise nor the inclination to micro-manage war from Washington. (36)

Something is **bull**(-shit).

"Man, those folks are just making fun of us," I said. "What're you talking about?" "All that 'Yo baby, give me five' bullshit." "So who's mister sensitive all of a sudden? Kurt don't mean nothing by it." (D,83)

"With the unions in the shape they're in, the churches are the only game in town. That's where the people are, and that's where the values are, even if they've been buried under a lot of bullshit." (D,141)

"Some people say," I interrupted, "that the church is too upwardly mobile." The reverend's [Wright's] smile faded. "That's a lot of bull," he said sharply. "People who talk that mess reflect their own confusion." (D,283)

To be on the back (front) **burner**.

Such a shift in emphasis is not easy: Old habits die hard, and there is always a fear on the part of many minorities that unless racial discrimination, past and present, stays on the front burner, white America will be let off the hook and hard-fought gains may be reversed. (H,248)

Business as usual.

How can we cut through the apathy and the partisanship and the business-as-usual culture in Washington? When we wonder this, we need to rediscover the hope that people have been in our shoes and they've lived to cross those bridges. (15)

So yes, I've had enough. And if you've had enough too, then we got some work to do. If you've had enough, then we have some checks to write, and some calls to make, and some doors to knock on. [...] And we're gonna change business-as-usual in Washington, and we're gonna set this country in a new direction. (50)

And in nine days, nearly half the nation will have the chance to join us in saying that we are tired of business-as-usual in Washington, we are hungry for change, and we are ready to believe again. (100)

We are going to make sure that we start focusing on energy, health care, on revamping our education system so that it's competitive in the 21st century, and as I'm talking about today, that we are not going back to business as usual when it comes to our budget. (204)

The chief **business** of the American people is business.

Calvin Coolidge once said that "the chief business of the American people is business," and indeed, it would be hard to find a country on earth that's been more consistently hospitable to the logic of the marketplace. (H,149)

To be like nobody's **business**.

For the first few years of our marriage, Michelle and I went through the usual adjustments all couples go through [...]. I invariably left the butter out after breakfast and forgot to twist the little tie around the bread bag; Michelle could rack up parking tickets like nobody's business. (H,338)

To go about one's **business**.

"Tim seems all right to me," he said. "He's going about his business. Don't bother nobody. Seems to me we should be worrying about whether our own stuff's together instead of passing judgment on how other folks are supposed to act." (D,102)

Of course, there is another story to be told, by the millions of Americans who are going about their business every day. They are on the job or looking for work, starting businesses, helping their kids with their homework, and struggling with high gas bills, insufficient health insurance, and a pension that some bankruptcy court somewhere has rendered unenforceable. (H,24)

To mind one's (own) **business**.

I took a step forward, but Roy pulled me back. "Mind your own business, brother," he whispered. "But −" "They may be police. I tell you, Barack, you don't know what it's like to spend a night in a Nairobi jail." (D,365)

46 [sic] percent of Americans have concluded that the United States should "mind its own business internationally and let other countries get along the best they can on their own." (H,303)

According to a recent Pew survey, 42% of Americans agree with the statement that the U.S. should "mind its own business internationally and let other countries get along the best they can on their own." (36)

According to a Pew survey, 42% of Americans now agree with the statement that the U.S. should "mind its own business internationally and let other countries get along the best they can on their own." (71)

Render unto **Caesar** the things which are Caesar's.

The reluctance on the part of many evangelicals to be drawn into politics – their inward focus on individual salvation and willingness to render unto Caesar what is his – might have endured indefinitely had it not been for the social upheavals of the sixties. (H,200)

A **call** to arms.

Now is the time for serious leadership to get us started down the path of energy independence. Now is the time for this call to arms. I hope some of the ideas I've laid out today can serve as a basis for this call. (43)

To be a wake-up **call**.

People like Herblock [Herbert Block] and Tony Auth and others jolt us awake from our political cynicism with a few ingenious images and a clever phrase that can often speak more truth than a thousand words. And this is the kind of wake-up call our politics need today more than ever. (8)

To go beyond the **call** (of duty).

A number of my Senate staff [...] read the manuscript on their own time and provided me with editorial suggestions, policy recommendations, reminders, and corrections. Thanks to all of them for literally going beyond the call of duty. (H,364)

To kick the **can** down the road.

We should help the auto industry, but what we should expect is that any additional money that we put into the auto industry, any help that we provide, is designed to assure a long-term, sustainable auto industry and not just kicking the can down the road. (203)

Yes we **can**.

It's hard to imagine that there are hundreds of thousands of parents every year who are forced to turn to kids who've worked hard and studied hard all through school and tell them "No, we can't send you to college." But it's harder to imagine that any of us could rest until those parents can start saying "yes we can" to their kids. (8)

Where we are met with cynicism, and doubt, and those who tell us that we can't, we will respond with that timeless creed that sums up the spirit of a people in three simple words: Yes. We. Can. (100)

Can we send a message to all those weary travelers beyond our shores who long to be free from fear and want that the United States of America is, and always will be, "the last best hope of Earth?" We say; we hope; we believe – yes, we can. (106)

We were told this wasn't possible. We were told the climb was too steep. We were told our country was too cynical – that we were just being naive; that we couldn't really change the world as it is. But then a few people in Iowa stood up to say, "Yes we can." (106)

It's the simple truth [...] that in this country, justice can be won against the greatest odds; hope can find its way back to the darkest corners; and when we are told that we cannot bring about the change that we seek, we answer with one voice – yes we can. (113)

We can prove that the one thing more powerful than the politics of anything goes is the will and determination of the American people. We can change this country. Yes we can. (195)

A man touched down on the moon, a wall came down in Berlin, a world was connected by our science and imagination. And this year, in this election, she [Ann Nixon Cooper] touched her finger to a screen, and cast her vote, because after 106 years in America, through the best of times and the darkest of hours, she knows how America can change. Yes we can. (197)

And tonight, I think about all that she's [Ann Nixon Cooper, 106 years old] seen throughout her century in America – the heartache and the hope; the struggle and the progress; the times we were told that we can't, and the people who pressed on with that American creed: Yes we can. (197)

At a time when women's voices were silenced and their hopes dismissed, she [Ann Nixon Cooper] lived to see them stand up and speak out and reach for the ballot. Yes we can. (197)

She [Ann Nixon Cooper] was there for the buses in Montgomery, the hoses in Birmingham, a bridge in Selma, and a preacher from Atlanta who told a people "We Shall Overcome." Yes we can. (197)

This is our moment. This is our time – to put our people back to work and open doors of opportunity for our kids; to restore prosperity and promote the cause of peace; to reclaim the American Dream and reaffirm that fundamental truth – that out of many, we are one; that while we breathe, we hope, and where we are met with cynicism, and doubt, and those who tell us that we can't, we will respond with that timeless creed that sums up the spirit of a people: Yes We Can. (197)

When the bombs fell on our harbor and tyranny threatened the world, she [Ann Nixon Cooper] was there to witness a generation to rise to greatness and a democracy was saved. Yes we can. (197)

When there was despair in the dust bowl and depression across the land, she [Ann Nixon Cooper] saw a nation conquer fear itself with a New Deal, new jobs and a new sense of common purpose. Yes we can. (197)

To play one's trump (best) **card**.

And I would know that Ray had flashed his trump card, one that, to his credit, he rarely played. I was different, after all, potentially suspect; I had no idea who my own self was. Unwilling to risk exposure, I would quickly retreat to safer ground. (D,82)

We can pounce on some gaffe by a Hillary supporter as evidence that she's playing the race card, or we can speculate on whether white men will all flock to John McCain in the general election regardless of his policies. (107)

To pull the **carpet** (rug) out from under someone.

When you've worked hard your whole life, and paid into the system, and done everything right, you shouldn't have the carpet pulled out from under you when you least expect it and can least afford it. Health care shouldn't be some kind of either-or tradeoff where our seniors get left out in the cold. (180)

The **carrot** and the stick.

Like Adlai Stevenson, I believe there are times to be tough. But statements like "I don't do carrots" coming from someone who wants to be our chief diplomat at the U.N. certainly give me pause. (9)

I think we need to ratchet up tough but direct diplomacy with Iran [...] and present a set of carrots and sticks in [for] changing their calculus about how they want to operate. You know, in terms of carrots, I think that we can provide economic incentives that would be helpful [...]. But we also have to focus on the sticks, and [...] in order for us to change Iran's behavior, we may have to tighten up those sanctions. (211)

To fight like **cats** and dogs.

"Back then, almost everybody with any power in Washington had served in World War II. We might've fought like cats and dogs on issues. A lot of us came from different backgrounds, different neighborhoods, different political philosophies." (H,25-26)

To break the glass **ceiling**.

At its heart, this has always been the essence of the women's movement in America – the quest to ensure that our daughters will have the same opportunities as our sons. Now, I realize that one day, my girls will discover that this journey is not over – that there are doors left to be open[ed] and glass ceilings yet to be shattered. (34)

But it also means binding our particular grievances – for better health care, and better schools, and better jobs – to the larger aspirations of all Americans – the white woman struggling to break the glass ceiling, the white man whose [i.e, who's] been laid off, the immigrant trying to feed his family. (107)

So it was for the workers who stood out on the picket lines; the women who shattered glass ceilings; the children who braved a Selma bridge for freedom's cause. (119)

I saw my grandmother, who helped raise me, work her way up from a secretary at a bank to become one of the first women bank vice presidents in the state. But I also saw how she ultimately hit a glass ceiling – how men no more qualified than she was kept moving up the corporate ladder ahead of her. (134, 135)

I saw my grandmother, who helped raise me, work her way up from the secretarial pool to middle management at a bank. But I also saw her hit a glass ceiling, as men no more qualified than she was moved up the corporate ladder ahead of her. (160)

That's why all of us are here today – because of women who came before us. [...] Women like my friend Hillary Clinton who put those 18 million cracks in that glass ceiling so that my daughters – and all our sons and daughters – could dream a little bigger and reach a little higher. (160)

To yank one's **chain**.

"They'll [colleges] train you so good, you'll start believing what they tell you about equal opportunity and the American way and all that shit. They'll give you a corner office and invite you to fancy dinners, and tell you you're a credit to your race. Until you want to actually start running things, and then they'll yank on your chain and let you know that you may be a well-trained, well-paid nigger, but you're a nigger just the same." (D,97)

To **chalk** up something.

This [the crumbling of the social compact] is not just happening by chance. It's not something we can just chalk up to temporary shocks. It's happening in part because of the choices we're making, and the way that we're making those choices. It's happening because we've gone too far from being a country where we're all in this together, to a country where everyone's on their own. (90)

Change is never (not) easy.

I'm sure you'll all agree that we have songs left to sing and bridges left to cross. And if there's anything we can learn from this living saint [John Lewis] sitting beside me, it is that change is never easy, but always possible. That it comes not from violence or militancy or the kind of politics that pits us against each other [...]; but from a strong message of hope, and from the courage to turn against the tide so that the tide eventually may be turned. (3)

They [civil rights acts] remind us that in America, ordinary citizens can somehow find in their hearts the courage to do extraordinary things. That change is never easy, but always possible. And it comes not from violence or militancy or the kind of politics that pits us against each other [...]; but from great discipline and organization, and from a strong message of hope. (15)

Change never comes without a fight.

We were thrilled yesterday when a great American statesman, General Colin Powell, joined our cause. But we cannot let up. And we won't. Because one thing we know is that change never comes without a fight. (183, 184, 187, 188)

We're going to have to work, and struggle, and fight for every single one of those 10 days to move our country in a new direction. We cannot let up. And we won't. Because one thing we know is that change never comes without a fight. (189)

Character is like a tree and reputation like its shadow.

It serves us then to reflect on whether that element of Lincoln's character, and the American character – that aspect which makes tough choices, and speaks the truth when least convenient, and acts while still admitting doubt – remains with us today. Lincoln once said that "character is like a tree and reputation like its shadow. The shadow is what we think of it; the tree is the real thing." (12)

To be a (good-time) **Charlie**.

"Remember what that's like? Effort? Damn it, Bar, you can't just sit around like some good-time Charlie, waiting for luck to see you through." "A good-time what?" "A good-time Charlie. A loafer." (D,95)

I suddenly felt like puncturing that certainty of hers [his mom's], letting her know that her experiment with me had failed. Instead of shouting, I laughed. "A good-time Charlie, huh? Well, why not? Maybe that's what I want out of life. I mean, look at Gramps. He didn't even go to college". (D,95)

To cut to the **chase**.

Certainly it eliminated any sense of shame I once had in asking strangers for large sums of money. By the end of the campaign, the banter and small talk that had once accompanied my solicitation calls were eliminated. I cut to the chase and tried not to take no for an answer. (H,113)

To be (get) a reality **check**.

We've been warned, in these last few weeks, that this kind of change isn't possible. That we're peddling false hope. That we need a reality check. (104)

To give a blank **check**.

This was a vote about whether or not to go to war. That's the truth as we all understood it then, and as we need to understand it now. And we need to ask those who voted for the war: how can you give the President a blank check and then act surprised when he cashes it? (92)

Make no mistake: we can't succeed in Afghanistan or secure our homeland unless we change our Pakistan policy. We must expect more of the Pakistani government, but we must offer more than a blank check to a General who has lost the confidence of his people. (139)

And in return for their support, the American people must be assured that the [economic recovery] deal reflects the basic principles of transparency, fairness, and reform. First, there must be no blank check when American taxpayers are on the hook for this much money. (161)

For the auto industry to completely collapse would be a disaster in this kind of environment, not just for individual families, but the repercussions across the economy would be dire. So it's my belief that we need to provide assistance to the auto industry. But I think that it can't be a blank check. (201)

What I also have said is that we can't just write a blank check to the auto industry. Taxpayers can't be expected to pony up more money for an auto industry that has been resistant to change. (203)

We started off with the automakers coming before Congress asking for a blank check, and I like many said that's not going to fly; we're going to have to make sure that we've got a mechanism to force the kind of restructuring that is necessary so that we have a sustainable auto industry. (218)

To grin like a **Cheshire** cat.

Still, I'd felt bad after that particular episode; it was the one trick my mother always had up her sleeve, that way she had of making me feel guilty. She made no bones about it, either. "You can't help it," she told me once. "Slipped it into your baby food. Don't worry, though," she added, smiling like the Cheshire cat. "A healthy dose of guilt never hurt anybody. It's what civilization is built on, guilt. A highly underrated emotion." (D,96)

Let the **chips** fall where they may.

It's a course that further divides Wall Street from Main Street; where struggling families are told to pull themselves up by their bootstraps because there's nothing government can do or should do – and so we should give more to those with the most and let the chips fall where they may. (106)

To run **circles** around someone (something).

He [Marcus] had caught me in a lie. Two lies, really – the lie I had told about Tim and the lie I was telling about myself. In fact, that whole first year seemed like one long lie, me spending all my energy running around in circles, trying to cover my tracks. (D,102)

These companies [foreign automakers] are running circles around their American counterparts. Ford is only making 20,000 Escape Hybrids this year, and GM's brand won't be on the market until 2007. This isn't just costing us energy efficiency – it's decimating American businesses and costing American workers their jobs. (26)

Some of the biggest corporations in America, giants of industry like GM and Ford, are watching foreign competitors based in countries with universal health care run circles around them, with a GM car containing twice as much health care cost as a Japanese car. (74)

Be a good **citizen**, and think about the other guy.

As a cartoonist, Herb [Block] was always able to illustrate deeply-held convictions about complicated political issues with a few brief strokes. And so it was with this simple, graceful, yet profoundly challenging philosophy that was passed down to him from his parents: "Be a good citizen, and think about the other guy." (8)

That's the America we love – the America we hope for – but that's not the America we can have by leaving this country on autopilot and going about our own business. That America takes work. It takes a belief that we're all connected as one people – that we rise and fall as one nation. [...] Be a good citizen. Think about the other guy. (8)

I'm not sure, but I do know that I've met enough good citizens who think about the other guy and want to change this [rising college tuition costs]. And I believe there are enough members of both parties who want to start this country down the path of making college affordable and accessible for every American. (8)

Be a good citizen, think about the other guy, but most importantly, do something about it. Whether it's through cartoons or campaigns, by taking it to the streets or taking it to your editor, tackling the biggest issues or lending a simple hand to your neighbor, these are the ways we leave our mark on the land we love – the same way Herblock [Herbert Block] left his mark on the pages of the Washington Post every day. (8)

As happy as a **clam**.

He [Tim] planned to major in business. His white girlfriend was probably waiting for him up in his room, listening to country music. He was happy as a clam, and I wanted nothing more than for him to go away. (D,102)

To come **clean**.

Time and again, President Bush has refused to come clean to Congress. Why was it that 14 of 16 members of the Intelligence Committee were kept in the dark for four and a half years? The only reason that some Senators are now being briefed is because the story was made public. (54)

To keep (something) **clean**.

It was with that mind-set that I had entered the 2004 U.S. Senate race. For the duration of the campaign I did my best to say what I thought, keep it clean, and focus on substance. When I won the Democratic primary [...] it was tempting to believe that I had proven my point. (H,18)

To have something (available) at the **click** of a mouse [computer!].

Yet, because we haven't updated technology in the rest of the health care industry, a single transaction still costs up to twenty-five dollars – not one dime of which goes toward improving the quality of our health care. Doctors are forced to fumble through paperwork and don't have all of the information about each patient at the click of a mouse. (21)

To go over the **cliff**.

And if you can demonstrate that you went bankrupt because of medical expenses, then there must be a process that relieves that debt and lets you get back on your feet. I don't accept an America where we let someone go over a cliff just because they get sick. That is not who we are. (95)

To get one's **clock** cleaned.

(I am convinced [...] that antitax, antigovernment, antiunion sentiments grow anytime people find themselves standing in line at a government office with only one window open and three or four workers chatting among themselves in full view.) Progressives in particular seem confused on this point, which is why we so often get our clocks cleaned in elections. (H,60)

To turn back the **clock**.

In 2009, we will have a window of opportunity to renew our global leadership and bring our nation together. If we don't seize that moment, we may not get another. This election is a turning point. The American people get to decide: are we going to turn back the clock, or turn the page? (92)

I know it is tempting – after another presidency by a man named George Bush – to simply turn back the clock, and to build a bridge back to the 20th century. (104)

I do not believe that government should stand in the way of innovation, or turn back the clock to an older era of regulation. But I do believe that government has a role to play in advancing our common prosperity. (109)

There are some who believe that we must try to turn back the clock on this new world; that the only chance to maintain our living standards is to build a fortress around America; to stop trading with other countries, shut down immigration, and rely on old industries. I disagree. Not only is it impossible to turn back the tide of globalization, but efforts to do so can make us worse off. (124)

To be made out of whole **cloth**.

And although Gramps's relationship with my mother was already strained by the time they reached Hawaii [...] it was this desire of his to obliterate the past, this confidence in the possibility of remaking the world from whole cloth, that proved to be his most lasting patrimony. (D,21-22)

To be a dark **cloud**.

That means a peaceful democratic transition in 2008, and support for economic growth and opportunity – including the lifting of sanctions – once the dark cloud of Mugabe's rule is lifted, and Zimbabweans are able again to reach for the new horizon they deserve. (80)

To be in (belong to) the old boys **club**.

Do you think Dick Cheney is delighted to support John McCain because he thinks John McCain's going to bring change? Do you think John McCain and Dick Cheney have been talking about how to shake things up, and get rid of the lobbyists and the old boys club in Washington? (195)

To be left out in the **cold**.

When you've worked hard your whole life, and paid into the system, and done everything right, you shouldn't have the carpet pulled out from under you when you least expect it and can least afford it. Health care shouldn't be some kind of either-or tradeoff where our seniors get left out in the cold. (180)

Confidence of success is almost success.

My grandfather would shake his head and get out of his chair to flip on the TV set. "Now there's something you can learn from your dad," he would tell me. "*Confidence*. The secret to a man's success." (D,8)

To use a **cookie-cutter**.

The IMF and World Bank need to recognize that there is no single, cookie-cutter formula for each and every country's development. There is nothing wrong, of course, with a policy of "tough love" when it comes to providing development assistance to poor countries. (H,318)

To have a **corner** on something.

And when I'm President, we're going to have a government that helps us win these fights [for equal education]. Not because it's up to me alone. Not because I have a corner on all the best ideas. But because I understand that we need more than a new campaign or candidate – we need a movement. (93)

To turn the **corner**.

"I was just starting to know him. It was getting to the point where…where he might have explained himself. Sometimes I think he might have really turned the corner, found some inner peace. When he died, I felt so…so cheated. As cheated as you must have felt." (D,219)

To cut **corners**.

He hadn't cut corners, though, or played all the angles. He was diligent and honest, no matter what it cost him. He had led his life according to principles that demanded a different kind of toughness, principles that promised a higher form of power. (D,50)

That is not how we should be doing business in the U.S. Senate, and that's not how we should be prosecuting this war on terrorism. When we're sloppy and cut corners, we are undermining those very virtues of America that will lead us to success in winning this war. (69)

In our government, we see campaign contributions and lobbyists used to cut corners and win favors that stack the deck against businesses and consumers who play by the rules. (89)

Too often we've excused and even embraced an ethic of greed, corner cutting and inside dealing that has always threatened the long-term stability of our economic system. (109)

You shouldn't have to pay higher taxes because some big corporations cut corners to avoid paying taxes. All of us have a responsibility to pay our fair share. That's accountability. (169)

Countries that out-teach us today will out-compete us tomorrow.

I don't accept that we can't give every single child in America a world-class education. We know countries that out-teach us today will out-compete us tomorrow.

But it's bigger than that. The America we believe in isn't a country where millions of children are robbed of their opportunity by failing schools. And the answer isn't just a snappy slogan. (88)

This [America's competitive edge] starts with providing every American with a world-class education, from cradle to adulthood. We know that in this economy, countries that out-educate us today will out-compete us tomorrow. (89)

Don't ask what your **country** can do for you, ask what you can do for your country.

The class of 1960 would find themselves at the beginning of a decade where social and racial strife threatened to tear apart the very fabric of the nation. They would hear a young President [Kennedy] urge them to ask what they could do for their country. And they would answer the call to sit at lunch counters and take those Freedom Rides; they would march for justice and live for equality. (58)

We're the party of a young President [Kennedy] who asked what we could do for our country, and who put us on a path to the moon. We're the party of a man who overcame his own disability, who told us that the only thing we had to fear was fear itself; and who faced down fascism and liberated a continent from tyranny. (104)

I was born the year his [Ted Kennedy's] brother John called a generation of Americans to ask their country what they could do. And I came of age at a time when they did it. (116)

You know, Ted Kennedy often tells a story about the fifth anniversary celebration of the Peace Corps. He was there, and he asked one of the young Americans why he had chosen to volunteer. And the man replied, "Because it was the first time someone asked me to do something for my country." (116)

To be like **crabs** in a bucket.

"They're the only ones that pay their dues into the Chamber. They understand business, what it means to cooperate. They pool their money. Make each other loans. We don't do that, see. The black merchants around here, we're all like crabs in a bucket." (D,182)

To fall through the **cracks**.

Think of how many [returning soldiers] we turn away [from proper medical care] – of how many we let fall through the cracks. We have to do better than this. (114)

Think of how many [returning soldiers] we turn away [from proper medical care] – of how many we let fall through the cracks; of how many suffer in silence. We have to do better than this. (131)

No longer can we allow Wall Street wrongdoers to slip through regulatory cracks. No longer can we allow special interests to put their thumbs on the economic scales. No longer can we allow the unscrupulous lending and borrowing that leads only to destructive cycles of bubble and bust. (221)

To be a **credit** to someone (something).

"They'll [colleges] train you so good, you'll start believing what they tell you about equal opportunity and the American way and all that shit. They'll give you a corner office and invite you to fancy dinners, and tell you you're a credit to your race. Until you want to actually start running things, and then they'll yank on your chain and let you know that you may be a well-trained, well-paid nigger, but you're a nigger just the same." (D,97)

To **crop** up like dandelions.

But there was an inescapable difference between what I was now hearing and what I remembered, as if the images of my childhood had been run in reverse. In these stories, For Sale signs cropped up like dandelions under a summer sun. (D,156)

To bear one's **cross**.

No one expected self-sacrifice from me [...]. As far as they were concerned, my color had always been a sufficient criterion for community membership, enough of a cross to bear. (D,278)

To be at the **crossroads**.

I believe that as we stand on the crossroads of history, we can make the right choices, and meet the challenges that face us. (2)

America now finds itself at a similar crossroads. As gas prices rise, the Middle East grows ever more unstable, and the ice caps continue to melt, we face a now-or-never, once-in-a-generation opportunity to set this country on a different course. (48)

We meet here today at a time where we find ourselves at a crossroads in America's history. It's a time where you can go to any town hall or street corner or coffee shop and hear people express the same anxiety about the future. (50)

My friends, we meet here today at a time where we find ourselves at a crossroads in America's history. It's a time when you can go to any town hall or street corner or coffee shop and hear people express the same anxiety about the future. (57)

The decisions that have been made [about Iraq] have led us to this crossroads – this moment of great peril. We have a choice. We can continue down the road that has weakened our credibility and damaged our strategic interests in the region. Or we can take a turn toward the future. That road will not be smooth, and there are risks involved with any approach. (79)

The news from Iraq is very bad, but it can change if we say enough. Let this be the day that begins the painful and difficult work of moving from this crossroad[s]. (79)

To be (get) ahead of the **curve**.

Since the founding, the American political tradition has been reformist, not revolutionary. What that means is that for a political leader to get things done, he or she ideally should be ahead of the curve, but not too far ahead. I want to push the envelope but make sure I have enough folks with me that I'm not rendered politically impotent. (B,109)

Lenders must get ahead of the curve rather than just reacting to crisis. They should actively look at all borrowers, offer workouts, and reduce the principal on mortgages in trouble. (109)

To be **cut** and dried.

Not only was the idea of an invasion increasingly popular, but on the merits I didn't consider the case against the war to be cut-and-dried. Like most analysts, I assumed that Saddam had chemical and biological weapons and coveted nuclear arms. (H,294)

To **cut** (nip) and run.

The administration has narrowed an entire debate about war into two camps: "cut-and-run" or "stay the course." If you offer any criticism or even mention that we should take a second look at our strategy and change our approach, you are branded "cut-and-run." If you are ready to blindly trust the administration no matter what they do, you are willing to "stay the course." (B,68)

The Administration has narrowed an entire debate about war into two camps: "cut-and-run" or "stay the course." If you offer any criticism or even mention that we should take a second look at our strategy and change our approach, you're branded cut-and-run. (36)

That policy-by-slogan will no longer pass as an acceptable form of debate in this country. "Mission Accomplished," "cut and run," "stay the course" – the American people have determined that all these phrases have become meaningless in the face of a conflict that grows more deadly and chaotic with each passing day. (71)

To be (kept) in the **dark**.

Time and again, President Bush has refused to come clean to Congress. Why was it that 14 of 16 members of the Intelligence Committee were kept in the dark for four and a half years? The only reason that some Senators are now being briefed is because the story was made public. (54)

To be a **dark horse**.

For whatever reason [...], it became fashionable among wealthy donors to promote my cause, and small donors around the state began sending checks through the internet at a pace we had never anticipated. Ironically, my dark-horse status protected me from some of the more dangerous pitfalls of fund-raising. (H,113)

The **days** are numbered.

The days of running a 21st century economy on a 20th century fossil fuel are numbered, and we need to realize that before it's too late. Our persistent dependence on oil is a danger our government has known about for years. [...] It's a danger they have failed to prepare for, listen to, or seriously try to guard against. (26)

The good old **days**.

And if we don't take these steps now, we will someday look back on today's $3 per gallon gasoline as the good old days. At that point, no amount of drilling on the Outer Continental Shelf will solve our problems. (64)

There are brighter (better) **days** ahead.

If we do what we must do, then I have no doubt that all across the country [...] the people will rise up in November [...], and this country will reclaim its promise, and out of this long political darkness a brighter day will come. (2)

The audacity of hope. In the end, that is God's greatest gift to us, the bedrock of this nation; the belief in things not seen; the belief that there are better days ahead. (2)

We're going through hard times. And, historically, what has always brought us through hard times is that national character, that sense of optimism, that willingness to look forward, that, that sense that better days are ahead. (211)

To be **dead** on arrival.

It's the same approach George W. Bush floated a few years ago. It was dead on arrival in Congress. But if Senator McCain were to succeed where George Bush failed, it very well could be the beginning of the end of our employer-based health care system. (172)

To be in a **deadlock**.

It occurred without warning. Only a few months earlier, Harold [Washington] had won reelection, handily beating Vrdolyak and Byrne, breaking the deadlock that had prevailed in the city for the previous four years. (D,287)

In his Manichean struggle, compromise came to look like weakness, to be punished or purged. You were with us or against us. You had to choose sides. It was Bill Clinton's singular contribution that he had tried to transcend this ideological deadlock. (H,34)

In 1993, President Clinton took a stab at creating a system of universal coverage, but was stymied. Since then, the public debate has been deadlocked, with some on the right arguing for a strong dose of market discipline. (H,183)

To be a (no) big **deal**.

"Yeah, I know – but it's probably a little scary for her, seeing some big man block her way. It's really no big deal." He [Obama's grandfather] turned around and I saw now that he was shaking. "It *is* a big deal. It's a big deal to me." (D,88)

To be (strike) a sweetheart **deal**.

And I will finally end the abuse of no-bid contracts once and for all – the days of sweetheart deals for Halliburton will be over when I'm in the White House. (169, 170)

To stack the **deck**.

It is painfully obvious that corruption stifles development – it siphons off scarce resources that could improve infrastructure, bolster education systems, and strengthen public health. It stacks the deck so high against entrepreneurs that they cannot get their job-creating ideas off the ground. (67)

In our government, we see campaign contributions and lobbyists used to cut corners and win favors that stack the deck against businesses and consumers who play by the rules. (89)

Deeds speak louder than words. (**Deeds**, not words.)

We can make claims on their behalf, so long as we understand that our values must be tested against fact and experience, so long as we recall that they demand deeds and not just words. (H,69)

It is my hope that upon his [President Bush] return from Mexico he will get to work, converting his words into deeds to help push comprehensive immigration reform forward. (78)

We do need to stand for democracy. And I will. But democracy is about more than a ballot box. America must show – through deeds as well as words – that we stand with those who seek a better life. (85)

An assertive Russia and a rising China remind us – through words and deeds – that the primacy of our power does not mean our power will go unchallenged. A new age of nuclear proliferation has left the world's most deadly weapons unlocked by more and more countries, with thousands of weapons and stockpiles poorly secured all over the world. (87)

The Scripture tells us that we are judged not just by word, but by deed. And if we are to truly bring about the unity that is so crucial in this time, we must find it within ourselves to act on what we know; to understand that living up to this country's ideals and its possibilities will require great effort and resources; sacrifice and stamina. (99)

He [Dr. Martin Luther King] led with words, but he also led with deeds. He also led by example. He led by marching and going to jail and suffering threats and being away from his family. He led by taking a stand against a war, knowing full well that it would diminish his popularity. (99)

Current incidents of discrimination, while less overt than in the past – are real and must be addressed. Not just with words, but with deeds – by investing in schools and our communities; by enforcing our civil rights laws and ensuing fairness in our criminal justice system. (107)

Since CGI [Clinton Global Initiative] is about deeds, not just words, let me tell you about four specific commitments that I will make on four issues that CGI has focused on – climate change, poverty, education, and health – if I have the opportunity to serve as President of the United States. (164)

After that war (World War II] was over [...]. those troops came home to a grateful nation, a nation that welcomed them with the GI Bill and a chance to live out in peace the dreams they had fought for, and so many died for, on the battlefield. We owe it to all our veterans to honor them as we honored our Greatest Generation, not just with words, but with deeds. (212)

To make a **dent**.

And this is a budget that tells all those veterans still waiting for help to keep waiting. There are roughly 480,000 compensation and pension claims still unprocessed, but this budget only calls for 113 new employees to help deal with this backlog – not enough to make a dent. (7)

We could open up every square inch of America to drilling and we still wouldn't even make a dent in our oil dependency. We could open up ANWR today, and at its peak, which would be more than a decade from now, it would give us enough oil to take care of our transportation needs for about a month. Clearly, this is not a solution. (26)

The President's energy proposal would reduce our oil imports by 4.5 million barrels per day by 2025. Not only can we do better than that [reducing oil imports], we must do better than that if we hope to make a real dent in our oil dependency. (48)

To make a pact with the **devil**.

There's a school of thought that sees [...] the Constitution only as a betrayal of the grand ideals set forth by the Declaration of Independence; that agrees with early abolitionists that the Great Compromise between North and South was a pact with the Devil. (H,96)

To roll (the) **dice**.

We can't afford to roll the dice by privatizing Social Security, and wagering the nest egg of millions of Americans on Wall Street. We can't afford to gamble on more of the same trickle down philosophy that showers tax breaks on big corporations and the wealthiest few. (167)

To be a **die-hard**.

And just then, the owner [of a restaurant] comes out. And I said, "Sir, I understand you're a die-hard Republican." He said yes. And I said, "Well, how's business?" He said, "Not so good because my customers can't afford to eat out right now." So I said, "Well, who do you think has been running the economy for the last eight years?" And he said, "The Republicans." Well, I said, "If you keep hitting your head against a wall and it starts to hurt, at some point don't you stop hitting it against the wall?" Maybe you should try the Democrats for a change. (183)

You can't change **direction** with a new driver who follows the same old map.

But another thing I know is this – we can't steer ourselves out of this crisis by heading in the same, disastrous direction. We can't change direction with a new driver who wants to follow the same old map. And that's what this election is all about. (158)

But another thing I know is that we can't steer ourselves out of this crisis by heading in the same, disastrous direction. We can't change direction with a new driver who wants to follow the same old map. And that's what this election is all about. (160)

Disorder breeds disorder.

Moreover, we fool ourselves in thinking that, in the words of one commentator, "we must learn to watch others die with equanimity," and not expect consequences. Disorder breeds disorder; callousness toward others tends to spread among ourselves. (H,319)

To get something out of the **ditch**.

You know, there were a lot of noteworthy moments in the debate, but there's one that sticks out this morning. It's when Governor Palin said to Joe Biden that our plan to get our economy out of the ditch was somehow a job killing plan. (171)

To run something into the **ditch**.

We cannot afford four more years of out of touch, on your own, leadership in the White House. John McCain likes to rail against the Washington herd, but the truth is, when it comes to the issues that really matter in your lives, he's been running in that herd for 26 years, and they've run this economy into a ditch. This election is our chance to stand up and say – enough is enough. (155)

Now, this didn't happen by accident. Our falling GDP is a direct result of eight years of the trickle down, Wall Street first/Main Street last policies that have driven our economy into a ditch. (193)

Do unto others as you would have them do unto you.

In the end then, what is called for is nothing more, and nothing less, than what all the world's great religions demand – that we do unto others as we would have them do unto us. Let us be our brother's keeper, Scripture tells us. Let us be our sister's keeper. Let us find that common stake we all have in one another, and let our politics reflect that spirit as well. (107)

To treat someone like a **dog**.

"I don't care how many mouths you have to feed, you cannot treat your own people like dogs. Here ..." Auma snapped open her purse and took out a crumpled hundred-shilling note. "You see!" she shouted. "I can pay for my own damn food." (D,313)

This is a revolving **door**.

By passing this bill, we will ban gifts and meals and end subsidized travel on corporate jets. We will close the revolving door between Pennsylvania Avenue and K Street. (86)

And I have laid out far-reaching plans that I intend to sign into law as President to bring transparency to government, and to end the revolving door between industries and the federal agencies that oversee them. (109)

To keep the wolf [famine] from knocking on the **door**.

As a peasant in 11th century China, you knew that no matter how hard you worked, the local warlord might take everything you had – and that famine might come knocking on your door any day. (19)

To open the **door** to someone or something.

Harold Washington did open up the door to a lot of organizations and minorities. What would have been real empowerment was not done. And I think what was unfortunate, was that Harold Washington instead of actually getting contacts back [...] should have been helping to foster in the black community the sense that they need to organize even more and build even more and broaden their base. (O,148-149)

No, people don't expect government to solve all their problems. But they sense, deep in their bones, that with just a change in priorities, we can make sure that every child in America has a decent shot at life, and that the doors of opportunity remain open to all. (2)

The chance to go to college – the chance to unlock so many doors of opportunity and possibility – has always been a foundation of the American Dream. [...] And it's a chance given to me by my parents, who weren't rich but believed that in a generous America, you don't have to be rich to achieve your potential – that it can be realized through hard work and education. (8)

We should all be grateful where opportunity has opened the doors of success for Americans of every background. [...] I think it is wonderful that Asian Americans, Latinos, African Americans, and others are represented in all parties and across the political spectrum. When such representation exists, then those [minority] groups are less likely to be taken for granted by any political party. (20)

At its heart, this has always been the essence of the women's movement in America – the quest to ensure that our daughters will have the same opportunities as our sons. Now, I realize that one day, my girls will discover that this journey is not over – that there are doors left to be open[ed] and glass ceilings yet to be shattered. (34)

All over the country, patients and their families are waiting today for Congress and the President to open the door to the cures of tomorrow. At the dawn of the 21st century, we should approach this [stem cell] research with the same passion and commitment that have led to so many cures and saved so many lives throughout our history. (62)

With each passing day, we draw closer together to our neighbors to the south [Latin America]. This convergence creates new challenges, but it also opens the door to a more hopeful future. (78)

In recent years, the doors of Congress and the White House have been thrown wide open to an army of Washington lobbyists who have turned our government into a game only they can afford to play. (86)

And it's a Washington that has thrown open its doors to lobbyists and special interests who've riddled our tax code with loopholes that let corporations avoid paying their taxes while you're paying more. (105)

President Clinton signed legislation that opened the door for faith-based groups to play a role in a number of areas, including helping people move from welfare to work. (130)

But it's also a great opportunity because if we can seize this moment, we can open the door to a new economy for the 21st century that will bring new energy, new jobs, and new hope to families in places like Elkhart [Indiana]. (149)

I come here [to the Congressional Hispanic Caucus] tonight as the first African American nominee of the Democratic Party because generations before me did that same work to break barriers and to open doors. (154)

This is our moment. This is our time – to put our people back to work and open doors of opportunity for our kids; to restore prosperity and promote the cause of peace; to reclaim the American Dream and reaffirm that fundamental truth – that out of many, we are one; that while we breathe, we hope, and where we are met with cynicism, and doubt, and those who tell us that we can't, we will respond with that timeless creed that sums up the spirit of a people: Yes We Can. (197)

We also know that the success of American businesses, small and large, depend on their ability to sell their products across the globe. That's why we must engage in strong, robust trade and open doors for American products. (218)

To shut (close) the **door** on someone or something.

We don't need another President who shuts the door on the American people when they make policy. The American people are not the problem in this country – they are the answer. And it's time we had a President who acted like that. (92)

To do something behind closed **doors**.

George Bush has spent most of his Administration denying that we have a problem, and making deals with Big Oil behind closed doors. (124)

To be (put something) at the **doorstep**.

It's easy for us to lay all of the problems of the world at George Bush's doorstep. His judgments will be subject to the harsh light of history, and the verdict will not be kind. But the question is what comes next. (97)

And then there are those who would lay all of the problems of the Middle East at the doorstep of Israel and its supporters, as if the Israeli-Palestinian conflict is the root of all trouble in the region. (120)

We did not arrive at the doorstep of our current economic crisis by some accident of history. This was not an inevitable part of the business cycle that was beyond our power to avoid. (122)

To let someone **down**.

As if it was me who had kept her grandma on her knees all her life. To hell with Regina. To hell with her high-horse, holier-than-thou, you-let-me-down look in her eyes. She didn't know me. She didn't understand where I was coming from. (D,92-93)

To be (go) **downhill** (from here).

Mr. Rush's name recognition stood at about 90 percent, while mine stood at 11 percent. His approval rating hovered around 70 percent – mine at 8. In that way I learned one of the cardinal rules of modern politics: Do the poll before you announce. Things went downhill from there. (H,106)

To **drink** from a fire hose.

There's a saying that senators frequently use when asked to describe their first year on Capitol Hill: "It's like drinking from a fire hose." The description is apt, for during my first few months in the Senate everything seemed to come at me at once. (H,71)

To **drive** someone to do something.

As the night wore on, the two of them would solicit my help in composing dirty limericks. Eventually, the conversation would turn to laments about women. "They'll drive you to drink, boy," Frank would tell me soberly. "And if you let 'em, they'll drive you into your grave." (D,77)

At the **drop** of a hat.

There was no doubt that the man could talk. At the drop of a hat Mr. Keyes could deliver a grammatically flawless disquisition on virtually every topic. On the stump, he could wind himself up into a fiery intensity, his body rocking, his brow running with sweat. (H,210)

To give someone his **due**.

Pride in our country, respect for our armed services [...], an insistence that there was no easy equivalence between East and West – in all this I had no quarrel with Reagan. And when the Berlin Wall came tumbling down, I had to give the old man his due, even if I never gave him my vote. (H,289)

To **dust** oneself off.

But our time of standing pat, of protecting narrow interests and putting off unpleasant decisions – that time has surely passed. Starting today, we must pick ourselves up, dust ourselves off, and begin again the work of remaking America. (229)

To turn to **dust**.

He [Obama's father], too, had probably believed he was acting out some grand design, that he wasn't simply fleeing from possible inconsequence. And, in fact, he had returned to Kenya, hadn't he? But only as a divided man, his plans, his dreams, soon turned to dust.... (D,277)

To fall on deaf **ears**.

President Kennedy once said – "the pursuit of peace is not as dramatic as the pursuit of war – and frequently the words of the pursuer fall on deaf ears." In the fall of 2002, those deaf ears were in Washington. They belonged to a President who didn't tell the whole truth to the American people. (92)

To be on the cutting (leading) **edge** of something.

See, in this new world, knowledge really is power. A new idea can lead not just to a new product or a new job, but [to] entire new industries and a new way of thinking about the world. And so you need to be the Idea Generation. The generation who's always thinking on the cutting edge, who's wondering how to create and keep the next wave of American jobs and American innovations. (16)

With 230 New Leaders serving more than 100,000 kids annually, New Leaders for New Schools has been at the cutting edge of this process – a process we need to expand nationally. (46)

The VA [Veterans Administration] will also be at the cutting edge of my plan for universal health care, with better preventive care, more research and specialty treatment, and more Vet Centers, particularly in rural areas. (87)

But that doesn't mean we have to accept an America of lost opportunity and diminished dreams. Not when we still have the most productive, highly-educated, best-skilled workers in the world. Not when we still stand on the cutting edge of innovation, and science, and discovery. (105)

And to ensure that America stays on the cutting edge, we'll expand broadband access, expand funding for basic research, and pass comprehensive immigration reform so that we continue to attract the best and the brightest to our shores. (109)

We need to invest in biomedical research and stem cell research, so that we're at the leading edge of prevention and treatment. And we need to finally pass universal health care so that every American has access to health insurance that they can afford. (124)

We'll invite the service and participation of American citizens, and cut through the red tape to make sure that every agency is meeting cutting edge standards. (124)

We will make sure that every doctors [doctor's] office and hospital in this country is using cutting edge technology and electronic medical records so that we can cut red tape, prevent medical mistakes, and help save billions of dollars each year. (210)

Dr. Steven Chu is a Nobel prize-winning physicist who has been working at the cutting edge of our nation's efforts to develop new and cleaner forms of energy. He blazed new trails as a scientist, teacher and administrator, and has recently led the Berkeley National Laboratory in pursuing new alternative and renewable energies. (214)

Nancy's [Sutley] been at the cutting edge of this [environmental] effort, working as the regional administrator for the EPA, at the state level in Sacramento, and recently as the deputy mayor of Energy and the Environment in Los Angles. (214)

I want a proactive vision of getting out, talking to people, talking to farmers, talking to ranchers, being at the cutting edge of environmental and energy policy so that commercial interests are just one group among many groups that are being listened to and being brought together to craft the kind of policies that we want to see. (216)

To set someone on **edge**.

So why did such comments always set me on edge? There was a trick there somewhere, although what the trick was, who was doing the tricking, and who was being tricked, eluded my conscious grasp. (D,82)

To be **either**-or.

When I'm President, we will no longer accept the false choice between being tough on crime and vigilant in our pursuit of justice. Dr. King said it's not either-or, it's both-and. We can have a crime policy that's both tough and smart. (91)

To use one's **elbow**.

He [Sadik] gestured to the crowd along First Avenue. "Everybody looking out for number one. Survival of the fittest. Tooth and claw. Elbow the other guy out of the way. That, my friend, is New York. But…" (D,119)

At the **end** of the day.

But at the end of the day, the students and I took the time to walk down to the Mall and the Washington Monument, and then spent a few minutes gazing at the White House. (H,43)

But the American people sent us here [to the Senate] to be their voice. They understand that those voices can at times become loud and argumentative, but they also hope that we can disagree without being disagreeable. And at the end of the day, they expect both parties to work together to get the people's business done. (10)

We will all need to sacrifice and we will all need to pull our weight because now more than ever, we are all in this together. What this crisis has taught us is that at the end of the day, there is no real separation between Main Street and Wall Street. (168, 169, 170, 171, 174, 175)

But Nancy [Killefer] also understands that at the end of the day, government services are delivered by people. That's why she's always worked tirelessly to empower employees to take matters into their own hands: to rethink outmoded ways of doing things, to embrace new systems and technologies, and to take initiative in developing better practices. (220)

Something is (not) the **end** (of the world).

"I did warn you [...]. That's all [Reverend] Smalls is – a politician who happens to wear a collar. Anyway, it's not the end of the world. You should just be glad you learned your lesson early." (D,162)

The **end** justifies the means.

I understand that Republicans are getting a lot of pressure to do this [and debate] from factions outside the chamber. But we need to rise above an "ends justify the means" mentality because we're here to answer to the people – all of the people – not just the ones wearing our party label. (10)

To make (both) **ends** meet.

So did the young man who lived in the crumbling apartment a few blocks away and was trying to make ends meet by mixing records at dance parties. As it had for the men in Smitty's barbershop, the election had given both these people a new idea of themselves. (D,158)

If he's ambitious he will do his best to learn the white man's language and use the white man's machines, trying to make ends meet the same way the computer repairman in Newark or the bus driver in Chicago does, with alternating spurts of enthusiasm or frustration but mostly resignation. (D,315)

But for the average American woman, the decision to work isn't simply a matter of changing attitudes. It's a matter of making ends meet. Consider the facts. Over the last thirty years, the average earnings of American men have grown less than 1 percent after being adjusted for inflation. (H,337)

Our government has to be looking out for these people who are working hard every day trying to make ends meet and right now we've got a set of policies that are not reflective of that. (B,80)

The teacher who works another shift at Dunkin Donuts after school just to make ends meet – she needs us to reform our education system so that she gets better pay, and more support, and her students get the resources they need to achieve their dreams. (100)

It is time for new leadership for children going to overcrowded schools in East L.A.; for the teacher I met who is working at Dunkin Donuts to make ends meet; for the young people who are ready to go to college but can't afford it. (104)

So we need to significantly extend unemployment insurance and expand it to include folks who are currently left out. That way, we can help them make ends meet while they're out of work. (111)

It's something [the difficulty of juggling jobs and parenting] I hear all the time from working parents, especially working women – many of whom are working more than one job to make ends meet. (134, 135)

We [Obama and his top economic advisors] agreed that the main risk we face today is doing too little in the face of our growing economic troubles. That's why today, I'm announcing a two-part emergency plan to help struggling families make ends meet and get our economy back on track. (144)

But you need relief right now. That's why yesterday, I announced a two-part emergency plan to help struggling families make ends meet and get our economy back on track. (146)

He [Joe Biden] was born in Scranton, Pennsylvania. His family didn't have much money. Joe Sr. worked different jobs, from cleaning boilers to selling cars, sometimes moving in with the in-laws or working weekends to make ends meet. But he raised his family with a strong commitment to work and to family. (151)

Enough is enough.

So the amendment we're offering today is our effort to say enough is enough. Our amendment requires all federal agencies to follow competitive bidding procedures for any Katrina-related contracts exceeding $500,000. (49)

We can either extend the Bush policies that we know don't work; or at this moment, in this election, we can come together and say enough is enough, we're going to finally solve this problem [health care] once and for all. (121)

The only change he [Senator McCain] offers is completing the Bush agenda. Privatizing your Social Security. Taxing your health benefits. [...] It's time for us to say, Enough is enough! (155)

We cannot afford four more years of out of touch, on your own, leadership in the White House. John McCain likes to rail against the Washington herd, but the truth is, when it comes to the issues that really matter in your lives, he's been running in that herd for 26 years, and they've run this economy into a ditch. This election is our chance to stand up and say – enough is enough. (155)

This time – this election – is our chance to stand up and say: enough is enough! We can do this because Americans have done this before. Time and again, we've battled back from adversity by recognizing that common stake that we have in each other's success. (156, 157, 158)

At this defining moment, we have the chance to finally stand up and say: enough is enough! We can do this because Americans have done this before. Time and again, we've battled back from adversity by recognizing that common stake that we have in each other's success. (161, 163, 166, 167)

We are not a country where a man I met should have to file for bankruptcy after he had a stroke, because he faced nearly \$200,000 in medical costs that he couldn't afford and his insurance company didn't cover. That's not right – and it's not who we are. That is not who we are, and that is not who we have to be. Enough is enough – it's time for change. (173)

We've tried it John McCain's way. We've tried it George Bush's way. And we're here [in Indianapolis] today to say enough is enough. We can't afford four more years of their "fundamental economics." (188)

To push the **envelope**.

Since the founding, the American political tradition has been reformist, not revolutionary. What that means is that for a political leader to get things done, he or she ideally should be ahead of the curve, but not too far ahead. I want to push the envelope but make sure I have enough folks with me that I'm not rendered politically impotent. (B,109)

The quick kill is prized without regard to long-term consequences for the financial system and the economy. And while this may benefit the few who push the envelope as far as it will go, it's [i.e., it] doesn't benefit America and it doesn't benefit the market. Just because it makes money doesn't mean it's good for business. (89)

Companies like Enron and WorldCom took advantage of the new regulatory environment to push the envelope, pump up earnings, disguise losses and otherwise engage in accounting fraud to make their profits look better. (109)

Past **error** is no excuse for its perpetuation.

So we know what this war has cost us – in blood and in treasure. But in the words of Robert Kennedy, "past error is no excuse for its perpetuation." And yet, John McCain refuses to learn from the failures of the Bush years. (108)

Everyone (has to fend) for himself.

In Washington, they call this the Ownership Society. But in our past there has been another term for it – Social Darwinism, every man and woman for him or herself. It's a tempting idea, because it doesn't require much thought or ingenuity. It allows us to say to those whose health care or tuition may rise faster than they can afford – tough luck. It allows us to say to the Maytag workers who have lost their job – life isn't fair. It let's [sic] us say to the child born into poverty – pull yourself up by your bootstraps. (19, 25)

In Washington, they call this the Ownership Society. But in our past there has been another term for it – Social Darwinism, every man and woman for him or herself. It allows us to say to those whose health care or tuition may rise faster than they can afford – tough luck. It allows us to say to the women who lose their jobs when they have to take care for a sick child – life isn't fair. It let's [sic] us say to the child born into poverty – pull yourself up by your bootstraps. (34)

We know this as the Ownership Society. But in our past there has been another term for it – Social Darwinism – every man or woman for him or herself. It allows us to say to those whose health care or tuition may rise faster than they can afford – tough luck. It allows us to say to the child who was born into poverty – pull yourself up by your bootstraps. It let's [sic] us say to the workers who lose their job when the factory shuts down – you're on your own. (35)

It's called the Ownership Society in Washington. But in our past there has been another term for it – Social Darwinism – every man or woman for him or herself. It allows us to say to those whose health care or tuition may rise faster than they can afford – life isn't fair. It allows us to say to the child who didn't have the fore-sight to choose the right parents or be born in the right suburb – pick yourself up by your bootstraps. It lets us say to the guy who worked twenty or thirty years in the factory and then watched his plant move out to Mexico or China – we're sorry, but you're on your own. (50, 57, 65)

To lead by (be an) **example**.

"What about Yusuf?" Auma asked. "Couldn't he do more?" Sayid shook his head. "My brother, he talks like a book, but I'm afraid he does not like to lead by example." Auma turned to me. (D,381)

Where there is no **experience**, the wise man is silent.

"Of course, I have not even one wife, so I shouldn't carry on so. Where there is no experience, I believe the wise man is silent." "Achebe?" I asked. Sayid laughed and clutched my hand "No, Barry. That one was only me." (D,386)

To keep an **eye** on someone (something).

We must be careful to keep our eyes on the prize – equal rights for every American. We must continue to fight for the Employment Non-Discrimination Act. We must vigorously expand hate crime legislation and be vigilant about how these laws are enforced. (B,44)

Finally, I think that real reform must include real oversight and accountability. Our bill sets up an independent Office of Public Integrity to keep an eye on lob-byists and to make sure they comply with the rules. (39)

To look someone (square) in the **eye**.

Like most of my values, I learned about empathy from my mother [...]. Whenever she saw even a hint of such behavior in me she would look me square in the eyes and ask, "How do you think that would make you feel?" (H,66)

Assuming we're able to bridge some of our ideological differences and keep the U.S. economy growing, will I be able to look squarely in the eyes of those workers in Galesburg and tell them that globalization can work for them and their children? (H,172)

In a nation torn by war and divided against itself, he [Bobby Kennedy] was able to look us in the eye and tell us that no matter how many cities burned with violence, no matter how persistent the poverty or the racism, no matter how far adrift America strayed, hope would come again. (35)

To not bat an **eye** (-lid).

"I'm telling you, Barack, he had the whole thing figured out. And you know what? The whole time we're talking, he's not batting an eye. Acting like what he's doing is the most natural thing in the world. It was unbelievable." (D,268)

To turn a blind **eye** towards something.

To suggest that our racial attitudes play no part in these disparities is to turn a blind eye to both our history and our experience – and to relieve ourselves of the responsibilities to make things right. (H,233)

We must help Pakistan invest in the provinces along the Afghan border, so that the extremists' program of hate is met with one of hope. And we must not turn a blind eye to elections [in Pakistan] that are neither free nor fair – our goal is not simply an ally in Pakistan, it is a democratic ally. (85)

If the last few months have taught us anything, it's that we can all suffer from the excesses of a few. Turning a blind eye to the cronyism in our midst can put us all in jeopardy. And we cannot accept that in the United States. (89)

The public interest was not protected. We do American business – and the American people – no favors when we turn a blind eye to excessive leverage and dangerous risks. (109)

While I certainly don't fault Senator McCain for all of the problems we're facing right now, I do fault the economic philosophy he's followed during his 26 years in Washington. It's a philosophy that says it's ok to turn a blind eye to practices that reward financial manipulation instead of sound business decisions. (161)

To keep one's **eyes** on (take off) the ball.

Six years after we took our eye off the ball in Afghanistan – the origin of the 9/11 attacks – we still don't have our priorities straight. That's why it's time to stop funding a failed policy, to remove our combat brigades from Iraq, and to increase our military, political, and economic commitment to Afghanistan. (97)

To keep one's **eyes** open.

"So what it is you're telling me – that I shouldn't be going to college?" Frank's shoulders slumped, and he fell back in his chair with a sigh "No. I didn't say that. You've got to go. I'm just telling you to keep your eyes open. Stay awake." (D,97)

In some ways he [Frank] was as incurable as my mother, as certain in his faith, living in the same sixties time warp that Hawaii had created. Keep your eyes open, he had warned. It wasn't as easy as it sounded. Not in sunny L.A. (D,98)

To roll one's **eyes**.

Since none of the three actually lived in Altgeld [...] I had asked them once what motivated them to do what they did. Before I could finish the question, they had all rolled their eyes as if on cue. (D,167)

Now, when the folks in Washington hear me speak, this is usually when they start rolling their eyes. "Oh, there he goes talking about hope again. He's so naive. He's a hope peddler. He's a hope-monger." (88)

To see through someone else's **eyes**.

That last aspect of Paul's character – a sense of empathy [...] is at the heart of my moral code, and it is how I understand the Golden Rule – not simply as a call to sympathy or charity, but as something more demanding, a call to stand in somebody else's shoes and see through their eyes. (H,66)

I am obligated to try to see the world through George Bush's eyes, no matter how much I may disagree with him. That's what empathy does – it calls us all to task, the conservative and the liberal, the powerful and the powerless, the oppressed and the oppressor. (H,68)

My third piece of advice is to cultivate a sense of empathy – to put yourself in other people's shoes – to see the world from their eyes. Empathy is a quality of character that can change the world – one that makes you understand that your obligations to others extend beyond people who look like you and act like you and live in your neighborhood. (55)

The world doesn't just revolve around you. There's a lot of talk in this country about the federal deficit. But I think we should talk more about our empathy deficit – the ability to put ourselves in someone else's shoes; to see the world through [the eyes of] those who are different from us – the child who's hungry, the laid-off steelworker, the immigrant woman cleaning your dorm room. (58)

There's a lot of talk in this country about the federal deficit. But I think we should talk more about our empathy deficit – the ability to put ourselves in someone else's shoes; to see the world through [the eyes of] those who are different from us – the child who's hungry, the laid-off steelworker, the immigrant woman cleaning your dorm room. (61)

You know, there's a lot of talk in this country about the federal deficit. But I think we should talk more about our empathy deficit – the ability to put ourselves in someone else's shoes; to see the world through the eyes of those who are different from us – the child who's hungry, the steelworker who's been laid off, the family who lost the entire life they built together when the storm came to town. (66)

The second thing we need to do as fathers is pass along the value of empathy to our children. Not sympathy, but empathy – the ability to stand in somebody else's shoes; to look at the world through their eyes. (123)

To be in (get into, fly into) the **face** of someone or something.

Ray's face suddenly glistened with anger. "Look," he said. "I'm just getting along, all right? [...] It's their world, all right? They own it, and we in it. So just get the fuck outta my face." (D,83)

There's no silver bullet. A solution to our energy dilemma won't come overnight. But we don't have to accept the wait-and-see attitude anymore. It flies in the face of our history and our founding principles. (26)

To do an about **face**.

But now he [John McCain] has done an about face and wants to make them [tax cuts] permanent, just like he wants a permanent occupation in Iraq. No matter what the costs, no matter what the consequences, John McCain seems determined to carry out a third Bush-term. (108)

To keep a straight **face**.
I don't know a single legislator who doesn't anguish on a regular basis over the votes he or she has to take. [...] At other times, a bill appears on the floor that's so blatantly one-sided or poorly designed that one wonders how the sponsor can maintain a straight face during debate. (H,128)

To make a long **face**.

I apologized for being late and poured myself some coffee. "So," I said, taking a seat on the windowsill. "Why all the long faces?" "We're quitting," Angela said. "Who's quitting?" Angela shrugged. "Well...I am, I guess. I can't speak for every-body else." (D,170-171)

To take at **face** value.

They know too much, we have all seen too much, to take my parents' brief union – a black man and a white woman, an African and an American – at face value. As a result, some people have a hard time taking me at face value. (D,xv)

To face **facts**.

When I tried to run for the US Senate, my media consultant, David Axelrod, had to sit me down to explain the facts of life. Our campaign plan called for a bare-bones budget, a heavy reliance on grassroots support and "earned media" – that is, an ability to make our own news. (H,110)

To get (have) one's fifteen minutes of **fame**.

Andy Warhol said that we all get our fifteen minutes of fame. I've already had an hour and a half. I'm so overexposed, I'm making Paris Hilton look like a recluse. (B,121)

To play **fast** and loose.

Tensions arise not because we have steered a wrong course but simply because we live in a complex and contradictory world. I firmly believe, for example, that since 9/11, we have played fast and loose with constitutional principles in the fight against terrorism. (H,56)

Father knows best.

All of which may explain why, as disturbed as I might have been by Ronald Reagan's election in 1980, as unconvinced as I might have been by his John Wayne, *Father Knows Best* pose, his policy by anecdote, and his gratuitous assaults on the poor, I understood his appeal. (H,31)

Straight answers to critical questions – for the most part, that is what both the Levin Amendment and the Warner Amendment call for. Members of both parties and the American people have now made clear that it is not enough for the President to simply say "we know best" and "stay the course." (36)

You either live up to your **father**'s expectations or make up for his mistakes.

Someone once said that every man is trying to either live up to his father's expectations or make up for his father's mistakes, and I suppose that may explain my particular malady as well as anything else. (H,3)

Let us never negotiate out of **fear**, but let us never fear to negotiate.

President Kennedy said it best: "Let us never negotiate out of fear, but let us never fear to negotiate." Only by knowing your adversary can you defeat them or drive wedges between them. (85)

The only thing we have to **fear** is fear itself.

It was [...] as if Dr. King had never been shot, and the Kennedys continued to beckon the nation, and war and riot and famine were nothing more than tempo-rary setbacks, and there was nothing to fear but fear itself. (D,67)

We're the party of a young President [Kennedy] who asked what we could do for our country, and who put us on a path to the moon. We're the party of a man who overcame his own disability, who told us that the only thing we had to fear was fear itself; and who faced down fascism and liberated a continent from tyranny. (104)

So it was for the Greatest Generation that conquered fear itself, and liberated a continent from tyranny, and made this country home to untold opportunity and prosperity. (119)

That's why we remember that some of the most famous words ever spoken by an American came from a President [FDR] who took office in a time of turmoil – "The only thing we have to fear is fear itself." (176)

When there was despair in the dust bowl and depression across the land, she [Ann Nixon Cooper, 106 years old] saw a nation conquer fear itself with a New Deal, new jobs and a new sense of common purpose. Yes we can. (197)

A **feather** in one's cap.

He [Reverend Wright] sat patiently and listened to my pitch, and when I was finished he gave a small nod. "I'll try to help you if I can," he said. "But you should know that having us involved in your effort isn't necessarily a feather in your cap." (D,283)

To be six **feet** under.

Reverend Wright shook his head. "I'm not the church, Barack. If I die tomorrow, I hope the congregation will give me a decent burial. I like to think a few tears will be shed. But as soon as I'm six feet under, they'll be right back on the case, figuring out how to make this church live up to its mission." (D,281-282)

To drag one's **feet**.

These [chemical] plants are stationary weapons of mass destruction spread all across the country. Their security is light, their facilities are easily entered, and their contents are deadly. Unfortunately, the chemical lobby is one of the most powerful ones in Washington. They have dragged their feet, in terms of wanting to move this issue forward. (B,160)

We know that cyber-espionage and common crime is already on the rise. And yet while countries like China have been quick to recognize this change, for the last eight years we have been dragging our feet. (140)

It is time to set a new course for this economy, and that change must begin now. [...] I urge Congress to move as quickly as possible on behalf of the American people. For every day we wait and point fingers and drag our feet, more Americans will lose their jobs. (221)

To get back on one's **feet**.

"It's a long road we're traveling," he said, "but tonight showed me what we can do when we put our minds to it. That good feeling you got right now, we got to keep it going till we got this neighborhood back on its feet." (D,154)

And because Franklin Roosevelt had the courage to act on this idea, individual Americans were able to get back on their feet and build a shared prosperity that is still the envy of the world. (14)

Justice Brown believes [...] that the New Deal, which helped save our country and get it back on its feet after the Great Depression, was a triumph of our own "Socialist revolution." She has equated altruism with communism. She equates even the most modest efforts to level life's playing field with somehow inhibiting our liberty. (20)

In Congress, with the help of the American Legion, I worked to ensure that our hospitalized soldiers don't get billed for their meals. And I've also sponsored the Sheltering All Veterans Everywhere Act, which would strengthen the VA programs our homeless vets need to get back on their feet. (23)

We all know what happened to the families on the Gulf Coast due to Hurricane Katrina, and it will be a long time before these families can rebuild their lives. [...] And the federal response so far has been inadequate to get these families effectively back on their feet. (40)

He [President Bush] pledged that he would provide the Gulf Coast with the federal assistance it needed to get back on its feet. With the bill now before us, the total amount of federal funding for hurricane recovery will exceed $100 billion. (49)

And if you can demonstrate that you went bankrupt because of medical expenses, then there must be a process that relieves that debt and lets you get back on your feet. I don't accept an America where we let someone go over a cliff just because they get sick. That is not who we are. (95)

We'll make sure that if you can demonstrate that you went bankrupt because of medical expenses, then you can relieve that debt and get back on your feet. (105)

When I'm President, we'll reform our bankruptcy laws so that we give Americans who find themselves in debt a second chance. We'll make sure that if you can demonstrate that you went bankrupt because of medical expenses, you can relieve that debt and get back on your feet. (122)

We also know that it's not enough to just get families back on their feet. We need to help hardworking families get ahead. We need [...] to give families the help they need to build that nest egg and provide a better life for their children. (132)

When I'm President, we'll reform our bankruptcy laws so that we give Americans who find themselves in debt a second chance. And we'll make sure that if you can demonstrate that you went bankrupt because of medical expenses, you can relieve that debt and get back on your feet. (132)

I've seen the flood damage here in Iowa and I've visited communities that have been devastated in my home state of Illinois. Now is the time for America to stand by those who have suffered so much, while helping them to get back on their feet. We need to make sure that these communities have access to the disaster assistance that can help businesses reopen and people rebuild their lives. (143)

If you are a bank or lender that is getting money from the rescue plan that passed Congress, and your customers are making a good-faith effort to make their mortgage payments and re-negotiate their mortgages, you will not be able to foreclose on their home for three months. We need to give people the breathing room they need to get back on their feet. (178)

For those responsible homeowners in danger of losing their homes, I've proposed a three-month moratorium on foreclosures so that we give people the breathing room they need to get back on their feet. (179)

We need to help small businesses get back on their feet. To fuel the real engine of job creation in this country, I'll eliminate all capital gains taxes on investments in small businesses and start-up companies. (179, 180, 181)

For those responsible homeowners in danger of losing their homes, I've proposed a three-month moratorium on foreclosures so that we give people the breathing room they need to get back on their feet. (180, 181)

I'll help small businesses get back on their feet by eliminating capital gains taxes and giving them emergency loans to keep their doors open and hire workers. (182, 183, 185, 187, 189)

I'll put a three-month moratorium on foreclosures so that we give homeowners the breathing room they need to get back on their feet. (182, 187, 188)

I'll help responsible homeowners refinance their mortgages on affordable terms and put in place a three-month moratorium on foreclosures to give folks the breathing room they need to get back on their feet. (184, 189)

In this situation you could see the spigot completely shut off so that it would not potentially permit GM to get back on its feet. And I think that what we have to do is to recognize that these are extraordinary circumstances. (201)

As part of my economic recovery plan, A, we're going to be focusing on jobs and getting businesses back on their feet; but B, we're also going to be focusing on updating the financial system; and C, we're going to be focusing on the budget [...]. (217)

To land on one's **feet**.

Since then Chalabi had fallen out with his U.S. patrons [...]. But he appeared to have landed on his feet; immaculately dressed, accompanied by his grown daughter, he was now the interim government's acting oil minister. (H,299)

To lay something at someone's **feet**.

This isn't to lay the blame for our energy problems entirely at the feet of our President. This is an issue that politicians from both parties clamor about when gas prices are the headline of the month, only to fall back into a trance of inaction once things calm down. (43)

To sit on the **fence**.

So to Democrats and Republicans in the House who are now on the fence, let me say this: do not make the same mistake twice. For the sake of our families, our economy, and our country, step up to the plate and pass this [rescue] plan. (171)

To play second **fiddle**.

When did the headlines about skyrocketing tuition start getting crowded out by Michael Jackson and Martha Stewart, and when did this national priority start playing second fiddle to the latest partisan food fight in Washington? (8)

To level the playing **field**. (To be on a level playing **field**).

Finally, to help workers gain higher wages and better benefits, we need once again to level the playing field between organized labor and employers. Since the early 1980s, unions have been steadily losing ground. (H,181)

Justice Brown believes [...] that the New Deal, which helped save our country and get it back on its feet after the Great Depression, was a triumph of our own "Socialist revolution." She has equated altruism with communism. She equates even the most modest efforts to level life's playing field with somehow inhibiting our liberty. (20)

I want to take Judge Roberts at his word that he doesn't like bullies and he sees the law and the Court as a means of evening the playing field between the strong and the weak. But given the gravity of the position to which he will undoubtedly ascend and the gravity of the decisions in which he will undoubtedly participate during his tenure on the [Supreme] Court, I ultimately have to give more weight to his deeds and the overarching political philosophy that he appears to have shared with those in power than to the assuring words that he provided me in our meeting. (27)

It is not easy for him [Judge John Roberts] to talk about his values and his deeper feelings. That is not how he is trained. He did say he doesn't like bullies and has always viewed the law as a way of evening out the playing field between the strong and the weak. (27)

And so, in the coming weeks, I will be laying out a 21st century economic agenda for America. It's an agenda that will level the playing field for more Americans to ensure that America can compete and thrive in a global economy. (89)

They [people] know we can't go back to yesterday or wall off our economy from everyone else. Their problem is not that the world is flat. It's that our playing field isn't level. It's that opportunity is no longer equal. And that's something we cannot accept anymore. (89)

Instead, it was the hand of industry lobbyists tilting the playing field in Washington, an accounting industry that had developed powerful conflicts of interest, and a financial sector that fueled over-investment. (109)

These steps are all paid for, and designed to restore balance and fairness to the American economy after years of Bush Administration policies tilted the playing field in favor of the wealthy and the well-connected. (124)

To cut a fine (dashing) **figure** (of a person).

The first time Toot brought Gramps over [...], her father took one look at my grandfather's black, slicked-black hair and his perpetual wise-guy grin and offered his unvarnished assessment. "He looks like a wop." My grandmother didn't care. To her, a home economics major fresh out of high school and tired of respectability, my grandfather must have cut a dashing figure. (D,14-15)

To (not) lift a **finger**.

They [school children in South Carolina] are overwhelmingly black and Latino and poor. And when they look around and see that no one has lifted a finger to fix their school since the 19th century; when they are pushed out the door at the sound of the last bell – some into a virtual war zone – is it any wonder they don't think their education is important? (96)

We've been extending a hand to Wall Street, but not lifting a finger for Main Street. And we wonder why polls show folks are more downbeat about their future than they've been in nearly fifty years. (111)

To point a **finger**.

It is time to set a new course for this economy, and that change must begin now. [...] I urge Congress to move as quickly as possible on behalf of the American people. For every day we wait and point fingers and drag our feet, more Americans will lose their jobs. (221)

To put a **finger** on something.

One day before Christmas, I asked Ruby to stop by my office so I could give her a present for Kyle. I was on the phone when she walked in, and out of the corner of my eye I thought I saw something different about her, but I couldn't quite put my finger on what is was. (D,191-192)

To snap one's **finger**.

I think if you talk to the average person right now, that they would say, "Well, look, you know, we're having a tough time right now. We've had tough times before. And we don't expect that a new president can snap his fingers and suddenly everything's going to be OK." (201)

To be baptized by **fire**.

For that is how most of my colleagues, Republican and Democrat, enter the Senate, their mistakes trumpeted, their words distorted, and their motives questioned. They are baptized in that fire; it haunts them each and every time they cast a vote, each and every time they issue a press release or make a statement. (H,133)

To draw **fire**.

For the better part of the month, I traveled Illinois without drawing fire, before being selected to deliver the keynote address at the Democratic National Convention – seventeen minutes of unfiltered, uninterrupted airtime on national television. (H,18)

To put **fire** under someone's feet. (To hold someone's feet to the **fire**).

I've had the opportunity to take a look at your Covenant for a New America. It is filled with outstanding policies and prescriptions for much of what ails this country. So I'd like to congratulate you all on the thoughtful presentations you've given so far about poverty and justice in America, and for putting fire under the feet of the political leadership here in Washington. (60)

If one is a **fish**, one does not try to fly.

"Our women have carried a heavy load. If one is a fish, one does not try to fly – one swims with other fish. One only knows what one knows. [...] I only know what I have seen. What I have not seen doesn't make my heart heavy." (D,406)

There are other **fish** in the sea.

"So fine – I figure there're more fish in the sea. I go ask Pamela out. She tells me she ain't going to the dance. I say cool. Get to the dance, guess who's standing there, got her arms around Nick Cook." (D,73)

To go on a **fishing** spree (expedition).

And if someone wants to know why their own government has decided to go on a fishing expedition through every personal record or private document [...], this legislation gives people no rights to appeal the need for such a search in a court of law. (37)

To give someone (high) **five**.

"Man, those folks are just making fun of us," I said. "What're you talking about?" "All that 'Yo baby, give me five' bullshit." "So who's mister sensitive all of a sudden? Kurt don't mean nothing by it." (D,83)

I had a slight scare when at 3:50 the pizzas had not yet arrived, but the delivery person got there ten minutes before the children were scheduled to eat. Michelle's brother, Craig, knowing the pressure I was under, gave me a high five. (H,350)

To raise a red **flag**.

Taken together, the questionable design of this points [immigration] program and the fundamental shift away from family preferences in the allocation of visas raise enough red flags that we should not rubber stamp this proposal and allow it to go forward. (82)

To go with the **flow**.

Ray looked at me and smiled: "I can tell you worry too much, Barack. That's my problem, as well. I think we need to learn to go with the flow. Isn't that what you say in America? *Just go with the flow. ...*" (D,267)

To be a **fly** in a net (web).

"I thought I could start over, you see. But now I know you can never start over. Not really. You think you have control, but you are like a fly in somebody else's web. Sometimes I think that's why I like accounting." (D,266)

To be (caught) flat-**footed**.

As the flood waters recede in New Orleans and the survivors of Katrina begin to rebuild their lives, one truth has become achingly clear over the past few weeks: [...] Katrina caught the government off-guard, flat-footed, and dangerously disorganized. The most tragic consequence of this slow response was the incalculable loss of human life. (26)

To follow in someone's **footsteps**.

It is now our turn to follow in the footsteps of all those generations who sacrificed and struggled and faced down the greatest odds to perfect our improbable union. (112)

It is easier to **forgive** than forget.

Except in Auma I had also sensed a willingness to put the past behind her, a capacity to somehow forgive, if not necessarily to forget. Roy's memories of the

Old Man seemed more immediate, more taunting; for him the past remained an open sore. (D,265)

To bear **fruit**.

Almost a year had passed since my arrival in Chicago, and our labor had finally begun to bear fruit. Will's and Mary's street corner group had grown to fifty strong; they organized neighborhood cleanups, sponsored career days for area youth, won agreements from the alderman to improve sanitation services. (D,226)

To add **fuel** to the fire.

And there will be 30-second attack ads and negative mail pieces, and we will be criticized as caring more about the rights of terrorists than the protection of Americans. And I know that the vote before us was specifically designed and timed to add fuel to the fire. (69)

To be in a **funk**.

It was Dr. Martha Collier who eventually lifted me out my funk. She was the principal of Carver Elementary, one of the two elementary schools out in Altgelt. The first time I called her for an appointment, she didn't ask too many questions. (D,231)

To write one's own **future**.

But our Party – the Democratic Party – has always been at its best when we rose above these divisions; when we called all Americans to a common purpose, a higher purpose; when we stood up and said that we will write our own future, and the future will be what we want it to be. (104)

To be the only **game** in town.

"With the unions in the shape they're in, the churches are the only game in town. That's where the people are, and that's where the values are, even if they've been buried under a lot of bullshit." (D,141)

To play a shell **game**.

So when you read the fine print, it's clear that John McCain is pulling an old Washington bait and switch. It's a shell game. He gives you a tax credit with one hand – but raises your taxes with the other. (172)

To talk a good **game**.

Ray's face suddenly glistened with anger. "Look," he said. "I'm just getting along, all right? Just like I see you getting along, talking your game with the teachers when you need them to do you a favor." (D,83)

They'll talk a good game – a sermon on Sunday, maybe, or a special offering for the homeless. But if push comes to shove, they won't really move unless you can show them how it'll help them pay their heating bill. (D,141)

To play **games**.

Perhaps if we had been living in New York or L.A., I would have been quicker to pick up the rules of the high-stake game we were playing. As it was, I learned to slip back and forth between my black and white worlds, understanding that each possessed its own language and customs and structures of meaning, convinced that with a bit of translation on my part the two worlds would eventually cohere. (D,82)

And for eight years in the Illinois legislature, I had gotten some taste of how the game had come to be played. (H,16)

It's not that the games that are played in this town are new or surprising to the public. People are not naive to the existence of corruption and they know it has worn the face of both Republicans and Democrats over the years. (44)

As people have looked away [from a government gone astray] in disillusionment and frustration, we know what's filled the void. The cynics, and the lobbyists, and the special interests who've turned our government into a game only they can afford to play. They write the checks and you get stuck paying the bills, they get the access while you get to write a letter, they think they own this government, but we're here today to take it back. The time for that politics is over. It's time to turn the page. (76)

For too long, the American people have seen lobbyists treat the legislative process like a game, using targeted contributions to maximize their leverage. Far too long, people have felt like their voice and their interests have been drowning in a sea of lobbyist money in Washington. (86)

In recent years, the doors of Congress and the White House have been thrown wide open to an army of Washington lobbyists who have turned our government into a game only they can afford to play. (86)

Too many in Washington see politics as a game. And that is why I believe this election cannot be about who can play this game better. It has to be about who can put an end to the game-playing. (88)

Now, Senator Clinton is certainly not the only one in Washington to play this game [of running a "textbook" campaign]. It's gone on for years, and I understand the reasoning behind it. It's a game that usually gets politicians where they need to go. But I don't believe it gets America where we need to go. (94)

They [middle-class white Americans] are anxious about their futures, and feel their dreams slipping away; in an era of stagnant wages and global competition, opportunity comes to be seen as a zero sum game. (107)

We're here because we can't afford to keep doing what we've been doing for another four years. We can't afford to play the same Washington games with the same Washington players and expect a different result. Not this time. Not now. (112)

Somewhere along the way, between all the bickering and the influence-peddling and the game-playing of the last few decades, Washington and Wall Street have lost touch with these values. (113)

Because that's how you play the game in Washington. When you can't win on the strength of your ideas, you make a big election about small things. (194, 195, 196)

I have a low tolerance of nonsense and turf battles and game-playing, and I send this message very clearly. And so over time, I think, people start trusting each other, and they stay focused on mission, as opposed to personal ambition or grievance. (219)

Give and take.

But I had come to appreciate the give-and-take that the blogs afforded, and in the days following the posting of my letter, in true democratic fashion, more than six hundred people posted their comment. (H,41)

Genuine bipartisanship, though, assumes an honest process of give-and-take, and that the quality of the compromise is measured by how well it serves some agreed-upon goal, whether better schools or lower deficits. (H,131)

To **give** one's all.

What is required of us now is a new era of responsibility – a recognition, on the part of every American, that we have duties to ourselves, our nation and the world; duties that we do not grudgingly accept but rather seize gladly, firm in the knowledge that there is nothing so satisfying to the spirit, so defining of our character, than giving our all to a difficult task. This is the price and the promise of citizenship. (229)

To **go** down.

"Get to the dance, guess who's standing there, got her arms around Rick Cook. 'Hi, Ray,' she says, like she don't know what's going down. Rick Cook! Now you know that guy ain't shit. Sorry-assed motherfucker got nothing on me, right? Nothing." (D,73)

God doesn't make junk

The secretary shook her head, and Dr. Collier frowned [...]. Her office was sparsely furnished , the walls bare except for a few community service awards and a poster of a young black boy that read "God Don't Make No Junk." (D,231-232)

The **golden** rule. (Matthew 7,12)

That last aspect of Paul's character – a sense of empathy [...] is at the heart of my moral code, and it is how I understand the Golden Rule – not simply as a call to sympathy or charity, but as something more demanding, a call to stand in somebody else's shoes and see through their eyes. (H,66)

Whose Christianity would we teach in the schools? [...] Or should we just stick to the Sermon on the Mount – a passage so radical that it's doubtful that our Defense Department would survive its application? (H,218)

This is not to say that I'm unanchored in my faith. There are some things that I'm absolutely sure about – the Golden Rule, the need to battle cruelty in all its forms, the value of love and charity, humility and grace. (H,224)

Which passages of Scripture should guide our public policy? Should we go with Leviticus, which suggests slavery is ok and that eating shellfish is abomination? How about Deuteronomy, which suggests stoning your child if he strays from the faith? Or should we just stick to the Sermon on the Mount [with the golden rule] – a passage that is so radical that it's doubtful that our own Defense Department would survive its application? So before we get carried away, let's read our bibles. Folks haven't been reading their bibles. (60)

To be a **good**-for-nothing.

The secretary shook her head, and Dr. Collier frowned. "Hold all calls," she said as I followed her into her office, "except for that good-for-nothing building engineer. I want to tell him just what I think of his sorry ass." (D,231)

Too **good** to be true.

Most everyone knew that some of these deals were just too good to be true, but all that money flowing made it tempting to look the other way and ignore the unscrupulous practice of some bad actors. (89)

What's **good** for me is good enough.

In recent years, we have seen a dangerous erosion of the rules and principles that have allowed our market to work and our economy to thrive. Instead of thinking about what's good for America or what's good for business, a mentality has crept into certain corners of Washington and the business world that says, "what's good for me is good enough." (89)

We will not tolerate a market that is rigged by lobbyists who don't represent the interests of the real Americans or most businesses. And we will not tolerate "what's good for me is good enough" any longer – because the only thing that's good enough is what's best for America. (89)

On Wall Street, easy money and an ethic of "what's good for me is good enough" blinded greedy executives to the danger in the decisions they were making. On Main Street, lenders tricked people into buying homes they couldn't afford. (190, 191, 192)

Government is not the solution to our problem; government is the problem.

Or, as Ronald Reagan succinctly put it: "Government is not the solution to our problem; government is the problem." (H,147)

Government of the people, by the people, and for the people.

It's time for us to stand up and tell George Bush that the government in this country is not based on the whims of one person, the government is of the people, by the people and for the people. (92)

George Washington is rightly revered for his leadership of the Continental Army, but one of his greatest acts of patriotism was his insistence on stepping down after two terms [as president], thereby setting a pattern for those who would follow, reminding future presidents that this is a government of and by and for the people. (129)

It [Obama's campaign] grew strength from the young people who rejected the myth of their generation's apathy; who left their homes and their families for jobs that offered little pay and less sleep; from not-so-young people who braved the bitter cold and scorching heat to knock on the doors of perfect strangers; from the millions of Americans who volunteered, and organized, and proved that more than two centuries later, a government of the people, by the people and for the people has not perished from this Earth. This is our victory. (197)

And yet, they [early patriots] were willing to put all they were and all they had on the line – their lives, their fortunes and their sacred honor – for a set of ideals that continue to light the world. That we are equal. That our rights to life, liberty and the pursuit of happiness come not from our laws, but from our maker. And that government of, by and for the people can endure. It was these ideals that led us to declare independence and craft our constitution, producing documents that were imperfect but had within them, like our nation itself, the capacity to be made more perfect. (226, 227)

[It] is not whether our **government** is too big or too small, but whether it works.

The question we ask today is not whether our government is too big or too small, but whether it works – whether it helps families find jobs at a decent wage, care they can afford, a retirement that is dignified. Where the answer is yes, we intend to move forward. Where the answer is no, programs will end. (229)

The **government** that people count on most is the one that's closest to the people.

But when a disaster strikes – a Katrina, a shooting, or a six-alarm blaze – it's City Hall we lean on. It's City Hall we call first, and City Hall we depend on to get us through tough times. Because whether it's a small town or a big city, the government that people count on most is the one that's closest to the people. (125)

Greatness is never a given. It must be earned.

In reaffirming the greatness of our nation, we understand that greatness is never a given. It must be earned. Our journey has never been one of shortcuts or settling for less. It has not been the path for the fainthearted – for those who prefer leisure over work, or seek only the pleasures of riches and fame. Rather it has been the risk-takers, the doers, the makers of things – some celebrated, but more often men and women obscure in their labor – who have carried us up the long, rugged path toward prosperity and freedom. (229)

To be **green** (behind one's ears).

I think that experience question would be answered during the course of the campaign. Either at the end of that campaign, people would say, "He looked good on paper but the guy was kind of way too green," or at the end of the campaign they say, "He's run a really strong campaign and we think he's got something to say and we think he could lead us." (B,84)

As **grim** as a hearse.

Except my mother hadn't looked satisfied. She had just sat there, studying my eyes, her face as grim as a hearse. "Don't you think you're being a little casual about your future?" she said. (D,95)

To close one's **grip** around something.

When Democrats rush up to me at events and insist that we live in the worst of political times, that a creeping fascism is closing its grip around our throats, I may mention the internment of Japanese Americans under FDR, the Alien and Sedition Acts under John Adams, or a hundred years of lynching under several dozen administrations as having been possibly worse, and suggest we all take a deep breath. (H,21-22)

To be **grist** for someone's mill.

If Clinton's policies were hardly radical, his biography (the draft letter saga, the marijuana puffing, the Ivy League intellectualism, the professional wife who didn't bake cookies, and most of all the sex) proved perfect grist for the conservative base. (H,35)

To be on solid **ground**.

I really have to make sure that everything I do focuses on the substance and the issues. If I stay focused on that, I'll have my good days and my bad days, but at least I'll always feel I'm on solid ground. (B,77)

To get something off the **ground**.

It is painfully obvious that corruption stifles development – it siphons off scarce resources that could improve infrastructure, bolster education systems, and strengthen public health. It stacks the deck so high against entrepreneurs that they cannot get their job-creating ideas off the ground. (67)

To hit the **ground** running.

We are going to hit the ground running. We're going to have clear plans of action. We intend to have the kind of economic recovery plan that is going to put 2.5 million people into jobs. (204)

We want ideas from everybody. But what I don't want to do is to somehow suggest that because you served in the last Democratic administration that you're somehow barred from serving again, because we need people who are going to be able to hit the ground running. (205)

And so what I can assure you is that my team is very active in reviewing what's already been done, to ensure that when we hit the ground running on January 20th, that any taxpayer money is going to be properly spent. (209)

Over the past few weeks, Vice President-Elect Biden and I have been working with our national security appointees so that we're ready to hit the ground running on January 20th. Today, I'm pleased to complete our team by announcing my choices to lead the intelligence community and the CIA. (223)

Here at home, transitions also remind us that what we hold in common as Americans far outweighs our political differences. Throughout the current transition, President Bush and his Administration have extended a hand of cooperation, and provided invaluable assistance to my team as we prepare to hit the ground running on January 20th. (225)

To stand one's **ground**.

The receptionist looked up with an icy stare, but we stood our ground. "Have a seat," she said finally. The parents sat down, and everyone fell into silence. Shirley started to light a cigarette, but Angela elbowed her in the ribs. (D,239)

To be caught off **guard**.

As the flood waters recede in New Orleans and the survivors of Katrina begin to rebuild their lives, one truth has become achingly clear over the past few weeks: [...] Katrina caught the government off-guard, flat-footed, and dangerously disorganized. The most tragic consequence of this slow response was the incalculable loss of human life. (26)

The failure to prepare for emergencies can have devastating consequences. We learned that lesson the hard way after Hurricane Katrina. The nation must not be caught off-guard when faced with the prospect of an avian flu pandemic. The consequences are too high. (28)

To feel something in one's **gut**.

Whether we're from red states or blue states, we feel in our gut the lack of honesty, rigor, and common sense in our policy debates, and dislike what appears to be a continuous menu of false or cramped choices. (H,9)

To listen to one's **gut**.

And when I was invited to speak out against George Bush's plan to invade Iraq as a Senate candidate five years ago, I didn't listen to those who warned me that it was [a] politically risky position to take, I listened to my gut, and I said loud and clear that this was the wrong war at the wrong time and Congress should stand up and say so. (94)

Old **habits** die hard.

Such a shift in emphasis is not easy: Old habits die hard, and there is always a fear on the part of many minorities that unless racial discrimination, past and present, stays on the front burner, white America will be let off the hook and hard-fought gains may be reversed. (H,248)

To count with (on) one **hand**.

We just spent three entire weeks arguing over the filibuster, but I can count on one hand the number of times we've talked about health care since I was sworn in last January. Yet, when I come back here and talk to families in Illinois, that's all they tell me about. (21)

To extend one's **hand**.

In this century, we need a strong European Union that deepens the security and prosperity of this continent, while extending a hand abroad. In this century – in this city [Berlin] of all cities – we must reject the Cold War mind-set of the past, and resolve to work with Russia when we can. (141)

Will we extend our hand to the people in the forgotten corners of this world who yearn for lives marked by dignity and opportunity; by security and justice? Will we lift the child in Bangladesh from poverty, shelter the refugee in Chad, and banish the scourge of AIDS in our time? (141)

That's why we need a Small Business Rescue Plan – so that we're extending our hand to the shops and restaurants; the start-ups and small firms that create jobs and make our economy grow. (176)

We also need a new lending facility that reaches out to states and localities – we can't extend a hand to banks on Wall Street without reaching out to Main Street so states can make payroll and deliver services. (179)

Here at home, transitions also remind us that what we hold in common as Americans far outweighs our political differences. Throughout the current transition, President Bush and his Administration have extended a hand of cooperation, and provided invaluable assistance to my team as we prepare to hit the ground running on January 20th. (225)

To those leaders around the globe who seek to sow conflict, or blame their society's ills on the West: Know that your people will judge you on what you can build, not what you destroy. To those who cling to power through corruption and deceit and the silencing of dissent, know that you are on the wrong side of history; but that we will extend a hand if you are willing to unclench your fist. (229)

To fight with one **hand** tied behind one's back.

Our enemies are fully aware that they can use oil as a weapon against America. And if we don't take this threat as seriously as the bombs they build and the guns they buy, we will be fighting the War on Terror with one hand tied behind our back. (43)

To give someone a **hand**.

I'll be a President who stands up for the American family by giving all working parents a hand. To help with childcare, I'll expand the Child and Dependent Care tax credit, so that working families can receive up to a 50 percent credit for their child care expenses. (126)

That means giving folks a hand with children – from expanding the childcare tax credit to an additional 7.5 million working moms, to providing afterschool and summer learning opportunities for an additional three million children. (135)

To lend a (helping) **hand**.

When laid off from their job or confronted with a family emergency, blacks and Latinos have less savings to draw on, and parents are less able to lend their children a helping hand. (H,243)

And perhaps the world's fate depends not just on the events of its battlefields; perhaps it depends just as much on the work we do in those quiet places that require a helping hand. (H,322)

Be a good citizen, think about the other guy, but most importantly, do something about it. Whether it's through cartoons or campaigns, by taking it to the streets or taking it to your editor, tackling the biggest issues or lending a simple hand to your neighbor, these are the ways we leave our mark on the land we love – the same way Herblock [Herbert Block] left his mark on the pages of the Washington Post every day. (8)

When World War II required the most massive homefront mobilization in history and we needed every single American to lend a hand, we had to decide: Do we listen to the skeptics who told us it wasn't possible to produce that many tanks and planes? (19)

To play one's **hand**.

I knew I was on precarious grounds. I wasn't close enough to any of them to be sure my play wouldn't backfire. At that particular moment, though, I had no other hand to play. The boys outside moved on down the street. (D,172)

What we're going to have to do is make the best decisions that we can with the hand that we're dealt. And what I think that is going to mean, although we haven't finalized our actual plan, is that we focus single-mindedly on job creation, increasing demand, getting the economy back on track, fixing our financial markets. (218)

To put one's **hand** in the pot.

"We got a lot of different personalities here," he told me. "Got the Africanist over here. The traditionalist over here. Once in a while, I have to stick my hand in the pot – smooth things over before stuff gets ugly. But that's rare." (D,282)

To tip one's **hand**.

But if Michelle was impressed, she certainly didn't tip her hand when we went to lunch. I did learn that she had grown up on the South Side, in a small bungalow just north of the neighborhoods where I had organized. (H,328-329)

What one **hand** gives, the other hand takes away.

So when you read the fine print, it's clear that John McCain is pulling an old Washington bait and switch. It's a shell game. He gives you a tax credit with one hand – but raises your taxes with the other. (172)

He [Senator McCain] talks about giving every family a $5,000 credit to buy health care, but he didn't mention last night that he'll also tax your benefits for the first time in history. It's an old Washington bait and switch. He gives you a tax credit with one hand, but raises your taxes with the other. (174)

To get a **handle** on something.

We can begin a debate about the real challenges America faces as the baby boomers begin to retire. About getting a handle on the growing cost of health care and prescription drugs. About increasing individual and national savings. About strengthening our pension system for the 21st century. (14)

One's **hands** are tied.

Democrats, for the most part, have taken the bait. At best, we may try to avoid the conversation about religious values altogether, fearful of offending anyone and claiming that – regardless of our personal beliefs – constitutional principles tie our hands. (60)

To have all **hands** on deck.

Yes, there must be more money spent on this disease. But there must also be a change in hearts and minds; in cultures and attitudes. Neither philanthropist nor scientist, neither government nor church, can solve this problem on their own – AIDS must be an all-hands-on-deck effort. (72)

The fact is, the challenges we face today – from saving our planet to ending poverty – are simply too big for government to solve alone. We need all hands on deck. (130)

Energy independence will require an all-hands-on-deck effort from America – effort from our scientists and entrepreneurs; from businesses and from every American citizen. (147)

Breaking our oil addiction will take nothing less than a complete transformation of our economy. It will take an all-hands-on-deck effort from America – effort from our scientists and entrepreneurs; from businesses and from every American citizen. (148, 149)

The pursuit of a new energy economy requires a sustained, all-hands-on deck effort, because the foundation of our energy independence is right here in America, in the power of wind and solar and new crops and new technologies, in the innovation of our scientists and entrepreneurs and the dedication and skill of our workforce. (214)

To have one's **hands** full.

We became friends and we kept in touch over email while he [Seamus Ahern] was in Iraq. One day he sent me one that said "I'm sorry I haven't written more often – I've been a little busy over here." I had to tell him "Don't worry – I know you've got your hands full." (23)

To sit on one's **hands**.

We are more compassionate than a government that lets veterans sleep on our streets and families slide into poverty; that sits on its hands while a major American city drowns before our eyes. (152)

Folks, we don't need a commission to figure out what happened. We know what happened. Too many in Washington and on Wall Street weren't minding the store. CEOs got greedy. Lobbyists got their way. Politicians sat on their hands until it was too late. (157)

To take something into one's own **hands**.

People across the country have been taking America's energy future into their own hands with the same sense of innovation and optimism that sent the Wright brothers into the sky, led Dr. Salk to a cure for polio, and fueled Henry Ford's confidence that his workers could afford cars they made. (26)

It's about all the people who are paying a price because of our broken immigration system; all the communities that are taking immigration enforcement into their own hands; and all the neighborhoods that are seeing rising tensions as citizens are pit against new immigrants. (133)

But Nancy [Killefer] also understands that at the end of the day, government services are delivered by people. That's why she's always worked tirelessly to empower employees to take matters into their own hands: to rethink outmoded ways of doing things, to embrace new systems and technologies, and to take initiative in developing better practices. (220)

To throw up one's **hands**.

This doesn't mean, however, that we should just throw up our hands and tell workers to fend for themselves. I would make this point to President Bush toward the end of the CAFTA debate, when I and a group of other senators were invited to the White House for discussions. (H,176)

Promising high-quality teachers in every classroom and then leaving the support and the pay for those teachers behind is wrong. Labeling a school and its students as failures one day and then throwing your hands up and walking away from them the next is wrong. (96)

But what I do oppose is using public money for private school vouchers. We need to focus on fixing and improving our public schools; not throwing our hands up and walking away from them. (137)

We need to fix and improve our public schools, not throw our hands up and walk away from them. We need to uphold the ideal of public education, but we also need reform. (138)

We need to focus on fixing and improving our public schools; not throwing our hands up and walking away from them. We need to stop the tired old attacks, and start getting results for our children. (145)

To have **hang**-ups.

In such surroundings, my racial stock caused my grandparents few problems, and they quickly adopted the scornful attitude local residents took toward visitors who expressed such hang-ups. (D,25)

To be **hard** and fast.

What is needed is a blueprint for an expeditious yet responsible exit from Iraq. A hard and fast, arbitrary deadline for withdrawal offers our commanders in the field, and our diplomats in the region, insufficient flexibility to implement that strategy. (59)

To play **hardball**.

We lose elections and hope for the courts to foil Republican plans. We lose the courts and wait for a White House scandal. And increasingly we feel the need to match the Republican right in stridence and hardball tactics. (H,39)

To have one's **hat** (cap) in hand.

The last thing I want to see happen is for the auto industry to disappear. But I'm also concerned that we don't put 10 or 20 or 30 or whatever billion dollars into an industry, and then, six months to a year later, they come back hat in hand and say, "Give me more." (211)

To take one's **hat** off to someone.

"Who knows? Maybe you'll be the exception. In which case I will doff my hat to you." Sadik tipped his coffee cup toward me in mock salute, his eyes searching for any immediate signs of change. (D,119)

To throw one's **hat** in the ring.

Well, I thought about it [running for the state Senate], and then I did what every wise man does when faced with a difficult decision: I prayed, and I asked my wife. And after consulting with these higher powers, I threw my hat in the ring and I did what every person on a campaign does – I talked to anyone who'd listen. (50, 57)

To (not) **have** what it takes.

It's impossible not to feel at some level as if you have been personally repudiated by the entire community, that you don't quite have what it takes, and that everywhere you go the word "loser" is flashing through the people's minds. (H,107)

To wreak **havoc**.

We can choose to go another four years with the same reckless fiscal policies that have busted our budget, wreaked havoc in our economy, and mortgaged our children's future on a mountain of debt. (144)

The radical idea that government has no role to play in protecting ordinary Americans has wreaked havoc on our economy. And we cannot let this dangerous philosophy spread to health care. (161)

To make **hay** (while the sun shines).

For years, conservatives in the United States have been making hay over problems at the UN: the hypocrisy of resolutions singling out Israel for condemnation, the Kafkaesque election of nations like Zimbabwe and Libya to the UN Commission on Human Rights, and most recently the kickbacks that plagued the oil-for-food program. (H,320)

To bang one's **head** against a (stone, brick) wall.

And just then, the owner [of a restaurant] comes out. And I said, "Sir, I understand you're a die-hard Republican." He said yes. And I said, "Well, how's business?" He said, "Not so good because my customers can't afford to eat out right now." So I said, "Well, who do you think has been running the economy for the last eight years?" And he said, "The Republicans." Well, I said, "If you keep hitting your head against a wall and it starts to hurt, at some point don't you stop hitting it against the wall?" Maybe you should try the Democrats for a change. (183)

To be turned on its **head**.

I felt as if my world had been turned on its heads; as if I had woken up to find a blue sun in the yellow sky, or heard animals speaking like men. All my life, I had carried a single image of my father, one that I had sometimes rebelled against but had never questioned, one that I had later tried to take as my own. (D,220)

To bury one's **head** into something.

The illness, along with the numerous moves, had made her something of a loner – cheerful and easy-tempered but prone to bury her head in a book or wander off on solitary walks – and Toot began to worry. (D,19)

To do something **head** first.

Congratulations! After four long years of endless studying [in medical school], sleepless nights, and constant stress, who's ready to kick back, relax, and jump head first into their residency? And who wishes people would stop making that joke? I thought so. It's an honor to be back at the University of Chicago. (21)

To go to one's **head**.

"And somebody else'd say, 'Take that glass way from Jimmy – that wine done gone to his head.' They'd all be laughing, but I could tell they weren't laughing inside. Sometimes, if I was around, my uncles'd start talking about me." (D,260)

To hold one's **head** high.

And if that child should ever get the chance to travel the world, and someone should ask her where she is from, we believe that she should always be able to hold her head high with pride in her voice when she answers "I am an American." (106)

To lose one's **head**.

[Peggy] Noonans's piece lays the groundwork for a different if equally familiar story line: the cautionary tale of a young man who comes to Washington, loses his head with all the publicity, and ultimately becomes either calculating or partisan. (H,124)

To make one's **head** spin.

Auma explained, "She says that things are changing so fast it makes her head spin. She says that the first time she saw television, she assumed the people inside the box could also see her." (D,393)

To put one's **head** in the sand.

History shows us that there is no substitute for presidential leadership in a time of economic crisis. FDR and Harry Truman didn't put their heads in the sand, or hand accountability over to a Commission. Bill Clinton didn't put off hard choices. (156)

To rain down on one's **head**.

They told me about their fallen leader, Tom Daschle of South Dakota, who had seen millions of dollars' worth of negative ad rain down on his head – full-page newspaper ads and television spots. (H,19)

To scratch one's **head**.

Some of the statements [about the nuclear non-proliferation policy] by our own officials have been confusing, contradictory, and problematic. At times, I have been left scratching my head about what exactly is our policy and how Administration statements square with this policy. (17)

To turn (away) one's **head**.

We cannot turn our heads any longer. Challenging as it is, fixing the health care system is not an impossible problem to solve. I'm not saying it will be easy, or that all the solutions are right in front of us. We may not be able to build agreement on every detail right away, but where we do agree, we should act now to bring down skyrocketing costs. (21)

To be at the **heart** of something.

We need solutions that strike at the very heart of our dependence on oil. Right now, the largest consumers of oil in this country are the cars we drive. And right now, we also have the technology to build cars that travel much further on a gallon of gas. [...] So the technology is on the shelf. It's ready and available for our car companies to use. (26)

The ideal of public education has always been at the heart of this bargain. [...] It was the driving force behind Thomas Jefferson's declaration that "... talent and virtue, needed in a free society, should be educated regardless of wealth, birth or other accidental condition." (30, 46)

At its heart, this has always been the essence of the women's movement in America – the quest to ensure that our daughters will have the same opportunities as our sons. Now, I realize that one day, my girls will discover that this journey is not over – that there are doors left to be open[ed] and glass ceilings yet to be shattered. (34)

But Sandra O'Connor was an independent voice on a host of important women's issues – and her story exemplifies the equality of opportunity at the heart of the women's movement. (34)

His [Bobby Kennedy] was a politics that, at its heart, was deeply moral – based on the notion that in this world, there is a right and there is a wrong, and it's our job to organize our laws and our lives around recognizing the difference. (35)

We're willing to respect that labor and reward it with a few basic guarantees – wages that can raise a family, health care if we get sick, a retirement that's dignified, working conditions that are safe. The struggle to secure these guarantees has always been at the heart of the labor movement – and the opposition has always been powerful. (65)

No amount of American forces can solve the political differences that lie at the heart of somebody else's civil war. As the President's own military commanders have said, escalation only prevents the Iraqis from taking more responsibility for their own future. (73)

There is no military solution to this war. At this point, no amount of soldiers can solve the grievances at the heart of someone else's civil war. The Iraqi people – Shia, Sunni, and Kurd – must come to the table and reach a political settlement themselves. (79)

There is no military solution to this war [in Iraq]. No amount of U.S. soldiers [...] can solve the grievances that lay [i.e., lie] at the heart of someone else's civil war. (81)

There is no military solution in Iraq. Only Iraq's leaders can settle the grievances at the heart of Iraq's civil war. We must apply pressure on them to act, and our best leverage is reducing our troop presence. (85)

And no matter how brilliant and bravely our troops and their commanders perform, they cannot and should not bear the responsibility of resolving grievances at the heart of Iraq's civil war. (87)

Because America can only prosper when all Americans prosper – brown, black, white, Asian, and Native American. That's the idea that lies at the heart of my campaign, and that's the idea that will lie at the heart of my presidency. Because we are all Americans. (128)

All for one and one for all. It's the idea that's at the heart of LULAC [League of United Latin American Citizens]. It's the idea that's at the heart of America. And it's what this election is all about. It's about the future we can build together. (133)

It goes back to the idea that's at the heart of LULAC [League of United Latin American Citizens] – that it's all for one and one for all. That's the idea we need to reclaim in this country. And that's the idea that we can reclaim in this election. (133)

That's the truth at the heart of your Opportunity Compact – that we cannot have a thriving Wall Street and a struggling Main Street. That when wages are flat, prices are rising, and more and more Americans are mired in debt, our economy as a whole suffers. (145)

Tim [Kaine] and I share a philosophy. It's a pragmatic, progressive philosophy that was at the heart of my campaign and will be at the heart of this administration. It's a philosophy that measures the strength of an idea not by whether it's Republican or Democrat, but whether it can actually solve a problem and make a difference in people's lives. (222)

To be close to one's **heart**.

Then, I saw a house that had been hit with one of the Hezbollah's Katyusha rockets. The family who lived in the house was lucky to be alive. [...] It is an experience I keep close to my heart. (77)

To be **heart** and soul.

The real job of organizing working America – politics and policy, vision and mission, heart and soul – belongs to each of you. And if you have the courage to succeed, labor will rise again. And hope will rise again. (25)

To break one's **heart**.

"I suppose. Maybe even if she'd been black it still wouldn't have worked out. I mean, there are several black ladies out there who've broken my heart just as good." I smiled and scraped the cut-up peppers into the pot, and then turned back to Auma. (D,211)

Auma sipped on her tea. "That's when David died. While he was living with Roy. His death broke everybody's heart – Roy's especially. The two of them were really close, you see. But Ruth never understood that." (D,339)

My little girls can break my heart. They can make me cry just looking at them eating their string beans. (B,21)

I won't pretend that simple words of condolence could ever ease the pain of the loss for the families they [killed soldiers] leave behind. I am the father of two little girls, and when I see the parents who have come here today to lay wreaths for the children they lost, my heart breaks with theirs. (18)

Too many young men and women have died. Too many have been maimed. Too many hearts have been broken. I fervently wish I had been wrong about this war; that my concerns had been unfounded. (59)

Today we grieve for the families who have lost loved ones, the hearts that have been broken, and the young lives that could have been. America, it's time to start bringing our troops home. (76)

I am the father of two young girls, and I cannot imagine what it is to lose a child. My heart breaks for the families who've lost a loved one. These are things I cannot know. But there are also some things I do know. I know that our sadness today is mixed with pride; that those we've lost will be remembered by a grateful nation. (117)

To do something to one's **heart's** content.

We might live as Indonesians lived – but every so often my mother would take me to the American Club, where I could jump in the pool and watch cartoons and sip Coca-Cola to my heart's content. (H,274)

To have a big **heart**.

"Yes, Barry, your father suffered," she repeated. "I am telling you, his problem was that his heart was too big. When he lived, he would just give to everybody who asked him. And they all asked." (D,336)

To have a **heart** of gold.

Like the janitor, Mr. Reed, or the black girl who churned up my dust as she raced down a Texas road 75, my father became a prop in someone else's narrative. An attractive prop – the alien figure with the heart of gold, the mysterious stranger who saves the town and wins the girl – but a prop nonetheless. (D,26)

To have a heavy **heart**.

"Our women have carried a heavy load. If one is a fish, one does not try to fly – one swims with other fish. One only knows what one knows. [...] I only know what I have seen. What I have not seen doesn't make my heart heavy." (D,406)

To have a soft **heart**.

"Your mother has a soft heart," Lolo would tell me one day after my mother tried to take the blame for knocking a radio off the dresser. "That's a good thing in a woman. But you will be a man someday, and a man needs to have more sense." (D,39)

To open one's **heart**.

I think that we get there [curing epilepsy and other diseases] the same way that so many of you got us here – by continuing to share your stories and your children's stories with the faith that more and more Americans will open their hearts to listen. (6)

To speak (from) one's **heart**.

I popped open a beer. "It was short, anyway." Regina ignored my sarcasm. "You spoke from the heart, Barack. It made people want to hear more [...]. When they pulled you away, it was as if –" (D,108)

To take something to **heart**.

History will not judge the architects of this war kindly. But the books have yet to be written on our efforts to right the wrongs we see in Iraq. The history has yet to be told about how we turned from this moment, found our way out of the desert, and took to heart the lessons of war that too many refused to heed back then. (81)

To win one's **heart**.

If we want to win the hearts and minds of people in Caracas, Jakarta, Nairobi, or Tehran, dispersing ballot boxes will not be enough. We'll have to make sure that the international rules we're promoting enhance, rather than impede, people's sense of material and personal security. (H,317)

To turn up the **heat**.

We've reached Americans of all political stripes who are more interested in turning the page than turning up the heat on our opponents. That's how Democrats will win in November and build a majority in Congress. (104)

Heaven helps those who help themselves.

We shouldn't help those in need without helping them help themselves. That's why I'll partner with the private sector in creating a new fund for Small and Medium Enterprise, so we're investing in ideas that can create growth and jobs in the developing world. (164)

To move **heaven** and earth.

But while President Bush and Senator McCain were ready to move heaven and earth to address the crisis on Wall Street, President Bush has failed to address the crisis on Main Street – and Senator McCain has failed to fully acknowledge it. (184, 185)

To be the Achilles **heel**.

More than anything else, these comments [by Osama bin Laden on America's dependency on foreign oil] represent a realization of American weakness shared by the rest of the world. It's a realization that for all of our military might and economic dominance, the Achilles heel of the most powerful country on Earth is the oil we cannot live without. (43)

To be at the **heels**.

Even Du Bois's learning and Baldwin's love and Langston's humor eventually succumbed to its corrosive force, each man [...] finally forced to withdraw, one to Africa, one to Europe, one deeper into the bowels of Harlem, but all of them in the same weary flight, all of them exhausted, bitter men, the devil at their heels. (D,86)

To give someone **hell**.

It wasn't until [...] after we had ridden over to the Fleet Center and heard strangers shout "Good Luck!" and "Give 'em hell, Obama!," after we had visited with a very gracious and funny Teresa Heinz Kerry in her hotel room, until finally it was just Michelle and me sitting backstage and watching the broadcast, that I started to feel just a tad bit nervous. (H,358-359)

To go to **hell**.

They had rallied behind him when white Democratic committeemen, Vrdolyak and others, announced their support for the Republican candidate, saying that the city would go to hell if it had a black mayor. (D,148)

He himself [Obama's grandfather], he would never allow himself to be beaten by a white man. This is how he lost many jobs. If the white man he worked for was abusive, he would tell the man to go to hell and leave to find other work. [Granny's story] (D,407)

To **hell** with someone (something).

Regina hadn't enjoyed herself. What was it that she'd said before she left? *You always think it's about you.* [...] To hell with Regina. To hell with her high-horse, holier-than-thou, you-let-me-down look in her eyes. (D,92-93)

Till **hell** freezes over.

Using charts and photos to build a compelling case, [Adlai] Stevenson declared to Soviet Ambassador Zorin that he was prepared to wait "until Hell freezes over" for Zorin's response to the U.S. charges. (9)

To be at the **helm**.

Steven [Chu] is uniquely suited to be our next secretary of Energy, as we make this pursuit a guiding purpose of the Department of Energy as well as a national mission. The scientists at our national labs will have a distinguished peer at the helm. His appointment should send a signal to all that my administration will value science [...]. (214)

When President Lincoln established the Department of Agriculture nearly a century and a half ago, he called it the people's department, for it meant – it was meant to serve the interests of those who lived off the land. And I know it will be the people's department once more when Tom [Vilsack] is at the helm. (216)

To strengthen our economy, we must also strengthen the small businesses that are its backbone. I can think of no one better to lead this effort as an administrator of the Small Business Administration than Karen Mills. With Karen at the helm, America's small businesses will have a partner in Washington, helping them create jobs and spur growth in communities across this country. (218)

To be a **Herculean** task.

We know how hard Kenyans are willing to work, the tremendous sacrifices that Kenyan mothers make for their children, the Herculean efforts that Kenyan fathers make for their families. (67)

To be joined at the **hip**.

That was the world in which my grandparents had been raised, the dab-smack, landlocked center of the country, a place where decency and endurance and the pioneer spirit were joined at the hip with conformity and suspicion and the potential for unblinking cruelty. (D,13)

History does not move in a straight line.

I understand these fears – nowhere is it ordained that history moves in a straight line, and during difficult economic times it is possible that the imperatives of racial equality get shunted aside. (H,248)

History repeats itself.

Iran's President Ahmadinejad's regime is a threat to all of us. His words contain a chilling echo of some of the world's most tragic history. Unfortunately, history has a terrible way of repeating itself. (77)

Hit and run.

Al Qaeda terrorists train, travel, and maintain global communication in this safe-haven [in Pakistan]. The Taliban pursues a hit and run strategy, striking in Afghanistan, then skulking across the border to safety. (85)

To be in the **hole**.

Sometimes I would tiptoe into the kitchen for a soda, and I could hear [...] Gramps's heavy sigh after he had hung up the phone, his hands fumbling through the files in his lap like those of a cardplayer who's deep in the hole. (D,55)

George Bush has put us in a hole, and John McCain's policies will keep us there. I want to take us in a new and better direction. I reject the belief that we should either shrink from the challenges of globalization, or fall back on the same tired and failed approaches of the last eight years. (124)

Some of the choices that we make are going to be difficult. And I have said before and I will repeat again: It is not going to be quick, and it is not going to be easy for us to dig ourselves out of the hole that we are in. (198)

To dig oneself out of (into) the **hole**.

If we're serious about avoiding such a future, then we'll have to start digging ourselves out of this hole. On paper, at least, we know what to do. We can cut and consolidate nonessential programs. We can rein in the spending on health-care costs. (H,188-189)

But this is a different hole that we've dug ourselves into. You know, Japan found itself in a somewhat similar situation in the '90s, made some poor decisions, didn't squarely face some of the problems in its banking system and, despite significant stimulus, still saw this thing drag on for almost a decade. (219)

Holier-than-thou.

Regina hadn't enjoyed herself. What was it that she'd said before she left? *You always think it's about you.* [...] To hell with Regina. To hell with her high-horse, holier-than-thou, you-let-me-down look in her eyes. (D,92-93)

To be on the **hook**.

And in return for their support, the American people must be assured that the [economic recovery] deal reflects the basic principles of transparency, fairness, and reform. First, there must be no blank check when American taxpayers are on the hook for this much money. (161)

To get (be) off the **hook**.

Such a shift in emphasis is not easy: Old habits die hard, and there is always a fear on the part of many minorities that unless racial discrimination, past and present, stays on the front burner, white America will be let off the hook and hard-fought gains may be reversed. (H,248)

After getting thrown off a **horse** it is best to get back on right away.

Although they didn't say this at the time, I suspect that they saw a trip to the convention as a bit of useful therapy for me, on the theory that the best thing to do after getting thrown off a horse is to get back on right away. (H,355)

To be a Trojan **horse**.

And just this week, researchers found that ducks infected with the virus were contagious for up to 17 days, causing the animals to become – in the research-ers' words – "medical Trojan horses" for transmitting the disease to humans. (24)

I know there are those who dismiss such beliefs [in a common effort to improve life] as happy talk. They claim that our insistence on something larger, something firmer and more honest in our public life is just a Trojan horse for higher taxes and the abandonment of traditional values. (152)

To be on (off) one's high **horse**.

Regina hadn't enjoyed herself. What was it that she'd said before she left? *You always think it's about you.* [...] To hell with Regina. To hell with her high-horse, holier-than-thou, you-let-me-down look in her eyes. (D,92-93)

To be a **hotbed** (for something).

The Senate became a hotbed of isolationism, passing a Neutrality Act that pre-vented the United Sates from lending assistance to countries invaded by the Axis powers, and repeatedly ignoring the President's appeals as Hitler's armies marched across Europe. (H,283)

The most segregated **hour** in American life occurs on Sunday morning.

The fact that so many people are surprised to hear that anger in some of Reverend Wright's sermons simply reminds us of the old truism that the most segregated hour in American life occurs on Sunday morning. That anger is not always productive; indeed, all too often it distracts attention from solving real problems. (107)

A **house** divided against itself cannot stand.

He [Lincoln] neither demonized the fathers and sons who did battle on the other side nor sought to diminish the terrible costs of his war. In the midst of slavery's dark storm and the complexities of governing a house divided, he somehow kept his moral compass pointed firm and true. (L,74)

I'm left then with Lincoln, who like no man before or since understood both the deliberative function of our democracy and the limits of such deliberation. We remember him for the firmness and depth of his convictions – his unyielding opposition to slavery and his determination that a house divided could not stand. (H,97)

He [Lincoln] did not equivocate or duck or pass the challenge on to future generations. He did not demonize the fathers and sons who did battle on the other side, nor seek to diminish the terrible costs of his war. In the midst of slavery's dark storm and the complexities of governing a house divided, he kept his moral compass pointed firm and true. (12)

In a nation torn by war and divided against itself, he [Bobby Kennedy] was able to look us in the eye and tell us that no matter how many cities burned with violence, no matter how persistent the poverty or the racism, no matter how far adrift America strayed, hope would come again. (35)

The class of 1860 would find their country torn apart by civil war in less than a year. Many of them would listen to their President [Lincoln] tell them that a house divided cannot stand, and they would answer the call to save a union and free a people. (58)

And that is why, in the shadow of the Old State Capitol, where Lincoln once called on a divided house to stand together, where common hopes and common dreams still [exist?], I stand before you today to announce my candidacy for President of the United States. (76)

To build a **house** on sand (rock).

And yet, three conversations during the course of my visit would remind me of just how quixotic our efforts in Iraq still seemed – how, with all the American blood, treasure, and the best of intentions, the house we were building might be resting on quicksand. (H,297-298)

At the end of the Sermon on the Mount, Jesus closes by saying, "Whoever hears these words of mine, and does them, shall be likened to a wise man who built his house upon a rock: and then the rain descended, and the floods came, and the winds blew, and beat upon that house, and it fell not, for it was founded upon a rock" [Matthew 7,24-25]. (123)

So I resolved many years ago that [...] I would be a good father to my girls; that if I could give them anything, I would give them that rock – that foundation – on which to build their lives. And that would be the greatest gift I could offer. (123)

That is our ultimate responsibility as fathers and parents. We try. We hope. We do what we can to build their house upon the sturdiest rock. And when the winds come, and the rains fall, and they beat upon that house, we keep faith that our Father will be there to guide us, and watch over us, and protect us. (123)

To put the (one's) **house** in order.

[Clinton] would accomplish what Reagan never did, putting the nation's fiscal house in order even while lessening poverty and making modest new investments in education and job training. (H,158)

"I said it's possible, not probable," he said. "I tend to be cautiously optimistic that if we get our fiscal house in order and improve our educational system, their children will do just fine." (H,175)

We have to make tough choices and smart investments today so that as the economy recovers, the deficit starts to come down. We cannot have a solid recovery if our people and our businesses don't have confidence that we're getting our fiscal house in order. (221)

To cross (jump over) **hurdles**.

From what I've observed, there are countless politicians who have crossed these hurdles and kept their integrity intact, men and women who raise campaign contributions without being corrupted, garner support without being held captive by special interests, and manage the media without losing their sense of self. (H,128)

To be the tip of the **iceberg**.

And let's be clear, the Supreme Court's ruling on equal pay is just the tip of the iceberg in terms of what's at stake in this election. [...] But the Supreme Court also affects women's lives in so many other ways – from decisions on equal pay, to workplace discrimination, to Title IX, to domestic violence, to civil rights and workers' rights. (134)

To get the (wrong) **idea**.

I grew quiet, embarrassed by my outburst. "Yeah, well...I'm just saying that I'll be back, that's all. I don't want you or the leaders to get the wrong idea." Johnnie smiled gently. "Ain't nobody gonna get the wrong idea, Barack. Man, we're just proud to see you succeed." (D,276)

Ideology is not a foreign policy.

We must remember that ideology is not a foreign policy. We must not embark on war based on untested theories, political agendas or wishful thinking that has little basis in fact or reality. (81)

No **ifs**, ands, or buts.

If you [college students] commit to serving your community or your country, we will make sure you can afford your tuition. No ifs, ands, or buts. You invest in America, America will invest in you, and together, we will move this country forward. (180)

If you [college students] commit to serving your community or your country, we will make sure you can afford your tuition. No ifs, ands or buts. You invest in America, America will invest in you, and together, we will move this country forward. (181, 182, 183, 184, 187, 188, 189)

Within an **inch** (of one's life).

Yesterday, he [President Bush] cast his vote – early – for Senator McCain. And that's no surprise, because when it comes to the policies that matter for middle class families, there's not an inch of daylight between George Bush and John McCain. (189)

To be in red **ink**.

When we believe that force is the only way to accomplish our ends in the world, when our leaders exaggerate or fudge the truth, we haven't set aside childish things. When we run our budget into red ink for things that we want instead of things that we need, we're indicating that we're not yet full-grown. (58)

To glow like **jack-o'-lanterns**.

Old faces and young faces all glow like jack-o'-lanterns in the shifting lamplight laughing and shouting, slumped in dark corners or gesticulating wildly for cigarettes or another drink. (D,389)

To (not) take a **joke**.

The tennis pro who told me during a tournament that I shouldn't touch the schedule of matches pinned up to the bulletin board because my color might rub off; his thin-lipped, red-faced smile – "Can't you take a joke?" – when I threatened to report him. (D,80)

Something is no guarantee of good **judgment**.

My experience tells me that real change and security come when we're willing to make foreign policy decisions based not on what's popular in Washington, but what's right for America – based on a real understanding of the world. That's why

I resisted the tide in my campaign for the US Senate and opposed the war in Iraq from the start. As we saw then, longevity in Washington is no guarantee of good judgment. (88)

There were a couple of guys named Cheney and Rumsfeld who had two of the longest resumes in Washington and they led us into the worst foreign policy fiasco in our history. Time served doesn't guarantee judgment. A resume does nothing about character. (88)

The inseparable twin of racial **justice** is economic justice.

But social justice is not enough. As Dr. King once said, "The inseparable twin of racial justice is economic justice." That's why Dr. King went to Memphis in his final days to stand with striking sanitation workers. (138)

Because you know that civil rights and equal treatment under the law are necessary, but not sufficient, to seize America's promise – as Dr. King once said, "the inseparable twin of racial justice is economic justice." (145)

To hold the **key** (to something).

Recent developments in stem cell research may hold the key to improved treatments, if not cures, for those effected by Alzheimer's disease, diabetes, spinal injury and countless other conditions. (62)

The **Kikuyu** are money-grubbing but industrious.

Even Jane or Zeituni could say things that surprised me. "The Luo are intelligent but lazy," they would say. Or "The Kikuyu are money-grubbing but industrious." Or "The Kalenjins – well, you can see what's happened to the country since they took over." (D,348)

To go for the **kill**.

Republicans, sensing that this was the time to go in for the kill, announced that if Democrats continued in their obstructionist ways, they would have no choice but to invoke the dreaded "nuclear option" (H,82)

To do something in a **knee-jerk** fashion.

Obviously, how we approach and deal with a country like Iran is not something that we should, you know, simply do in a knee-jerk fashion. I think we've got to think it through. (198)

To bring to one's **knees**.

You must choose: Will the groundbreaking [medical] miracles you discover over the next generation reach only the luckiest few? Or will history look back at this moment as the time when we finally made care available at a cost that won't bring the world's largest economy to its knees? (21)

In the face of tyranny, a band of patriots brought an Empire to its knees. In the face of secession, we unified a nation and set the captives free. In the face of Depression, we put people back to work and lifted millions out of poverty. (76)

To bring out the long **knives**.

I see my invitations to the White House for what they are – exercises in common political courtesy – and am mindful of how quickly the long knives can come out when the Administration's agenda is threatened in any serious way. (H,48)

To tie the **knot**.

While it's true that marriage rates have declined steadily since the 1950s, some of the decline is a result of most Americans delaying marriage to pursue an education or establish a career; by the age of forty-five, 89 percent of women and 83 percent of men will have tied the knot at least once. (H,332)

One **knows** what one knows.

"Our women have carried a heavy load. If one is a fish, one does not try to fly – one swims with other fish. One only knows what one knows. [...] I only know what I have seen. What I have not seen doesn't make my heart heavy." (D,406)

To **know** one when one sees one.

Rove may or may not have thought the White House bill [tax cuts] was good policy, but he knew a political winner when he saw one. Either the senator voted aye and helped pass the President's program, or he voted no and became a plump target during the next election. (H,130)

To (not) **know** the half of something.

Johnnie was there [...]. So were Angela, Shirley, and Mona, who told my mother what a fine job she'd done raising me. ("You don't know the half of it," my mother replied with a laugh.) (D,440)

Knowledge is power.

See, in this new world, knowledge really is power. A new idea can lead not just to a new product or a new job, but [to] entire new industries and a new way of thinking about the world. And so you need to be the Idea Generation. The generation who's always thinking on the cutting edge, who's wondering how to create and keep the next wave of American jobs and American innovations. (16)

At the dawn of the 21st century, in a world where knowledge truly is power and literacy is the skill that unlocks the gates of opportunity and success, we all have a responsibility as parents and librarians, educators and citizens, to instill in our children a love of reading so that we can give them the chance to fulfill their dreams. (22)

To be at the bottom of the **ladder**.

And we need to help folks at the bottom of the ladder. Almost 60 percent of Americans who benefited from raising the minimum wage were women. I won't leave any working people behind. (126)

To climb (move up) the **ladder** (to success).

As long as our best and brightest [African American] youth see more opportunity in climbing the corporate ladder than in building the communities from which they came, organizing will remain decidedly handicapped. (O,39)

We welcome success stories here in America. We admire those who have climbed to the top of the ladder. We just need to be sure that the ladder doesn't get taken away from the rest of us. We want a system based on fairness – not special favors. (90)

Through education in particular, every American could climb the ladder of social and economic mobility, and achieve the American Dream. (109)

I saw my grandmother, who helped raise me, work her way up from a secretary at a bank to become one of the first women bank vice presidents in the state. But I also saw how she ultimately hit a glass ceiling – how men no more qualified than she was kept moving up the corporate ladder ahead of her. (134, 135)

Finally, we've got to do more to help folks at the bottom of the ladder climb into the middle class. (135)

To get **laid**.

Otherwise, our worries seemed indistinguishable from those of the white kids. Surviving classes. Finding a well-paying gig after graduation. Trying to get laid. I had stumbled upon one of the well-kept secrets about black people: that most of us weren't interested in revolt. (D,98)

To land in one's **lap**.

Teaching keeps you sharp. The great thing about teaching constitutional law is that all the tough question land in your lap: abortion, gay rights, affirmative action. And you need to be able to argue both sides. I have to be able to argue the other side as well as Scalia does. I think that's good for one's politics. (B,152)

Better **late** than never.

Senator McCain is making some proposals about how to deal with our housing crisis. And I'm glad he's finally decided to offer a plan. Better late than never. But don't expect any real answers. Don't expect it to actually help struggling families. (111)

To work oneself into a **lather**.

And sometimes our ideological predispositions are just so fixed that we have trouble seeing the obvious. Once, while still in the Illinois Senate, I listened to a Republican colleague work himself into a lather over a proposed plan to provide school breakfasts to preschoolers. (H,59)

To rest (sit) on one's **laurels**.

Those of us concerned about protecting those rights can't afford to sit on our laurels upon reauthorization of this bill [Voting Rights Act]. We must take advantage of this rare united front and fight to ensure unimpeded access to the polls for all Americans. (63)

(To increase) by **leaps** and bounds.

Nondenominational evangelical churches are growing by leaps and bounds, eliciting levels of commitment and participation from their membership that no other American institution can match. (H,201-202)

To pull someone's **leg**.

She [Regina] stared at me, puzzled, trying to figure out whether I was pulling her leg. "Well, you could have fooled me," she said finally, trying to match my tone. (D,108)

To be **legendary**.

By now, the Bush Administration's record on climate change is almost legendary. This is the administration that commissioned government experts and scientists to do a study on global warming, only to omit the part from the final report that said it was caused by humans. (48)

To be **legion**.

He [Obama's father] studied econometrics, worked with unsurpassed concentration, and graduated in three years at the top of his class. His friends were legion, and he helped organize the International Students Association, of which he became the first president. (D,9)

To cut the **legs** from something.

From a national-security posture, there's not a better thing we could do [...] than to drive the price of oil down to twenty-five bucks a barrel. It's the single biggest thing we could do to effectuate change and cut the legs out of some of the fundamentalist impulses in the Middle East. (B,99)

To be (act) like **lemmings**.

In the parking lot afterward, Marty looked stunned. "They're not interested," he told me, shaking his head. "Like a bunch of lemmings running towards a cliff." I had felt bad for Marty. I had felt worse for Angela. (D,169)

To learn a **lesson**.

"I [Marty] told you Chicago's polarized and that politicians use it to their own advantage. That's all [Reverend] Smalls is – a politician who happens to wear a collar. Anyway, it's not the end of the world. You should just be glad you learned your lesson early." (D,162)

There was another lesson to be learned [from Obama's *Time* article in 2005 where he compares himself to Lincoln]: As soon as Ms. Noonan's column hit, it went racing across the internet, appearing on every right-wing website as proof of what an arrogant, shallow boob I was. (H,124)

But here in Washington, we have also learned some tough lessons. We have learned that to make pragmatic policy choices, we must insist on assessments grounded solely in the facts, and not seek information to suit any ideological agenda. (223)

Life is hard.

I sensed Mark hesitate, like a rock climber losing his footing. Then, almost immediately, he regained his composure and waved for the check. "Who knows?" he said. "What's certain is that I don't need the stress. Life's hard enough without all that excess baggage." (D,344)

Life is not fair.

In Washington, they call this the Ownership Society. But in our past there has been another term for it – Social Darwinism, every man and woman for him or herself. It's a tempting idea, because it doesn't require much thought or ingenuity. It allows us to say to those whose health care or tuition may rise faster than they can afford – tough luck. It allows us to say to the Maytag workers who have lost their job – life isn't fair. It let's [sic] us say to the child born into poverty – pull yourself up by your bootstraps. (19)

In Washington, they call this the Ownership Society. But in our past there has been another term for it – Social Darwinism, every man and woman for him or herself. It allows us to say to those whose health care or tuition may rise faster than they can afford – tough luck. It allows us to say to the women who lose their jobs when they have to take care for a sick child – life isn't fair. It let's [sic] us say to the child born into poverty – pull yourself up by your bootstraps. (34)

It's called the Ownership Society in Washington. But in our past there has been another term for it – Social Darwinism – every man or woman for him or herself.

It allows us to say to those whose health care or tuition may rise faster than they can afford – life isn't fair. It allows us to say to the child who didn't have the foresight to choose the right parents or be born in the right suburb – pick yourself up by your bootstraps. It lets us say to the guy who worked twenty or thirty years in the factory and then watched his plant move out to Mexico or China – we're sorry, but you're on your own. (50, 57, 65)

Life is short.

In our weekly meetings, though, he [Marty] would remind me of the choice I'd made, that there was no risk in my modest accomplishments, that the men in fancy suits downtown were still calling the shots. "Life is short, Barack," he would say. "If you're not trying to really change things out here, you might as well forget it." (D,229)

Life, liberty and the pursuit of happiness.

"We hold these truths to be self-evident, that all men are created equal, that they are endowed by their Creator with certain unalienable Rights, that among these are Life, Liberty and the pursuit of Happiness." (H,53)

Our pride is based on a very simple premise, summed up in a declaration made over two hundred years ago. "We hold these truths to be self-evident, that all men are created equal. That they are endowed by their Creator with certain inalienable [sic] rights. That among these are life, liberty and the pursuit of happiness." (2)

It is the light of opportunity that led my father across the ocean. It is the founding ideals that the flag draped over my grandfather's coffin stands for – it is life, and liberty, and the pursuit of happiness. (113)

I remember, when living four years in Indonesia as a child, listening to my mother reading me the first lines of the Declaration of Independence – "We hold these truths to be self-evident, that all men are created equal. That they are endowed by their Creator with certain unalienable rights, that among these are Life, Liberty and the pursuit of Happiness." (129)

And yet, they [early patriots] were willing to put all they were and all they had on the line – their lives, their fortunes and their sacred honor – for a set of ideals that continue to light the world. That we are equal. That our rights to life, liberty and the pursuit of happiness come not from our laws, but from our maker. And that government of, by and for the people can endure. It was these ideals that led us to declare independence and craft our constitution, producing documents that were imperfect but had within them, like our nation itself, the capacity to be made more perfect. (226, 227)

We remain a young country, but in the words of Scripture, the time has come to set aside childish things [I Corinthians 13,11]. The time has come to reaffirm our enduring spirit; to choose our better history; to carry forward that precious gift, that noble idea, passed on from generation to generation: the God-given promise that all are equal [All men are created equal], all are free, and all deserve a chance to pursue their full measure of happiness. (229)

To risk **life** and limb.

And yet, our government will not help pay for these [phone] calls. And it will not help pay for those meals. Think about the sacrifice these kids have made for their country, many of them literally risking life and limb. (11)

But to me, the most striking evidence of our progress [in voting rights] can be found right across this building, in my dear friend, Congressman John Lewis, who was on the front lines of the civil rights movement, risking life and limb for freedom. (63)

A thousand points of **light**.

I am not suggesting that every progressive suddenly latch on to religious terminology or that we abandon the fight for institutional change in favor of a thousand points of light. I recognize how often appeals to private virtue become excuses for inaction. (H,215)

If you're **light**, you're all right, if you're black, get back.

Since my first frightening discovery of bleaching creams in *Life* magazine, I'd become familiar with the lexicon of color consciousness within the black community – good hair, bad hair; thick lips or thin; if you're light, you're all right, if you're black, get back. (D,192-193)

To do something in the **light** of day.

And those of us who manage the public's dollars will be held to account – to spend wisely, reform bad habits, and do our business in the light of day – because only then can we restore the vital trust between a people and their government. (229)

To shed (shine a) **light** on something.

And it's time to shed some sunlight not only on companies that abuse the tax code, but also on the secretive offshore tax havens that shelter them. We'll create a list of countries where tax evaders hide their income and cost America untold billions of dollars every year. (90)

To be in the **line** of fire.

But wasn't there a reality to the class division, I wondered? I mentioned the conversation I'd had with his assistant, the tendency of those with means to move out of the line of fire. He [Rev. Wright] took off his glasses and rubbed what I now saw to be a pair of tired eyes. (D,283)

To be on the front **line**.

The men and women of the intelligence community have been on the front lines in this world of new and evolving dangers. They have served in the shadows, saved American lives, advanced our interests, and earned the respect of a grateful nation. (223)

To draw the **line** somewhere (in the sand).

This internal debate has raged between integration and nationalism, between accommodation and militancy, between sit-down strikes and boardroom negotiations. The lines between these strategies have never been simply drawn, and the most successful black leadership has recognized the need to bridge these seemingly divergent approaches. (O,37)

"And you must learn from his life. If you have something, then everyone will want a piece of it. So you have to draw the line somewhere. If everyone is family, no one is family. Your father, he never understood this, I think." (D,337)

Anyway, the divisions in Kenya didn't stop there; there were always finer lines to draw. Between the country's forty black tribes, for example. They, too, were a fact of life. You didn't notice the tribalism so much among Auma's friends, younger university-educated Kenyans. (D,348)

Whatever the explanation, after Reagan the lines between Republican and Democrat, liberal and conservative, would be drawn in more sharply ideological terms. This was true, of course, for the hot-button issues of affirmative action, crime, welfare, abortion, and school prayer. (H,32-33)

In a country as diverse as ours, there will always be passionate arguments about how we draw the line when it comes to government action. That is how democracy works. But our democracy might work a bit better if we recognized that all of us possess values that are worthy of respect. (H,57)

It would have been typical of today's politics for each side to draw a line in the sand: for death penalty opponents to harp on racism and police misconduct and for law enforcement to suggest that my bill coddled criminals. (H,58)

But at a certain point, we have to draw a line. At a certain point, the American people have to have some confidence that we are not simply going down this blind alley in perpetuity. (73)

To be in the **lion**'s den.

At the foot of that cross, inside the thousands of churches across the city, I imagined the stories of ordinary black people merging with the stories of David and Goliath, Moses and Pharaoh, the Christians in the lion's den, Ezekiel's field of dry bones. Those stories – of survival, and freedom, and hope – became our story. (107)

To get the **lion**'s share.

Our current immigration system delivers the lion's share of green cards – about 63% – to family members of Americans and legal permanent residents, while roughly 16% of visas are allocated to employment-based categories. (82)

To bite one's **lip**.

Gramps is probably too busy telling one of his jokes or arguing with Toot over how to cook the steaks to notice my mother reach out and squeeze the smooth, sinewy hand beside hers. Toot notices, but she's polite enough to bite her lip and offer dessert; her instincts warn her against making a scene. (D,17)

To keep a stiff upper **lip**.

The whole thing seems so fragile in retrospect, so haphazard. And perhaps that's how my grandparents intended it to be, a trial that would pass, just a matter of time, as long as they maintained a stiff upper lip and didn't do anything drastic. (D,22)

You can put **lipstick** on a pig, but it's still a pig.

John McCain says he's about change too, and so I guess his whole angle is, "Watch out George Bush – except for economic policy, health care policy, tax policy, education policy, foreign policy and Karl Rove-style politics – we're really going to shake things up in Washington." That's not change. That's just calling something [that's] the same thing something different. You know you can put lipstick on a pig, but it's still a pig. You know you can wrap an old fish in a piece of paper called change, it's still going to stink after eight years. We've had enough of the same old thing. (no number; just this remark from Obama's spontaneous comment on September 9, 2008, at Lebanon, Virginia)

To be too **little** too late.

In the few weeks before the primary, my campaign recovered a bit [...]. But it was too little too late. I arrived at my victory party to discover that the race had already been called and that I had lost by thirty-one points. (H,107)

Now Senator McCain wants to turn Bush's policy of "too little, too late" into a policy of "even less, even later". That's not the change we need right now. That's what got us into this mess in the first place. (122)

Live and let live.

Beyond that, the party cultivated a certain live-and-let-live philosophy: a philosophy anchored in acquiescence toward or active promotion of racial oppression in the South; a philosophy that depended on a broader culture. (H,26-27)

Half a **loaf** (of bread) is better than none.

If I look at an issue or if I look at how I approach campaigning, if it's something that is consistent with my broader values and is just a matter of tactics – having to take half a loaf – then that's something I'm comfortable with, and that's sort of the nature of the process. If it's something that violates my core beliefs, then it's not worth it. (B,59)

When **locusts** fight, it is always the crow who feasts.

"The lawyers are eating very well off this case, I believe. How does the saying go? When locusts fight, it is always the crow who feasts." Is that a Luo expression?" I asked. Sayid's face broke into a bashful smile. "We have similar expressions in Luo," he said., " but actually I must admit that I read this particular expression in a book by Chinua Achebe. The Nigerian writer [...]. We share more than divides us." (D,382)

Look at yourself before you pass judgment.

Look at yourself before you pass judgment. Don't make someone else clean up your mess. It's not about you. They were such simple points, homilies I had heard a thousand times before, in all their variations, from TV sitcoms and philosophy books, from my grandparents and from my mother. (D,110)

Look before you leap.

Just as important, the painstaking process of building coalitions forces us to listen to other points of view and therefore look before we leap. When we're not defending ourselves against a direct and imminent threat, we will often have the benefit of time. (H,310)

To find (make, close) **loopholes**.

It [a new bill] will close two loopholes that guarantee banks and private lenders an additional $2 billion in taxpayer subsidies a year on top of the interest that college students and their families pay. (8)

And it's a Washington that has thrown open its doors to lobbyists and special interests who've riddled our tax code with loopholes that let corporations avoid paying their taxes while you're paying more. (105)

I'll close the loophole that allows investors with multiple homes to renegotiate their mortgage in bankruptcy court, but not victims of predatory lending. (105)

And for all of George Bush's professed faith in free markets, the markets have hardly been free – not when the gates of Washington are thrown open to high-priced lobbyists who rig the rules of the road and riddle our tax code with special interest favors and corporate loopholes. (122)

So when I'm President, I'll shut down the corporate loopholes and tax havens, and I'll use the money to help pay for a middle-class tax cut that will provide $1,000 of relief to 95% of workers and their families. (132)

It's time to crack down on speculators who manipulate the market. It's time to close the loopholes that allow them to game the system. It's time to make Washington work for the American people, not the special interests. (143)

Lord knows what.

So unless we want to stay dependent forever on a region of the world that's dangerous, politically unstable, and willing to do lord-knows-what with the price of oil, we must find new sources of energy here in America. (13)

To cut one's **losses**.

Their [Obama's grandparents'] principal excitement now came from new drapes or a stand-alone freezer. [...] At some point in my absence, they had decided to cut their losses and settle for hanging on. They saw no more destinations to hope for. (D,58)

I was about to cut our losses and go ahead with Ms. Broadnax when the murmur rose from the back of the gym and the director walked through the door surrounded by a number of a number of aides. (D,244)

To get **lost**.

"You take good care of Barry now," she said. "Make sure he doesn't get lost again." Once we were back on the highway, I asked Auma what Zeituni had meant about me getting lost. Auma shrugged. "It's a common expression here," she said. "Usually, it means the person hasn't seen you in a while. 'You've been lost,' they'll say. Or 'Don't get lost.' [...]." (D,307)

Loud and clear.

And when I was invited to speak out against George Bush's plan to invade Iraq as a Senate candidate five years ago, I didn't listen to those who warned me that it was [a] politically risky position to take, I listened to my gut, and I said loud and clear that this was the wrong war at the wrong time and Congress should stand up and say so. (94)

Tough **love**.

The IMF and World Bank need to recognize that there is no single, cookie-cutter formula for each and every country's development. There is nothing wrong, of course, with a policy of "tough love" when it comes to providing development assistance to poor countries. (H,318)

The **Luo** are intelligent but lazy.

Even Jane or Zeituni could say things that surprised me. "The Luo are intelligent but lazy," they would say. Or "The Kikuyu are money-grubbing but industrious." Or "The Kalenjins – well, you can see what's happened to the country since they took over." (D,348)

What's good (bad) for **Main Street**, is good (bad) for Wall Street.

When folks are hurting out there on Main Street, that's not good for Wall Street. When the changes in our economy are leaving too many people behind, the competitiveness of our country risks falling behind. (90)

That is why the principle that I spoke about at NASDAQ is even more urgently true today: in our 21st century economy, there is no dividing line between Main Street and Wall Street. The decisions made in New York's high-rises have consequences for Americans across the country. (109)

When all is said and done, losses will be in the many hundreds of billions. What was bad for Main Street was bad for Wall Street. Pain trickled up. (109)

Even as we are doing whatever's required to stabilize the financial system [...] we [must] also recognize that a strong Main Street will reinforce and help a strong Wall Street, and that we can't separate those two things. (203)

To **make** or break.

Forty or fifty years ago, that force would have been the party apparatus: the big-city bosses, the political fixers, the power brokers in Washington who could make or break a career with a phone call. Today, that force is the media. (H,120)

To be a self-made **man**.

Although Chicago has always had one of the more vibrant black business communities in the country, in the sixties and seventies only a handful of self-made men [...] would have been considered wealthy by the standards of white America. (H,240)

Out of **many**, one.

It's that fundamental belief – I am my brother's keeper, I am my sister's keeper – that makes this country work. It's what allows us to pursue our individual dreams, yet still come together as a single American family. "E pluribus unum." Out of many, one. (2)

It is a belief that says if this nation was truly founded on the principles of freedom and equality, it could not sit idly by while millions were shackled because of the color of their skin. [...] That if out of many, we are truly one, then we must not limit ourselves to the pursuit of selfish gain, but that which will help all Americans rise together. (35)

We leave this state [South Carolina] with a new wind at our back, and take this journey across the country we love [... with] the same message we had when we were up and when we were down – that out of many, we are one; that while we breathe, we hope. (100)

This is our moment. This is our time – to put our people back to work and open doors of opportunity for our kids; to restore prosperity and promote the cause of peace; to reclaim the American Dream and reaffirm that fundamental truth – that out of many, we are one; that while we breathe, we hope, and where we are met with cynicism, and doubt, and those who tell us that we can't, we will respond with that timeless creed that sums up the spirit of a people: Yes We Can. (197)

To be all over the **map**.

I don't have a crystal ball, and economists are all over the map on this. I think we should anticipate that 2009 is going to be a tough year. And if we make some good choices, I'm confident that [...] we can start seeing an upward trajectory on the economy. (219)

To be off the **map**.

Its President denies the Holocaust and threatens to wipe Israel off the map. The danger from Iran is grave, it is real, and my goal will be to eliminate this threat. (120)

Today we **march**, tomorrow we vote

During the immigration marches back in 2006, we had a saying: "Today, we march. Tomorrow, we vote." Well, that was the time to march. And now comes the time to vote. (133)

To be close to (off) the **mark**.

My wife offers a simpler explanation – that boys and their fathers don't always have much to say to each other unless and until they trust – and this may come closer to the mark, for I often felt mute before him, and he never pushed me to speak. (D,66)

To make (leave) one's **mark**.

I came to see that in her (Michelle's) own mind, two visions of herself were at war with each other – the desire to be the woman her mother had been [...] and the desire to excel in her profession, to make her mark on the world and realize all those plans she'd had on the very first day that we met. (H,341)

Be a good citizen, think about the other guy, but most importantly, do something about it. Whether it's through cartoons or campaigns, by taking it to the streets or taking it to your editor, tackling the biggest issues or lending a simple hand to your neighbor, these are the ways we leave our mark on the land we love – the same way Herblock [Herbert Block] left his mark on the pages of the Washington Post every day. (8)

We are here because we believe that this is our time. Our time to make a mark on history. Our time to write a new chapter in the American story. And then someday, someday, if our kids get the chance to stand where we are and look back at the beginning of the 21st century, they can say that this was the time when America renewed its purpose. (50)

Ladies and gentlemen, this is our time. Our time to make a mark in history. Our time to write a new chapter in the American story. Our time to leave our children a country that is freer and kinder, more prosperous and more just than the place we grew up. (57)

Making your mark on the world is hard. If it were easy, everybody would do it. It takes patience, it takes commitment, and it comes with plenty of failure along the way. The real test is not whether you avoid failure, because you won't, it's whether you let it harden or shame you into inaction, or whether you learn from it; whether you choose to persevere. (58)

Making your mark on the world is hard. If it were easy, everybody would do it. It takes patience, it takes commitment, and it comes with plenty of failure along the way. The real test is not whether you avoid this failure, because you won't, it's whether you let it harden or shame you into inaction, or whether you learn from it; whether you choose to persevere. (61)

I believe it's time for this generation to make its own mark – to write our own chapter in the American story. After all, those who came before us did not strike a blow against injustice so that we would allow injustice to fester in our time. (91)

There is a moment in the life of every generation, if it is to make its mark on history, when its spirit has to come through, when it must choose the future over the past, when it must make its own change from the bottom up. (104)

It is because of these aspirations [for freedom, prosperity, etc.] that all free people – everywhere – became citizens of Berlin. It is in the pursuit of these aspirations that a new generation – our generation – must make our mark on the world. (141)

To be a **means** to an end.

For half of the world's population, roughly three billion people around the world living on less than two dollars a day, an election is at best a means, not an end; a starting point, not deliverance. (H,317)

All **men** are created equal.

"We hold these truths to be self-evident, that all men are created equal, that they are endowed by their Creator with certain unalienable Rights, that among these are Life, Liberty and the pursuit of Happiness." (H,53)

Our pride is based on a very simple premise, summed up in a declaration made over two hundred years ago. "We hold these truths to be self-evident, that all men are created equal. That they are endowed by their Creator with certain inalienable [sic] rights. That among these are life, liberty and the pursuit of happiness." (2)

And we're the party of Jefferson, who wrote the words that we are still trying to heed – that all of us are created equal – and who sent us West to blaze new trails, to make new discoveries, and to realize the promise of our highest ideals. (104)

I remember, when living four years in Indonesia as a child, listening to my mother reading me the first lines of the Declaration of Independence – "We hold these truths to be self-evident, that all men are created equal. That they are endowed by their Creator with certain unalienable rights, that among these are Life, Liberty and the pursuit of Happiness." (129)

And yet, they [early patriots] were willing to put all they were and all they had on the line – their lives, their fortunes and their sacred honor – for a set of ideals that continue to light the world. That we are equal [All men are created equal]. That our rights to life, liberty and the pursuit of happiness come not from our laws, but from our maker. And that government of, by and for the people can endure. It was these ideals that led us to declare independence and craft our constitution, producing documents that were imperfect but had within them, like our nation itself, the capacity to be made more perfect. (226, 227)

We remain a young country, but in the words of Scripture, the time has come to set aside childish things [I Corinthians 13,11]. The time has come to reaffirm our enduring spirit; to choose our better history; to carry forward that precious gift, that noble idea, passed on from generation to generation: the God-given promise that all are equal [All men are created equal], all are free, and all deserve a chance to pursue their full measure of happiness. (229)

To clean up one's **mess**.

Look at yourself before you pass judgment. Don't make someone else clean up your mess. It's not about you. They were such simple points, homilies I had heard a thousand times before, in all their variations, from TV sitcoms and philosophy books, from my grandparents and from my mother. (D,110)

To go the extra **mile**.

Nothing brightens my day more than dealing with somebody, anybody, who takes pride in their work or goes the extra mile – an accountant, a plumber, a three-star general, the person on the other end of the phone who actually seems to want to solve the problem. (H,60)

If publishing involves the intersection of art and commerce, Jenny and Steve have consistently erred on the side of making this book as good as it could possibly be. Their faith in this book has led them to go the extra mile time and time again, and for that I am tremendously grateful. (H,363)

To be out of one's **mind**.

And if you had come up to me a few years earlier and told me I'd be there [at the 2004 Democratic Convention at Boston], I would've politely told you that you were out of your mind. (55)

Don't make the same **mistake** twice.

So to Democrats and Republicans in the House who are now on the fence, let me say this: do not make the same mistake twice. For the sake of our families, our economy, and our country, step up to the plate and pass this [rescue] plan. (171)

Just because it makes **money** doesn't mean it's good for business.

The quick kill is prized without regard to long-term consequences for the financial system and the economy. And while this may benefit the few who push the envelope as far as it will go, it's [i.e., it] doesn't benefit America and it doesn't benefit the market. Just because it makes money doesn't mean it's good for business. (89)

Money is how we keep score.

Rather than vilify the rich, we hold them up as role models, and our mythology is steeped in stories of men on the make – the immigrant who comes to this country with nothing and strikes it big, the young man who heads West in search of his fortune. As Ted Turner famously said, in America money is how we keep score. (H,149)

Money matters.

Now, if we are going to learn from schools that work, we must begin by admitting the obvious: money matters. In too many places, kids are going to school in trailers where rats are more numerous than computers. (30)

To throw good **money** after bad.

But resources must be focused on the right priorities. No one wants to put good money after bad, or ignore the underlying causes at the root of these problems [i.e., climate change, poverty, etc.]. (164)

You can't make **money** unless you spend money.

"I told you, these are Just [sic] samples," he [Roy] said as he folded the carvings back in their wrapping. "An investment, so I will know what the market wants. You can't make money unless you spend money, eh, Barack?" "That's what they say." (D,360)

We are all **mortal**.

I am reminded by a quote from the late President Kennedy given in a speech at American University in 1963 about threats posed by the Soviet Union. "Let us not be blind to our differences – but let us also direct attention to our common interests and to the means by which those differences can be resolved ... For in the final analysis, our most basic common link is that we all inhabit this small planet. We all breathe the same air. We all cherish our children's future. And we are all mortal." (32)

To keep one's **mouth** shut.

But whether I was meeting with two people or fifty [...], whether people were friendly, indifferent, or occasionally hostile, I tried my best to keep my mouth shut and hear what they had to say. (H,6)

It takes a **movement** to lift a nation.

It takes a movement to lift a nation. It will take a movement to go into our cities and say that it's not enough to just fix our criminal justice system; what we really need is to make sure that our kids don't end up there in the first place. (91)

One man cannot make a **movement**.

And I will stand up for you, and fight for you, and wake up every day thinking about how to make your lives better. But the truth is, one man cannot make a movement. (91)

Mumbo-jumbo.

Although my father had been raised a Muslim, by the time he met my mother he was a confirmed atheist, thinking religion to be so much superstition, like the mumbo-jumbo of witch doctors that he had witnessed in the Kenyan villages of his youth. (H,204)

To face the **music**.

I looked at my watch: ten past two. Time to face the music. I got out of my car and rang the church doorbell. Angela answered, and led me into a room where the other leaders were waiting. (D,170)

To make (new) **music**.

Behind me, Billie was on her last song. I picked up the refrain, humming a few bars. Her voice sounded different to me now. Beneath the layers of hurt, beneath the ragged laughter, I heard a willingness to endure. Endure – and make music that wasn't there before. (D,112)

To call someone **names**.

When people at dinner parties ask me how I can possibly operate in the current political environment, with all the negative campaigning and personal attacks, I may mention Nelson Mandela, Aleksandr Solzhenitsyn, or some guy in a Chinese or Egyptian prison somewhere. In truth, being called names is not such a bad deal. (H,22)

A **nation** cannot prosper long when it favors only the prosperous.

Its [the market's] power to generate wealth and expand freedom is unmatched, but this crisis has reminded us that without a watchful eye, the market can spin out of control – and that a nation cannot prosper long when it favors only the prosperous. (229)

To be **neat** and tidy.

Throughout the fifties and early sixties, the GOP, too, tolerated all sorts of philosophical fissures [...]. Accommodating these regional and temperamental differences, on civil rights, federal regulation, or even taxes, was neither neat nor tidy. (H,27)

To wring someone's **neck**.

And yet, as the campaign progressed, I found him [Alan Keyes] getting under my skin in a way that few people ever have. When our paths crossed during the campaign, I often had to suppress the rather uncharitable urge to either taunt him or wring his neck. (H,211)

Love your **neighbor** (as yourself).

We know that we've been called in churches and mosques, synagogues and Sunday schools to love our neighbors as ourselves; to be our brother's keeper; to be our sister's keeper. That we have individual responsibility, but we also have collective responsibility to each other. (50, 57, 65)

To have the **nerve**.

The lobbyists who ruled George Bush's Washington are now running John McCain's campaign, and they actually had the nerve to say that the American people won't care about this. Talk about out of touch! (115)

To get on someone's **nerves**.

The man [Marty] was starting to get on my nerves. I asked him if he ever worried about becoming too calculating, if the idea of probing people's psyches and gaining their trust just to build an organization ever felt manipulative. He sighed. (D,158-159)

And outside of specific policy measures, two years from now, I want the American people to say, "Government's not perfect; there are some things Obama does that get on my nerves. But you know what? I feel like the government's working for me." (219)

To have (build) a **nest egg**.

We also know that it's not enough to just get families back on their feet. We need to help hardworking families get ahead. We need [...] to give families the help they need to build that nest egg and provide a better life for their children. (132)

I'll make sure every working woman has the chance to not just get by, but get ahead – to save, invest, build a nest egg, and provide a better life for their children. (135)

But if my opponent [Senator McCain] had his way, the millions of Floridians who rely on it would've had their Social Security tied up in the stock market this week. Millions would've watched as the market tumbled and their nest egg disappeared before their eyes. (160)

We can't afford to roll the dice by privatizing Social Security, and wagering the nest egg of millions of Americans on Wall Street. We can't afford to gamble on more of the same trickle down philosophy that showers tax breaks on big corporations and the wealthiest few. (167)

The state pension funds of teachers and government employees lost billions upon billions of dollars. Hardworking Americans who invested their nest egg to watch it grow are now watching it disappear. (168, 169)

To cast a (wide) **net**.

This is an extraordinarily difficult war we are prosecuting against terrorism. There are going to be situations in which we cast too wide a net and capture the wrong person. But what is avoidable is refusing to ever allow our legal system to correct these mistakes. (68)

To have a safety **net**.

Almost all the family's younger members were unemployed, including the two or three who had managed, against stiff competition, to graduate from one of Kenya's universities. If Jane or Zeituni ever fell ill, if their companies ever closed or laid them off, there was no government safety net. (D,329)

There is the absolutism of the free market, an ideology of no taxes, no regulations, no safety net – indeed, no government beyond what's required to protect private property and provide for the national defense. (H,37)

But the irony of this all-out assault against every existing form of social insurance is that these safety nets are exactly what encourage each of us to be risk-takers and entrepreneurs who are free to pursue our individual ambitions. (14)

The third part of my agenda will be to modernize and strengthen America's safety net for working Americans. Like all of you, I believe in free trade. But we have to acknowledge that for millions of Americans, its burdens outweigh its benefits. (89)

For far too long, the same politicians in Washington who have been cutting back the safety net for working people have been protecting golden parachutes for the well-off – so workers lose their pensions and their health care, while CEOs get multi-million dollar pay-offs. (95)

We have to give them [the American people] a way out by cutting costs, putting more money in their pockets, and rebuilding a safety net that's become badly frayed over the last decades. (105)

That's what FDR did in confronting capitalism's gravest crisis, when he forged the social safety net, built the Hoover Dam, created the Tennessee Valley Authority, and invested in an Arsenal of Democracy. (124)

You know, at this point [Great Depression] you already had 25, 30 percent unemployment across the country, and we didn't have many social safety nets that emerged out of the New Deal. So there's no doubt that Franklin Roosevelt had to recreate an entire economic structure that had entirely collapsed, and we've got some strengths that he didn't, he didn't have. (211)

To tighten the **net**.

We can work together to track terrorists down with a stronger military, we can tighten the net around their finances, and we can improve our intelligence capabilities. (76)

The old boy **network**.

John McCain actually said that if he's President, he'll take on the – quote "ol' boys [sic] network" in Washington. I am not making this up. This is someone who's been in Congress for twenty-six years – who put seven of the most powerful Washington lobbyists in charge of his campaign – and now he tells us that he's the one who will take on the ol' boy network. The ol' boy network? In the McCain campaign, that's called a staff meeting. (157)

So while he [Senator McCain] isn't offering real solutions, he can't talk enough about how greedy Wall Street is, and how he's going to take on that ol' boy network in Washington. (157)

He [Senator McCain] said he would take on the ol' boy network, but he seemed to forget that he took seven of the biggest lobbyists in Washington from that network and put them in charge of your campaign. (158)

So when you hear John McCain talk about taking on the ol' boy network in Washington – know this, on the McCain campaign, that's called a staff meeting. (160)

To give a **nod**.

Domestically, our cultural debates [...] seemed so fierce precisely because Bill Clinton's Third Way, a scaled-back welfare state without grand ambition but without sharp edges, seemed to describe a broad, underlying consensus on bread-and-butter issues, a consensus to which even George W. Bush's first campaign, with its "compassionate conservatism," would have to give a nod. (D,ix-x)

In every **nook** and cranny.

I saw them on every street and along every major thoroughfare, in every direction and every nook and cranny, in barbershop windows and posted on abandoned buildings, in front of bus stops and behind grocery store counters – Hull signs everywhere, dotting the landscape like daisies in spring. (H,112)

To slip through the **noose**.

It is to insist that across Illinois, and across America, a constant cross-pollination is occurring [...]. Identities are scrambling, and then cohering in new ways. Beliefs keep slipping through the noose of predictability. Facile expectations and simple explanations are being constantly upended. (H,51)

To have a good **nose** (for something).

I don't think there's a magic trick here [Obama's executive style]. I think I've got a good nose for talent, so I hire really good people. And I've got a pretty healthy ego, so I'm not scared of hiring the smartest people, even when they're smarter than me. (219)

To hold one's **nose**.

Supporters of this Conference Report have argued that we should just hold our noses and support the legislation, because it's not going to get any better. That does not convince me that I should support this report. I believe we owe it to the nation to do whatever we can to make this legislation better. We don't have to settle for a PATRIOT Act that sacrifices our liberties or our safety – we can have one that secures both. (37)

To end on a happy **note**.

But if his [Obama's father's] assessment is relatively clear-eyed, he is careful to end on a happy note: One thing other nations can learn from Hawaii, he says, is the willingness of races to work together toward common development. (D,26)

Nothing is ever simple in a bureaucracy.

Thankfully, this body [the Senate] acted to change this law in 2003 so that wounded soldiers wouldn't have to pay for their meals. But, we're dealing with a bureaucracy here, and as we all know, nothing is ever simple in a bureaucracy. (11)

It's **now** or never.

America now finds itself at a similar crossroads. As gas prices rise, the Middle East grows ever more unstable, and the ice caps continue to melt, we face a now-or-never, once-in-a-generation opportunity to set this country on a different course. (48)

To look out for (take care of) **number** one.

He [Sadik] gestured to the crowd along First Avenue. "Everybody looking out for number one. Survival of the fittest. Tooth and claw. Elbow the other guy out of the way. That, my friend, is New York. (D,119)

Numbers don't lie.

The numbers don't lie. At a time when income inequality is growing sharper, the Bush tax cuts gave the wealthiest 1 percent of Americans a tax cut that was twice as large as the middle class. (90)

To drive someone **nuts**.

We held a series of joint meetings with Mexicans in the Southeast Side to craft a common environmental strategy for the region. I drove Johnnie nuts trying to cram him with the things it had taken me three years to learn. (D,289)

A young teacher [...] spoke about what she called "These Kids Syndrome" – the tendency to explain away the shortcomings and failures of our education system by saying that "these kids can't learn" or "these kids don't want to learn" or "these kids are just too far behind." And after a while, "these kids" become somebody else's problem. And this teacher looked at me and said, "When I hear that term it drives me nuts. They're not 'these kids.' They're our kids. All of them." (96)

One of the teachers here told me about what she called "These Kids Syndrome" – our willingness to find a million excuses for why "these kids" can't learn [...]. "When I hear that term [these kids], it drives me nuts," the teacher told me. "They're not 'these' kids, they're our kids." (215)

To put something in a **nutshell**.

So here's John McCain's radical plan in a nutshell: he taxes health care benefits for the first time in history; millions lose the health care they have; millions pay more for the health care they get; drug and insurance companies continue to profit; and middle class families watch the system they rely on begin to unravel before their eyes. (172, 173)

To give a **once-over**.

"It's too late for me girl," Shirley muttered, but the pack [of cigarettes] went into her purse. A group of men in suits and ties came out of the door behind the receptionist's desk and gave our contingent the once-over as they walked to the elevator. (D,239-240)

Opportunity doesn't come easy.

We believe that there is a place in the American economy for every American's dream. And we know when we extend that dream of opportunity to more Americans, all of us gain. Americans know that opportunity doesn't come easy. You have to work for it. (90)

To be a night **owl**.

Michelle liked to wake up early and could barely keep her eyes open after ten o'clock. I was a night owl and could be a bit grumpy (mean, Michelle would say) within the first half hour or so of getting out of bed. (H,338)

To be on one's **own**.

The boats were out of their moorings, their distant sails like the wings of doves across Lake Michigan. Marty had told me that he would be busy those first few days, and so I was left on my own. (D,145)

We simply cannot tell our heroes that when it comes to dealing with TBI or epilepsy, they're on their own. I know CURE won't, and I will go back to Washington and make sure the federal government won't either. (6)

After a lifetime of hard work and contributions to this country, do we tell our seniors that they're on their own, or that we're here for them to provide a basic standard of living? Is the dignity of life in their latter years their problem, or one we all share? (14)

If we privatize Social Security, what will we tell retirees whose investments in the stock market went badly? We're sorry? Keep working? You're on your own? When people's expected benefits get cut and they have to choose between their groceries and their prescriptions, what will we say then? That's not our problem? (14)

Our vision of America is not one where big government runs our lives; it's one that gives every American the opportunity to make the most of their lives. It's not one that tells us we're on our own, it's one that realizes that we rise or fall together as one people. (25)

We know this as the Ownership Society. But in our past there has been another term for it – Social Darwinism – every man or woman for him or herself. It allows us to say to those whose health care or tuition may rise faster than they can afford – tough luck. It allows us to say to the child who was born into poverty – pull yourself up by your bootstraps. It let's [sic] us say to the workers who lose their job when the factory shuts down – you're on your own. (35)

It's called the Ownership Society in Washington. But in our past there has been another term for it – Social Darwinism – every man or woman for him or herself. It allows us to say to those whose health care or tuition may rise faster than they can afford – life isn't fair. It allows us to say to the child who didn't have the foresight to choose the right parents or be born in the right suburb – pick yourself up by your bootstraps. It lets us say to the guy who worked twenty or thirty years in the factory and then watched his plant move out to Mexico or China – we're sorry, but you're on your own. (50, 57, 65)

And as long as there are those who try to privatize our government and decimate our social programs and peddle a philosophy of trickle-down and on-your-own, I ask you to keep marching for a vision of America where we rise or fall as one nation under God. (65)

This [the crumbling of the social compact] is not just happening by chance. It's not something we can just chalk up to temporary shocks. It's happening in part because of the choices we're making, and the way that we're making those choices. It's happening because we've gone too far from being a country where we're all in this together, to a country where everyone's on their own. (90)

I talked about the need to put the policies of George W. Bush behind us – policies that have essentially said to the American people: "you are on your own"; because we need to pursue policies that once again recognize that we are in this together. (109)

It's a philosophy that says unless you're a big campaign donor or a special interest lobbyist, "you're on your own." And it's a philosophy that's come to dominate Washington over the last seven and a half years. (111)

It's time to end the Bush-McCain approach that tells the American people – "you're on your own" – because we know we're all in this together as Americans. That's what brought us here today. And that's the idea we'll restore in the White House when I'm President of the United States. (111)

In Washington, they call this the Ownership Society, but what it really means is – you're on your own. Out of work? Tough luck. No health care? The market will fix it. Born into poverty? Pull yourself up by your own bootstraps – even if you don't have boots. You're on your own. (152)

For eight long years, there's been a very different philosophy in the White House. They call it the Ownership Society, but what it really means is you're on your own. Job shipped overseas? Tough luck. Pension disappeared? That's the breaks. No health care? The emergency room will fix it. You're on your own. (153)

We cannot afford four more years of out of touch, on your own, leadership in the White House. John McCain likes to rail against the Washington herd, but the truth is, when it comes to the issues that really matter in your lives, he's been running in that herd for 26 years, and they've run this economy into a ditch. This election is our chance to stand up and say – enough is enough. (155)

Now that this [economic] crisis has hit, John McCain is calling for the firing of the Security and Exchange Commissioner. Well here's what I say: In 47 days, you can fire the whole Trickle-Down, On-Your-Own, Look-the-Other-Way crowd in Washington who have led us down this disastrous path. (158)

We don't need any more out-of-touch, on-your-own leadership in Washington. We need a President who will change this economy so that it finally works for your family. We need a President who knows that America's strength and leadership abroad depends on the strength of our economy at home. (165)

We don't need any more out-of-touch, on-your-own leadership in Washington. We need a President who will change this economy so that it finally works for your family. We need a President who will fight for the middle class every single day. (166)

They call this the Ownership Society, but what it really means is – you're on your own. Your job doesn't give you health care? The market will fix it. Pre-existing condition? Tough luck. Insurance company won't pay for your treatment? Too bad, you're on your own. This approach hasn't worked these past eight years, it won't work now, and it's time to turn the page. (172)

They call this the Ownership Society, but what it really means is – you're on your own. Your job doesn't give you health care? The market will fix it. Pre-existing condition? Tough luck. Insurance company won't pay for your treatment? Too bad, you're on your own. This approach hasn't worked these past eight years, it won't work now, and it's time for change. (173)

To be (get) run through the **paces**.

We have a long and rigorous election process and, if I ever did decide to run [for President], I'm confident that I'd be run through the paces pretty good. (B,110)

To turn the **page**.

America is ready to turn the page. America is ready for a new set of challenges. This is our time. A new generation is prepared to lead. (B,125)

As people have looked away [from a government gone astray] in disillusionment and frustration, we know what's filled the void. The cynics, and the lobbyists, and the special interests who've turned our government into a game only they can afford to play. They write the checks and you get stuck paying the bills, they get the access while you get to write a letter, they think they own this government, but we're here today to take it back. The time for that politics is over. It's time to turn the page. (76)

It's our turn to write a new chapter in the American story. Let's write that next chapter. Let's turn that next page. Let's bring a new generation of leadership to America, and let's change this country together. (84)

It's time to turn the page on the era of Bush-Cheney diplomacy and reach out to the rest of the world again. Refusing to engage in tough, smart diplomacy with world leaders we don't like doesn't show your strength, it shows your stubbornness, and we don't need another eight years of that. (84)

These Americans are saying it's time for a change. It's time to turn the page. It's time for a new generation of leadership in Washington. It's time for a new generation of leadership to solve the health care crisis once and for all. (84)

It's time to turn the page on the diplomacy of tough talk and no action. It's time to turn the page on Washington's conventional wisdom that agreement must be reached before you meet, that talking to other countries is some kind of reward, and that Presidents can only meet with people who will tell them what they want to hear. (85)

What could have been a call to a generation has become an excuse for unchecked presidential power. A tragedy [9/11] that united us was turned into a political wedge issue used to divide us. It's time to turn the page. It is time to write a new chapter in our response to 9/11. (85)

To meet the dangers and seize the opportunities of this new century, the old formulas will not do. We need to turn the page on the Bush-Cheney policy of not talking to leaders we don't like. That doesn't make us look tough. It makes us look arrogant. (88)

We need something new. We need to turn the page. There are those who tout their experience working the system in Washington – but the problem is that the system in Washington isn't working for us and hasn't for a long time. (88)

We'll also turn the page on an approach that gives repeated tax cuts to the wealthiest 1 percent of Americans even though they don't need them and didn't ask for them. (90)

And I'll turn the page on the imperial presidency that treats national security as a partisan issue – not an American issue. I will call for a standing, bipartisan Consultative Group of congressional leaders on national security. I will meet with this Consultative Group every month, and consult with them before taking major military action. The buck will stop with me. (92)

I'll turn the page on a growing empire of classified information, and restore the balance we've lost between the necessarily secret and the necessity of openness in a democratic society by creating a new National Declassification Center. (92)

In 2009, we will have a window of opportunity to renew our global leadership and bring our nation together. If we don't seize that moment, we may not get another. This election is a turning point. The American people get to decide: are we going to turn back the clock, or turn the page? (92)

There are those who suggest that there are easy answers to the challenges we face. We can look, they say, to Washington experience – the same experience that got us into this war. Or we can turn the page to something new, to unite this country and to seize this moment. (92)

These discussions have to take place on a bipartisan basis, and support for these decisions will be stronger if they draw on bipartisan counsel. We're not going to secure this country unless we turn the page on the conventional thinking that says politics is just about beating the other side. (92)

When I said that as President I would lead direct diplomacy with our adversaries, I was called naive and irresponsible. But how are we going to turn the page on the failed Bush-Cheney policy of not talking to our adversaries if we don't have a President who will lead that diplomacy? (92)

I don't want to see homeless veterans on the street. I don't want to send another generation of children through corridors of shame. I don't want this future for my daughters and I do not accept this future for America. It is time to turn the page. (94)

In this election, we have the chance to turn the page on the last six years of being told that the only way for Democrats to look tough on national security is to talk, and act, and vote like George Bush Republicans. (94)

It's a chance to turn the page by offering the American people a fundamentally different choice in 2008 – not just in the policies we offer, but in the kind of leadership we offer. (94)

But what it [President Bush's State of the Union address] did do was give us an urgent reminder why it's so important to turn the page on the failed politics and policies of the past, and change the status quo in Washington so we can finally start making progress for ordinary Americans. (102)

But the choice before you is about what comes next. Because we need to do more than turn the page on the failed Bush-Cheney policies; we have to turn the page on the politics that helped make those policies possible. (104)

We've reached Americans of all political stripes who are more interested in turning the page than turning up the heat on our opponents. That's how Democrats will win in November and build a majority in Congress. (104)

And tonight, because of you – because of a movement you built that stretches from Vermont's Green Mountains to the streets of San Antonio, we can stand up with confidence and clarity to say that we are turning the page, and we are ready to write the next great chapter in America's history. (106)

If we could inspire a nation to come together again, then we could turn the page on the politics that's shut us out, and told us to settle. We could write a new chapter in the American story. (106)

America, this is our moment. This is our time. Our time to turn the page on the policies of the past. Our time to bring new energy and new ideas to the challenges we face. Out time to offer a new direction for the country we love. (119)

Together we'll turn the page on the failed policies of the past. We'll bring new energy and new ideas to meet the challenges we face. We'll ensure that our daughters have the same rights, the same dreams, the same freedom to pursue their vision of happiness as our sons. (134)

Joe [Biden] won't just make a good Vice President – he will make a great one. After decades of steady work across the aisle, I know he'll be able to help me turn the page on the ugly partisanship in Washington, so we can bring Democrats and Republicans together to pass an agenda that works for the American people. (151)

It's time that we turned the page on the failed policies of the past and brought new energy and ideas to the challenges we face. And if you're willing to work with me, and fight with me, and stand with me this fall, we won't just win the election, we will transform this nation. (154)

And I hope you'll join me. I hope you'll walk with me so that we can turn the page on the failed policies of the past. And if you'll make that commitment [...], we won't just win an election, we will transform this nation. (160)

We need to stop giving those tax cuts to corporations and CEOs on Wall Street, and start standing up for families out on Main Street. We need to turn the page on the failed policies of the last eight years, and finally put working people first. (165, 166)

It's a philosophy [...] that says even common-sense regulations are unnecessary and unwise; a philosophy that lets lobbyists shred consumer protections and puts the needs of special interests ahead of working people. And what we have seen over the last few weeks is the final verdict on this failed philosophy. It is time to turn the page. (167)

They call this the Ownership Society, but what it really means is – you're on your own. Your job doesn't give you health care? The market will fix it. Pre-existing condition? Tough luck. Insurance company won't pay for your treatment? Too bad, you're on your own. This approach hasn't worked these past eight years, it won't work now, and it's time to turn the page. (172)

Senator McCain's campaign has announced that they plan to turn the page on the discussion about our economy and spend the final weeks of this campaign launching Swiftboat-style attacks on me. Think about that for a second. Turn the page on the economy? We're facing the worst economic crisis since the Great Depression, and John McCain wants us to "turn the page?" Well, I know the policies he's supported these past eight years and wants to continue are pretty hard to defend. I can understand why Senator McCain would want to "turn the page" and ignore the economy. (173)

We're not going to let John McCain distract us from what we need to do to move this country forward. Because November 4th, you and I are going to turn the page on the disastrous economic policies of George W. Bush and John McCain. (173)

You're trying to pay your bills every week and stay above the water – you can't ignore it [the economy]. You're worrying about whether your job will be there a month from now – you can't ignore it. You're worrying about whether you can pay your mortgage and stay in your house – you can't turn the page. (173)

It's time to turn the page on eight years of economic policies that put Wall Street before Main Street but ended up hurting both. We need policies that grow our economy from the bottom-up, so that every American, everywhere has the chance to get ahead. (174, 184, 187, 188, 189)

Senator McCain's campaign announced last week that they plan to "turn the page" on the discussion about our economy and spend the final weeks of this election attacking me instead. His campaign actually said, and I quote, "if we keep talking about the economy, we're going to lose." (174, 175)

It is time to turn the page on eight years of economic policies that put Wall Street before Main Street but ended up hurting both. We need policies that grow our economy from the bottom-up, so that every American, everywhere has the chance to get ahead. (175, 176, 179, 180, 181, 182, 183)

My opponent's campaign announced last week that they plan to "turn the page" on the discussion about our economy so they can spend the final weeks of this election attacking me instead. Senator McCain's campaign actually said, and I quote, "if we keep talking about the economy, we're going to lose." (176)

They can try to "turn the page" on the economy and deny the records of the last eight years. They can run misleading ads and pursue the politics of anything goes. But it's not going to work. Not this time. (176)

It is time to turn the page on eight years of economic policies that put Wall Street before Main Street but end[ed] up hurting both. We need policies that grow our economy from the bottom-up, so that every American, everywhere has the chance to get ahead. (177)

Last week, in the midst of the most serious economic crisis of our time, his [Senator McCain's] campaign announced that they plan to "turn the page" on the discussion about our economy so they can spend the final weeks of this election attacking me instead. They said, and I quote, "if we keep talking about the economy, we're going to lose." (177)

Last week, Senator McCain's campaign announced that they were going to "turn the page" on the discussion about our economy so they can spend the final weeks of this election attacking me instead. His campaign actually said, and I quote, "if we keep talking about the economy, we're going to lose." (178)

They [Americans] can't afford four more years of the economic theory that says we should give more and more to millionaires and billionaires and hope that prosperity trickles down to everyone else. We've seen where that's led us and we're not going back. It's time to turn the page. (178)

My opponent's campaign announced earlier this month that they want to "turn the page" on the discussion about our economy so they can spend the final weeks of this election attacking me instead. Senator McCain's campaign actually said, and I quote, "if we keep talking about the economy, we're going to lose." (179, 180, 181)

In one week, you can turn the page on policies that have put the greed and irresponsibility of Wall Street before the hard work and sacrifice of folks on Main Street. (190, 191)

In six days, you can turn the page on policies that have put the greed and irresponsibility of Wall Street before the hard work and sacrifice of folks on Main Street. (192)

In five days, you can turn the page on policies that have put the greed and irresponsibility of Wall Street before the hard work and sacrifice of folks on Main Street. (193)

In four days, you can turn the page on policies that have put the greed and irresponsibility of Wall Street before the hard work and sacrifice of folks on Main Street. (194)

In two days, you can turn the page on policies that have put the greed and irresponsibility of Wall Street before the hard work and sacrifice of folks on Main Street. (195)

Tomorrow, you can turn the page on policies that have put the greed and irresponsibility of Wall Street before the hard work and sacrifice of folks on Main Street. (196)

To grease (oil) the **palm**.

"To get a job these days, even as a clerk, requires that you know somebody," Sayid said as we approached Granny's compound. "Or you must grease the palm

of some person very heavily. That's why I would like to start my own business."
(D,382)

To give (have) a golden **parachute**.

A bill [...] to provide shareholders with an advisory vote on executive compensation. [...] Requires [...] to disclose compensation agreements or understandings
with the principal executive officer of either the issuer or acquiring issuer regarding any type of (golden parachute) compensation. (W,263-264)

Shareholder approval of golden parachute compensation. [...] The proxy solicitation material containing the disclosure required by subparagraph (A) shall
require a separate shareholder vote to approve such agreements or understandings.
(W,266)

For far too long, the same politicians in Washington who have been cutting back
the safety net for working people have been protecting golden parachutes for the
well-off – so workers lose their pensions and their health care, while CEOs get
multi-million dollar pay-offs. (95)

The recklessness of some of these executives has helped cause this mess, even as
they walk away with multimillion dollar golden parachutes while taxpayers are
left holding the bag. (159)

I sure wish he [Senator McCain] joined me when I blew the whistle on the fired
CEOs of Fannie Mae and Freddie Mac who tried to walk away with golden
parachutes. (163)

Instead of allowing interests to put their thumbs on the economic scales and CEOs
run off with excessive golden parachutes, we're going to ensure openness, accountability and transparency in our markets so that people can trust the value of the
financial product they're buying. (217)

Part and parcel.

I have said repeatedly that I intend to close Guantanamo, and I will follow through
on that. I've said repeatedly that America doesn't torture, and I'm going to make
sure that we don't torture. Those are – those are part and parcel of an effort to
regain America's moral stature in the world. (201)

I said during the campaign that my plan represented a net tax cut. [...] Now, the
reason that's important is not only is that good for families who are struggling, but
it's also part and parcel of what we need when it comes to stimulus. (203)

So the way to think about it is, short term we've got to focus on boosting the
economy and creating 2.5 million jobs, but part and parcel of that is a plan for a
sustainable fiscal situation long term, and that's going to require some reforms in
Washington. (203)

And so part – part and parcel of our overall economic plan is going to be a mechanism to get our mid-term and long-term budgets under control. And I – I want to be very clear, we are going to make some difficult choices on the budget. (218)

To have the **patience** of Job.

This book would not have been possible without the extraordinary support of a number of people. I have to begin with my wife, Michelle. Being married to a senator is bad enough; being married to a senator who is also writing a book requires the patience of Job. (H,363)

Patriotism is supporting your country all the time, and your government when it deserves it.

As Mark Twain, that greatest of American satirists and proud son of Missouri, once wrote, "Patriotism is supporting your country all the time, and your government when it deserves it." We may hope that our leaders and our government stand up for our ideals, and there are many times in our history when that's occurred. But when our laws, our leaders or our government are out of alignment with our ideals, then the dissent of ordinary Americans may prove to be one of the truest expression[s] of patriotism. (129)

Equal **pay** for an equal day's work (for equal work).

It becomes harder to argue that women shouldn't get equal pay for an equal day's work, or that they shouldn't get the support they need to be good workers and good parents at the same time. (34)

I'll make sure that women get equal pay for an equal day's work, because that's what's right and that's what families need to get ahead. (132)

And I'll give working parents the support they need by making childcare affordable and expanding paid leave – and we'll make sure that women get equal pay for equal work. (146)

And now is the time to keep the promise of equal pay for an equal day's work, because I want my daughters to have exactly the same opportunities as your sons. (152)

Pay as you go.

A complete disdain for pay-as-you-go budgeting – coupled with a generally scornful attitude towards oversight and enforcement – allowed far too many to put short-term gain ahead of long term consequences. (109)

Now, contrary to what John McCain may say, every single proposal that I've made in this campaign is paid for – because I believe in pay-as-you-go. (122)

It's time to put an end to the run-away spending and the record deficits – it's not how you would run your family budget, and it must not be how Washington handles your tax dollars. It's time to return to the fiscal responsibility and pay as you go budgeting that we had in the 1990s. (169)

To make one's **peace**.

That's how things were; you couldn't change it, you could just live by the rules, so simple once you learned them. And so Lolo had made his peace with power, learned the wisdom of forgetting. (D,45-46)

To take someone down a **peg** (or two).

I've got a wife who knocks me down a peg anytime I start believing what they're writing about me is true. (B,90)

To watch every **penny**.

And we saw the largest decline in consumer spending in 28 years as wages failed to keep up with the rising cost of living, and folks have been watching every penny and tightening their belts. (193)

People who are hungry, people who are out of a job are the stuff of which dictatorships are made.

But FDR also understood that capitalism in a democracy required the consent of the people [...]. As he would explain in 1944, "People who are hungry, people who are out of a job are the stuff of which dictatorships are made." (H,155)

People will judge you on what you can build, not what you can destroy.

To those leaders around the globe who seek to sow conflict, or blame their society's ills on the West: Know that your people will judge you on what you can build, not what you destroy. To those who cling to power through corruption and deceit and the silencing of dissent, know that you are on the wrong side of history; but that we will extend a hand if you are willing to unclench your fist. (229)

To **pick** oneself up.

But our time of standing pat, of protecting narrow interests and putting off unpleasant decisions – that time has surely passed. Starting today, we must pick ourselves up, dust ourselves off, and begin again the work of remaking America. (229)

To be no **picnic**.

I offered stiff resistance to this regimen, but in response to every strategy I concocted [...], she [Obama's mother] would patiently repeat her most powerful defense: "This is no picnic for me either, buster." (D,48)

A **picture** is worth a thousand words.

People like Herblock [Herbert Block] and Tony Auth and others jolt us awake from our political cynicism with a few ingenious images and a clever phrase that can often speak more truth than a thousand words. And this is the kind of wake-up call our politics need today more than ever. (8)

To get a (complete) **picture**.

220,000 young Americans gave up on their dream to go to college last year for the simple reason that they could not afford the price of tuition [...]. Add to that the rising cost of health care, and a falling family income, and you begin to get a picture of what these kids are facing. (8)

Fortunately, those who work in the field know what [educational] reforms really work: [...] Meaningful, performance-based assessments that can give us a fuller picture of how a student is doing. (30)

To look at the big **picture**.

"We gotta talk, Barack [...]. Can't think about this thing in isolation ... got to look at the big picture. You don't understand the forces at work out here. Is big, man. All kinds of folks ready to stab you in the back." (D,195)

To be a **pie** in the sky.

And a handful I met with conformed to the prototypes found in Richard Wright novels or Malcolm X speeches: sanctimonious graybeards preaching pie-in-the-sky, or slick Holy Rollers with flashy cars and a constant eye on the collection plate. (D,279)

And Kennedy's was not a pie-in-the-sky-type idealism either. He believed we would always face real enemies, and that there was no quick or perfect fix to the turmoil of the 1960s. Rather, the idealism of Robert Kennedy – the unfinished legacy that calls us still – is a fundamental belief in the continued perfection of America. (35)

What we are seeing here [...] is that a green, renewable energy economy isn't some pie-in-the-sky, far-off future, it is now. It is creating jobs, now. It is providing cheap alternatives to $140-a-barrel oil, now. And it can create millions of additional jobs and entire new industries if we act now. (127)

Most importantly, this [energy] plan will ensure that we control the energy we use with resources and technology that are available today. The steps I just spoke about are not far-off, pie-in-the-sky solutions, they are now. (136)

When all is said and done, my [energy] plan will create entire new industries and thousands of new businesses, while working to strengthen our national security and save our planet. These steps are not far-off, pie-in-the-sky solutions – the American people are ready to make this change. (143)

To have (give) a slice of the **pie**.

No longer was economic policy a matter of weighing trade-offs between competing goals of productivity and distributional justice, of growing the pie and slicing the pie. You were for either tax cuts or tax hikes, small government or big government. (H,33)

But FDR also understood that [...] by giving workers a larger share of the economic pie, his reforms would undercut the potential appeal of government-managed, command-and-control systems. (H,154-155)

Reagan's central insight – that the liberal welfare state had grown complacent and overly bureaucratic, with Democrat policy makers more obsessed with slicing the economic pie than with growing the pie – contained a good deal of truth. (H,156-157)

Yes, we have to make sure that the economic pie is sliced more fairly, but we also have to make sure that the economic pie is growing. Yes, we need to provide immediate help to families who are struggling in places like Flint [Michigan], but we also need a serious plan to create new jobs and industry. (124)

Recently, I heard Senator McCain say that I'm more concerned with who gets your piece of pie than with growing the pie. But make no mistake about it, after eight years of Bush-McCain economics, the pie is shrinking. (184)

Yesterday, I heard Senator McCain say that I'm more concerned with who gets your piece of pie than with growing the pie. But make no mistake about it, after eight years of Bush-McCain economics, the pie is shrinking. (185)

I've tried to bring together the best economic minds, people who don't always agree with each other but [who] all share a commitment to making sure that we're growing the pie and that equal opportunity is a reality in our economy, that the American dream remains alive. (205)

To be like a **pig** on the spit.

I sat there, roasting like a pig on a spit, as the pastors went on to discuss a joint Thanksgiving service in the park across the street. When the meeting was over, Reverend Reynolds and a few of the others thanked me for coming. (D,161)

To **pinch-hit** for someone.

I have the distinct honor today of pinch-hitting for one of my personal heroes – and a hero to this country, Senator Edward Kennedy. Teddy wanted to be here very much, but as you know, he's had a very long week and is taking some much-needed rest. He called me up a few days ago and I said that I'd be happy to be his stand-in, even if there was no way I could fill his shoes. (116)

To be a **pipe-dream**.

I did feel that there was something to prove – to the people of Altgelt, to Marty, to my father, to myself. That what I did counted for something. That I wasn't a fool chasing pipe dreams. (D,230)

To fall into the **pit**.

"I did not mean to speak so freely, Bernard. You must respect your elders. They clear the way for you so that your path is easier. But if you see them falling into a pit, then you must learn to what?" "Step around," Bernard said. "You are right. Diverge from the path and make your own." (D,390-391)

Which perhaps indicates a second, more intimate theme in this book – namely how, I or anybody in public office, can avoid the pitfalls of fame, the hunger to please, the fear of loss, and thereby retain that kernel of truth, that singular voice within each of us that reminds us of our deepest commitments. (H,11)

To be at the wrong (right) **place** at the wrong (right) time.

Under this bill [Habeas Corpus Amendment], people who may have been simply at the wrong place at the wrong time – and there may be just a few – will never get a chance to appeal their detention. (68)

The best-laid **plans** (of mice and men) often go astray.

For these men, the issues America faced were never abstract and hence never simple. War might be hell and still the right thing to do. Economies could collapse despite the best-laid plans. People could work hard all their lives and still lose everything. (H,36)

To have a lot on one's **plate**.

My economic team has been in conversations with them [the Treasury and the Federal Reserve]. Obviously, they've got a lot on their plate. It's not just the financial system that they're focused on at this moment. We've still got the auto industry and how that's going to be dealt with. (217)

To step up to the **plate**.

Although we have begun to step up to the plate in the Senate, it is unfortunate that none of the avian flu bills that have been introduced have passed into law. Frankly, there's been a lot of talk, but not enough action. And this isn't just true of the Congress. (28)

I will continue to reach out to leaders in both parties and do whatever I can to help pass a rescue plan. To the Democrats and Republicans who opposed this plan yesterday, I say – step up to the plate and do what's right for this country. (168)

And to the Democrats and Republicans who have opposed this plan, I say – step up to the plate and do what's right for the country, because the time to act is now. (169)

So to Democrats and Republicans in the House who are now on the fence, let me say this: do not make the same mistake twice. For the sake of our families, our economy, and our country, step up to the plate and pass this [rescue] plan. (171)

And I think Congress was right to say that the taxpayers expect and deserve better than that before they are stepping up to the plate for any kind of bailout [of the automakers]. (209)

To **play** dumb.

We either exaggerate the degree to which policies we don't like impinge on our most sacred values, or play dumb when our own preferred policies conflict with important countervailing values. (H,57)

To **play** one off the other.

It's the freedom of the relativist, the rule breaker, the teenager who has discovered his parents are imperfect and has learned to play one off the other – the freedom of the apostate. (H,92)

E **pluribus** unum.

It's that fundamental belief – I am my brother's keeper, I am my sister's keeper – that makes this country work. It's what allows us to pursue our individual dreams, yet still come together as a single American family. "E pluribus unum." Out of many, one. (2)

To be in the **pocket** of someone or something.

It is an American tradition to attribute the problem with our politics to the quality of our politicians. At times, this is expressed in very specific terms: The president is a moron, or Congressman So-and-So is a bum. Sometimes a broader indictment is issued, as on "They're all in the pockets of the special interests." (H,102)

Because after one president in the pocket of the oil companies – we can't afford another. For the sake of our economy, our security, and the future of our planet, we must end the age of oil in our time. (148)

To have something in one's hip **pocket**.

I don't presume to have this grand strategy in my hip pocket. But I know what I believe, and I'd suggest a few things that the American people should be able to agree on, starting points for a new consensus. (H,303)

To reach a **point** of no return.

Maybe the critics are right. Maybe there's no escaping our great political divide, an endless clash of armies, and any attempts to alter the rules of engagement are futile. Or maybe the trivialization of politics has reached a point of no return. (H,41)

To have a **poker** face.

Roy maintained a poker face, as if the conversation didn't concern him. Both he and Amy had the sheen of too many beers, and I saw Jane sneak an anxious look at Kezia. I decided to change the subject, and asked Zeituni if she'd been to Garden Square before. (D,363)

A new **politics** for a new time.

Change comes to Washington. Change happens because the American people demand it – because they rise up and insist on new ideas and new leaders, a new politics for a new time. (152)

To be a **pork barrel**.

It seems to champion compromise, modesty, and muddling through; to justify logrolling, deal-making, self-interest, pork barrels, paralysis, and inefficiency – all the sausage-making that no one wants to see and that the editorialists throughout our history have often labeled as corrupt. (H,94)

To stir the **pot**.

Maybe that would have been possible had the election not been so close, or had the war in Iraq not been still raging, or had the advocacy groups, pundits, and all manner of media not stood to gain by stirring the pot. (H,19-20)

Often, reporters will go out of their way to stir up the pot, asking questions in such a way as to provoke an inflammatory response. One TV reporter I know back in Chicago was so notorious for feeding you the quote he wanted that his interviews felt like an Abbott and Costello routine. (H,126)

Power concedes nothing without a demand.

When African nations were just gaining independence, industrialized nations had decades of experience building their domestic economies and navigating the international financial system. And, as Frederick Douglass once stated: "Power concedes nothing without a demand. It never did, and it never will." As a result, many African nations have been asked to liberalize their markets without reciprocal concessions from mature economies. (67)

Don't believe for a second this election is over. Don't think for a minute that power concedes. We have to work like our future depends on it in this last week [of the election], because it does. (190, 191, 192, 193, 194)

Don't believe for a second this election is over. Don't think for a minute that power concedes. We have to work like our future depends on it in these last few days [of the election], because it does. (195)

Don't believe for a second this election is over. Don't think for a minute that power concedes. We have to work like our future depends on it in the next twenty-four hours [of the election], because it does. (196)

To be the **price** for something.

What is required of us now is a new era of responsibility – a recognition, on the part of every American, that we have duties to ourselves, our nation and the world; duties that we do not grudgingly accept but rather seize gladly, firm in the knowledge that there is nothing so satisfying to the spirit, so defining of our character, than giving our all to a difficult task. This is the price and the promise of citizenship. (229)

To pay the **price**.

Ray assured me that we would never talk about whites as whites in front of whites without knowing exactly what we were doing. Without knowing that there might be a price to pay. But was that right? Was there still a price to pay? That was the complicated part, the thing that Ray and I never could seem to agree on. (D,81)

I had nothing to escape from except my own inner doubt. I was more like the black students who had grown up in the suburbs, kids whose parents had already paid the price of escape. (D,99)

"You know, your father and Sarah were actually very similar [...]. Most women in Kenya put up with anything. I did, for a long time. But Sarah also paid a price for her independence." (D,335)

That a new generation would not pay any price or bear any burden that its elders might dictate. And then, with the walls of the status quo breached, every form of "outsider" came streaming through the gates: feminists, Latinos, hippies, Panthers, welfare moms, gays, all asserting their rights, all insisting on recognition, all demanding a seat at the table and a piece of the pie. (H,28)

Moreover, whenever I write a letter to a family who has lost a loved one in Iraq [...], I'm reminded that the actions of those in power have enormous consequences – a price that they themselves almost never have to pay. (H,48)

If we aren't willing to pay a price for our values, if we aren't willing to make some sacrifices in order to realize them, then we should ask ourselves whether we truly believe in them at all. (H,68)

The blood of slaves reminds us that our pragmatism can sometimes be moral cowardice. Lincoln, and those buried at Gettysburg, remind us that we should pursue our own absolute truths only if we acknowledge that there may be a terrible price to pay. (H,98)

The leaders [...] broke ranks and chose to endorse me over Hynes, support that proved critical in giving my campaign some semblance of weight. It was a risky move on their part; had I lost, those unions might have paid a price in access, in support, in credibility with their members. (H,118-119)

When they [soldiers] come home with injuries, the government that asked these kids to serve should provide them with the best possible care and support. This is a small price to pay for those who sacrificed so much for their country. (11)

America and the American people have paid a high price for the decision to invade Iraq and myriad mistakes that followed. I believe that history will not judge the authors of this war kindly. (59)

Once again, we are told that the opposition is to blame. Once again, we hear ominous warnings that the opposition is "set to pay a very heavy price, regardless of who they are." Meanwhile, the cause of the strife [in Zimbabwe] – President Mugabe's disastrous rule – remains unaddressed. (80)

We face real threats. Any President needs the latitude to confront them swiftly and surely. But we've paid a heavy price for having a President whose priority is expanding his own power. (92)

All too often, we seek to ignore the profound institutional barriers that stand in the way of ensuring opportunity for all children, or decent jobs for all people, or health care for those who are sick. We long for unity, but are unwilling to pay the price. (99)

And the price our families and communities are paying reflects the price America is paying. The most conservative estimates say that Iraq has now cost more than half a trillion dollars, more than any other war in our history besides World War II. (108)

At a time when we're on the brink of recession – when neighborhoods have For Sale signs outside every home, and working families are struggling to keep up with rising costs – ordinary Americans are paying a price for this war. (108)

When you're spending over $50 to fill up your car because the price of oil is four times what it was before Iraq, you're paying a price for this war. When Iraq is costing each household about $100 a month, you're paying a price for this war. When a National Guard unit is over in Iraq and can't help out during a hurricane in Louisiana or with floods here in West Virginia, our communities are paying a price for this war. (108)

And now we're paying the price. Now we've fallen behind the rest of the world. Now we're forced to beg Saudi Arabia for more oil. Now we're facing gas prices over $4 a gallon. (127)

It's about all the people who are paying a price because of our broken immigration system; all the communities that are taking immigration enforcement into their own hands; and all the neighborhoods that are seeing rising tensions as citizens are pit against new immigrants. (133)

For eight years, we have paid the price for a foreign policy that lectures without listening; that divides us from one another – and from the world – instead of calling us to a common purpose. (139)

We faced down fascism with the greatest war-time alliance the world has ever known. We stood shoulder to shoulder with out NATO allies against the Soviet threat, and paid a far smaller price for the first Gulf War because we acted together with a broad coalition. (139)

When special interests put their thumb too heavily on the scale, and distort the free market, those who compete by the rules come in last. And when government fails to meet its obligation – to provide sensible oversight and stand on the side of working people and invest in their future – America pays a heavy price. (142)

When special interests put their thumb on the scale, and distort the free market, the people who compete by the rules come in last. And when government fails to meet its obligation – to provide sensible oversight and stand on the side of working people and invest in their future – America pays a heavy price. (144, 146)

Somewhere along the way, we let a reckless few game the system, we let special interests tilt the scale and distort the free market, we stopped making the investments in our children and our workers to help us rise together. And today, we're all paying the price. (145)

But the price he [John McCain] paid for his party's nomination was to reverse himself on position after position, and now he embraces the failed Bush policies and politics that helped break Washington in the first place – and that doesn't exactly meet my definition of a maverick. (149)

And while we pay a heavy price in Iraq – and Americans pay record prices at the pump – Iraq's government is sitting on a $79 billion dollar budget surplus from windfall oil profits. (150)

CEOs and executives got reckless. Lobbyists got what they wanted. Politicians in both parties looked the other way until it was too late. And it is the American people who have paid the price. (159)

To be a **prima donna**.

Given all the hype surrounding my election, I hope people have gotten a sense that I am here to do the work and not just chase cameras. The collateral benefit is that people really like me. I'm not some prima donna. (B,122)

To read the fine **print**.
Senator McCain has been eager to share some details of his health care plan – but not all. Like those ads for prescription drugs, you have to read the fine print to learn the full story. (180)

A **problem** facing any American is a problem facing all Americans.

It's about making sure that we have a government that knows that a problem facing any American is a problem facing all Americans. It's about making sure our government knows that when there's a Hispanic girl stuck in a crumbling school who graduates without learning to read or doesn't graduate at all, that isn't just a Hispanic-American problem, that's an American problem. (133)

A **promise** made is a promise kept.

We'll never rise together if we allow medical bills to swallow family budgets or let people retire penniless after a lifetime of hard work, and so today we must demand that when it comes to commitments made by working men and women on health care and pensions, a promise made is a promise kept. (25)

Pros and cons.

There were a handful of senators who also had young families, and whenever we met we could compare notes on the pros and cons of moving to Washington, as well as the difficulty in protecting family time from overzealous staff. (H,72)

Instead of an honest accounting of this military campaign's pros and cons, the Administration initiated a public relations offensive: shading intelligence reports to support its case. (H,293)

To pull no (ones') **punches**.

He [Paul Volcker] has served under both Republicans and Democrats, and is held in the highest esteem for his sound and independent judgment. He pulls no punches. He seems fairly opinionated. He has a long and distinguished record of service to our nation. (205)

When **push** come to shove.

"They'll talk a good game – a sermon on Sunday, maybe, or a special offering for the homeless. But if push comes to shove, they won't really move unless you can show them how it'll help them pay their heating bill." (D,141)

To be **ready**, willing, and able.

In Uruguay, President Bush has the opportunity to forge closer ties with President Tabaré Vázquez, and to show that the United States is ready, willing, and able to work productively with democratic-left governments. (78)

To have a track **record**.

Community-based programs that have a proven track record in preventing unwanted pregnancies – both by encouraging abstinence and by promoting the proper use of contraception – deserve broad support. (H,334)

He [Leon Panetta] will be a strong manager and a strong advocate for the CIA. He knows how to focus resources where they are needed, and he has a proven track record of building consensus and working on a bipartisan basis with Congress. (223)

The **rich** get richer and the poor get poorer.

It is social [sic] Darwinism, a view of America that says there is not a problem that cannot be solved by making sure that the rich get richer and the poor get poorer. It requires no sacrifice on the part of those of us who have won life's lottery and does not consider who our parents were or the education received or the right breaks that came at the right time. (20)

To sell (send) someone down the **river**.

Whenever we sat down with Rafiq to discuss our joint strategy, he would interrupt the discussion with long lectures about secret machinations afoot, and all the black people willing to sell their people down the river. (D,196)

To be on a long (winding) **road**.

"It's a long road we're traveling," he said, "but tonight showed me what we can do when we put our minds to it. That good feeling you got right now, we got to keep it going till we got this neighborhood back on its feet." (D,154)

To have been down the same **road** before.

Cars meandering across lanes and roundabouts, dodging potholes, bicycles, and pedestrians [...]. It all seemed strangely familiar, as if I had been down the same road before. (D,307)

To face **roadblocks**.

Statistically, the number of African Americans who occupy the top fifth of the income ladder remains relatively small. Moreover, every black professional und businessperson in Chicago can tell you stories of the roadblocks they still experience on account of race. (H,241)

We're tired of being divided, tired of running into ideological walls and partisan roadblocks, tired of appeals to our worst instincts and greatest fears. Americans everywhere are desperate for leadership. They are longing for direction. And they want to believe again. (57)

But we always knew that hope is not blind optimism. It's not ignoring the enormity of the task ahead or the roadblocks that stand in our path. It's not sitting on the sidelines or shrinking from a fight. (98)

To be on a **roll**.

I tried to change the subject, but Reggie was on a roll. "I'm telling you, Regina, it was wild. When the maids show up Monday morning, we were all still sitting in the hallway, looking like zombies." (D,109)

To go (be) through the **roof**.

All the while, [medical] costs just keep climbing. Family premiums are up nearly 65% over the last five years. Deductibles are up 50%. Co-payments for care and prescriptions are through the roof. (21)

Family premiums are up nearly 87% over the last five years, growing faster than workers' wages. Deductibles are up 50%. Co-payments for care and prescriptions are through the roof. (74)

To have a **roof** over one's head.

If cash was too short, the children could be sent upcountry for a time; that's where another brother, Abo, was staying, I was told, with an uncle in Kendu Bay, where there were always chores to perform, food on the table and a roof over one's head. (D,329)

These are middle-class families with two parents who both work at good-paying jobs that put a roof over their heads. They're saving every extra penny they have so that their children can someday do better than they did. (4)

I will change our bankruptcy laws to make it easier for families to stay in their homes. Right now, if you're a family that owns one house, bankruptcy judges are actually barred from helping you keep a roof over your head by writing down the value of your mortgage. (156)

To learn the **ropes**.

The path of least resistance [...] starts to look awfully tempting, and if the opinions of these insiders don't quite jibe with those you once held, you learn to rationalize the changes as a matter of realism, of compromise, of learning the ropes. (H,115)

To run **roughshod**.

At the end of the Civil War, when farmers and their families began moving into the cities to work in the big factories that were sprouting up all across America, we had to decide: Do we do nothing and allow the captains of industry and robber barons to run roughshod over the economy and workers by competing to see who can pay the lowest wage at the worst working conditions? (19)

Do we do nothing and allow the captains of industry and robber barons to run roughshod over the economy and workers by competing to see who can pay the lowest wage at the worst working conditions? (25)

The **rubber** hits the road.

This economic recovery plan will require their [governors and mayors] input, their participation. And you know, part of our job is to make sure that we are listening to what's happening on the ground, where the rubber hits the road, and not simply redesigning something out of Washington. (204)

It always feels like a bit of a homecoming when I meet with governors. Because while I stand here today as President-elect, I will never forget the eight years I served in the state Senate in Illinois. It is in state and local government that the rubber hits the road. (208)

To use a **rubber stamp**.

Taken together, the questionable design of this points [immigration] program and the fundamental shift away from family preferences in the allocation of visas raise enough red flags that we should not rubber stamp this proposal and allow it to go forward. (82)

There is no **rule** without an exception.

It's not just his decisions in these individual cases that give me pause − it's that decisions like these are the rule for Samuel Alito, not the exception. When it comes to how checks and balances in our system are supposed to work [...], Judge Alito consistently sides with the notion that a President should not be constrained by either Congressional acts or the check of the Judiciary. (38)

To change the **rules** (of the game).

To me, the threat to eliminate the filibuster on judicial nominations was just one more example of Republicans changing the rules in the middle of the game. (H,82)

The rules of the game have changed. And so we must change with them. But in a country of innovators and optimists − a country that pioneered the first moon landing, discovered the cure for polio, and led the technological revolution of the nineties − I have no doubt that we can. (5)

We're here today because when it comes to the global economy, the rules of the game have changed. This is a fact not only understood by a roomful of Silicon Valley CEOs, but by families I met all across Illinois during the campaign. (5)

Yes, the rules of the game have changed. And now it's time for us to prove to the world that we can still play better than anyone. The families I've met are ready to try. Their kids are ready. TechNet is ready. And in the coming months, I will do my best to work with my colleagues and make sure our government is ready too. (5)

What we don't expect is for one party – be it Republican or Democrat [sic] – to change the rules in the middle of the game so that they can make all the decisions while the other party is told to sit down and keep quiet. (10)

It's as if someone changed the rules in the middle of the game and no one bothered to tell these people. And, in reality, the rules have changed. It started with technology and automation that rendered entire occupations obsolete. (19, 25)

At the very moment that globalization is changing the rules of the game on the American worker [...], the people running Washington are responding with a philosophy that says government has no role in solving these problems. (65)

I meet these Americans every single day – people who believe they have been left on the sidelines by a global economy that has forever changed the rules of the game. (89)

To live by the **rules**.

That's how things were; you couldn't change it, you could just live by the rules, so simple once you learned them. And so Lolo had made his peace with power, learned the wisdom of forgetting. (D,45-46)

To obey the **rules** of the road.

The growing threat, then, comes primarily from those parts of the world on the margins of the global economy where the international "rules of the road" have never taken hold – the realm of weak or failing states, arbitrary rule, corruption, and chronic violence. (H,305)

Why conduct ourselves in this way? Because nobody benefits more than we do from the observance of international "rules of the road." We can't win converts to those rules if we act as if they apply to everyone but us. (H,309)

We have not come this far because we practice survival of the fittest. America is America because we believe in creating a framework in which all can succeed. Our free market was never meant to be a free license to take whatever you can get, however you can get it. And so from time to time, we have to put in place certain rules of the road to make competition fair, and open, and honest. (89)

As we do this [working on our nuclear policy], we'll be in a better position to lead the world in enforcing the rules of the road if we firmly abide by those rules. It's time to stop giving countries like Iran and North Korea an excuse. It's time for America to lead. (92)

The first challenge is to stem the fallout from the housing crisis and put in place rules of the road to prevent it from happening again. (105)

Our free market was never meant to be a free license to take whatever you can get, however you can get it. That is why we have to put in place rules of the road to make competition fair, and open, and honest. (109)

The goal must be ensuring that financial institutions around the world are subject to similar rules of the road – both to make the system stable, and to keep our financial institutions competitive. (109)

There were arguments for changing the rules of the road in the 1990s. Our economy was undergoing a fundamental shift, carried along by the swift currents of technological change and globalization. (109)

And for all of George Bush's professed faith in free markets, the markets have hardly been free – not when the gates of Washington are thrown open to high-priced lobbyists who rig the rules of the road and riddle our tax code with special interest favors and corporate loopholes. (122)

Businesses should live up to their responsibilities to create American jobs, look out for American workers, and play by the rules of the road. (152)

As we reform our regulatory system at home, we must address the same problems abroad so that financial institutions around the world are subject to similar rules of the road. (156)

But the American economy has worked in large part because we have guided the market's invisible hand with a higher principle – that America prospers when all Americans prosper. That is why we have put in place rules of the road to make competition fair, and open, and honest. (156, 157)

We must build upon these ideas I have laid out over the last several years about how to modernize our financial regulation in this country, and establish common-sense rules of the road for our financial system to help restore confidence in our financial system. (159)

What led us to this point was years and years of a philosophy in Washington and on Wall Street that viewed even common-sense regulations and oversight as unwise and unnecessary; that shredded consumer protections and loosened the rules of the road. (159)

Sixth, we need to start putting in place the rules of the road I've been calling for years to prevent this [economic crisis] from ever happening again. (161)

That means taking on the lobbyists and special interests in Washington. That means taking on the greed and corruption on Wall Street. That means putting in place the rules of the road and common-sense regulations for our finance system that I've been calling for since March. It is time to reform Washington. (166)

That means taking on the lobbyists and special interests in Washington. That means taking on the greed and corruption on Wall Street. That means putting in place the rules of the road and common-sense regulations for our finance system that I've been calling for since last March – regulations that would make our markets open, honest, and transparent. (167)

I will modernize our outdated financial regulations and put in the place the common-sense rules of the road I've been calling for since March – rules that will keep our market free, fair, and honest. (168, 169, 171)

And as I modernize the financial system to create new rules of the road to prevent another crisis, we will continue this [financial stability] fee to build up a reserve so that if this happens again, it will be the money contributed by banks that's put at risk. (169)

Over the past few days, he's [Senator McCain] talked a lot about getting tough on Wall Street, but over the past few decades, he's fought against the very rules of the road that could've stopped this mess. (170)

I will take on the corruption in Washington and on Wall Street to make sure a crisis like this can never, ever happen again. I'll put in place the common-sense regulations and rules of the road I've been calling for since March – rules that will keep our market free, fair, and honest. (174, 175, 176, 179, 180, 181)

Now none of us want to see unnecessary burdens on business. But after what we've seen on Wall Street, isn't it obvious by now that we need some common-sense rules of the road to protect consumers and our economy? (189)

It [government] should reward drive and innovation and growth in the free market, but it should also make sure businesses live up to their responsibility to create American jobs, and look out for American workers, and play by the rules of the road. (190, 191, 192)

I do think that we have to put in place a set of rules of the road [for the housing market], some financial regulations that prevent the kind of speculation and leveraging, that we saw, in the future. (211)

But the American economy has worked in large part because we've guided the market's invisible hand with a higher principle: that America prospers when all Americans prosper. That principle is why we put in place common-sense rules of the road to regulate our market, and it's why we need to restore and renew those rules today. (217)

These individuals [Mary Schapiro, Gary Gensler, and Daniel Tarullo] will help put in place new, common-sense rules of the road that will protect investors, consumers and our entire economy from fraud and manipulation by an irresponsible few. (217)

On [domestic] policy, have we helped this economy recover from what is the worst financial crisis since the Great Depression? Have we instituted financial regulations and rules of the road that assure this kind of crisis doesn't occur again? (219)

That is why we need to act boldly and act now to reverse these cycles. That's why we need to put money in the pockets of the American people, create new jobs, and invest in our future. That's why we need to re-start the flow of credit and restore the rules of the road that will ensure a crisis like this never happens again. (221)

To play by the **rules**.

But she had a quick mind and sound judgment, and a capacity for sustained work. Slowly she had risen, playing by the rules, until she reached the threshold where competence didn't suffice. (D,56)

And by the time I had dropped my friends off, I had begun to see a new map of the world, one that was frightening in its simplicity, suffocating in its implications. We were always playing on the white man's court, Ray had told me, by the white man's rules. (D,85)

In our government, we see campaign contributions and lobbyists used to cut corners and win favors that stack the deck against businesses and consumers who play by the rules. (89)

These anti-market, anti-business practices are wasteful, unproductive, and antithetical to the very spirit of capitalism. They benefit the undeserving few at the expense of hardworking Americans and entrepreneurs who play by the rules. (89)

You can't **run** away from yourself.

She took a step back, her hand on her hips. "Naive? *You're* calling *me* naive? Uh-uh. I don't think so. If anybody's naïve, it's you. You're the one who seems to think he can run away from himself." (D,108)

Easier **said** than done.

So we need to make investments in family literacy programs and early childhood education so that kids aren't left behind before they even go to school. And we need to get books in our kids' hands early and often. I know that this is often easier said than done. Parents today still have the toughest job in the world – and no one ever thanks you enough for doing it. (22)

Now, at a time when both parents are more likely to work longer hours outside the home, this is a lot easier said than done. We try to compete with these media messages, but it's nearly impossible to be there every moment our kids are watching television. (33)

When all is **said** and done.

But when all is said an done, China will still have more surplus labor in its countryside than half the entire population of the United States – which means Wal-Mart will be keeping suppliers there busy for a very, very long time. (H,173)

When all is said and done, losses will be in the many hundreds of billions. What was bad for Main Street was bad for Wall Street. Pain trickled up. (109)

When all is said and done, my plan to increase our fuel standards will save American consumers from purchasing half a trillion gallons of gas over the next eighteen years. (127)

When all is said and done, my plan to invest $150 billion in alternative energy will create entire new industries, thousands of new businesses, and up to five million new, green jobs that pay well and can't be outsourced. (136)

When all is said and done, my [energy] plan will create entire new industries and thousands of new businesses, while working to strengthen our national security and save our planet. These steps are not far-off, pie-in-the-sky solutions – the American people are ready to make this change. (143)

To be (rest) on shifting **sands**.

Such policies take us [...] to a brave new world in which gender differences have been erased, sex is purely recreational, marriage is disposable, motherhood is an inconvenience, and civilization itself rests on shifting sands. (H,335)

To tilt (tip) the **scale**.

I was deeply disturbed by some statements that were made by largely Democratic advocacy groups when ranking member Senator Leahy announced that he would support Judge [John] Roberts. Although the scales have tipped in a different direction for me, I am deeply admiring of the work and the thought that Senator Leahy has put into making his decision. (27)

Somewhere along the way, we let a reckless few game the system, we let special interests tilt the scale and distort the free market, we stopped making the investments in our children and our workers to help us rise together. And today, we're all paying the price. (145)

To make a **scene**.

Gramps is probably too busy telling one if his jokes or arguing with Toot over how to cook the steaks to notice my mother reach out and squeeze the smooth, sinewy hand beside hers. Toot notices, but she's polite enough to bite her lip and offer dessert; her instincts warn her against making a scene. (D,17)

To **sell** out.

But I suspect that the union leaders won't always see it that way. There may be times when they will see it as betrayal. They may alert their members that I have sold them out. I may get angry mail and angry phone calls. They may not endorse me the next time around. (H,119)

Every U.S. **senator** wakes up in the morning, looks in the mirror and looks at a future president.

There's a famous saying that every United States senator wakes up in the morning, looks in the mirror and looks at a future president. It's one of the congenital defects of serving in the Unites States Senate. (B,146)

In America, **separate** can never be equal

Fifty years ago this country decided that Linda Brown shouldn't have to walk miles and miles to school every morning when there was a white school but four blocks away because when it comes to education in America, separate can never be equal. (15)

And even when our government refused to hold up its end of the bargain [to educate everybody], ordinary people marched and bled, they took to the streets and fought in the courts, they stood up and spoke out until the day when the arrival of nine little children at a school in Little Rock made real the decision that in America separate could never be equal. (30)

And even when our government refused to hold up its end of the bargain [to educate everybody], ordinary people stood up and spoke out until the day when the arrival of nine little children at a school in Little Rock made real the decision that in America, separate could never be equal. (46)

It was ordinary Americans who marched and bled; who took to the streets and fought in the courts until the arrival of nine little children at a Little Rock school made the real decision that in America separate can never be equal. (96)

To be in the **shadow** of someone or something.

We have to finally bring undocumented immigrants out of the shadows. Yes, they broke the law. And they should have to pay a fine, and learn English, and go to the back of the line. That's how we'll put them on a pathway to citizenship. (133)

To get bent out of **shape**.

You might think that Washington would learn from Iraq. But we've seen in this campaign just how bent out of shape Washington gets when you challenge its assumptions. (92)

To be on the **shelf**.

We need solutions that strike at the very heart of our dependence on oil. Right now, the largest consumers of oil in this country are the cars we drive. And right now, we also have the technology to build cars that travel much further on a gallon of gas. [...] So the technology is on the shelf. It's ready and available for our car companies to use. (26)

To be on a sinking **ship**.

I took the turn into Altgelt [...]. But as I cut off the engine and started reaching for my briefcase, something stopped me short. The view, perhaps; the choking gray sky. I closed my eyes and leaned my head against the car seat, feeling like the first mate on a sinking ship. (D,166)

When one's **ship** comes in (home).

How lucky he [Obama's father] must have felt when his ship came sailing in! He must have known, when that letter came from Hawaii, that he had been chosen after all; that he possessed the grace of his name, the *baraka*, the blessings of God. (D,428)

All that **shit**.

"They'll [colleges] train you so good, you'll start believing what they tell you about equal opportunity and the American way and all that shit. They'll give you a corner office and invite you to fancy dinners, and tell you you're a credit to your race. Until you want to actually start running things, and then they'll yank on your chain and let you know that you may be a well-trained, well-paid nigger, but you're a nigger just the same." (D,97)

Not worth (a) **shit**.

"Get to the dance, guess who's standing there, got her arms around Rick Cook. 'Hi, Ray,' she says, like she don't know what's going down. Rick Cook! Now you know that guy ain't shit. Sorry-assed motherfucker got nothing on me, right? Nothing." (D,73)

Until the first time I heard a young mother use it on her child to tell him he wasn't worth shit, or watched teenage boys use it to draw blood in a quick round of verbal sparring. (D,194-195)

Someone's **shit** isn't so hot.

"Don't be thick, all right? I'm not just talking about one time. Look, I ask Monica out, she says no. I say okay...your shit's not so hot anyway." Ray stopped to see my reaction, then smiled. (D,73)

To feel like **shit**.

About halfway through the meeting, Marty arrived. After it was over, he came up and put a hand on my shoulder. "Feels like shit, huh?" It did. He helped me clean up, then took me out for coffee and pointed out some of my mistakes. (D,162)

To tell someone **shit**.

"I don't need no help!" he shouted, trying to steady himself "Not from nobody, you understand me! Punk-ass motherfucker...try to tell me shit..." His voice trailed off. (D,186)

To treat someone like **shit**.

"She said that often women needed to be beaten, because otherwise they would not do everything that was required of them. You see how we are? We complain, but still we encourage men to treat us like shit." (D,405)

To give (get) the **shivers**.

She [Auma] rubbed her eyes and laughed. "[...] I don't know, Barack. Sometimes I think it's just impossible for me to trust anybody completely. I think of what the Old Man made of his life, and the idea of marriage gives me, how do you say...the shivers." (D,210)

To be (put oneself, stand) in someone else's **shoes**.

Was the collaboration of some slaves any different than the silence of some Iranians who stood by and did nothing as Savac thugs murdered and tortured opponents of the Shah? How could we judge other men until we had stood in their shoes? (D,117)

That last aspect of Paul's character – a sense of empathy [...] is at the heart of my moral code, and it is how I understand the Golden Rule – not simply as a call to sympathy or charity, but as something more demanding, a call to stand in somebody else's shoes and see through their eyes. (H,66)

How can we cut through the apathy and the partisanship and the business-as-usual culture in Washington? When we wonder this, we need to rediscover the hope that people have been in our shoes and they've lived to cross those bridges. (15)

From the earliest days of our founding, they [questions about labor] have been asked and then answered by Americans [workers] who have stood in your shoes and shared your concerns about the future. (25)

My third piece of advice is to cultivate a sense of empathy – to put yourself in other people's shoes – to see the world from their eyes. Empathy is a quality of character that can change the world – one that makes you understand that your obligations to others extend beyond people who look like you and act like you and live in your neighborhood. (55)

The world doesn't just revolve around you. There's a lot of talk in this country about the federal deficit. But I think we should talk more about our empathy deficit – the ability to put ourselves in someone else's shoes; to see the world through [the eyes of] those who are different from us – the child who's hungry, the laid-off steelworker, the immigrant woman cleaning your dorm room. (58)

There's a lot of talk in this country about the federal deficit. But I think we should talk more about our empathy deficit – the ability to put ourselves in someone else's shoes; to see the world through [the eyes of] those who are different from us – the child who's hungry, the laid-off steelworker, the immigrant woman cleaning your dorm room. (61)

In this time of change and uncertainty, these questions [about economics, jobs, etc.] are expected – but I want you to know today they are by no means unique. Throughout our history, they have been asked and then answered by Americans who have stood in your shoes and shared your concerns. (65)

You know, there's a lot of talk in this country about the federal deficit. But I think we should talk more about our empathy deficit – the ability to put ourselves in someone else's shoes; to see the world through the eyes of those who are different from us – the child who's hungry, the steelworker who's been laid off, the family who lost the entire life they built together when the storm came to town. (66)

Like no other illness, AIDS tests our ability to put ourselves in someone else's shoes – to empathize with the plight of our fellow man. While most would agree that the AIDS orphan or the transfusion victim or the wronged wife contracted the disease through no fault of their own, it has too often been easy for some to point to the unfaithful husband or promiscuous youth or the gay man and say "This is your fault. You have sinned." I don't think that is a satisfactory response. My faith reminds me that we are all sinners. (72)

The other day I got head to [i.e., to head] out to California because the Service Employees' Union had organized an event where I would walk in the shoes of one of their members for a day. (88)

It's not easy to stand in somebody else's shoes. It's not easy to see past our differences. We've all encountered this in our lives. But what makes it even more difficult is that we have a politics in this country that seeks to drive us apart – that puts up walls between us. (99)

[Change] will require each of us to do our part in closing the moral deficit – the empathy deficit – that exists in this nation. It will take standing in one another's shoes and remembering that we are our brother's keeper; we are our sister's keeper. (103)

I have the distinct honor today of pinch-hitting for one of my personal heroes – and a hero to this country, Senator Edward Kennedy. Teddy wanted to be here very much, but as you know, he's had a very long week and is taking some much-needed rest. He called me up a few days ago and I said that I'd be happy to be his stand-in, even if there was no way I could fill his shoes. (116)

The second thing we need to do as fathers is pass along the value of empathy to our children. Not sympathy, but empathy – the ability to stand in somebody else's shoes; to look at the world through their eyes. (123)

The **shot** heard around the world.

On a spring morning in April 1775, a simple band of colonists [... took] up arms against the tyranny of an Empire. [...] They did so not on behalf of a particular tribe or image, but on behalf of a larger idea. The idea of liberty. The idea of God-given, inalienable [sic] rights. And with the first shot that fateful day – a shot heard around the world – the American Revolution, and America's experiment with democracy, began. (129)

To be a big **shot**.

"So they expected anything from him. 'Ah, Barack, you are a big shot now. You should give me something. You should help me.' Always these pressures from family. And he couldn't say no, he was so generous." (D,336)

To be a long **shot**.

It was a difficult race, in a crowded field of well-funded, skilled, and prominent candidates; without organizational backing or personal wealth, a black man with a funny name, I was considered a long shot. (D,viii)

To have a (fair) **shot** at something.

"No, I'm just asking you a question [...] trying to figure out what's going to happen to those boys. Who's going to make sure they get a fair shot? The alderman? The social workers? The gangs?" (D,172)

"Listen, Barack, your loyalty is admirable. But right now you need to worry about your own development. Stay here and you're bound to fail. You'll give up organizing before you gave it a real shot." (D,228)

And it was this acceptance, I think, that allowed me to come up with the thoroughly cockeyed idea of running for the United Sates Senate. An up-or-out strategy was how I described it to my wife, one last shot to test out my ideas before I settled into a calmer, more stable, and better-paying existence. (H,5)

I told them that they were right: government couldn't solve all their problems. But with a slight change in priorities we could make sure every child had a decent shot at life and meet the challenges we faced as a nation. (H,7)

I want to make real the American ideal that every child in this country has a shot at life. Right now, that's not true. (B,108)

No, people don't expect government to solve all their problems. But they sense, deep in their bones, that with just a change in priorities, we can make sure that every child in America has a decent shot at life, and that the doors of opportunity remain open. (2)

But there are also millions of middle-class families out there who are struggling to get by. They work hard, they love their children, and they're willing to do anything to give them the best possible shot in life. (4)

And even if you didn't go to a fine school like SIU [Southern Illinois University], in those days you still had a shot at the American dream. Because whether it was on the farm or in a factory, a middle-class job that paid a decent wage and good benefits was easy to come by. (13)

Our economic dominance has depended on individual initiative and belief in the free market; but it has also depended on our sense of mutual regard for each other, the idea that everybody has a stake in the country, that we're all in it together and everybody's got a shot at opportunity. (19, 34)

Yes, our greatness as a nation has depended on individual initiative, on a belief in the free market. But it has also depended on our sense of mutual regard for each other, the idea that everybody has a stake in the country, that we're all in it together, and everybody's got a shot at opportunity. (35)

We're the party of civil rights, and workers' rights, and women's rights who believes that every member of the American family deserves a shot at the American Dream. That's who we are. (50)

I asked them, "Before you quit, I want you to answer one question. What's gonna happen to those boys? Who will fight for them if not us? Who will give them a fair shot if we leave?" (58, 61)

Yes, our greatness as a nation has depended on individual initiative, on a belief in the free market. But it has also depended on our sense of mutual regard for each other, of mutual responsibility. The idea that everybody has a stake in the country, that we're all in it together and everybody's got a shot at opportunity. (65)

He [Theodore Roosevelt] devoted his presidency to busting trusts, breaking up monopolies, and doing his best to give American people a shot at the American dream once more. (86)

For homeowners facing foreclosure through no fault of their own, we'll create a fund and reform bankruptcy laws to give them a shot at avoiding foreclosure. We'll mandate that prospective homebuyers have access to accurate and complete information about their mortgage options. (95)

It's about giving all Americans a fair shot at the American dream. That's what most Americans are looking for. It's not a lot. Americans don't need government to solve all their problems, and they don't want it to. (133)

Now, with Joe Biden at my side, I am confident that we can take this country in a new direction; [...] we'll restore that fair shot at your dreams that is at the core of who Joe Biden and I are as a people, and what America is as a nation. (151)

[We need] common-sense regulations to prevent a crisis like this from ever happening again. Investments in the technology and innovation that will restore prosperity and lead to new jobs and a new economy for the 21st century. Bottom-up growth that gives every American a fair shot at the American dream. (174, 176)

We can restore a sense of fairness and balance that will give ever[y] American a fair shot at the American dream. And above all, we can restore confidence – confidence in America, confidence in our economy, and confidence in ourselves. (178)

To take a (cheap) **shot**.

We paint our faces red or blue and cheer our side and boo their side, and if it takes a late hit or cheap shot to beat the other team, so be it, for winning is all that matters. But I don't think so. (H,41)

To ride **shotgun**

He's [Senator McCain] supported four of the five Bush budgets that have taken us from the surpluses of the Clinton years to the largest deficits in history. John McCain has ridden shotgun as George Bush has driven our economy toward a cliff, and now he wants to take the wheel and step on the gas. (191)

To call (all) the **shots**.

In our weekly meetings, though, he [Marty] would remind me of the choice I'd made, that there was no risk in my modest accomplishments, that the men in fancy suits downtown were still calling the shots. (D,229)

To carry (put) something on one's **shoulder**.

And if none of this works – if you couldn't find affordable insurance and suffer an illness that leaves you thousands of dollars in debt – then you should no longer count on being able to start over by declaring bankruptcy because they've changed the law to put the burden of debt squarely on your shoulders. (14)

To lend a **shoulder**.

After all, Katrina may well be the most dramatic test you face in life, but it will by no means be the last. There will be quiet tests of character – the shoulder you lend a friend during their [sic] time of need; the way you raise your children; the care you give a loved one who's sick or dying; the integrity and honesty with which you carry yourself. (66)

To look over someone's **shoulder**.

Whether it's Medicaid reimbursements, the rising price of medical malpractice insurance, or having HMOs look over your shoulder, all the hard work and sacrifice you've put in during medical school isn't as rewarding as it once was. (21, 51)

So I'm here to gratefully acknowledge the importance of libraries and the work you do. I also want to work with you to insure that libraries continue to be sanctuaries for learning, where we are free to read and consider what we please, without the fear of Big Brother peering menacingly over our shoulders. (22)

When political groups try to censor great works of literature, you're [librarians] the ones putting Huck Finn and Catcher in the Rye back on the shelves, making sure that our right to free thought and free information is protected. And ever since we've had to worry about our government looking over our shoulders in the library, you've been there to stand up and speak out on privacy issues. (22)

To put (push) one's **shoulder** to the wheel.

It's this sense of mission that has compelled Americans of all backgrounds and beliefs to put aside their differences and push their shoulder against the wheel of history in search of a better day. (88)

But we've got work to do and we cannot rest. And I know that if you put your shoulders to the wheel of history and take up the cause of perfecting our union just as earlier generations of Americans did before you; [...] then not only will we help close the responsibility deficit in this country, [...] but I will come back here next year on the 100th anniversary of the NAACP, and I will stand before you as the President of the United States of America. (138)

And your chairman Julian Bond [of the NAACP] was but a 25-year old state legislator when he put his own shoulder to the wheel of history. (138)

To stand on someone's (giants') **shoulders**.

Dr. King told a gathering of organizers and activists and community members that they should not despair because the arc of the moral universe is long, but it bends towards justice. That's because of the work that each of us do to bend it towards justice. It's because of people like John Lewis and Fannie Lou Hamer and Coretta Scott King and Rosa Parks, all the giants upon whose shoulders we stand that we are beneficiaries of that arc bending towards justice. (63)

Everyone in this room stands on the shoulders of many Moses. They are the courageous men and women who marched and fought and bled for the rights and freedoms we enjoy today. (91)

And I know that I stand on their shoulders [of civil rights advocates], that their courage and sacrifice six decades ago makes it possible for me to run today for President of the United States. (93)

It is always humbling to speak before the NAACP. It is a powerful reminder of the debt we all owe to those who marched for us and stood up on our behalf; of the sacrifices that were made for us by those we never knew, and of the giants whose shoulders I stand on here today. (138)

To weigh heavy on one's **shoulders**.

I mention it not to add to the burden that must already weigh heavily on your shoulders, but to point out that your distinct commitment and compassion for the lives of your fellow human beings is a quality that has intrinsic value far outside the doctor's office or the operating room. (51)

To have nothing to **show**.

"How old are you anyway?" "Twenty-two." "See there. Don't waste your youth, Mr. Barack. Wake up one morning, an old man like me, and all you gonna be is tired, with nothing to show for it." (D,136)

"I'm sorry, Barack," Angela continued. "It has nothing to do with you. The truth is, we're just tired. We've all been at this for two years, and we've got nothing to show for it." (D,171)

To put up (pull down) the **shutters**.

Few minorities can isolate themselves entirely from white society – certainly not in the way that whites can successfully avoid contact with members of other races. But it is possible for minorities to pull down the shutters psychologically, to protect themselves by assuming the worst. (H,236)

To be **sick** and tired.

Reverend J.A. DeLaine [...] joined with Levi Pearson, a father who was sick and tired of seeing his children walk nine miles to school, and more than a dozen other Black parents to challenge unequal education. (93)

We're tired of more Americans going without health care, of more Americans falling into poverty, of more American kids who have the brains and the drive to go to college – but can't – because they can't afford it. We're ready for the Bush Administration to end, because we are sick and tired of being sick and tired. (95)

There's a bright **side** somewhere.

"The audacity of hope! I still remember my grandmother, singing in the house, 'There's a bright side somewhere ... don't rest till you find it ....'" "That's right!" "The audacity of hope! Times when we couldn't pay the bills." (D,294)

To be on the wrong **side**.

To those leaders around the globe who seek to sow conflict, or blame their society's ills on the West: Know that your people will judge you on what you can build, not what you destroy. To those who cling to power through corruption and deceit and the silencing of dissent, know that you are on the wrong side of history; but that we will extend a hand if you are willing to unclench your fist. (229)

To be only one **side** of the equation.

Now, building cars that use less oil is only one side of the equation. The other involves replacing the oil we use with home-grown biofuels. The Governors in this room have long known about this potential, and all of you have been leading the way on ethanol in your own states. (43)

But building cars that use less oil is only part of the equation. The other involves replacing the oil we use with the home-grown biofuels that will finally slow the warming of the planet. (48)

To sit on the **sidelines**.

I meet these Americans every single day – people who believe they have been left on the sidelines by a global economy that has forever changed the rules of the game. (89)

But we always knew that hope is not blind optimism. It's not ignoring the enormity of the task ahead or the roadblocks that stand in our path. It's not sitting on the sidelines or shrinking from a fight. (98)

You spoke of an America where working families [...] don't have to sit on the sidelines of the global economy because they couldn't afford the cost of a college education. (115)

Never again will we sit on the sidelines, or stand in the way of global action to tackle this global [energy] challenge. I will reach out to the leaders of the biggest carbon emitting nations and ask them to join a new Global Energy Forum that will lay the foundation for the next generation of climate protocols. (139)

To lower one's **sights**.

These are the indicators of crisis, subject to data and statistics. Less measurable but no less profound is a sapping of confidence across our land – a nagging fear that America's decline is inevitable, and that the next generation must lower its sights. (229)

To set one's **sights** high(er).

You know, they said this day would never come [Iowa caucus night]. They said our sights were set too high. They said this country was too divided; too disillusioned to ever come together around a common purpose. (98)

We also know that because of what Hillary [Clinton] accomplished, my daughters and yours look at themselves a little differently today. They're dreaming a little bigger and setting their sights a little higher today. (134)

Signs don't vote.

There is a saying in Illinois politics that "signs don't vote," meaning that you can't judge a race by how many signs a candidate has. But nobody in Illinois had ever seen during the course of an entire campaign the number of signs and billboards that Mr. Hull had put up in a single day [...]. (H,112)

The **sins** of the fathers are visited on the children.

He turned toward the campfire, and I thought his voice began to waver. "Perhaps I can never call this place home," he said. "Sins of the father, you know. I've learned to accept that." He paused for a moment, then looked at me. (D,355)

To do something by the **skin** of one's teeth.

The Sox won last night the way they have won all season – by playing aggressively, scrapping for every base and every run. [...] The four games against the Astros were decided by a total of six runs. Win by the skin of your teeth. Win or die trying, that's our motto this year. (31)

To get under someone's **skin**.

And yet, as the campaign progressed, I found him [Alan Keyes] getting under my skin in a way that few people ever have. When our paths crossed during the campaign, I often had to suppress the rather uncharitable urge to either taunt him or wring his neck. (H,211)

To **slash** and burn.

In fact, with their rigid doctrines, slash-and-burn style, and exaggerated sense of having been aggrieved, this new conservative leadership was eerily reminiscent of some of the New Left's leaders during the sixties. (H,33)

It's 24-hour, slash-and-burn, negative-ad, bickering, small-minded politics that doesn't move us forward. (B,25)

To wipe the **slate** clean (have a clean slate).

"So I told him, 'Roy and myself we're already adults. We have our own ways, our own memories, and what happened between all of us is hard to undo. But with George, the baby, he is a clean slate. You have a chance to really do right by him.' And he just nodded, as if ... as if ..." (D,218-219)

To have something up one's **sleeve**.

Still, I'd felt bad after that particular episode; it was the one trick my mother always had up her sleeve, that way she had of making me feel guilty. She made no bones about it, either. "You can't help it," she told me once. "Slipped it into your baby food. Don't worry, though," she added, smiling like the Cheshire cat. "A healthy dose of guilt never hurt anybody. It's what civilization is built on, guilt. A highly underrated emotion." (D,196)

To wear something on one's **sleeve**.

I don't think it's healthy for public figures to wear religion on their sleeve as a means to insulate themselves from criticism or dialogue with people who disagree with them. (B,93)

To **slice** and dice something.

The pundits like to slice-and-dice our country into Red States and Blue States; Red States of Republicans, Blue States for Democrats. But I've got news for them, too. [...] We are one people, all of us pledging allegiance to the stars and stripes, all of us defending the United States of America. (2)

We can continue to slice and dice this country into Red States and Blue States. We can exploit the divisions that exist in our country for pure political gain. Or this time, we can build on the movement we've started in this campaign – a movement that unites Democrats, Independents, and Republicans; a movement of young and old, rich and poor; white, black, Hispanic, Asian, and Native American. (112)

The attempts to play on our fears and exploit our differences to turn us against each other for pure political gain – to slice and dice this country into Red States and Blue States; blue-collar and white-collar; white and black, and brown. (113)

To get the (pink) **slip**.

We should make sure that [child] care is affordable, and that our kids can go to school earlier and longer so they have a safe place to learn while their parents are at work. And when a mom or a dad has to leave work to care for a sick child, we should make sure it doesn't result in a pink slip. (65)

To be on a slippery **slope**.

There's a slide. There is this big slippery slope of folks and communities that are sinking. The question is: What can organizing do about helping them, first, to stem the tide and then to build back up? (O,143)

To **smile** from one ear to the other.

Just then I noticed an American family sit down a few tables away from us. Two of the African waiters immediately sprang into action, both of them smiling from one ear to the other. (D,312)

To be up to **snuff**.

Look, we're not going to transform every school overnight. And there are some school systems – not just big-city school systems, there are rural schools and suburban schools – that just aren't up to snuff. But what we can expect is that each and every day we are thinking of new, innovative ways to make schools better. (215)

Sooner or later.

It's the timidity – the smallness – of our politics that's holding us back right now. The idea that some problems are just too big to handle, and if you just ignore them, sooner or later, they'll go away. (50, 57)

I want to see a stimulus package sooner rather than later. If it does not get done in the lame-duck session, it will be the first thing I get done as president of the United States. (198)

The **sooner** the better.

During my campaign I talked about the need to provide a tax cut to 95 percent of workers. Now, [it's time] for us to get that tax cut in place, that is going to put money into the pockets of the middle class and will help them in spending for their basic needs. That can help the economy. The sooner we do that the better. (204)

To sell one's **soul**.

"But when the so-called black committeemen came around election time, we'd all line up and vote the straight Democratic ticket. Sell our soul for a Christmas turkey. White folks spitting in our faces, and we'd reward 'em with the vote." (D,147)

You don't know if you want the whole bowl of **soup** unless you first have a taste.

"I asked her if the man would force the girl to sleep with him the night of the capture," Auma explained, "and she told me that no one knew what went on in a man's hut. But she also asked me how a man would know if he wanted the whole bowl of soup unless he first had a taste." (D,405)

To go **south**.

We recognize that things don't always work out as planned – a child gets sick, the company we work for shuts its doors, a parent contracts Alzheimer's, the stock market portfolio turns south. (H,177)

Speeches don't make unions.

Almost a century earlier, during the struggle for the soul of Chicago's stockyards, Hank Johnson, a leading African-American union organizer, told a crowd of laborers that in the end, speeches don't make unions. (25)

To get up to **speed** on something.

I had to hire staff and set up offices in Washington and Illinois. I had to negotiate committee assignments and get up to speed on the issues pending before the committees. (H,71)

Tim [Geithner] will waste no time getting up to speed. He will start his first day on the job [as Secretary of Treasury] with a unique insight into the failures of today's markets and a clear vision of the steps we must take to revive them. (203)

To break the **spell**.

I tried to imagine what would happen if Gramps walked into the barbershop at that moment, how the talk would stop, how the spell would be broken; the different assumptions at work. (D,148)

To fall (be) under a **spell**.

For an improbably short span it seems that my father fell under the same spell as my mother and her parents; and for the first six years of my life, even as that spell was broken and the worlds that they thought they'd left behind reclaimed each of them, I occupied the place where their dreams had been. (D,27)

To have a blind **spot**.

Of course, conservatives have their own blind spots when it comes to addressing problems in the culture. Take executive pay. In 1980, the average CEO made forty-two times what the hourly worker took home. By 2005, the ratio was 262 to 1. (H,61-62)

To (not) be in the **spotlight**.

The stories that give me such hope don't happen in the spotlight. They don't happen on the presidential stage. They happen in the quiet corners of our lives. They happen in the moments we least expect. (99)

The **stakes** are high.

This is not an easy posture to maintain in Washington. The stakes involved in Washington policy debates are often so high [...] that even small differences in perspectives are magnified. (H,48)

With hundreds of thousands of immigrants protesting in the streets and a group of self-proclaimed vigilantes called the Minutemen rushing to defend the Southern border, the political stakes were high for Democrats, Republicans, and the President. (H,264)

The times are too serious; the stakes are too high. And the change that's required, this new spirit of responsibility and honesty; of seriousness and sacrifice, starts with you. It starts with millions of people across the country, coming together to demand something better. (88)

The stakes could not be higher. Our children will grow up competing with children in Beijing and Bangalore and Berlin. And make no mistake – their governments are doing everything they can to give their countries an edge by investing in regional growth. (125)

And yet, at a time when the stakes could not be higher – when the challenges facing our country could not be greater – my opponent is talking about Britney and Paris. Well, I think the American people deserve better. Senator McCain and I have real differences and that's what we should be talking about. (146)

The times are too serious, the stakes are too high for this same partisan playbook. So let us agree that patriotism has no party. I love this country, and so do you, and so does John McCain. (152)

Florida, the stakes couldn't be higher. The choice couldn't be clearer. But still, we know that bringing the change we need won't be easy. We know we're up against a powerful, entrenched status quo in Washington. (160)

The times are too serious. The stakes are too high. At this moment, in this election, we need real change – change that's more than just a slogan, change that actually makes a difference in people's lives. (161)

The events of the last few weeks have shown us that the stakes in this election could not be higher. We are in a financial crisis as serious as any we've faced since the Great Depression. (170)

To put down (pull up) **stakes**.

What I needed was a community [...]. A place where I could put down stakes and test my commitments. And so, when I heard about a transfer program that Occidental had arranged with Columbia University, I'd been quick to apply. (D,115)

To raise the **stakes**.

That a desire for expanded prosperity has been given such a clear voice raises the stakes. Governments must now do more to address the basic needs and aspirations of their people in an effective, democratic, and sustainable way. (78)

If we **stand** together, we rise together.

For this has always been the way with us – at the edge of despair, in the shadow of hopelessness, ordinary people make the extraordinary decision that if we stand together, we rise together. And we do. (25)

To **stand** pat.

But our time of standing pat, of protecting narrow interests and putting off unpleasant decisions – that time has surely passed. Starting today, we must pick ourselves up, dust ourselves off, and begin again the work of remaking America. (229)

To gain **steam**.

But as the civil rights movement gained steam and they watched the marches and saw the boycotts and heard about the passage of voting rights, the workers in Memphis decided that they'd had enough, and in 1968, over 1,000 went on strike. (65)

To let off **steam**.

Blacks had no real power to act on the occasional slips into anti-Semitism or Asian-bashing, people would tell me; and anyway, black folks needed a chance to let off a little steam every once in a while – man, what do you think those folks say about us behind our backs? (D,203)

To be a **stick**-in-the-mud.

While in the state legislature, I never needed to spend more than $100,000 on a race; in fact, I developed a reputation for being something of a stick-in-the-mud when it came to fund-raising, coauthoring the first campaign finance legislation to pass in twenty-five years. (H,110)

To take **stock** of something.

At a time when she [his mother] should have been focused on getting well, at a time when she should have been taking stock of her life and taking comfort in her family, she was lying in a hospital bed, fighting with her insurance company because they didn't want to cover her treatment. (172)

One's **stomach** is tied in knots.

Two weeks of preparation and yet, the night of the meeting, my stomach was tied up in knots. At six forty-five only three people had shown up: a young woman with a baby who was drooling onto her tiny jumper, an older woman [...] and a drunken man. (D,184-185)

To be within a **stone**'s throw.

It's wonderful to be here today. I feel right at home in Bettendorf [Iowa], which is just a stone's throw from my home state of Illinois. But the truth is, we share more than the banks of a great river. (95)

To leave no **stone** unturned.

We can and we should help Israelis and Palestinians both fulfill their national goals: two states side by side in peace and security. Both the Israeli and Palestinian people have suffered from the failure to achieve this goal. The United States should leave no stone unturned in working to make that goal a reality. (77)

To (not) be etched in **stone**.

The exact details of these safeguards are not etched in stone. They can be reevaluated from time to time. The last time we had a major overhaul of the intelligence apparatus was 30 years ago in the aftermath of Watergate. (54)

To mind the **store**.

Folks, we don't need a commission to figure out what happened. We know what happened. Too many in Washington and on Wall Street weren't minding the store. CEOs got greedy. Lobbyists got their way. Politicians sat on their hands until it was too late. (157)

To weather a **storm**.

In the years to come, return this favor to those who are forced to weather their own storms – be it the loss of a job or a slide into poverty; an unexpected illness or an unforeseen eviction. (66)

A man of **straw**.

Well, what we need now is not straw men and misleading charges. What we need is honest leadership and real change, and that's why I'm running for President of the United States. (184)

The last **straw** will break the camel's back.

At a time like this, it's no wonder that the mortgage crisis was the straw that broke the camel's back. The equity that people own in their homes is often their largest source of savings, and as millions upon millions have seen those savings and their home equity decline or disappear altogether, so have their dreams for a better future. (105)

To be a two-way **street**.

Information sharing with state and local governments must be a two-way street, because we never know where the two pieces of the puzzle are that might fit together – the tip from Afghanistan, and the cop who sees something suspicious on Michigan Avenue. (85)

To take something to the **streets**.

Now, after the meeting in Altgelt, Will had an idea. "These mixed-up Negroes inside St. Catherine's ain't never gonna do nothing." He said. "If we wanna get something done, we gonna have to take it to the streets!" (D,173)

Be a good citizen, think about the other guy, but most importantly, do something about it. Whether it's through cartoons or campaigns, by taking it to the streets or taking it to your editor, tackling the biggest issues or lending a simple hand to your neighbor, these are the ways we leave our mark on the land we love – the same way Herblock [Herbert Block] left his mark on the pages of the Washington Post every day. (8)

To be of different **stripes**.

Undoubtedly, some of these views will get me in trouble. I am new enough on the national political scene that I serve as a blank screen on which people of vastly different political stripes project their own views. (H,11)

To earn one's **stripes**.

I have tremendous respect for Hillary Clinton. She's an outstanding leader in the Democratic Party. She's earned her stripes. (B,57)

To do something with the **stroke** of a pen.

Ultimately, Lyndon Johnson chose the right side of the battle [...]: upon signing the Civil Rights act of 1964, he would tell aide Bill Moyers that with the stroke of a pen he had just delivered the South to the GOP for the foreseeable future. (H,27)

The **survival** of the fittest.

"Everybody looking out for number one. Survival of the fittest. Tooth and claw. Elbow the other guy out of the way. That, my friend, is New York. But..." He shrugged and mopped up some egg with his toast. (D,119)

We have not come this far because we practice survival of the fittest. America is America because we believe in creating a framework in which all can succeed. Our free market was never meant to be a free license to take whatever you can get, however you can get it. And so from time to time, we have to put in place certain rules of the road to make competition fair, and open, and honest. (89)

To **swallow** something whole.

Still, as I look at his [Lincoln's] picture, it is the man and not the icon that speaks to me. I cannot swallow whole the view of Lincoln as the Great Emancipator. As a law professor and civil rights lawyer and as an African American, I am fully aware of his limited views on race. (L,74)

To be asleep at the **switch**.

We have been asleep at the switch, not just some of the regulatory agencies, but some of the congressional committees that might have been taking a look at this [financial] stuff. We have not been as aggressive, and we've had a White House that started with the premise that deregulation was always good. (217)

To pick up the **tab**.

By picking up part of the tab for the health care costs of their retirees, we'd be lifting a huge burden off the auto industry so that they'll invest in the technology that will finally reduce America's dependence on foreign oil. (26)

In the current Washington culture, lobbyists are expected to pick up the tab when they meet with members [of Congress] or staff. It is simply understood by all sides that the best way to get face time with a member or staffer in order to express your ideas on legislation is to buy them a meal. (45)

It's a piece of legislation I introduced called "Health Care for Hybrids," and it would allow the federal government to pick up part of the tab for the auto companies' retiree health care costs. (48)

We'll also reduce costs for business and their workers by picking up the tab for some of the most expensive illnesses. And we won't do all this twenty years from now, or ten years from now. We'll do it by the end of my first term as President of the United States. (121)

They [immigrants] need us to [...] cut costs for business and their workers by picking up the tab for some of the most expensive illnesses and conditions. (133)

We can guarantee health care for anyone who wants it, make it affordable for anyone who needs it, and cut costs for businesses and their workers by picking up the tab for some of the most expensive illnesses and conditions. (142)

We should be guaranteeing health care for anyone who wants it, making it affordable for anyone who needs it, and cutting costs for businesses and their workers by picking up the tab for some of the most expensive illnesses and conditions. (144)

And we'll reduce [health care] costs for business[es] and their workers by picking up the tab for some of the most expensive illnesses and conditions – because that's how we'll make our companies more competitive in the 21st century. (170)

We have to act to fix our broken economy and restore the credit markets. But taxpayers shouldn't be asked to pick up the tab for the very folks who helped create the crisis. (175)

To be on the **table**.

Finally, let there be no doubt: I will always keep the threat of military action on the table to defend our security and our ally Israel. Sometimes there are no alternatives to confrontation. (120)

Since the White House just made the announcement this morning, I have not had an opportunity, nor has my economic team, to look at all the details of the plan [to bail out the automakers]. So I wouldn't want to comment about what changes I would want to make before I've seen what's already on the table. (218)

To come to (be at, have at, bring to) the **table**.

If they [unorganized constituents] were brought to the table, a lot of times their agendas would be lost or manipulated, or what have you, not necessarily by him [Harold Washington], but by the various [political] forces because it was a big table and there were a lot of folks around it. (O,150)

It was here, in Springfield, where I saw all that is America converge – farmers and teachers, businessmen and laborers, all of them with a story to tell, all of them seeking a seat at the table, all of them clamoring to be heard. (76)

That's why I have a plan that will bring our combat troops home by March of 2008. Letting the Iraqis know that we will not be there forever is our last, best hope to pressure the Sunni and Shia to come to the table and find peace. (76)

Iran is highly dependent on imports and foreign investment, credit and technology. And an environment where our allies see that these types of investments in Iran are not in the world's best interests, could bring Iran to the table. (77)

There is no military solution to this war. At this point, no amount of soldiers can solve the grievances at the heart of someone else's civil war. The Iraqi people – Shia, Sunni, and Kurd – must come to the table and reach a political settlement themselves. (79)

It's time to move past the failed debates of yesterday, bring everyone to the table, and finally let the drug and insurance companies know that while they get a seat at the table, the[y] don't get to buy every chair. (84)

But it's time we had a Congress that tells the drug companies and the oil companies and the insurance industry that while they may get a seat at the table in Washington, they don't get to buy every chair. (86)

We have to stop giving countries the excuse that America will not come to the table. We have to lead, and that's what I intend to do. When you elect our next President, you will choose someone to make those tough judgments on Iraq, on Iran, on how to restore America's standing. (97)

And he [Tom Daschle] has the trust of folks from every angle of this issue [health care]: doctors, nurses and patients; unions and businesses; hospitals and advocacy groups – all of whom will have a seat at the table as we craft our [health] plan. (213)

If I'm having a debate about windpower, with my various – the various members of my energy team, having somebody like Ken [Salazar] at the table – who can say, here's our experience in Colorado; here's what we're seeing; here's how we can drive down unit costs; here's what we'd do [...] – that's going to be extraordinarily important. (216)

So if there's going to be a debate about oil shale, I want Ken [Salazar] at the table, because he can help sort through what are legitimate claims about, you know, how productive that approach might be, versus the kind of environmental degradation that is possible if we don't do it carefully. (216)

To put something on the **table**.

And so, Congress did the right thing when it rejected a plea for funds without a plan two weeks ago. The automakers have to come forward and put a more serious plan on the table, but more needs to be done. (212)

To be in a **tailspin**.

For months, the state of our economy has dominated the headlines – and the news hasn't been good. The sub-prime lending debacle has sent the housing market into a tailspin, and caused a broader contraction in the credit markets. (124)

Talent is (the) 21st century wealth.

As British Prime Minister Tony Blair has said, in this economy, "talent is 21st century wealth." If you've got the skills, you've got the education and you have the opportunity to upgrade and improve both, you'll be able to compete and win everywhere. (19)

Tony Blair once said that "Talent is the 21st century wealth," and I believe we all have a stake in nurturing that talent if we hope to prosper in this century. Ensuring our competitive edge also means investing more in the science and technology that has [sic] fueled so much of our nation's economic growth. (89)

Talk is cheap.

No one is exempt from the call to find common ground. Of course, in the end a sense of mutual understanding isn't enough, After all, talk is cheap; like any value, empathy must be acted upon. (H,68)

Less **talk**, more action.

But when you look at the record gas prices, and the possibility of more war and turmoil in the Middle East, it's clear that we need less talk and more action. We can start by producing more ethanol in America. (13)

Although we have begun to step up to the plate in the Senate, it is unfortunate that none of the avian flu bills that have been introduced have passed into law. Frankly, there's been a lot of talk, but not enough action. And this isn't just true of the Congress. (28)

To have a man-to-man **talk**.

I realized that he had time for me partly because he had nothing better to do. He was patient because he had no particular place he wanted to go. I needed to talk to him about that, as I'd promised Auma I would – a man-to-man talk…. (D,325)

To **talk** like a book.

"What about Yusuf?" Auma asked. "Couldn't he do more?" Sayid shook his head. "My brother, he talks like a book, but I'm afraid he does not like to lead by example." Auma turned to me. (D,381)

To **talk** the talk. (If you want to **talk** the talk, you've got to walk the walk.)

So let's be clear – there are a lot of people who have been in Washington longer than me; who have better connections and go to the right dinner parties and know how to talk the Washington talk. (88)

To cut through the red **tape**.

Declaring the era of big government over, Clinton signed welfare reform into law, pushed tax cuts for the middle class and working poor, and worked to reduce bureaucracy and red tape. (H,157)

I led a bipartisan effort to improve outpatient facilities at places like Walter Reed, and slash red tape, and reform the disability process – because recovering troops should go to the front of the line, and they shouldn't have to fight to get there. (114)

That's why I've pledged to build a 21st century VA [Veterans Administration] as President. It means no more red tape – it's time to give every service-member electronic copies of medical and service records upon discharge. (114, 131)

We'll invite the service and participation of American citizens, and cut through the red tape to make sure that every agency is meeting cutting edge standards. (124)

I led a bipartisan effort to improve outpatient facilities at places like Walter Reed, and to slash red tape, and reform the disability process – because recovering troops should go to the front of the line, and they shouldn't have to fight to get there. (131)

We must also stand up for affordable health care for every single veteran. That's why I've pledged to build a 21st century VA [Veterans Administration]. We need to cut through the red tape – every service-member should get electronic copies of medical and service records upon discharge. (150)

We will make sure that every doctors [doctor's] office and hospital in this country is using cutting edge technology and electronic medical records so that we can cut red tape, prevent medical mistakes, and help save billions of dollars each year. (210)

We don't just need to better serve veterans of today's wars, we need to build a 21st century VA [Veterans Administration] that will better serve all who've answered our nation's call. That means cutting red tape and easing transition into civilian life. (212)

To improve the quality of our health care while lowering its cost, we will make the immediate investment necessary to ensure that within five years, all of America's medical records are computerized. This will cut waste, eliminate red tape, and reduce the need to repeat expensive medical tests. (221)

To cut one's **teeth**.

Arne's [Duncan] somebody who has really been working on the ground, for example. He's not a creature of Washington. That's not where he cut his teeth. He cut his teeth working with kids individually, working in schools like this. (215)

To **tell** it like it is.

One of the guys sitting nearby must have overheard us, for he leaned over with a sagacious expression on his face. "You all talking about Malcolm, huh? Malcolm tells it like it is, no doubt about it." (D,87)

I stopped. The crowd was quiet now, watching me. Somebody started to clap. "Go on with it, Barack," somebody else shouted. "Tell it like it is." Then the others started in, clapping, cheering, and I knew that I had them, that the connection had been made. (D,106-107)

To take something on its own **terms**.

"Your mother had a soft heart [...]. That's a good thing in a woman. But you will be a man someday, and a man needs to have more sense." It had nothing to do with good or bad, he explained, like or dislike. It was a matter of taking life on its own terms. (D,39)

To be **thick**.

"Just 'cause a girl don't go out with you doesn't make her a racist." "Don't be thick, all right? I'm not just talking about one time. Look, I ask Monica out, she says no. I say okay...your shit's not so hot anyway." (D,73)

He would say that the white man was always improving himself, whereas the African was suspicious of anything new. "The African is thick," he would sometimes say to me. "For him to do anything, he needs to be beaten." [Granny's story] (D,407)

All **things** are possible (**Anything** is possible.).

If there is anyone out there [at Chicago on election night] who still doubts that America is a place where all things are possible, who still wonders if the dream of our founders is alive in our time; who still questions the power of democracy, tonight is your answer. (197)

What gives me hope is what I see when I look out across this mall. For in these monuments are chiseled those unlikely stories that affirm our unyielding faith – a faith that anything is possible in America. Rising before us stands a memorial to a man [George Washington] who led a small band of farmers and shopkeepers in revolution against the army of an Empire, all for the sake of an idea. (228)

To put (set) aside childish **things**.

We remain a young country, but in the words of Scripture, the time has come to set aside childish things [I Corinthians 13,11]. The time has come to reaffirm our enduring spirit; to choose our better history; to carry forward that precious gift, that noble idea, passed on from generation to generation: the God-given promise that all are equal [All men are created equal], all are free, and all deserve a chance to pursue their full measure of happiness. (229)

To have second **thoughts**.

Obviously, his parents, born and raised in Chicago and Gary, lost their own innocence long ago, and although they aren't bitter [...] one hears the pain in their voices as they begin to have second thoughts about having moved out of the city into a mostly white suburb, a move they made to protect their son from the possibility of being caught in a gang shooting and the certainty of attending an underfunded school. (D,xv)

To hang by a **thread**.

I know something about the anxiety of families hanging on by a thread as premiums have doubled these past eight years, and they're going into debt, and more than half – half – of all personal bankruptcies are caused in part by medical bills. (172)

I know something about the anxiety of families hanging on by a thread as premiums have doubled, and debt piles up, and more than half – half – of all personal bankruptcies are caused in part by medical bills. (173)

To cram (shove) something down one's **throat**.

I don't oppose all wars. [...] What I am opposed to is a dumb war. What I am opposed to is a rash war. What I am opposed to is the cynical attempt by Richard Perle and Paul Wolfowitz and other armchair, weekend warriors in this administration to shove their own ideological agendas down our throats, irrespective of the costs in lives lost and in hardships borne. (1)

Once a **thug**, always a thug.

"He grew up in Altgelt – in fact, I think him and Will used to be in school together. Wally was a big-time gang-banger before he became a Muslim." "Once a thug, always a thug," Angela said. (D,181)

To have a green **thumb**.

Zeituni shook her head. "Actually, he was well respected because he was such a good farmer. His compound in Alego was one of the biggest in the area. He had such a green thumb, he could make anything grow." (D,370)

To put the **thumb** (finger) on the scale.

We let the special interests put their thumbs on the economic scales. The result has been a distorted market that creates bubbles instead of steady, sustainable growth; a market that favors Wall Street over Main Street, but ends up hurting both. (109)

When special interests put their thumb too heavily on the scale, and distort the free market, those who compete by the rules come in last. And when government fails to meet its obligation – to provide sensible oversight and stand on the side of working people and invest in their future – America pays a heavy price. (142)

When special interests put their thumb on the scale, and distort the free market, the people who compete by the rules come in last. And when government fails to meet its obligation – to provide sensible oversight and stand on the side of working people and invest in their future – America pays a heavy price. (144, 146)

Instead of allowing interests to put their thumbs on the economic scales and CEOs run off with excessive golden parachutes, we're going to ensure openness, accountability and transparency in our markets so that people can trust the value of the financial product they're buying. (217)

No longer can we allow Wall Street wrongdoers to slip through regulatory cracks. No longer can we allow special interests to put their thumbs on the economic scales. No longer can we allow the unscrupulous lending and borrowing that leads only to destructive cycles of bubble and bust. (221)

To punch one's own **ticket**.

This may be difficult for all of you because one of the great things about graduating from Northwestern is that you can now punch your own ticket. You can take your diploma, walk of this stage, and go chasing after the big house and the nice suits and all the other things that our money culture says you should buy. (58)

After graduating from a great school like Xavier, you'll pretty much be able to punch your own ticket – which means you can take your diploma, walk of this stage, leave the city, and go chasing after the big house and the large salary and the nice suits and all the other things that our money culture says you should buy. (66)

A rising **tide** lifts all boats.

To stay competitive and keep investors happy in the global marketplace, U.S.-based companies have automated, downsized, outsourced, and offshored. [...] The result has been the emergence of what some call a "winner-take-all" economy, in which a rising tide doesn't necessarily lift all boats. (H,146)

This pattern – of a rising tide lifting minority boats – has certainly held true in the past. The progress made by the previous generation of Latinos and African Americans occurred primarily because the same ladders of opportunity that built the white middle class were for the first time made available to minorities as well. (H,246)

And when we've succeeded [to be good citizens], it's made America the place where dreams are possible, where freedoms of speech and press and worship are protected, and where the rising tide lifts the boats of the many instead of just the few. (8)

It has been the creation of a massive middle class, through decent wages and benefits and public schools – that has allowed us to prosper. And it has been the ability of working men and women to join together in unions that has allowed our rising tide to lift every boat. (65)

Our economy hasn't just been the world's greatest wealth creator – it's been the world's greatest job generator. It's been the tide that has lifted the boats of the largest middle-class in history. (89)

But through hard times and good, great challenge and great change, the promise of Janesville [Wisconsin] has been the promise of America – that our prosperity can and must be the tide that lifts every boat; that we rise or fall as one nation; that our economy is strongest when our middle-class grows and opportunity is spread as widely as possible. (105)

To stem the **tide**.

There's a slide. There is this big slippery slope of folks and communities that are sinking. The question is: What can organizing do about helping them, first, to stem the tide and then to build back up? (O,143)

To swim against the **tide**.

The bankruptcy of communism and socialism as alternative means of economic organization has only reinforced this assumption. In our standard economics text-books and in our modern political debates, laissez-faire is the default rule; anyone who would challenge it swims against the prevailing tide. (H,150)

To turn back (reverse) the **tide**.

I try to do my small part in reversing the tide. In my legal practice, I work mostly with churches and community groups, men and women who quietly build grocery stores and health clinics in the inner city, and housing for the poor. (D,438)

I'm sure you'll all agree that we have songs left to sing and bridges left to cross. And if there's anything we can learn from this living saint [John Lewis] sitting beside me, it is that change is never easy, but always possible. That it comes not from violence or militancy or the kind of politics that pits us against each other [...]; but from a strong message of hope, and from the courage to turn against the tide so that the tide eventually may be turned. (3)

After 9/11, our calling was to write a new chapter in the American story. [...] We had the might and moral-suasion that was the legacy of generations of Americans. The tide of history seemed poised to turn, once again, toward hope. (85)

As President, I will make it a focus of my foreign policy to roll back the tide of hopelessness that gives rise to hate. Freedom must mean freedom from fear, not the freedom of anarchy. (85)

These [Mobile Development] teams will work with civil society and local governments to make an immediate impact in peoples' [sic] lives, and to turn the tide against extremism. (85)

There are some who believe that we must try to turn back the clock on this new world; that the only chance to maintain our living standards is to build a fortress around America; to stop trading with other countries, shut down immigration, and rely on old industries. I disagree. Not only is it impossible to turn back the tide of globalization, but efforts to do so can make us worse off. (124)

Time heals all wounds.

Well, lessons can be just as easily unlearned as they are learned. Time may heal, but it can also cloud the memory and remove us further from that initial core of concern. And so what this all means is that today and every day, you have a responsibility to remember what happened here in New Orleans. (66)

Time will tell.

Time will tell. You will be tested by the challenges of this new century, and at times you will fail. But know that you have it within your power to try. That generations who have come before you faced these same fears and uncertainties in their own time. (58)

Desperate **times** call for desperate measures.

Desperate times called for desperate measures, and for many blacks, times were chronically desperate. If nationalism could create a strong and effective insularity, deliver on its promise of self respect [...], then the hurt it might cause [...] would be of little consequence. (D,199-200)

Tit for tat.

I believe every Senator on the other side of the aisle, if they were honest, would acknowledge that the same unyielding, unbending, dogmatic approach to judicial confirmation has in large part been responsible for the kind of poisonous atmosphere that exists in this Chamber regarding judicial nominations. It is tempting, then, for us on this side of the aisle to go tit for tat. (27)

It's easy to get caught up in the distractions and the silliness and the tit-for-tat that consumes our politics; the bickering that none of us are immune to, and that trivializes the profound issues – two wars, an economy in recession, a planet in peril. (112)

We are all in this **together**.

If the guiding philosophy behind the traditional system of social insurance could be described as "We're all in this together," the philosophy behind the Ownership Society seems to be "You're on your own." (H,178-179)

The GI Bill of Rights – a bill that has since provided education and training to nearly 8 million Americans, housing for 2 million families, and led to the creation of the great American middle-class. That was a bill that told our heroes "When you come home, we're here for you, because we're all in this together." (7)

The day Franklin Roosevelt signed the Social Security Act of 1935 into law, he began by saying that "Today, a hope of many years' standing is in large part fulfilled." It's now time to fulfill our hope for an America where we're in this together – for our seniors, for our children, and for every American in the years and generations yet to come. (14)

Our economic dominance has depended on individual initiative and belief in the free market; but it has also depended on our sense of mutual regard for each other, the idea that everybody has a stake in the country, that we're all in it together and everybody's got a shot at opportunity. (19, 34)

Yes, our greatness as a nation has depended on individual initiative, on a belief in the free market. But it has also depended on our sense of mutual regard for each other, the idea that everybody has a stake in the country, that we're all in it together, and everybody's got a shot at opportunity. (35)

Yes, our greatness as a nation has depended on individual initiative, on a belief in the free market. But it has also depended on our sense of mutual regard for each other, of mutual responsibility. The idea that everybody has a stake in the country, that we're all in it together and everybody's got a shot at opportunity. (65)

It's the idea that we are all in this together. From CEOs to shareholders, from financiers to factory workers, we all have a stake in each other's success, because the more Americans prosper, the more America prospers. (89)

This [the crumbling of the social compact] is not just happening by chance. It's not something we can just chalk up to temporary shocks. It's happening in part because of the choices we're making, and the way that we're making those choices. It's happening because we've gone too far from being a country where we're all in this together, to a country where everyone's on their own. (90)

It's time to end the Bush-McCain approach that tells the American people – "you're on your own" – because we know we're all in this together as Americans. That's what brought us here today. And that's the idea we'll restore in the White House when I'm President of the United States. (111)

Last September, I stood up at NASDAQ and said it's time to realize that we are in this together – that there is no dividing line between Wall Street and Main Street – and warned of a growing loss of trust in our capital markets. (156)

Across this country, Americans are worried about whether they can make their mortgage payments, or keep their jobs, or ensure that their retirement is secure. Truly, we are all in this together. (159)

Our country is being tested by a very serious [economic] crisis. We are all in this together, and we must come together as Democrats and Republicans, on Wall Street and on Main Street to solve it. And with the proper spirit of cooperation, I know we can. (162)

We will all need to sacrifice and we will all need to pull our weight because now more than ever, we are all in this together. What this crisis has taught us is that at the end of the day, there is no real separation between Main Street and Wall Street. (168, 169, 170, 171, 174, 175)

If we've learned anything from this economic crisis, it's that we're all connected; we're all in this together; and we will rise or fall as one nation – as one people. (175, 176, 179, 180, 181, 182, 184, 187, 188, 189)

We will all need to sacrifice and we will all need to pull our weight because now more than ever, we are all in this together. This country and the dream it represents are being tested in a way that we haven't seen in nearly a century. (176, 177, 179, 180, 181)

Now, I won't pretend that any of this will come easy or without cost. We will all need to tighten our belts, we will all need to sacrifice and we will all need to pull our weight because now more than ever, we are all in this together. (182)

Now, make no mistake: the change we need won't come easy or without cost. We will all need to tighten our belts, we will all need to sacrifice and we will all need to pull our weight because now more than ever, we are all in this together. (183, 184, 187, 188, 189)

To act as if there is no **tomorrow**.

Because I'm shy, I thought to myself; but I would never admit that to him. Ray pressed the advantage. "So what happens when we go out to a party with some sisters, huh? What happens? I tell you what happens. Blam! They on us like there's no tomorrow." (D,73)

Tooth and claw.

He gestures to the crowd along First Avenue. "Everybody looking out for number one. Survival of the fittest. Tooth and claw. Elbow the other guy out of the way. That, my friend, is New York. But..." He shrugged and mopped up some egg with toast. (D,119)

"Tooth and claw, Barack. Stop worrying about the rest of these bums out here and figure out how you're going to make some money out of this fancy degree you'll be getting." (D,119)

From **top** to bottom.

We know that global competition – not to mention any genuine commitment to the values of equal opportunity and upward mobility – requires us to revamp our educational system from top to bottom. (H,22)

To be over the **top**.

I'm surprised by the media interest in me and my candidacy. It's a little over the top, and I am not somebody who spends a lot of time reading my own press clippings. (B,89)

To put over the **top**.

There are other forces at work on a senator. As important as money is in campaigns, it's not just fund-raising that puts a candidate over the top. If you want to win in politics – if you don't want to lose – then organized people can be just as important as cash. (H,115)

Topsy-turvy

In the midst of this topsy-turvy time, in the wake of assassinations and cities burning and Vietnam's bitter defeat, economic expansion gave way to gas lines and inflation and plant closings. (H,29)

To carry the **torch**.

It's a torch he's [Ted Kennedy] carried as a champion for working Americans, a fierce proponent of universal health care, and a tireless advocate for giving every child in this country a quality education. (101)

It's a torch he's [Ted Kennedy] carried as the lion of the Senate, a man whose mastery of the issues and command of the levers of government – whose determined leadership and deft political skills – are matched only by his ability to tell a good story. (101)

To pass the **torch**.

In the year I was born, President Kennedy let out word that the torch had been passed to a new generation of Americans. He was right. It had. It was passed to his youngest brother [Ted]. From the battles of the 1960s to the battles of today, he has carried that torch, lighting the way for all who share his American ideals. (101)

The American people can't take four more years of the same failed policies and the same failed politics. We're not going to let George Bush pass the torch to John McCain. It's time for change. (189)

To be in an ivory **tower**.

So when Arne Duncan [Secretary of Education] speaks to – to educators across America, it won't be from up in some ivory tower, but from the lessons he's learned during his years changing our schools from the bottom up. (215)

To be on the fast **track**.

Oh, Michelle was full of plans that day, on the fast track, with no time, she told me, for distractions – especially men. But she knew how to laugh, brightly and easily, and I noticed she didn't seem in too much of a hurry to get back to the office. (H,329)

To be on the right (wrong) **track**.

Senator McCain said earlier this year that America has made "great progress economically" over the past eight years. He believes we're on the right track, and he's launching a new economic tour today with policies that are very much the same as those we have seen from the Bush Administration. (132)

But there's one thing that hasn't changed in those 19 months: the American people know this country is on the wrong track, and you know that we need new leadership in Washington. (155)

To be or get (back) on **track**.

We [Obama and his top economic advisors] agreed that the main risk we face today is doing too little in the face of our growing economic troubles. That's why today, I'm announcing a two-part emergency plan to help struggling families make ends meet and get our economy back on track. (144)

But you need relief right now. That's why yesterday, I announced a two-part emergency plan to help struggling families make ends meet and get our economy back on track. (146)

He's [Joe Biden] an expert on foreign policy whose heart and values are rooted firmly in the middle class. He has stared down dictators and spoken out for America's cops and firefighters. He is uniquely suited to be my partner as we work to put our country back on track. (151)

Some of the largest corporations in America – including major American car makers – are fighting to compete because of high health care costs. They're watching their foreign competitors prosper – unburdened by these costs – as they struggle to create the good jobs we need to get our economy back on track. (173)

These are three [financial] steps that we must take – right now – to begin to get our economy back on track. But we also need a new set of priorities. (179)

These are the [financial] steps that we must take – right now – to start getting our economy back on track. But we also need a new set of priorities to grow our economy and create jobs over the long-term. (182, 184, 185)

These are the [financial] steps we must take – right now – to start getting our economy back on track. But we also need a new set of priorities to grow our economy and create jobs over the long-term. (187, 188, 189)

Obviously the economy, talking to top economic advisers about how we're going to create jobs, how we get the economy back on track and what to do in terms of some long-term issues like energy and health care. (201)

But the basic principle is that we're going to provide tax cuts to the vast majority of Americans [...]; that those who have benefitted disproportionately over the last eight years, the very wealthiest among us, will pay a little bit more in order for us to be able to invest in the economy and get it back on track. (203)

I want to see it [the stimulus package] enacted right away. It is going to be of a size and scope that is necessary to get this economy back on track. I don't want to get into numbers right now. (203)

The right answer is that we have to first focus on getting the economy back on track. We've got to first focus on making sure that we're creating those 2.5 million jobs. We've got to make sure that the investments are made to sustain economic growth over the long term. (203)

And so what I intend to do over the next two months is to forge that [economic] team, make sure that it has concrete plans for us to put this economy back on track. And we are going to implement starting day one when I come into office. (205)

I think it is important for the American people, though, to have confidence that we've gone through recessions before, we've gone through difficult times before; that my administration intends to get this economy back on track; [...] that our future is bright if we make good decisions. (205)

If we do those things, then I'm confident that we can get back on track, but we're still going to need the economic recovery plan that I've been talking about and that I intend to get passed as soon as I'm sworn into office. (205)

I am absolutely confident that if we take the right steps over the coming months, that not only can we get the economy back on track, but we can emerge leaner, meaner, and ultimately more competitive and more prosperous. (212)

What we're going to have to do is make the best decisions that we can with the hand that we're dealt. And what I think that is going to mean, although we haven't finalized our actual plan, is that we focus single-mindedly on job creation, increasing demand, getting the economy back on track, fixing our financial markets. (218)

Once we get this economy back on track – and I am confident that we're going to do it – I'm confident that we're going to put people back to work, and I'm confident that businesses are going to start growing again. It's going to take some time, but we can get this done. (218)

But every economist that I've spoken to insists that the most important thing we can do even for our budget and even for our deficit is to get our economy back on track because if the economy keeps on weakening, that means tax revenues are down, that means more people are out of work, which means that they are seeking unemployment insurance, they are relying on the government for health care or helping look after their children. (218)

And if we do this right – and it's not easy – then what we can do is grow the economy, get it back on track over the first couple of years, and then we'll be in a position to make some tough choices. (218)

Fortunately, most of the proposals that we made apply not only to our long-term economic growth but also fit well into what we need to do short term to get the economy back on track. (219)

On the other hand, you've got countries like Sweden that went through this [economic crisis] and acted forcefully and boldly and in two years were back on track and were growing at a really healthy clip. (219)

To cover one's **tracks**.

He [Marcus] had caught me in a lie. Two lies, really – the lie I had told about Tim and the lie I was telling about myself. In fact, that whole first year seemed like one long lie, me spending all my energy running around in circles, trying to cover my tracks. (D,102)

To stop (dead) in one's **tracks**.

It was a perfect day, the sun cut with a steady breeze, the road empty except for a distant woman, walking with a basket of kindling on top of her head. After less than a quarter of a mile, Bernard stopped dead in his tracks, beads of sweat forming on his high, smooth forehead. (D,325)

Trial and error.

It's useful to remind ourselves, then, that our free-market system is the result neither of natural law nor the divine providence. Rather, it emerged through a painful process of trial and error, a series of difficult choices between efficiency and fairness, stability and change. (H,150)

To get into **trouble**.

Undoubtedly, some of these views will get me in trouble. I am new enough on the national political scene that I serve as a blank screen on which people of vastly different political stripes project their own views. (H,11)

The **truth** shall make you free.

What would happen once I relinquished that distance? It was nice to believe that the truth would somehow set me free. But what was wrong? What if the truth only disappointed, and my father's death meant nothing, and his leaving me behind meant nothing, and the only tie that bound me to him, or to Africa, was a name, a blood type, or white people's scorn? (D,302)

To have a kernel of **truth**.

Which perhaps indicates a second, more intimate theme in this book – namely how, I or anybody in public office, can avoid the pitfalls of fame, the hunger to please, the fear of loss, and thereby retain that kernel of truth, that singular voice within each of us that reminds us of our deepest commitments. (H,11)

Truth is the best corrective.

"So this idea about a golden age in Africa, before the white man came, seems only natural." "A corrective," Auma said. "Truth is usually the best corrective," Rukia said with a smile. (D,434)

To be **two-faced**.

Say one thing during the campaign and do another thing once in office, and you're a typical, two-faced politician. I lost some endorsements by not giving the right answer. A couple of times, a group surprised us and gave me their endorsement despite the wrong answer. (H,117)

To be an **underdog**.

No doubt some of this had to do with my status as an underdog in my Senate primary, as well as my novelty as a black candidate with an exotic background. Maybe it had also something to do with my style of communicating, which can be rambling, hesitant, and overly verbose (both my staff and Michelle often remind me of this), but which perhaps finds sympathy in the literary class. (H,120)

Everything that goes **up** must come down.

There's this weird confluence of events that's making all this possible. But my experience in these kinds of things is that what comes up must come down. (B,122)

Ups and downs.

That was the promise FDR made. And it was a promise that Washington kept for decades while folks like my grandparents and Michelle's parents moved through the ups and downs of middle-class life. (153)

There were multiple points throughout the election when I thought I could lose. Including the day I announced. And honestly, you know, we had a bunch of ups and downs in the campaign [...]. And if we lost, that wouldn't be such a terrible thing. And that's why I think I stayed pretty steady throughout this race, despite the ups and downs. (219)

Use it or lose it.

Well [We'll] invest your precious tax dollars in new and smarter ways, and well [we'll] set a simple rule – use it or lose it. If a state doesn't act quickly to invest in roads and bridges in their communities, theyll [they'll] lose the money. (210)

To speak with one **voice**.

To America's veterans, our country must speak with one voice: we honor your service, and we enter into a sacred trust with you from the moment you put on that uniform. That trust is simple: America will be there for you just as you have been there for America. (87)

God had a plan for his people. He told them to stand together and march together around the city, and [...] they should speak with one voice. And at the chosen hour, when the horn sounded and a chorus of voices cried out together, the mighty walls of Jericho came tumbling down. (99)

It's the simple truth [...] that in this country, justice can be won against the greatest odds; hope can find its way back to the darkest corners; and when we are told that we cannot bring about the change that we seek, we answer with one voice – yes we can. (113)

Hitch your **wagon** to a star.

At some level, your individual salvation depends on collective salvation. It's only when you hitch yourself up to something bigger than yourself that you're going to realize your true potential, and the world will benefit from that potential. (B,103)

You need to take up the challenges that we face as a nation and make them your own. [...] You need to take on the challenge because you have an obligation to yourself. Because our individual salvation depends on collective salvation. Because it's only when you hitch your wagon to something larger than yourself that you will realize your true potential. And if we're willing to share the risks and the rewards this new century offers, it will be a victory for each of you, and for every American. (19)

You need to take on the challenges that your country is facing because you have an obligation to yourself. Because our individual salvation depends on collective salvation. Because it's only when you hitch your wagon to something larger than yourself that you will realize your true potential. (21, 51)

I hope you choose to broaden, and not to contract, your ambit of concern. [...] It's because you have an obligation to yourself. Because our individual salvation depends on collective salvation. And because it's only when you hitch your wagon to something larger than yourself that you will realize your true potential – and become full-grown. (58, 61)

I ask you to take it [the harder path] because you have an obligation to yourself. Because our individual salvation depends on our collective salvation. And because it's only when you hitch your wagon to something larger than yourself that you will realize your true potential. (66)

Because it's only when you hitch your wagon to something larger than yourself that you realize your true potential and discover the role you'll play in writing the next great chapter in America's story. (116)

I hope both of you [Malia and Sasha] will take up that work, righting the wrongs that you see and working to give others the chances you've had. Not just because you have an obligation to give something back to this country that has given our family so much – although you do have that obligation. But because you have an obligation to yourself. Because it is only when you hitch your wagon to something larger than yourself that you will realize your true potential. (224)

To fall off the **wagon**.

You know, I have [stopped smoking], but what I said was that, you know, there are times where I've fallen off the wagon. (211)

Wait and see.

There's no silver bullet. A solution to our energy dilemma won't come overnight. But we don't have to accept the wait-and-see attitude anymore. It flies in the face of our history and our founding principles. (26)

Hard working families who've been hard hit by this economic crisis – folks who can't pay their mortgages or their medical bills or send their kids to college – they can't afford to wait and see. (184)

Senator McCain's economic advisor made it clear that Senator McCain still isn't ready to support a stimulus. He's taking a wait and see approach. And instead of offering a real plan to boost our economy, Senator McCain has offered a proposal that does nothing to create jobs. (184)

But that is all the more reason for Congress to act without delay. I know the scale of this plan is unprecedented, but so is the severity of our situation. We have already tried the wait-and-see approach to our problems, and it is the same approach that helped lead us to this day of reckoning. (221)

We cannot have a thriving **Wall Street** and a struggling Main Street (while Main Street suffers).

In the past few years, we have relearned the essential truth that in the long run, we cannot have a thriving Wall Street and a struggling Main Street. When wages are flat, prices are rising and more and more Americans are mired in debt, the economy as a whole suffers. When a reckless few game the system, as we've seen in this housing crisis, millions suffer and we're all impacted. (142)

In recent years, we have relearned the essential truth that in the long run, we cannot have a thriving Wall Street and a struggling Main Street. When wages are flat, prices are rising, and more Americans are mired in debt, the economy as a whole suffers. When a reckless few game the system, as we've seen in this housing crisis, millions suffer and we're all affected. (144, 146)

That's the truth at the heart of your Opportunity Compact – that we cannot have a thriving Wall Street and a struggling Main Street. That when wages are flat, prices are rising, and more and more Americans are mired in debt, our economy as a whole suffers. (145)

Let us remember that if this financial crisis taught us anything, it's that we cannot have a thriving Wall Street while Main Street suffers – in this country, we rise or fall as one nation; as one people. (197)

If this financial crisis has taught us anything, it's that we cannot have a thriving Wall Street while Main Street suffers – in this country, we rise and fall as one nation; as one people. And that is how we will meet the challenges of our time – together. (200)

I've sought leaders who [...] share my fundamental belief that we cannot have a thriving Wall Street without a thriving Main Street; that in this country, we rise and fall as one nation, as one people. (203)

But as difficult as these times are, I'm confident that we're going to rise to meet this challenge, if we're willing to band together and recognize that Wall Street cannot thrive so long as Main Street is struggling, if we're willing to summon a new spirit of ingenuity and determination and if Americans of great intellect, broad experience and good character are willing to serve in our government at its hour of need. (204)

To build (put up) **walls** around something.

We can try to build walls around us, and we can look inward, and we can respond by being frightened and angry about those disruptions [caused by globalization]. But that's not what we're about. We are a confident country, not a fearful one. We can meet these challenges. And that means every single one of us needs to learn more so we can compete more. (55)

It's not easy to stand in somebody else's shoes. It's not easy to see past our differences. We've all encountered this in our lives. But what makes it even more difficult is that we have a politics in this country that seeks to drive us apart – that puts up walls between us. (99)

And because we know that we can't or shouldn't put up walls around our economy, a long-term agenda will also find a way to make trade work for American workers. (122, 132)

When it comes to jobs, the choice in this election is not between putting up a wall around America or standing by and doing nothing. The truth is, we won't be able to bring back every job that we've lost, but that doesn't mean we should follow John McCain's plan to keep giving tax breaks to corporations that send American jobs overseas and promoting unfair trade agreements. (194, 195)

When it comes to jobs, the choice in this election is not between putting up a wall around America or standing by and doing nothing. The truth is, we won't be able to bring back every job that we've lost, but that doesn't mean we should follow John McCain's plan to keep promoting unfair trade agreements and keep giving tax breaks to corporations that send American jobs overseas. (196)

To make **walls** (of Jericho) fall.

And if enough of our voices join together, we can bring those walls tumbling down. The walls of Jericho can finally come tumbling down. That is our hope – but only if we pray together, and work together, and march together. (99)

God had a plan for his people. He told them to stand together and march together around the city, and [...] they should speak with one voice. And at the chosen hour, when the horn sounded and a chorus of voices cried out together, the mighty walls of Jericho came tumbling down. (99)

Together, we can renew our commitment to justice. Together, we can join our voices together, and in doing so make even the mightiest of walls fall down. (120)

To run into **walls**.

We're tired of being divided, tired of running into ideological walls and partisan roadblocks, tired of appeals to our worst instincts and greatest fears. Americans everywhere are desperate for leadership. They are longing for direction. And they want to believe again. (57)

To tear down **walls**.

The sweeping changes brought by revolutions in technology have torn down walls between business and government and people and places all over the globe. And with this new world comes [sic] new risks and new dangers. (57)

Just look at our history. Kennedy had a direct line to Khrushchev. Nixon met with Mao. Carter did the hard work of negotiating the Camp David Accords. Reagan was negotiating arms agreements with Gorbachev even as he called on him to "tear down this wall." (92)

The walls between old allies on either side of the Atlantic cannot stand. The walls between the countries with the most and those with the least cannot stand. The walls between races and tribes; natives and immigrants; Christian and Muslim and Jew cannot stand. These now are the walls we must tear down. (141)

To wave a (magic) **wand**.

I wish I could wave a magic wand and make gas prices go down, but I can't. What I can do – and what I will do – is push for a second stimulus package that will send out another round of rebate checks to the American people. (127)

War is hell.

For these men, the issues America faced were never abstract and hence never simple. War might be hell and still the right thing to do. Economies could collapse despite the best-laid plans. People could work hard all their lives and still lose everything. (H,36)

Let justice roll down like **water** and righteousness like a mighty stream.

We welcomed immigrants to our shores, we opened railroads to the west, we landed a man on the moon, and we heard a [Marin Luther] King's call to let justice roll down like water, and righteousness like a mighty stream. (76)

We'll be making real the words of Amos [5,24] that he [Dr. Martin Luther King] invoked so often, and "let justice roll down like water and righteousness like a mighty stream." (110)

Like **water** finding its level, you will arrive at a career that suits you.

From time to time he [Obama's father] would include advice, usually in the form of aphorisms I didn't quite understand ("Like water finding its level, you will arrive at a career that suits you"). (D,76)

To tread **water**.

For most folks, one income isn't enough to raise a family and send your kids to college. Sometimes, two incomes aren't enough. It's harder to save, it's harder to retire. You're doing your part, you're meeting your responsibilities, but it always seems like you're treading water or falling behind. (95)

Whenever I've been asked how I measure the strength of the American economy, my answer is simple: jobs and wages. I know we will be headed in the right direction again when we are creating jobs instead of losing them, and when Americans are gaining ground in terms of their incomes instead of treading water or falling behind. (218)

To (try to) stay above **water**.

You're trying to pay your bills every week and stay above the water – you can't ignore it [the economy]. You're worrying about whether your job will be there a month from now – you can't ignore it. You're worrying about whether you can pay your mortgage and stay in your house – you can't turn the page. (173)

To make (no) **waves**.

When we arrived the party was well on its way, and we steered ourselves toward the refreshments. The presence of Jeff and Scott seemed to make no waves. Ray introduced them around the room, they made some small talk. (D,84)

My **way** or the highway.

The President's stubborn inflexibility is both unacceptable and disturbingly familiar. This is not the time for my-way-or-the-highway intransigence from anyone involved. It's not the time for fear and panic. It's the time for resolve, responsibility, and reasonableness. (162)
So we need to act and act now. This cannot fall victim to the usual partisan politics or special-interest lobbying. But it also can't be negotiated by the Administration with the same my-way-or-the-highway mentality that is all too familiar. (163)

To make a **way** out of no way.

In the day-to-day work of the men and women I met in church each day, in their ability to "make a way out of no way" and maintain hope and dignity in the direst of circumstances, I could see the Word made manifest. (H,207)

To drive a **wedge** between something.

With the Shiites increasingly in control of the government, the U.S. is viewed as the military force that is keeping the Shiites in power, picking sides in the conflict, driving a wedge between the factions, and keeping the Sunnis out of the government [in Iraq]. (36)

President Kennedy said it best: "Let us never negotiate out of fear, but let us never fear to negotiate." Only by knowing your adversary can you defeat them or drive wedges between them. (85)

To (pull) carry one's (own) **weight**.

She [Obama's mother] hadn't traveled all this way to be a burden, she decided. She would carry her own weight. She found herself a job right away teaching English to Indonesian businessmen at the American embassy. (D,43)

We will all need to sacrifice and we will all need to pull our weight because now more than ever, we are all in this together. What this crisis has taught us is that at the end of the day, there is no real separation between Main Street and Wall Street. (168, 170, 171, 174, 175)

We will all need to sacrifice and we will all need to pull our weight because now more than ever, we are all in this together. This country and the dream it represents are being tested in a way that we haven't seen in nearly a century. (176, 177, 179, 180, 181)

Now, I won't pretend that any of this will come easy or without cost. We will all need to tighten our belts, we will all need to sacrifice and we will all need to pull our weight because now more than ever, we are all in this together. (182)

Now, make no mistake: the change we need won't come easy or without cost. We will all need to tighten our belts, we will all need to sacrifice and we will all need to pull our weight because now more than ever, we are all in this together. (183, 184, 187, 188, 189)

To throw one's **weight** around.

So long as Russia and China retain their own large military forces and haven't fully rid themselves of the instinct to throw their weight around [...] there will be times when we must again play the role of the world's reluctant sheriff. This will not change – nor should it. (H,306)

Eight teams, that would be three rounds to determine a national champion. It would – it would add three extra weeks to the season. You could trim back on the regular season. I don't know any serious fan of college football who has disagreed with me on this. So I'm going to throw my weight around a little bit. I think it's the right thing to do. (201)

To be all **well** and good.

My opponent [Senator McCain] has decided to start talking tough about CEO pay. He's suddenly a hard-charging populist. And that's all well and good. But I sure wish he was talking the same way over a year ago, when I introduced a bill that would've helped to stop the multi-million-dollar bonus packages that CEOs grab on their way out the door. (163)

To dry up the **well**.

This is the moment when we must defeat terror and dry up the well of extremism that supports it. This threat is real and we cannot shrink from our responsibility to combat it. (141)

To tap the **well**.

So we'll exempt start-up companies and small businesses from capital gains to give them an added boost. Because when more Americans tap that well of opportunity, all of us are better off. (90)

To be **well-fed** like a prize bull.

Together with Kezia, she went out of the room, and Billy fell onto the couch beside Roy. "So, you still crazy, *bwana*? Look at you now! Well-fed, like a prize bull! You must be enjoying yourself in the States." (D,385)

To take (be at) the **wheel**.

And yet, ultimately, such apostasy leaves me unsatisfied as well. Maybe I am too steeped in the myth of the founding to reject it entirely. Maybe like those who reject Darwin in favor of intelligent design, I prefer to assume that someone's at the wheel. (H,92)

He's [Senator McCain] supported four of the five Bush budgets that have taken us from the surpluses of the Clinton years to the largest deficits in history. John McCain has ridden shotgun as George Bush has driven our economy toward a cliff, and now he wants to take the wheel and step on the gas. (191)

To blow the **whistle**.

I sure wish he [Senator McCain] joined me when I blew the whistle on the fired CEOs of Fannie Mae and Freddie Mac who tried to walk away with golden parachutes. (163)

White as milk.

That my father looked nothing like the people around me – that he was black as pitch, my mother white as milk – barely registered in my mind. In fact, I can recall only one story that dealt explicitly with the subject of race. (D,10)

Continue to ask **why**, what if, and why not.

I've always believed that the incredible story of progress that is America has been built by those who ask why, what if, and why not – questions asked by the very students at this college [College of Agriculture at Southern Illinois University] every day they choose to confront the challenges of this new century. (13)

You'll find them [answers] by continuing to ask yourselves those questions – why, what if, and why not. And as you keep studying and researching here at school, remember that the answers you discover will not only have an impact where you live and learn, but across a world that is just waiting to hear from the next generation of dreamers. (13)

You're [young Americans] all sitting here because in each of you, someone saw a spark. It's the spark that keeps each of you asking the questions what if, why, and why not? The one that keeps you always searching for answers to those questions. The one that makes you say, "I don't have to be content with the present, because I have a role in changing the future." (16)

Win or die trying.

The Sox won last night the way they have won all season – by playing aggressively, scrapping for every base and every run. [...] The four games against the Astros were decided by a total of six runs. Win by the skin of your teeth. Win or die trying, that's our motto this year. (31)

To be a **win-win** (situation).

It's a win-win proposal for the industry – their retirees will be taken care of, they'll save money on health care, and they'll be free to invest in the kind of fuel-efficient cars that are the key to their competitive future. (43, 48)

To have the **wind** in one's back.

Now – at a time of rising costs and rising uncertainty – it's time for policies from Washington that put a little wind at the backs of the American people. Now is the time for us to come together as a nation behind a new compact for the 21st century – one that gives the American people a lift, so they can lift up this country anew. (90)

That's why I'm introducing an American Dream agenda – to put some wind at the backs of working people, to lower the cost of getting ahead, and to protect and extend opportunity for the middle class. (95)

We leave this state [South Carolina] with a new wind at our back, and take this journey across the country we love [... with] the same message we had when we were up and when we were down – that out of many, we are one; that while we breathe, we hope. (100)

But I know this, Ohio, the time for change has come. We have a righteous wind at our back. And in these last couple of days, I need you to knock on some doors for me, and make some calls for me, and go to barackobama.com. (195)

But I know this, Florida, the time for change has come. We have a righteous wind at our back. And in these final hours, you will knock on some doors for me, and make some calls for me, and go to barackobama.com. and find out where to vote. (196)

Something is out the **window**.

The world will [eventually] look more like Brazil, with its racial mix. America is getting more complex. The color line in America being black and white is out the window. That does break down barriers. (B,94)

To throw something out of the **window**.

Over the years, states have come up with common sense rules to make sure that insurance companies aren't just looking out for their own profits, but for your health. And we cannot toss those rules out the window. (161)

To be **window-dressing**.

This is not a time for window-dressing or putting a band-aid on a problem just to score political points. This is a time for real reform, and I think the Democrats' Honest Leadership and Open Government Act does this by including provisions that so far the Republican proposals do not. (39)

This is not a time for window-dressing or putting a band-aid on a problem just to score political points. This is a time for real reform. I think the Honest Leadership and Open Government Act, which has 41 cosponsors, established the right marker for reform. (44)

To scatter to the (four) **winds**.

For someone like me, who had barely known his father, who had spent much of his life traveling from place to place, his bloodlines scattered to the four winds, the home that Frasier and Marian Robinson had built for themselves and their children stirred a longing for stability and a sense of place that I had not realized was there. (H,331-332)

Winner take all.

Certainly Democrats aren't happy with the current situation, since for the moment at least they are on the losing side, dominated by Republicans who, thanks to winner-take-all elections, control every branch of government. (H,23)

To stay competitive and keep investors happy in the global marketplace, U.S.-based companies have automated, downsized, outsourced, and offshored [...]. The result has been the emergence of what some call a "winner-take-all" economy, in which a rising tide doesn't necessarily lift all boats. (H,146)

In other words, the Ownership Society doesn't even try to spread the risks and rewards of the new economy among all Americans. Instead, it simply magnifies the uneven risks and rewards of today's winner-take-all economy. (H,180)

Unfortunately, instead of establishing a 21st century regulatory framework, we simply dismantled the old one. [...]. We encouraged a winner take all, anything goes environment that helped foster devastating dislocations in our economy. (109)

Winning is all that matters.

We paint our faces red or blue and cheer our side and boo their side, and if it takes a late hit or cheap shot to beat the other team, so be it, for winning is all that matters. But I don't think so. (H,41)

The **winter** of our discontent.

At a moment when the outcome of our revolution was most in doubt, the father of our nation ordered these words to be read to the people: "Let it be told to the future world … that in the depth of winter, when nothing but hope and virtue could survive … that the city and the country, alarmed at one common danger, came forth to meet [it]." America. In the face of our common dangers, in this winter of our hardship, let us remember these timeless words. With hope and virtue, let us brave once more the icy currents, and endure what storms may come. (229)

To be **wise** to the world.

After all, I'm thirty-three now; I work as a lawyer active in the social and political life of Chicago, a town that's accustomed to its racial wounds and prides itself on a certain lack of sentiment. If I've been able to fight off cynicism, I nevertheless like to think of myself as wise to the world, careful not to expect too much. (D,xiv)

To fade into the **woodwork**.

I suppose the politically safe thing would be to move on from this episode [the controversial remarks by Rev. Jeremiah Wright] and just hope that it fades into the woodwork. [...] But race is an issue that I believe this nation cannot afford to ignore right now. (107)

To take at one's **word**.

I want to take Judge Roberts at his word that he doesn't like bullies and he sees the law and the Court as a means of evening the playing field between the strong and the weak. But given the gravity of the position to which he will undoubtedly ascend and the gravity of the decisions in which he will undoubtedly participate during his tenure on the [Supreme] Court, I ultimately have to give more weight to his deeds and the overarching political philosophy that he appears to have shared with those in power than to the assuring words that he provided me in our meeting. (27)

Well, on the gun issue. I believe in common-sense gun safety laws, and I believe in the Second Amendment. And so, lawful gun owners have nothing to fear. I've said that throughout the campaign. I haven't indicated anything different during the transition. And I think that people can take me at my word. (212)

Pretty **words** don't make it so.

"I don't believe that what happened to a kid in Soweto makes much difference to the people we were talking to. Pretty words don't make it so. So why do I pretend otherwise? I'll tell you why. Because it makes *me* feel important." (D,108)

If you **work** hard, your work will be rewarded.

This story could not exist without a basic social compact in this country. That compact says that if you work hard, your work will be rewarded. That everybody has an opportunity to make a decent living, to raise a family, to give their children the best chance of success, and to look forward to a secure retirement. (90)

To **work** like a dog.

"When I was in high school, I got to feeling ashamed of him. My old man, I mean. Working like a dog. Sitting there, getting drunk with his brothers. I swore I'd never end up like that." (D,260)

The **world** has changed, and we must change with it.

To the people of poor nations, we pledge to work alongside you to make your farms flourish and let clean waters flow; to nourish starved bodies and feed hungry minds. And to those nations like ours that enjoy relative plenty, we say we can no longer afford indifference to suffering outside our borders; nor can we consume the world's resources without regard to effect. For the world has changed, and we must change with it. (229)

The **world** is a place.

"I'm telling you, man, the world is a *place*." "Say, the world is a place, huh." "That's what I'm saying." We were walking back to the car after dinner in Hyde Park, and Johnnie was in an expansive mood. He often got like this, especially after a good meal and wine. (D,249)

"Whole panorama of life out there. Crazy shit going on. You got to ask yourself, is this kinda stuff happening elsewhere? Is there any precedent for all this shit? You ever ask yourself that?" "The world's a place," I repeated. "See there! It's serious, man." (D,251)

The **world** is (turned) upside down.

But in the eyes of the public, at least, foreign policy in the nineties lacked an overarching theme or grand imperatives. U.S. military action in particular seemed entirely a matter of choice, not necessity [...]. Then came September 11 – and Americans felt their world turned upside down. (H,290)

To be **worth** a mint.

"That's the short term. [...] But see, white folks ain't stupid. They just waiting for us to move out of the city so they can come back, 'cause they know that the value of the property we sitting on right now is worth a mint." (D,181)

To lick one's **wounds**.

Such concessions helped to lift the spirits of some of the parents, and after a few weeks licking our wounds, we started meeting again to make sure that CHA followed up on its commitments. (D,247)

What can (will) go **wrong**, goes wrong.

I still burn, for example, with the thought of my one loss in politics, a drubbing in 2000 at the hands of incumbent Democratic Congressman Bobby Rush. It was a race in which everything that could go wrong did go wrong, in which my own mistakes were compounded by tragedy and farce. (H,105)

Never in a million **years**.

When I was first asked to speak here, I thought to myself, never in a million years would I have guessed that I'd be serving in Congress with John Lewis. And then I thought, you know, there was once a time when John Lewis might never have guessed that he'd be serving in Congress. (3)

And as I stood up there next to John Lewis, not a giant in stature, but a giant of compassion and courage, I thought to myself, never in a million years would I have guessed that I'd be serving in Congress with John Lewis. And then I thought, you know, there was once a time when John Lewis might never have guessed that he'd be serving in Congress. (15)

To be in the golden **years**.

Unless we're willing to see seniors starve on the street, we're going to have to cover their retirement expenses one way or another – and since we don't know in advance which of us will be losers, it makes sense for all of us to chip in to a pool that gives us at least some guaranteed income in our golden years. (H,179)

Bibliography

Achebe, Chinua. 1967. *Arrow of God*. New York: John Day, 1967 (1st ed. 1964).

Ammer, Christine. 1992. *Southpaws & Sunday Punches and Other Sporting Expressions*. New York: Penguin, 1992.

Aron, Paul. 2008. *We Hold These Truths ... And Other Words that Made America*. Lanham, Maryland: Rowman & Littlefield, 2008.

Baker, Gerard. 2009. "The Speech That Failed to Fly [Barack Obama]." *The Times* (January 21, 2009), 3.

Barbour, Frances M. 1974. *A Concordance to the Sayings in Franklin's "Poor Richard"*. Detroit, Michigan: Gale Research Company, 1974.

Baron, Dennis. 2008. "Pig-Gate: Any Way You Spin It, Lipstick on a Pig Is Politics as Usual." *The Web of Language* – Blog (September 10, 2008), online. http://illinois.edu/blog/view?blogId

Bartlett, John. 2002. *Familiar Quotations*. Ed. Justin Kaplan. 17th ed. Boston: Little, Brown and Company, 2002.

Basler, Roy P. (ed.). 1953. *The Collected Works of Abraham Lincoln*. 8 vols. New Brunswick, New Jersey: Rutgers University Press, 1953

Beinart, Peter. 2008. "The *New* New Deal. What Barack Obama Can Learn from F.D.R. – and What the Democrats Need to Do." *Time* (November 24, 2008), cover and pp. 30-32.

Blassingame, John (ed.). 1985-1992. *The Frederick Douglass Papers*, 5 vols. New Haven, Connecticut: Yale University Press, 1985-1992.

Boas, George. 1969. *Vox Populi: Essays in the History of an Idea*. Baltimore: Johns Hopkins University Press, 1969.

Boller, Paul F. 1967. *Quotemanship: The Use and Abuse of Quotations for Polemical and Other Purposes.* Dallas, Texas: Southern Methodist University Press, 1967.

Breuillard, Jean. 1984. "Proverbes et pouvoir politique: Le cas de l'U.R.S.S." *Richesse du proverbe.* Eds. François Suard and Claude Buridant. Lille: Université de Lille, 1984. II, 155-166.

Brune, Tom. 2009. "Confident, Somber, Historic [Barack Obama]." *Newsday* (January 21, 2009), W8.

Bryan, George B., and Wolfgang Mieder. 2003. "The Proverbial Carl Sandburg (1878-1967). An Index of Folk Speech in His American Poetry." *Proverbium: Yearbook of International Proverb Scholarship*, 20 (2003), 15-49.

Burrell, Brian. 1997. *The Words We Live By. The Creeds, Mottoes, and Pledges that Have Shaped America.* New York: The Free Press, 1997.

Campbell, Karlyn Kohrs, and Kathleen Hall Jamieson. 2008. *Presidents Creating the Presidency: Deeds Done in Words.* Chicago, Illinois: University of Chicago Press, 2008.

Cary, Mary Kate. 2009. "Hungry for Words [Barack Obama]." *The New York Times* (January 21, 2009), online. http://roomfordebate.blogs.nytimes.com/2009/01/20/the-speech-the-experts-critique/

Cashill, Jack. 2008a. "Who Wrote *Dreams From My Father?*" *American Thinker* (October 9, 2008), online. http://www.americanthinker.com/2008/10/1.html.

Cashill, Jack. 2008b. "Evidence Mounts: Ayers Co-Wrote Obama's *Dreams.*" *American Thinker* (October 17, 2008), online. http://www.americanthinker.com/2008/10/.html.

Covington, Marti, and Maya Curry. 2008. "A Brief History of: 'Putting Lipstick on a Pig'." *Time* (September 11, 2008), online. http://www.time.com/time/nation/article/0,8599,1840392,00.html

Daniel, Jack L. 1973. "Towards an Ethnography of Afroamerican Proverbial Usage." *Black Lines*, 2 (1973), 3-12.

Denton, Robert E., and Dan F. Hahn. 1986. *Presidential Communication. Description and Analysis.* New York: Praeger, 1986.

Denton, Robert E., and Gary C. Woodward. 1998. *Political Communication in America.* 3rd ed. Westport, Connecticut: Praeger, 1998.

Dibbley, Dale Corey. 1993. *From Achilles' Heel to Zeus's Shield.* New York: Fawcett Columbine, 1993.

Doyle, Charles Clay. 1996. "On 'New' Proverbs and the Conservativeness of Proverb Dictionaries." *Proverbium: Yearbook of International Proverb Scholarship*, 13 (1996), 69-84.

Dundes, Alan. 2004. "'As the Crow Flies': A Straightforward Study of Lineal Worldview in American Folk Speech." *What Goes Around Comes Around: The Circulation of Proverbs in Contemporary Life. Essays in Honor of Wolfgang Mieder.* Eds. Kimberly J. Lau, Peter Tokofsky, and Stephen D. Winick. Logan, Utah: Utah State University Press, 2004. 171-187.

Editorial. 2009. "Inaugural Address Sounds Notes of Optimism and Reality [Barack Obama]." *Los Angeles Times* (January 21, 2009), A16.

Eggert, Sonja Brunhilde. 1998. *"Kleine Schritte sind besser als keine Schritte": Willy Brandts sprich-wörtliche Rhetorik.* Honors Thesis University of Vermont, 1998.

Fields, Wayne. 1996. *Union of Words. A History of Presidential Eloquence*. New York: The Free Press, 1996.

Frank, David A., and Mark Lawrence McPhail. 2005. "Barack Obama's Address to the 2004 Democratic National Convention: Trauma, Compromise, Consilience, and the (Im)possibility of Racial Reconciliation." *Rhetoric & Public Affairs*, 8, no. 4 (2005), 571-594.

Frost, Elizabeth (ed.). 1988. *The Bully Pulpit. Quotations from America's Presidents*. New York: Facts on File, 1988.

Gallacher, Stuart A. 1945. "'Vox Populi, Vox Dei'." *Philological Quarterly*, 24 (1945), 12-19.

Gerson, Michael. 2009. "The Conservative Revolutionary [Barack Obama]." *The Washington Post* (January 21, 2009), A11.

Griffin, Albert Kirby. 1991. *Religious Proverbs: Over 1600 Adages from 18 Faiths Worldwide*. Jefferson, North Carolina: McFarland, 1991.

Harnsberger, Thomas (ed.). 1964. *Treasury of Presidential Quotations*. Chicago: Follett, 1964.

Harrison, Maureen, and Steve Gilbert (eds.). 2007. *Barack Obama. Speeches 2002-2006*. Carlsbad, California: Excellent Books, 2007.

Hart, Gary. 2006. "American Idol [Barack Obama]." *The New York Times* (December 24, 2006), online. http://www.nytimes.com/20061/12/24/books/review/Hart.t.html

Hayes, Stephen F. 2008. "Obama and the Power of Words." *The Wall Street Journal* (February 26, 2008), online. http://online.wsj.com/public/article_print/SB120398899374792349.html

Hendrickson, Robert. 1984. *Salty Words [and Phrases]*. New York: Hearst Marine Books, 1984.

Hertzler, Joyce O. 1933-1934. "On Golden Rules." *International Journal of Ethics*, 44 (1933-1934), 418-436.

Hitchens, Christopher. 2007. "The Audacity of Hope." *Times* (May 6, 2007), online. http://entertainment.timesonline.co.uk/tol/arts_and_entertainment/books/non-fiction/article

Holly, Dan. 2004. "Onward and Upward. Memoirs of Genius, Biographies of Struggle and Essays of Nuance." *Black Issues Book Review*, 6, no. 6 (November 2004), 63.

Hunt, John Gabriel (ed.). 1997. *The Inaugural Addresses of the Presidents*. New York: Gramercy Books, 1997.

Jay, Antony (ed.). 1996. *The Oxford Dictionary of Political Quotations*. Oxford: Oxford University Press, 1996.

Kakutani, Michiko. 2006. "Obama's Foursquare Politics, With a Dab of Dijon." *The New York Times* (October 17, 2006), online. http://www.nytimes.com/2006/10/1/17/books/17kaku.html

Karabegović, Dženeta. 2007. "'No Lie Can Live Forever': Zur sprichwörtlichen Rhetorik von Martin Luther King." *Sprichwörter sind Goldes wert: Parömiologische Studien zu Kultur, Literatur und Medien*. Ed. Wolfgang Mieder. Burlington, Vermont: The University of Vermont, 2007. 223-240.

Kazin, Michael. 2006. "Rising Star [Barack Obama]: A Dashing Young Senator Lays Out His Vision for His Party and His Country." *The Washington Post* (October 22, 2006), online. http://www.washingtonpost.com/wp-dyn/content/article/2006/10/19/AR2006101901175.ht

King, Oona. 2007. "Obama: A Man with a Dream." *The Times* (London) (September 15, 2007), 5.

Klein, Joe. 2006. "The Fresh Face [Barack Obama]," *Time* (October 15, 2006), online. http://www.time.com/time/magazine/article/0,9171,1546362-3,00.html

Klüver, Reymer. 2008. "Von Schweinen und Kühen: Republikaner kritisieren McCains Wahlkampf, und US-Medien decken Verfehlungen seiner Mitbewerberin Palin auf." *Süddeutsche Zeitung* (September 16, 2008), 7.

Lepore, Jill. 2009. "The Speech: Have Inaugural Addresses Been Getting Worse?" *The New Yorker* (January 12, 2009), pp. 49-53.

Lim, Elvin T. 2008. *The Anti-Intellectual Presidency: The Decline of Presidential Rhetoric from George Washington to George W. Bush.* New York: Oxford University Press, 2008.

Lindfors, Bernth. 1970-1971. "Chinua Achebe's Proverbs." *Nigerian Field*, 35 (1970), 180-185; and 36 (1971), 45-48, 90-96, and 139-143.

Litovkina, Anna T., and Carl Lindahl (eds.). 2007. *Anti-Proverbs in Contemporary Societies.* Budapest: Akadémiai Kiadó, 2007 (=*Acta Ethnographica Hungarica*, 52, no. 1 [2007], 1-285).

Litovkina, Anna T., and Wolfgang Mieder. 2006. *Old Proverbs Never Die, They Just Diversify. A Collection of Anti-Proverbs.* Burlington, Vermont: The University of Vermont; Veszprém: The Pannonian University of Veszprém, 2006.

Lott, David Newton (ed.). 1961. *The Inaugural Addresses of the American Presidents from Washington to Kennedy.* New York: Holt, Rinehart and Winston, 1961.

Louis, Cameron. 2000. "Proverbs and the Politics of Language." *Proverbium: Yearbook of International Proverb Scholarship*, 17 (2000), 173-194.

Macrone, Michael. 1992. *By Jove! Brush Up Your Mythology.* New York: HarperCollins, 1992.

Major, Clarence. 1970. *Dictionary of Afro-American Slang.* New York: International Publishers, 1970.

Major, Clarence. 1994. *Juba to Jive. A Dictionary of African-American Slang.* New York: Penguin Books, 1994.

McCrum, Robert. 2007. "A Candidate's Tale [Barack Obama]." *The Guardian* (August 26, 2007), online. http://www.guardian.co.uk.books/2007/aug/26/features.review4/print

Medhurst, Martin J. 2003. "Presidential Speechwriting: Ten Myths that Plague Modern Scholarship." *Presidential Speechwriting. From the New Deal to the Reagan Revolution and Beyond.* Eds. Kurt Ritter and M.J. Medhurst. College Station, Texas: Texas A&M University Press, 2003. 3-19.

Meis, Morgan. 2008. "Idle Chatter. Barack Obama: *The Audacity of Hope.*" *The Smart Set. From Drexel University* (February 14, 2008), online. http://www.thesmartset.com/article/article02140801.aspx

Mieder, Wolfgang. 1971. "'Behold the Proverbs of a People': A Florilegium of Proverbs in Carl Sandburg's Poem 'Good Morning, America'." *Southern Folklore Quarterly*, 35 (1971), 160-168.

Mieder, Wolfgang. 1973. "Proverbs in Carl Sandburg's *The People, Yes.*" *Southern Folklore Quarterly*, 37 (1973), 15-36.

Mieder, Wolfgang. 1986. *Encyclopedia of World Proverbs*. Englewood Cliffs, New Jersey: Prentice-Hall, 1986.

Mieder, Wolfgang. 1989. *American Proverbs. A Study of Texts and Contexts*. Bern: Peter Lang, 1989.

Mieder, Wolfgang. 1990a. *Not By Bread Alone. Proverbs of the Bible*. Shelburne, Vermont: New England Press, 1990a.

Mieder, Wolfgang. 1990b. *Salty Wisdom: Proverbs of the Sea*. Shelburne, Vermont: The New England Press, 1990b.

Mieder, Wolfgang. 1993. *Proverbs Are Never Out of Season: Popular Wisdom in the Modern Ages*. New York: Oxford University Press, 1993.

Mieder, Wolfgang. 1997. *The Politics of Proverbs: From Traditional Wisdom to Proverbial Stereotypes*. Madison, Wisconsin: University of Wisconsin Press, 1997.

Mieder, Wolfgang. 1998. *"A House Divided": From Biblical Proverb to Lincoln and Beyond*. Burlington, Vermont: The University of Vermont, 1998.

Mieder, Wolfgang. 2000. *The Proverbial Abraham Lincoln: An Index to Proverbs in the Works of Abraham Lincoln*. New York: Peter Lang, 2000.

Mieder, Wolfgang. 2001. *"No Struggle, No Progress": Frederick Douglass and His Proverbial Rhetoric for Civil Rights*. New York: Peter Lang, 2001.

Mieder, Wolfgang. 2004. *Proverbs. A Handbook*. Westport, Connecticut: Greenwood Press, 2004.

Mieder, Wolfgang. 2005. *Proverbs Are the Best Policy: Folk Wisdom and American Politics*. Logan, Utah: Utah State University Press, 2005.

Mieder, Wolfgang. 2007. "Proverbs in the Works of Ralph Waldo Emerson." *Phraseology: An International Handbook of Contemporary Research*. Eds. Harald Burger, Dmitrij Dobrovol'skij, Peter Kühn, and Neal R. Norrick. Berlin: Walter de Gruyter, 2007. II, 337-348.

Mieder, Wolfgang. 2008a. "'Let Us Have Faith that Right Makes Might': Proverbial Rhetoric in Decisive Moments of American Politics." *Proverbium: Yearbook of International Proverb Scholarship*, 25 (2008a), 319-352.

Mieder, Wolfgang. 2008b. *"Proverbs Speak Louder Than Words": Folk Wisdom in Art, Culture, Folklore, History, Literature, and Mass Media*. New York: Peter Lang, 2008b.

Mieder, Wolfgang, and George B. Bryan. 1995. *The Proverbial Winston S. Churchill: An Index to Proverbs in the Works of Sir Winston Churchill*. Westport, Connecticut: Greenwood Press, 1995.

Mieder, Wolfgang, and George B. Bryan. 1996. *Proverbs in World Literature: A Bibliography*. New York: Peter Lang, 1996.

Mieder, Wolfgang, and George B. Bryan. 1997. *The Proverbial Harry S. Truman: An Index to Proverbs in the Works of Harry S. Truman*. New York: Peter Lang, 1997.

Mieder, Wolfgang, Stewart A. Kingsbury, and Kelsie B. Harder (eds.). 1992. *A Dictionary of American Proverbs*. New York: Oxford University Press, 1992.

Mieder, Wolfgang, Fred Shapiro, Charles C. Doyle, and Jane Garry (eds.). 2010. *Yale Dictionary of Modern Proverbs*. New Haven, Connecticut: Yale University Press, 2010 (in preparation).

Mieder, Wolfgang, and Janet Sobieski (eds.). 2006. *"Gold Nuggets or Fool's Gold?" Magazine and Newspaper Articles on the (Ir)relevance of Proverbs and Proverbial Phrases*. Burlington, Vermont: The University of Vermont, 2006.

Miller, Donald L. (ed.). 1989. *From George ... to George: 200 Years of Presidential Quotations*. Washington, D.C.: Braddock Communications, 1989.

Murphey, Dwight D. 2008. "Dreams from My Father: A Story of Race and Inheritance." *The Journal of Social, Political and Economic Studies*, 33, no. 2 (2008), 271-277 (here pp. 272-273).

Newcomb, Robert. 1957. *The Sources of Benjamin Franklin's Sayings of Poor Richard*. Diss. University of Maryland, 1957.

Newton-Small, Jay. 2008. "How Obama Writes His Speeches." *Time* (August 28, 2008), online. http://www.time.com/time/politics/article/0,8599,1837368,00.html

Nichols, Ray. 1996. "Maxims, 'Practical Wisdom,' and the Language of Action." *Political Theory*, 24 (1996), 687-705.

Obama, Barack: Websites for speeches, news conferences, and radio addresses:
  http://www.obama.senate.gov/
  http://www.barack.obama.com/
  http://www.obamaspeeches.com/

Obama, Barack. 1988 [1990]. "Why Organize? Problems and Promise in the Inner City." Ed. Peg Knoepfle. *After Alinsky: Community Organizing in Illinois*. Springfield, Illinois: Sangamon State University, 1990. 35-40 (roundtable discussion with remarks by Barack Obama on pp. 123-152). This essay was first published in August/September 1988 in *Illinois Issues*.

Obama, Barack. 1995 [2004]. *Dreams from My Father: A Story of Race and Inheritance*. New York: Three Rivers Press, 2004 (originally published 1995). All page references in parentheses are from this paperback edition.

Obama, Barack. 2005. "What I See in Lincoln's Eyes." *Time Magazine* (June 27, 2005), 74.

Obama, Barack. 2006. *The Audacity of Hope. Thoughts on Reclaiming the American Dream*. New York: Three Rivers Press, 2006.

Obama, Barack (editor not listed!). 2008a. *Barack Obama. What He Believes in From His Own Words. Resolutions and Bills Sponsored & Co-Sponsored by Senator Barack Obama During the 110th Session (First Half) of the U.S. Congress January 4, 2007 to December 19, 2007*. Rockville, Maryland: Arc Manor, 2008a.

Obama, Barack (editor not listed!). 2008b. *Change We Can Believe In. Barack Obama's Plan to Renew America's Promise*. With a foreword by Barack Obama. New York: Three Rivers Press, 2008b. With seven speeches on pp. 193-271.

Olive, David. 2008a. "Does Obama Talk the Talk? Will Senator's Smooth Delivery Spark a Renaissance in Political Oratory?" *Toronto Star* (February 9, 2008a), online. http://www.thestar.com/comment/columnists/article/301885

Olive, David (ed.). 2008b. *An American Story. The Speeches of Barack Obama*. Toronto: ECW Press, 2008b.

O'Toole, Fintan. 2009. "A Rhetoric That Made Newness Threaten Less [Barack Obama]." *The Irish Times* (January 21, 2009), 3.

Parker, Ashley. 2008. "What Would Obama Say?" *The New York Times* (January 20, 2008), online. http://www,nytimes.com/2008/01/20/fashion/20speechwriter.html

Prahlad, Sw. Anand. 1996. *African-American Proverbs in Context.* Jackson, Mississippi: University Press of Mississippi. 1996.

Preston, Peter. 2007. "His Hope Springs Eternal. Democrat Hopeful Barack Obama Looks Good and Writes Well in *The Audacity of Hope* – But Can His Third-Way Politics Carry Him to the Ultimate Prize?" *The Observer* (April 29, 2007), online. http://www.guardian.co.uk/books/2007/apr/29/politics

Rees, Nigel. 2008. "Yes We Can." The *"Quote ... Unquote" Newsletter*, 18, no. 1 (2009), 3 (citing Allegra Stratton in *The Guardian* of November 8, 2008).

Remini, Robert V., and Terry Golway (eds.). 2008. *Fellow Citizens: The Penguin Book of U.S. Presidential Inaugural Addresses.* New York: Penguin Books, 2008.

Ritter, Kurt, and Martin J. Medhurst (eds.). 2003. *Presidential Speechwriting. From the New Deal to the Reagan Revolution and Beyond.* College Station, Texas: Texas A&M University Press, 2003.

Rogak, Lisa (ed.). 2007. *Barack Obama in His Own Words.* New York: Carroll & Graf, 2007.

Rogers, C.D. 2005. "Dreams from My Father: A Story of Race and Inheritance." *The Florida Bar Journal* (October 2005), 83-84.

Room, Adrian. 2000. *Brewer's Dictionary of Modern Phrase & Fable.* London, Cassell, 2000.

Safire, William. 1978. *Safire's Political Dictionary.* 3rd ed. New York: Random House, 1978.

Safire, William. 2009. "No Memorable Theme [Barack Obama]." *The New York Times* (January 21, 2009), online. http://roomfordebate.blogs.nytimes.com/2009/01/20/the-speech-the-experts-critique/

Sandburg, Carl. 1970. *The Complete Poems of Carl Sandburg.* New York: Harcourt, Brace, Jovanovich, 1970.

Sanger, David E. 2009. "[Inaugural] Speech Spanned History and Confronted Bush." *The New York Times* (January 21, 2009), online. http://www.nytimes.com/2009/o1/21/us/politics/w21assessS2.html

Schäfer, Ingo. 1983. *Populäre Sprachformen und politische Argumentation: Zur Funktion der Idiomatik in den Schriften Mao Zedongs.* Frankfurt am Main: Haag & Herchen, 1983.

Scheven, Albert. 1981. *Swahili Proverbs.* Washington, D.C.: University Press of America, 1981.

Schlesinger, Robert. 2008. *White House Ghosts: Presidents and Their Speechwriters.* New York: Simon & Schuster, 2008.

Schneider, Peter. 2008. "Noch ein Berliner. Barack Obama an der Siegessäule: Berlin, die USA und ihre Präsidenten – Geschichte einer ungewöhnlichen Liebesbeziehung." *Die Zeit*, no. 31 (July 24, 2008), 7.

Shapiro, Fred R. 2006. *The Yale Book of Quotations.* New Haven, Connecticut: Yale University Press, 2006.

Shesol, Jeff. 2009. "Powerful Words [Barack Obama]." *The New York Times* (January 21, 2009), online. http://www.nytimes.com/2009/o1/21/us/politics/w21assessS2.html

Smitherman, Geneva. 1977. *Talkin and Testifyin. The Language of Black America.* Detroit, Michigan: Wayne State University Press, 1977.

Smitherman, Geneva. 1994. *Black Talk. Words and Phrases from the Hood to the Amen Corner.* Boston: Houghton Mifflin Company, 1994.

Stevenson, Burton. 1948. *The Home Book of Proverbs, Maxims, and Famous Phrases.* New York: Macmillan, 1948.

Stevenson, Burton. 1949. *The Home Book of Bible Quotations.* New York: Harpers & Brothers, 1949.

Stewart, Gordon. 2009. "Giving No Offense [Barack Obama]." *The New York Times* (January 21, 2009), online. http://www.nytimes.com/2009/o1/21/us/politics/w21assessS2.html

Templeton, John Marks. 1997. *Worldwide Laws of Life.* Philadelphia, Pennsylvania: Templeton Foundation Press, 1997.

Tomasky, Michael. 2006. "The Phenomenon [of Barack Obama]." *The New York Review of Books*, 53, no. 19 (November 30, 2006), online. http://www/nybooks.com/articles/19651

Tulis, Jeffrey K. 1987. *The Rhetorical Presidency.* Princeton, New Jersey: Princeton University Press, 1987.

Viellard, Stéphane. 2001. "Le statut du proverbe dans le discours soviétique de la première moitié du XX-ème siècle." *Russkii iazyk: Peresekaia granitsy.* Eds. Marguerite Guiraud-Weber and I.B. Shatunovskii. Dubna: Mezhdunarodnyi Universitet, 2001. 54-65.

Watkins, Paul. 1995. "A Promise of Redemption [Barack Obama]." *The New York Times* (August 5, 1995), BR17.

Wilkinson, P.R. 1993. *Thesaurus of Traditional English Metaphors.* London: Routledge, 1993.

Wills, Garry. 1992. *Lincoln at Gettysburg. The Words That Remade America.* New York: Touchstone, 1992.

Wills, Garry. 2008. "Two Speeches [by Lincoln and Obama] on Race." *The New York Review of Books* (May 1, 2008), 4, 6, and 8.

Wilson, F.P. 1970. *The Oxford Dictionary of English Proverbs.* Oxford: Clarendon Press, 1970.

Wolffe, Richard. 2008. "In His Candidate's Voice. The Speech Lit a Fire. Meet Obama's Editor." *Newsweek* (January 6, 2008), online. http://www.newsweek.com/id/84756

Zeleny, Jeff. 2008. "Obama's Speechwriter Moves to the White House." *The New York Times* "The Caucus Blog" (November 26, 2008), online. http://thecaucus.blogs.nytimes.com/2008/11/26/

Zimmer, Ben. 2008. "Who First Put 'Lipstick on a Pig'? The Origins of the Porcine Proverb." *Slate Magazine* (September 10, 2008), online. http://www.slate.com/id/2199805/